ORGANIZING
CIVIL SOCIETY

ORGANIZING CIVIL SOCIETY

THE POPULAR SECTORS
AND THE
STRUGGLE FOR DEMOCRACY IN CHILE

Philip Oxhorn

The Pennsylvania State University Press
University Park, Pennsylvania

Library of Congress Cataloging-in-Publication Data

Oxhorn, Philip.
   Organizing civil society : the popular sectors and the struggle
for democracy in Chile / by Philip Oxhorn.
      p.   cm.
  Includes bibliographical references and index.
  ISBN 0-271-01435-0 (cloth)
  ISBN 0-271-01436-9 (paper)
  1. Political participation—Chile—Santiago. 2. Poor—Chile
—Santiago—Political activity. 3. Democracy—Chile—Santiago.
4. Social movements—Chile—Santiago. I. Title.
JL2681.094 1995
323′.042′0983315—dc20   94-34682
                                                    CIP

For Gabriel, so that his Chile will be that much better for what has gone before.

CONTENTS

PREFACE

It is impossible to study the urban poor without become emotionally attached to their cause. Working with these people on a day-to-day basis, watching them persevere against what often appear to be insurmountable odds and still have the generosity to share what little they have with a "gringo," invariably leads one to admire their efforts and hope that they do, in the end, succeed. Their enthusiasm and idealism are contagious. The "objective" participant/observer must struggle with his or her own prejudices, trying not to see what one wants to see, but instead understand what is really happening—the good, the bad; the successful, the not so successful.

As the present work evolved, the challenge has always been to avoid a romanticized vision of the shantytown organizations, yet at the same time convey what is genuinely novel and progressive about them. Moreover, one has to learn that it is acceptable to be critical of these organizations and their members. One must understand the limitations and problems inherent in the shantytown organizational activity that emerged during the Chilean military regime to understand if this kind of activity is the best, or even the most appropriate, mechanism for helping Chile's urban poor to achieve better lives for themselves.

I have tried to deal with this almost inevitable "pro-poor" bias over the years as the present work has undergone numerous revisions. Benefitting from both time and distance, the following is an effort to present an objective, albeit sympathetic, account of what actually happens at the "base" level of society when democracy is lost. Its goal is that we not only learn about the urban poor and their prospects, but that we also learn about the Chilean political system as a whole and the numerous changes that it has undergone since the imposition of military rule in 1973.

In Chapter 1, I will develop a theoretical framework for understanding popular-sector organizational activity and its relationship to the larger political system. Chapter 2 will provide the context for understanding the emergence of base-level organizations in Santiago shantytowns by analyzing the nature of the previous democratic regime, its breakdown, and the general evolution of the authoritarian regime imposed in September 1973. Chapter 3 will then focus specifically on the development of base-level organizational activity in the slums. It will contrast base-level organizational activity prior to the coup with what has taken place since 1973 in terms of the theoretical framework developed in Chapter 1. The notion of a popular collective identity is examined in Chapter 4. Chapter 5 focuses on the political demands that are associated with the emerging collective identity, while Chapter 6 looks at how the various political tendencies in Chile viewed the popular sectors and their organizations in 1986. The challenges facing autonomous popular-sector collective action will be discussed in Chapter 7, which examines the interaction between popular organizations and political parties in the context of the opposition's unsuccessful efforts to pressure the military regime into accepting an early transition to democracy in the mid-1980s. Chapter 8 then analyzes the dynamics of the transition and current democratic regime, in which political parties play a central role, from the perspective of popular-sector organizations. Finally, Chapter 9 situates the Chilean experience in a comparative perspective by assessing the political significance of popular-sector organizational activity in terms of both the existence of a popular collective identity and the translation of this collective identity into popular-sector collective action. The chapter ends with a discussion of the future possibilities for popular-sector organizational activity and its contribution to the continued democratization of civil society under the current democratic regime.

ACKNOWLEDGMENTS

The project on which this book is based had its inception in 1984. Since that time, a number of people and institutions have contributed to the present study in important ways, although I assume full responsibility for any errors or omissions.

To begin with, I thank Terry Karl, Philippe Schmitter, and Sidney Verba, who have taught, prodded, and encouraged me over the years. It was Terry Karl who first encouraged me to pursue my interests in democratic theory and grassroots organizing by studying the Chilean case (even though I knew no Spanish at the time) and who was particularly supportive during the most trying periods of attempting to conduct fieldwork in an authoritarian country. Philippe Schmitter's insightful comments have enabled me to write a much better theoretical chapter than would otherwise have been the case. Sidney Verba has been both extremely supportive of my project and contributed the invaluable insights of someone who knows a great deal about the general themes that inspired this book.

It is not possible to list the names of all of the countless Chileans who made this study possible by sharing with me their experiences and thoughts. To all of the *pobladores* who opened their lives up to me, I owe more than mere words can say. This general debt also includes the many politicians who were willing to discuss the political situation in Chile and the particular situation in the *poblaciones*.

My work in Chile was also facilitated by the institutional and intellectual support of a number of people and organizations. During most of my stay in Chile, I was formally affiliated with the Facultad Latinoamericana de Ciencias Sociales (FLACSO). The researchers at FLACSO were generous with their time and resources. In particular, I thank Carlos Portales and

Manuel Antonio Garretón, who always showed a special interest in my work and made time in their busy schedules to talk to me about it. I owe a very special debt of gratitude to Sergio Bitar, who took me into his home when I first arrived in Santiago and has helped my work progress in uncountable ways ever since.

Manuel Barrera, the director of the Centro de Estudios Sociales (CED), was also very helpful in commenting on my earlier work while I was in Chile and in offering me the resources of his research institute. Similarly, I am indebted to Guillermo Campero of the Instituto Latinoamericano de Estudios Transnacionales (ILET), who shared with me the findings of his own larger study of shantytown organizations that was in progress while I was conducting my field research. He also provided useful comments on my earlier work while I was in Chile.

A fellowship from the Helen Kellogg Institute at the University of Notre Dame during the fall of 1988 allowed me to make substantial progress in writing several chapters contained in the present work. I express special thanks to Samuel Valenzuela, now at Notre Dame, who was an important influence on my choosing to study Chile and who helped design my initial proposal for the work while he was at Harvard.

McGill University generously provided me with the institutional support that I needed to complete the final revisions of the work. Research on developments after 1987 was made possible by generous grants from the Social Science Research Grants Committee, McGill University, the Fonds pour la Formation de Chercheurs et l'Aide à la Recherche, Government of Quebec, and the Social Sciences and Humanities Research Council, Canada. I also thank Ton Salman, Hudson Meadwell, John Hall and, in particular, Pierre Gratton, for their comments on earlier versions of this book. I owe a very special thanks to Carmen Sorger, who proved invaluable as my research assistant during the final phases of this project, Michael Fleet, who generously provided me with a wealth of insightful comments on the entire manuscript, and Sandy Thatcher, whose encouragement and advice have meant a great deal to me.

Finally, I thank Cynthia Sanborn, who has been a good friend for many years now. And last, but by no means least, I give special thanks to Rosa Liencura, who has taught me more than anyone about life in Chilean shantytowns, where she worked as a social worker, and has made many sacrifices so that I could finish this book.

LIST OF ILLUSTRATIONS

LIST OF TABLES

ABBREVIATIONS

ACHIP	Asociación Chilen ade Investigaciones Para La Paz
AD	Democratic Alliance
AN	National Advancement
APRA	American Popular Revolutionary Alliance
CEB	Christian base community
CED	Centro de Estudios Sociales
CEDLA	Interuniversity Center of Latin American Research and Documentation
CEPAL	Comisión Económica para América Latina y el Caribe
CERC	Centro de Estudios de la Realidad Contemporánea
CESOC	Centro de Estudios Sociales Ltda.
CIDU	Centro Interdisciplinario de Desarollo Urbano y Regional
CIEPLAN	Corporación de Investigaciones Económicas Para Latinoamerica
CLASCO	Consejo Latinoamericano de Ciencias Sociales
CNI	National Intelligence Center
COAPO	Coordinadora de Agrupaciones Poblacionales
CODECO	Consejo de Desarrollo Comunal
COPACHI	Committee of Cooperation for Peace in Chile
CORFO	State Development Corporation
CUP	Unitary Command for Pobladores
DC	Christian Democratic Party
DESAL	Center for Latin American and Social Development
DESCO	Centro de Estudios y Promoción del Desarollo
DINA	National Intelligence Directorate
DOS	Division of Social Organizations
DR	Radical Democracy

ECO	Educación y Comunicaciones
EURE	Revista Latinoamericana de Estudios Urbano Regionales
FLACSO	Facultad Latinoamericana de Ciencias Sociales
FOCh	Chilean Workers' Federation
FPMR	Manuel Rodríguez Patriotic Front
GDP	Gross Domestic Product
GNP	Gross National Product
IC	Christian Left
ICHEH	Instituto Chileno de Estudios Humanísticas
ILADES	Instituto Latinoamericano de Doctrina y Estudios Sociales
ILET	Instituto Latinoamericano de Estudios Transnacionales
LASA	Latin American Studies Association
MAN	National Action Movement
MAPU	Unitary Popular Action Movement
MDP	Popular Democratic Movement
METRO	Coordinadora Metropolitana de Pobladores
MIDA	Movement of the Allendista Democratic Left
MIR	Revolutionary Left Movement
MOC	Unitary Popular Action Movement—Worker Peasant
MUN	National Union Movement
PAIS	Partido Amplio de Izquierda Socialista
PC	Communist Party
PEM	Minimal Employment Program
PH	Humanist Party
PL	Liberal Party
PN	National Party
POHJ	Occupational Program for Heads of Household
PPD	Party for Democracy
PR	Radical Party
PS	Socialist Party
PS(A)	Almeyda branch of the Socialist Party
PSD	Social Democratic Party
PS(N)	Nuñez branch of the Socialist Party
RN	National Renovation Party
SUR	Sur Profesionales
PET	Program de Economia del Trabajo
UDI	Independent Democratic Union
UP	Popular Unity
VECTOR	Centro de Estudios Económicos y Sociales

1

"BRINGING THE BASE BACK IN"

Toward the Democratization of Civil Society Under Authoritarian Regimes

The *toma* (illegal land seizure) in a low-income area of Santiago on 17 July 1986 was unremarkable in itself. It could not have been more spontaneous. Several families had camped out on a vacant lot three weeks earlier. Suddenly (no one really knew how it happened), a rumor spread that a *toma* was in process, and more than eight hundred people decided to occupy the land. Like all other *tomas* since 1973, it was violently repressed. Within twenty-four hours, *Carabineros*[1] forcibly evicted the 185 participating families. Many lost everything that they owned as the ramshackle squatter settlement was dismantled. In the words of one observer, " It was savage. The *pacos*[2] destroyed everything."[3] And like almost every other *toma* after the military took power, the people involved failed to achieve their primary goal: a place to live. In the end, the best they could hope for was that the government would replace their lost belongings.

More important than the *toma* itself was what it revealed about life in Santiago's shantytowns during the period of military rule: the willingness

---

1. This is the name of the national paramilitary police.
2. Popular slang for "police."
3. Unless otherwise indicated, all quotes are from interviews conducted by the author in Santiago, Chile.

of other, equally poor but *organized*, shantytown dwellers to make sacrifices so that the *toma*'s participants could cope with what otherwise would have been a disastrous situation. Almost immediately after the *Carabineros* had arrived, the local *olla comune* (soup kitchen) offered to help in any way that it could. The *olla* had been formed in 1983 by a small group of *pobladores* (shantytown dwellers). Before the *toma*, it was feeding between two hundred and three hundred people a week. Soon, the *olla* was providing all the meals for another three hundred people who had participated in the *toma* and were now living in the local Catholic church. The members of the *olla* did the cooking (except on weekends, when the *toma* participants did their own cooking) and searched for food donations.

The members of the *olla* also took charge of the equally important task of organizing what was a chaotic, disorganized mass of people. They had already learned from their own experience that organization was the key to successfully defending the poor's interests, and realized that for an organization to be strong, it could not be dependent on outsiders. The *olla*'s members were more than willing to help, but they refused to do so in a patronizing or paternalistic fashion. As the *olla*'s president (who only recently had learned to read through the *olla*'s literacy workshop) pointed out at the time: "I want to help, but I cannot take over their responsibilities for them."

It was not easy to organize the people who had participated in the *toma* after they had already been evicted from the land. To begin with, no one even knew the names of all of the people who had participated in the *toma* and what they had lost. To deal with this problem, the *olla*'s leaders organized those who could write to collect the needed information. Leaders also had to be found for the new organization, so the *olla* held elections to form a ten-person committee. This committee would work with the members of the *olla* to help take care of the people's various needs. The committee would also represent the *toma*'s participants in dealings with the municipal government and various nongovernmental human rights groups that had become concerned about the people's plight. The *olla*'s leadership was prepared to train the new leaders, but with the goal of creating an autonomous organization among a group of *pobladores* with no previous organizational experience. The members of the *olla* wanted to share their own organizational know-how. They took it upon themselves to help people who were even less fortunate, despite the risks that this entailed in a repressive environment and the obvious lack of anything tangible they could hope to gain in return.

The efforts of the *olla* in the aftermath of the July 17 *toma* are just one example of how literally tens of thousands of Santiago's poor had learned the value of autonomous organization, self-help, and solidarity during the military regime. These are the terms in which the members of the *olla* understood the *toma*'s failure. To remedy what they saw as the *toma*'s shortcomings, they decided to help their fellow *pobladores* acquire the capacity to define and defend their own interests collectively. It is a graphic illustration of one of my central themes here: the way in which the repressive policies of the military regime led to the emergence of a rich set of participatory and democratic organizational experiences among Chile's poor that helped them cope with their most pressing problems. The *olla*'s reaction to the *toma*'s failure demonstrated how the urban poor were attempting to restructure the social fabric of Chilean society, which was virtually destroyed by the violent dismantling of the state's social welfare apparatus. Moreover, it stood in dramatic contrast to the individualistic authoritarian model for social relations that the military regime was attempting to impose by force on Chile.

From a more historical perspective, both the *toma* and the *olla* were noteworthy for the virtually complete absence of political parties. Prior to the military coup, political parties dominated all forms of social mobilization in Chile. For the urban poor, this generally prevented the emergence of any autonomous forms of organization, as popular organizations quickly became overwhelmed by narrow partisan interests. The military regime changed all of that. The emergence of autonomous organizations like the *olla* reflected the cessation of traditional political party activity under an authoritarian regime and a subsequent attempt by the urban poor to re-create a public space for the expression of lower-class, or "popular-sector,"[4] interests. This is a second theme: how the violence unleashed by the 1973 military coup shifted the locus of political activity to the grassroots level and away from political parties, where some of Chile's most disadvantaged groups played an active role in rebuilding their society. In particular, the book explores the ways in which popular organizations in the 1980s were different from those that had existed prior to the coup. It emphasizes popular organizations' newfound autonomy from political parties by analyzing how the authoritarian experience led to and shaped their emergence.

The central role that repression and the absence of political-party activity played in conditioning the activities of organizations like the *olla* raises an

---

4. For a discussion of the significance of this and other concepts, see the Glossary.

important question: How were such organizations affected by the resurgence of political-party activity beginning in the mid-1980s and the disappearance of political repression after the transition to democracy in 1989? This question serves as the basis for the third theme: the changing ways in which popular organizations, and the popular sectors more generally, influence Chilean politics. More specifically, I examine the political demands and aspirations of the leaders of popular organizations, as well as the nature of the relationship between political parties and popular organizations once political parties began to reassume their dominant political role in the mid-1980s. In this way, I offer insights into the role that the popular sectors as a collective actor might play in the future, now that democracy has been restored in Chile.

The Chilean experience is not isolated. It forms part of a broader context that includes the role played by grassroots movements in recent democratization processes in both Southern Europe and Latin America. Contrary to the more conservative political behavior exhibited by the urban poor in other contexts (Cornelius 1975), organizations of the urban poor formed an important element in the broad social fronts—"popular upsurges"—that mobilized to pressure reluctant elites to expand partial processes of democratization. As a result, the urban poor helped to push such transition processes further than would otherwise have been the case (O'Donnell and Schmitter 1986, 53).

Moreover, organizational experiences similar to those found in Chilean shantytowns can be seen as forming a vital part of a more subtle process of democratization, one that takes place within a society—as opposed to political institutions or regimes—and has been referred to as the "invisible transition" (Garretón 1989c, and 1989a). At this microlevel of society, the grassroots-level, (or base-level) organizations have historically tended to be highly egalitarian and participatory (Castells 1983). Their importance as forums for the practice and learning of modern norms and behaviors appropriate for political democracy has frequently been noted (O'Donnell and Schmitter 1986; Tocqueville 1969; Mill 1972). In particular, the democratic nature of a variety of organizations that have emerged in the context of a generalized economic crisis throughout Latin America in the 1980s has been stressed in a number of studies focusing on urban marginals in various countries.[5]

5. For a general survey of different country cases, see Escobar and Alvarez 1992; Eckstein 1989; and Calderón 1986. For Peru, see Tovar 1986a and 1986b; Stokes 1988; and Barrig

With this in mind, I focus on the democratizing aspects of popular organizations in the shantytowns of Santiago, Chile. I argue that they formed part of a democratization process in civil society that was distinct from a process of democratic transition at the political-regime level. As such, the ability of the popular sectors to represent their interests effectively in the political realm is dependent on two factors: (1) on the emergence of a popular collective identity within the popular sectors, and (2) on the ability of the popular sectors to translate such a collective identity into collective action. Whether popular sectors can realize their interests and begin to democratize civil society as a whole will depend on the progress that the popular sectors are able to make along these two distinct but interrelated dimensions. In order to understand why this is the case, I shall develop a theoretical model to explain a process of democratization of civil society under authoritarian regimes.

THE PARADOX OF AUTHORITARIAN RULE FOR THE DEVELOPMENT OF CIVIL SOCIETY

The imposition of authoritarian rule affects the development of civil society in important, sometimes contradictory, ways. The policies followed by an authoritarian regime may, for example, foster the development of the kind of atomized, individualistic, market-centered civil society that was associated with the spread of capitalism in early liberal thought (Ferguson 1966). Such development would tend to exacerbate the effects that high levels of socioeconomic inequality have historically had in preventing the emergence of strong civil societies in Latin America.[6] "Strong" civil societies in this sense are characterized by their institutionalized social pluralism. Such civil societies provide the foundations for stable democracies in Western Europe and North America. Conversely, the historical weakness of civil societies in Latin America has contributed to democratic instability throughout the region (Schmitter 1986).

1986. The Brazilian case is discussed in Cardoso 1983; Alvarez 1990; Mainwaring 1989; Salles 1983; and Singer 1981.

6. For a much more detailed discussion of the concept of civil society and the relative underdevelopment of Latin American civil societies, see the Glossary.

Paradoxically, however, the same policies (at least under certain circumstances, which will be discussed in greater detail below) can cause civil society to develop in a completely different direction. As a response to the imposition of authoritarian rule, the historical underdevelopment of Latin American civil society may actually begin to reverse itself (Oxhorn 1995). To the extent that authoritarian rule causes the multiplication of different organizations in society and, in particular, if the cessation of traditional forms of political activity enhances the autonomy of such organizations to define and pursue their own interests, the type of variegated civil society to which Schmitter (1986) referred may actually begin to emerge in embryonic form under the authoritarian regime. Indeed, an important axis for opposition to the authoritarian regime may come to reflect this basic conflict between these two competing tendencies within civil society.

Recent experiences in many Latin American countries have given rise to a number of studies of base-level organizations under authoritarian regimes.[7] Frequently, however, these studies tend toward the descriptive and do not provide a general framework or model for understanding organizational activity to place it in a comparative perspective. In what follows, a theoretical model for understanding base-level organizational activity under an authoritarian regime will be developed. It will be argued that *under certain circumstances, the resumption of significant base-level organizational activity is not only possible under an authoritarian regime, but also a direct result of the authoritarian experience itself.* Two sets of factors are critical to understanding such a possibility and form the basis for this theoretical model: those related to the nature of the authoritarian regime and others related to a country's preauthoritarian heritage.

The Nature and Level of Repression

The nature and level of coercion under an authoritarian regime form the first set of factors affecting the reemergence of base-level organizational

---

7. In large part due to the particular populist characteristics of Peru's military regime from 1968 to 1978, this phenomenon was perhaps most studied here. See Tovar 1985; Collier 1976; and McClintock 1981. On Brazil, see Perlman 1976; and Mainwaring 1986, 1987, and 1989. On Mexico, see Cornelius 1975. Among recent works on the Chilean case, see Oxhorn 1991 and 1988; Schneider 1991; Campero 1987; Espinoza 1985 and 1983; and Razeto et al. 1986. Also see Escobar and Alvarez 1992.

activity. Repression can contribute to this in several ways. Rather than eliminating self-organized and autonomously defined political space, repression can have the effect of shifting the locus of political activity to nonparty arenas by effectively proscribing traditional political-party activity. These nonparty arenas typically will be at the base level where their suppression is more difficult, given the greater possibilities for concealing such activity and for either sheltering or replacing leaders than at the intermediate and elite levels.

For such a shift to take place, the level of repression must be neither too great nor too indiscriminate. Massive, indiscriminate repression can close all potential political space through intimidation, fear, and the elimination of any potential leadership. More selective repression, on the other hand, can channel potential organizational activity into those areas that either are not being directly repressed or are, for one reason or another, actually tolerated by the regime. It is this latter element, as will be discussed below, that is important in explaining the significance of such bodies as the Catholic Church in promoting base-level organizational activity under many Latin American authoritarian regimes.[8] Thus, selective repression targeted primarily at political parties and elites is most conducive to a shift in the locus of political activity to the base level.

Repression under authoritarian regimes may also indirectly favor the expansion of territorially rather than functionally based organizations. Labor organizations are by far the most important functionally based organizations. These organizations, along with political parties, were typically the most heavily repressed by the authoritarian regimes that were prevalent in Latin America during most of the past two decades. This is in part due to the nature of these regimes and to the relative vulnerability of union organizers, especially those connected with parties of the Left. Territorial organizations, especially those in the slums and shantytowns of major cities, are much more difficult to repress, at least while they remain confined to relatively small communities.[9] Labor leaders tend to be easily

---

8. Peru provides perhaps a unique example of an authoritarian regime actually encouraging a wide variety of organizational activity within civil society in order to establish its own social base and, to a lesser extent, weaken the political power of Peru's dominant political party, the American Popular Revolutionary Alliance (APRA). See Tovar 1985; Stepan 1978; and Sanborn 1988.

9. It might also be argued that such territorially based organizations are viewed as less of a threat by the regime, given the greater immediate capacity of organized labor to wreak havoc on the economy. To the extent that this is the case, it would further contribute to the spread of such organizations. However, such a perception would appear to be somewhat problematic,

identifiable and the success of the organization in large part depends on the organizers' ability to bring in as many potential members as possible in order to increase the effectiveness of collective bargaining and the ultimate threat of a strike. In contrast, territorial organizations do not require the participation of even a majority of the community to be minimally effective in meeting the needs of their members and the atomization of groups is not so detrimental an impediment to effective organization. Leaders are not so visible as in the more confined and monitored space of a firm or factory, and potential leaders may also be more readily available at the community level. The very conditions necessary for a viable union organization that make labor leaders more vulnerable do not exist in the same way at the territorial level.[10]

More generally, a "re-territorialization" of political activity at the base level can be seen as an indirect result of authoritarian regimes. The policies of deliberate atomization, the destruction of networks of representation, and the emphasis on centralized and technocratic policymaking that have characterized authoritarian regimes in Latin America and Southern Europe all appear to contribute to the development of organizations based on narrowly circumscribed territorial domains in these countries (O'Donnell and Schmitter 1986). The combination of these efforts to depoliticize society with the limits to the state's repressive capacity at the base level leaves space for territorially differentiated political activities that largely escape the ability of the authoritarian regime to control.

It is important to emphasize that repression creates a new political dynamic by shifting the locus of political activity to the base level. As will be stressed throughout the rest of the book, this is due to the politicization of new issues by the regime and the nature of the community-based organizations that emerge. It also is a reflection of the fact that people without previous political experience start participating for the first time.

---

given the distinctly antipopular character of many of these regimes (Garretón, 1989a) and the more general perceptions of both the state and the dominant classes associated with the idea of "popular sectors" as discussed in the Glossary.

10. Moreover, repression of the labor movement, especially the common practice of blacklisting experienced union organizers, can directly contribute to the strengthening of territorially based organizations in popular sectors. To a marked degree this has been the case in Chile, where many experienced labor leaders found themselves unable to obtain employment and as a result became active in organizing the urban poor. Since many of these labor leaders were members of the Communist Party or closely associated with it, this also helps explain the Communist Party's marked success in gaining support in Chilean shantytowns after the coup. See Oxhorn 1986.

Only a small percentage of the people involved in popular organizations tend to be former political-party activists. Moreover, this new political dynamic affects party activists, who begin to participate in politics in different ways that political parties are less able to control. As a result, previous patterns of party organization and relations with social organizations may no longer be viable, regardless of the intentions of party elites.

The Authoritarian Regime's Socioeconomic Model

A distinctive feature of the authoritarian regimes in Latin America in recent decades is their "foundational" dynamic: their attempt to transform society as a whole in a determined direction (Garretón 1989a and 1986). While these projects for transforming society vary among the different countries, they have resulted in a variety of similar neoconservative socioeconomic policies (Foxley 1983). These, in turn, often create new political needs, regardless of whether a regime's transformative project is in some sense "successful."

The social costs associated with these neoconservative policies are typically reflected in a prolonged period of urban unemployment rates characteristic of an economic depression, a substantial fall in real wages, the weakening of organized labor, and a regressive redistribution of national income. They may leave the popular sectors with few alternatives to the creation of self-help organizations in their narrowly circumscribed territorial communities. This tendency is exacerbated by the progressive dismantling of the state's social welfare apparatus. The focus of politics is changed as state institutions are eliminated and/or privatized, while new institutions are created. This, in turn, alters the potential nature of self-defined and autonomously generated political space, something of special importance in many Latin American countries where the state has traditionally been the principal referent for political activity.

It should be noted, of course, that neoconservative economic policies have also been implemented by democratic governments as a response to the economic crisis that characterized Latin American countries in the 1980s and the conditions imposed on debtor countries by international and private lending institutions for securing needed foreign capital. In many Latin American countries, however, the shift toward neoconservative economic policies preceded the economic crisis of the 1980s and these were implemented by authoritarian regimes as an integral part of a much larger project for transforming society. In fact, these earlier policies actually contributed to the severity of the subsequent "crisis" due to the extensive foreign borrowing on which they tended to rely. As part of a larger project being implemented by an authoritarian regime, the alternatives open to the urban poor, in particular, were much more limited and the new political needs being created were much more fundamental.[11]

In summing up, it must be pointed out that the influences of these factors associated with the authoritarian regime tend to vary over time. As Garretón (1989a) has shown, these regimes generally go through distinct phases. While the characteristics of any one phase may also be present in the others, these regimes generally pass through three distinct phases before entering a terminal phase in which the authoritarian regime breaks down and is replaced.

During the regime's *reactive phase*, which generally follows the installation of the authoritarian regime, the repressive element of these regimes predominates. Human rights abuses are the most widespread and brutal during this period as the authoritarian regime seeks to eliminate its "adversaries" and disarticulate the fundamental processes of the previous political system.

The regime passes into a *foundational* or *transformative phase* once it begins to claim legitimacy on the basis of a new project for society. In this

11. At least in the case of Peru, the implementation of such policies by a democratically elected government in response to the economic crisis in the 1980s actually has had the opposite effect, weakening base-level organizational activity as many turned to traditional patterns of activity that were much more closely linked to political parties, electoral politics, and the state as a referent for political activity (Tovar 1986b). Such traditional alternatives would not exist under most authoritarian regimes. Moreover, the Peruvian case is somewhat of an anomaly given the unique nature of the Peruvian military regime. It lacked the same type of economic project and neoconservative policies characteristic of the Southern Cone authoritarian regimes. A significant number of leftist political parties also were able to establish themselves in the shantytowns for the first time under military rule. This, combined with the state's active role in promoting base-level organizational activity, severely circumscribed the development of autonomous popular-sector organizations. These factors contributed to the general tendency for popular-sector mobilizations toward the end of the military regime to focus on the satisfaction of immediate economic needs caused by rapid economic decline in the latter part of the 1970s, rather than on demands for broad political change (Tovar 1986a and 1986b; Stephens 1983). The resurgence of traditional patterns of political activity after the transition to democracy therefore represents not so much the reversal or weakening of nontraditional patterns of political activity, but rather the relative inability of such nontraditional patterns to become institutionalized.

phase, the military regime attempts to develop a new model for economic development, social relations, and the political system that will provide for a successor to the military regime and is usually of a neoconservative mold.

The failure of the regime's foundational project, especially its economic base, normally gives passage to a phase of the *administration of recurrent crises*. In this phase, the regime moves from crisis to crisis and its primary problem is ensuring its own survival. Similarly, the relationships between repression, the regime's project for transforming society, and the general tendency for the "reterritorialization" of base-level organizations will also vary over time and in different ways, depending on the particular phase through which the regime is passing. But one could also expect a cumulative effect. The combination of a worsening socioeconomic situation and increasing desperation in certain sectors can contribute to a decrease in the effectiveness of repression, as people overcome their earlier fear and the level of repression required to maintain a given situation rises as a function of the growing strength of the opposition and/or increased participation in base-level organizational activity. In the same vein, one can also expect a time lag between the installation of the authoritarian regime and the emergence of significant base-level organizational activity that will vary according to the specific characteristics of each national situation.

The Preauthoritarian Heritage
The Existence of an Umbrella Organization

The most important factor in a country's preauthoritarian heritage for understanding the reemergence of base-level organizational activity under authoritarian rule is the presence of a "protective umbrella" that can provide base-level organizations with the necessary organizational space to begin functioning in a repressive environment. In Latin America, this role has been typically filled by the Catholic Church or other religious organizations (Levine and Mainwaring 1989; Garretón 1989c; Valenzuela and Valenzuela 1986a).

In order to be effective, such a protective umbrella must be viewed as legitimate and enjoy the confidence of potential members of base-level organizations. This, in turn, can strengthen the umbrella institution's second important requirement: relative immunity from the regime's repression. Under the protection of an institution endowed with these attributes, groups can again form with at least a minimal level of protection from state violence, and thereby begin to reconstruct a social fabric that has been severely torn by the imposition of authoritarian rule.

The church's relative immunity from repression stems from the historic importance of the Catholic Church in Latin America. This immunity also reflects the reluctance of many authoritarian regimes to openly challenge the church at a time when they are trying to legitimize their rule by allegedly safeguarding Christian values in the face of an atheistic Communist threat. A key variable in determining the church's capacity to serve as a protective umbrella for base-level organizations is the willingness of the national church hierarchy to do so. In this way, the reforms of the Catholic Church in many Latin American countries in the wake of Vatican II and the growing acceptance of more progressive church doctrines, most notably liberation theology, were critical in allowing the church to offer an alternative sphere for organizational activity after the imposition of authoritarian rule in such countries as Brazil and Chile.[12]

In addition to providing the necessary physical space for conducting organizational meetings, the church frequently provides other essential resources. These include material resources such as food, clothing, and the materials that various workshops use in order to produce goods either for the group members' own consumption or for sale. The church also provides important intangible resources in the form of leadership training, as well as the church laypeople and clergy who often provide an essential impetus to the formation of new groups and help new groups to overcome initial challenges and problems.

Finally, it is worth noting that the importance of the church's role in the reemergence of base-level organizational activity under authoritarian regimes will favor territorially rather than functionally based organizations. The church itself is a territorially based organization whose resources tend to be focused at the base level around local parishes. It is here that these resources are often most effective, given the trust that the local parish's priests and nuns are able to develop in their communities through constant direct contact. The Church's explicit acceptance of organizational activity can then be transformed into an initial legitimacy that helps attract potential members who are still uncertain as to the benefits of participating in an organization and who may fear the possible repression that such participation can invite.

12. On the Brazilian case, see Mainwaring 1986. For Chile, see Smith 1982 and Correa and Viera-Gallo 1986. Also see the selections in Levine 1986, and Levine and Mainwaring 1989.

The Authoritarian Regime is Preceded by an Extended Period of Political Democracy

The final set of factors relates to a country's democratic history and focuses on the distinction between cases of *democratization* following authoritarian rule and cases of *re-democratization*. Where an authoritarian regime has been immediately proceeded by a lengthy period of political democracy, civil society may possess the values and behavioral norms conducive to organizing at the base level. There is also a greater likelihood that people will view democratic and participatory base-level organizations as a symbolic repudiation of the authoritarian regime and model, and therefore as an important means of expressing their opposition to the regime. Perhaps more important, the popular sectors are more likely to perceive possibilities for changing the political system and pressuring the state for improved living conditions through organizing as a result of previous popular gains made during the country's democratic period (cf. Mainwaring 1987).

A country that has had a democratic regime for an extended period prior to the imposition of authoritarian rule has an important asset for reestablishing base-level organizational activity in the form of a pool of individuals with actual organizing experience. Such people may have gained experience by participating within the political parties or the labor movement. But many may also have gained organizational experience working in the local organizations of the preceding regime, such as neighborhood councils, women's groups, youth groups, etc. Regardless of the extent of their organizational experiences, the presence of these people facilitates the emergence of new organizations and they may actually be key catalysts for the emergence of organizations when other factors are favorable.

This theoretical model for explaining base-level organizational activity under authoritarian regimes is summarized schematically in Figure 1. The model developed here focuses on the emergence of base-level organizational activity as a function of the authoritarian regime itself, in combination with certain elements of a country's preauthoritarian heritage. It rejects the argument implicit in much of the literature on democratic transitions (O'Donnell and Schmitter 1986), that the emergence of such activity is dependent on the initiation of a regime or even policy change. This model provides for the possibility that a process of democratization within civil society can begin independently of an actual democratic transition under the authoritarian regime. This process, which in its most general terms has

Figure 1. The resurrection of the civil society under an authoritian regime

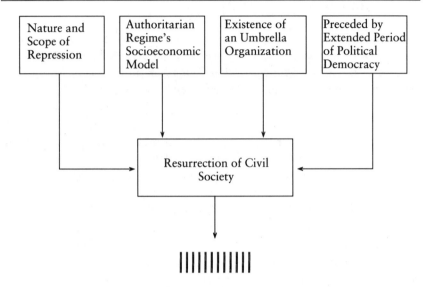

been described as the "invisible transition" (Garretón 1989a and 1989c), will be the focus of the remainder of this chapter.

AUTHORITARIAN REGIMES AND THE DEMOCRATIZATION OF CIVIL SOCIETY

The implied paradox that an authoritarian regime can, under certain circumstances, contribute to the democratization of civil society is a complex proposition. It revolves around the specific characteristics of the base-level organizations that are likely to develop according to the model in Figure 1. But before examining these characteristics and the potential for these organizations to somehow transform civil society, it is first necessary to discuss the concept of a democratic civil society.

The concept or ideal of a "democratic" civil society is frequently presented as the basis for a fundamental critique of political democracy (Barber 1984 and 1974; Pateman 1970; Bachrach 1967; Duncan and Lukes 1963). According to this perspective, a democratic civil society is one in which there is a maximum amount of direct citizen participation in the decision-making processes that affect their lives. This necessarily requires a multiplicity of relatively small, participatory, and democratically structured organizations that can be both functionally and territorially based. Because people spend such a proportionately large part of their time at the workplace in a modern society, industrial democracy is viewed as essential to genuine democracy.

From this perspective, political democracy in general, and its liberal variant in particular, must be fundamentally transformed because they tend to circumscribe the scope of "politics" and citizen participation. This circumscription results in an excessive elite bias in the institutions of political democracy and, ultimately, an unacceptable reduction in individual freedom and the possibilities for personal growth and development. The direct democracy of ancient Greece and certain Swiss cantons well into the eighteenth century, or, alternatively, the small, agriculturally based community envisioned by Rousseau, are often held as models to be emulated in modern nation-states, although the mechanisms for doing so generally remain vague or unsatisfactory for complex large-scale industrial societies, which lack the greater homogeneity and consensus characteristic of small polities. Carrying this argument to its extreme, some authors have actually concluded that true democracy and freedom can exist only in a situation of anarchy, in which the state ceases to exist entirely (Taylor 1982).

Questions dealing with how a democratic civil society might relate to political democracy at the regime level will be discussed in Chapter 9. Here I am looking specifically at the *process* by which civil society becomes more democratic. This approach is consistent with the study's focus on the resurrection of civil society under authoritarian regimes, and in this regard the model developed above suggests a novel conclusion: The democratization of civil society is not only conceptually distinct from the instauration of liberal democratic institutions; it can begin prior to, and independently of, an actual democratic transition.

The basis for this conclusion lies in the nature of the organizations whose emergence under authoritarian rule is predicted by the model developed above. These organizations' relatively small size, with an average of ten to twenty-five members, and their direct association with a territorially circumscribed community provide them with a dynamic and certain inherent qualities that are fundamental to a process of democratization at the level of civil society.

While a general definition of political democracy would be incomplete if it focused only on participation, participation is the principal defining quality of democracy at the level of civil society (cf. Mansbridge 1980). The myriad of organizations that characterizes the base level of civil society provides the most abundant, effective, and efficacious mechanisms for direct citizen participation. It is at this level, as opposed to the level of the political regime in modern nation-states, that the ideal of direct democracy is most feasible, given both the relatively small size of these organizations and the more immediate nature of the issues they address for potential members.[13] The ideal of a "democratic civil society" is thus virtually synonymous with that of a "participatory society" or "participatory democracy" (cf. Held 1987).

This parallel can be illustrated more clearly by looking at democracy in terms of five contrasting dimensions in the relationship between rulers and the ruled: participation, accountability, accessibility, responsiveness, and competitiveness (Schmitter 1983). No democracy will necessarily score equally well on each of these dimensions. An improvement on one dimension can be accompanied by a decrease on another, and new institutional arrangements may contribute to one dimension while undermining another. Similarly, if a distinction is drawn between the levels of the political regime and civil society, certain dimensions may be favored over others and a given dimension may have a qualitatively different meaning depending on the level that is being examined.

At the level of civil society, small organizations by their very nature allow for maximum citizen participation in the decision-making processes that affect them most directly. At this level, the dimensions of accountability, accessibility, and responsiveness are at least potentially subsumed under the dimension of participation within the sphere of issues over which the organization or unit of civil society has the capacity to control. Indeed, these other criteria become relevant for evaluating democratic performance to the extent that the ideal of direct democracy becomes unobtainable (Schmitter 1983). Actions on behalf of the interests of large sectors of civil society at the national level, such as the work of civil rights organizations, consumer advocacy groups, environmental protection lobbies, etc., frequently do not involve active popular participation, yet all are democratic to the extent that they increase accountability and responsiveness to large

13. The size of modern nation-states makes the ready application of the participatory mechanisms that are characteristic of the base level difficult, if not impossible, while decisions taken at the national level may often appear too remote or complex to motivate active participation.

blocs of citizens. At the base level of civil society, however, such activities seem less relevant, given the greater prevalence of participatory mechanisms for pursuing the interests of organized groups of citizens; they are potentially even detrimental if a normative value is placed on direct participation for both personal development and as a school for democratic socialization. Even the most basic attribute of political democracy, the right to vote, is qualitatively distinct at the base level of civil society where, at a minimum, the smaller size of organizational units means that an individual's vote is more significant in terms of the final outcome.

By their very nature, the small size and face-to-face contact that are characteristic of base-level organizations tend to generate equal status and decision-making processes based on consensus within the organization. The continual direct interaction of members often generates greater empathy among them, as individuals make others' interests their own (Mansbridge 1980).

These characteristics of base-level organizations are more than incidental consequences of the organizations' relatively small size.[14] People join organizations for a variety of reasons, many of which are unrelated to tangible material incentives. For instance, the opportunity to hold office or to contribute to the achievement of a worthwhile cause, and the satisfaction derived from simply belonging to and interacting within a group, are important intangible incentives for participating in organizations. Because the latter category of incentives is immediately available to potential members, they tend to be especially important in the absence of material incentives or where there is little or no progress in the achievement of purposive goals related to the attainment of some worthwhile cause. Moreover, while an organization will use a variety of incentives in order to attract and retain members, it will tend to rely predominantly on a single type of incentive. This, in turn, significantly influences and constrains both the strategies that the organization can follow in the pursuit of its objectives and the behavior of the organization's leaders as they seek to ensure the organization's survival. The strategies followed by an organization and the behavior of its leaders must be consistent with the type of incentives the organization uses to attract members.

Significantly, organizations tend to be more democratic internally in the *absence* of material benefits to membership. The presence of material benefits provides a relatively unambiguous measure of the value of belong-

14. The following is drawn from the arguments developed in Wilson 1973.

ing to an organization. When members join organizations in order to contribute to the achievement of worthwhile goals, members generally demand institutionalized means for influencing the definition of purposes and the tactics used to achieve them. Where membership is motivated more by the satisfaction of belonging to and interacting with a group, organizational democracy is frequently both an important aspect of such satisfaction, as well as a by-product of the social ties among members that precede their membership in a particular organization. More generally, this is a reflection of the "symbolic-expressive" aspects of all political organizations and underlines the importance of particular organizational forms: "Organizational forms and procedures are mechanisms for legitimating participation and outcomes. They may give reassurance that things are done appropriately, in particular in situations where it is difficult to demonstrate how a specific decision accomplishes objectives" (Olsen 1983, 9).

The factors that contribute to these democratic characteristics of smaller organizations are accentuated if the organizations are based on territorially circumscribed communities. In varying degrees, communities possess three principal attributes (Taylor 1982). First, the members of a community share common beliefs and values (although communities vary greatly with respect to the range of beliefs and values that are shared, the degree to which these are articulated, and the strength of the individual's attachment to them). Second, relationships between members of communities are direct and multifaceted. Finally, communities are characterized by the existence of reciprocity covering a wide range of arrangements and relations, including mutual aid, cooperation, and forms of sharing. Thus, the tendencies toward equal status within organizations, consensus-oriented decision-making, empathy between members, and organizational democracy in general should be significantly strengthened when the organization is territorially based around a preestablished community.

Such appears to have been the experience of certain Swiss cantons well into the eighteenth century. Here, according to Benjamin Barber's detailed study of the history of one such canton, there existed what Barber calls "Neighborhood Democracy." Within historically defined geographic boundaries, immediacy, smallness, kinship, and collective necessity created the ideal conditions for consensus. As a result, according to Barber's account, democracy in the canton of Raetia was largely unconcerned with the interests of relative majorities and minorities, and the individual felt the obligation to participate in the realization of the communal will (Barber 1974).

In the urban shantytowns of Latin America, similar patterns suggesting the presence of communities appear to be emerging, albeit in a less idyllic form than that described by Barber.[15] Solidarity and mutual self-help seem to characterize many aspects of life in the shantytowns of major Latin American cities.[16] People know each other quite well and are in constant contact with one another. Neighbors baby-sit each other's children and share in each other's and community celebrations. The members of these communities frequently help mitigate family crises, often by pooling their own limited resources to help meet family emergencies resulting from a sudden illness, injury, or death. Limited barter economies may emerge as an alternative for individuals to help make ends meet when employment is scarce. Other collective attempts to resolve the problems of poverty and unemployment include soup kitchens, committees that attempt to provide basic health care, handicraft workshops, neighborhood employment committees that look for jobs for their members, and small businesses, especially in construction-related fields, which seek contracts for small-scale projects such as the construction of low-cost, subsidized housing for their own members and members of their communities. There are also numerous cultural groups and groups for the young, the old, women, and married couples.[17] These various organizations, regardless of their purposes or

15. For the Brazilian case, see Perlman 1976. The Peruvian experience is discussed in Tovar 1986a. On Chile, see Baño 1985; Campero 1987; Oxhorn 1988 and 1986. Also see Evers 1985. The following is based on these works, as well as the author's own observations of various Chilean shantytowns. It should be recognized, however, that the significance of such phenomena varies greatly from community to community and that an alternative democratic mode of social organization is at best still in embryonic form. One of the purposes of this study is to suggest that the emergence of such a democratic alternative in civil society may actually be related to the imposition of authoritarian rule, although it would be naive to ignore the important barriers that prevent its full development, both under authoritarian and democratic political regimes.

16. For example, one study estimated that more than 70 percent of the adults in domestic households in Santiago shantytowns are actively involved in mutual-assistance networks based on trust and reciprocity. See Hardy and Razeto 1984.

17. While not examined directly in the present study, many of the solidaristic and communitarian values discussed here as part of a community identity within shantytowns are often reinforced through the efforts of the Catholic Church in the shantytowns themselves, especially through the promotion of Christian base communities. This is particularly true where the prior existence of such values in shantytowns conditioned the nature of particular base communities and their interest in liberation theology. See Levine and Mainwaring 1989 and Levine 1986. On the Chilean case specifically, see Campero 1987 and Smith 1982.

goals, tend to be democratically organized and emphasize the importance of each member's participation in the group. An alternative identity as a "neighbor" (*vecino*) begins to emerge and popular organizations often seek to demonstrate and develop an alternative democratic life-style (Tovar 1986a).

While a clear pattern appears to be emerging in Latin American shanty-towns, it still remains a relatively limited phenomenon in which only a minority of the population living in these areas participates. It is also a phenomenon whose wider social implications and potential for social transformation generally only have been hinted at (cf. Castells 1983). In order for these egalitarian and participatory patterns to begin to affect society at large, the specific organizations that embody them in the urban slums would somehow have to coalesce into a single, coherent *social movement* that can persist over time.

A social movement differs from an interest group in that its members *knowingly* pursue goals whose benefits are not limited exclusively to those same members.[18] In other words, social movements, as opposed to interest groups, pursue some form of public good. In general terms, the aim of a social movement is to transform society in some way on the basis of the value commitments and ideals of its members, but in a way that also would transform the ideals and commitments of everyone in that society. In the case of the urban marginals being analyzed in this study, a new collective identity, one that encapsulates the egalitarian and participatory ideals represented by their organizations, would have to emerge in order for urban marginals to begin to influence society at large in fundamental ways.[19]

If civil society is to be fully democratized through the influence of base-level organizations in urban slums, these organizations must form a new social movement that would represent the values and organizational pat-

18. I am indebted to Philippe Schmitter for this definition of a social movement.

19. It is at this juncture that Katznelson's distinction between level 3 (shared dispositions) and level 4 (collective action) of class is particularly useful. See Katznelson 1986 and 1981. The similarities between Katznelson's description of collective action as a class and the concept of a "social movement" as developed here should also be noted. I shall return to these issues at the conclusion of this chapter. Katznelson's theoretical framework for understanding class formation and its usefulness for analyzing the development of popular organizations are discussed in the Glossary.

It also should be noted that this definition of a social movement is not meant to imply that the existence of a social movement is determined by its success in transforming society at any level, or that all of the movement's activities necessarily reflect the ultimate objective of societal transformation. Rather, the definition is intended to highlight the potential challenges social movements face in attempting to organize collective action.

terns described above as being associated with small, territorially based organizations. They must form, to borrow the phrase commonly used in Latin America, a genuine *movimiento poblacional* (shantytown movement) that goes beyond being an atomized conglomeration of markedly similar organizations linked by few organic ties. While it may ultimately prove to be impossible, these community-based organizations must begin to operate effectively at levels that progressively encompass more than a single community. And they must do so in the pursuit of goals that similarly will benefit large numbers of people living in more than one community.[20]

THE POTENTIAL FOR ACHIEVING A DEMOCRATIC CIVIL SOCIETY

A number of variables will influence the ability of base-level organizations that emerge under an authoritarian regime (and are responsible for the resurrection of civil society) to form a social movement and transform civil society. Of these variables, three are particularly significant: (1) the level of *institutionalization* that these organizations are able to achieve during the authoritarian period, (2) the type of *transition process* that their respective countries undergo, and (3) the nature of their relations with the *political-party system*.

The Institutionalization of Base-Level Organizations

Institutionalization is defined here as "the process by which organizations and procedures acquire value and stability" (Huntington 1968, 12). The

20. This is an important distinction. It explains why the existence of a large number of shantytown organizations may have little direct impact in transforming a society as a whole, while at the same time it highlights the difficulties that are confronted when organizers in the shantytowns attempt to establish organizational ties across shantytown boundaries. Individual shantytown organizations may exist for many years, obtaining important benefits for their members and the members of the communities in which they are based, but their potential to transform society is severely circumscribed by their refusal and/or inability to pursue goals that will benefit *all* shantytown dwellers. In this regard, although there has been a significant increase in organizational activity in the shantytowns throughout Latin America, at best this activity still represents the potential foundations for future social movements in these countries and the embryonic emergence of the alternative values and organizational styles that will serve as the model for such movements.

ability of organizations that develop under an authoritarian regime to transform civil society is in large part dependent upon their ability to outlive the authoritarian regime and translate their experiences to a new political context. The level of institutionalization that these organizations acquire during the authoritarian period will help determine their capacity to continue functioning once a transition has taken place. Moreover, even before a transition process begins, the potential for a new collective identity to emerge, and thus the possibilities for the formation of a new social movement based upon urban marginals, is a direct function of the institutionalization of the organizations, which themselves form the basis for such a collective identity.

Huntington offers a useful model for measuring the level of institutionalization that organizations possess (Huntington 1968). For Huntington, an organization's level of institutionalization is a function of four sets of factors. The first set of factors Huntington labels *adaptability-rigidity.* In general, the first obstacle an organization must overcome is the most important. If it can adapt successfully to its first organizational challenge, the probability is increased that the organization will be able to adapt to future challenges. Adaptability can be measured according to three variables: organizational age or how long the organization has been functioning; generational age, which is represented by the successful renovation of the organization's leadership; and the ability of an organization to survive changes in its principal functions. The latter variable is particularly important because it signifies that an organization has become more than a simple instrument for achieving certain ends and represents the "triumph of organization over function."

Implicit in the notion of adaptability is an organization's efforts at self-evaluation and reform. It is important that organizations actively involve themselves in efforts to identify and improve upon organizational weaknesses. This aspect of adaptability is particularly relevant to the study of base-level organizational activity in Latin America, where the phenomena is often relatively new and immediate organizational objectives, such as finding solutions to hunger, poor housing, unemployment, etc., do not change.

The second set of factors in Huntington's model is labeled an organization's *complexity-simplicity.* Organizational complexity reflects a higher level of institutionalization. Complexity refers to the multiplication of organizational subunits, both hierarchically and functionally, and the differentiation of various types of subunits. A large number of objectives is another indicator of organizational complexity.

Organizational *autonomy-subordination* is the third set of factors. Autonomy refers to an organization's independence from other groups and a low level of vulnerability to external influences. An autonomous organization is able to maintain its own interests, which can be distinguished from the interests of outside groups. Regarding the types of organizations that are the object of this study, their interests should be distinguishable from the interests of both political parties and the Catholic Church if they are to be considered autonomous.[21]

Finally, the *coherence-disunity* of an organization is an important aspect of institutionalization. An organization's coherence is closely related to its autonomy. Autonomy is a means for achieving organizational coherence and permits an organization to develop a spirit and style that become distinct signs of its conduct. By studying the actual experiences of individual organizations according to these four sets of factors, a relative assessment of the level of institutionalization that they have achieved at a given point in time should be possible. The stronger the indicators of institutionalization are, then the more likely it is that an organization will survive the transition process.

The Transition to Democracy

An important intervening variable in this process of the democratization of civil society is the type of transition from authoritarian rule that a country experiences. A principal conclusion of this study is that this process can begin prior to a democratic transition, but it is highly unlikely that the

21. The relationship between these organizations and political parties will be discussed in detail, both theoretically in this chapter and in terms of the Chilean situation throughout the empirical chapters of this study. Regarding the relationship between the church and base-level organizations in general, it is important to point out that the church's own institutional interests tend to set important limits on the political role it is capable of fulfilling. Tensions frequently emerge as base-level organizations that initially depended on the church become increasingly politicized and seek to expand their goals and activities beyond the more narrow church conception of the proper role for such groups. Institutionalization for these organizations therefore entails a necessary distancing from the church. See Oxhorn 1986; Portes and Johns 1986; Levine and Mainwaring 1989. On the limits to the potential political role of the church in Chile, see Garretón 1989a.

potential for the democratization of civil society will be exhausted under an authoritarian regime. The nature of the regime that succeeds it will have important consequences for the continuation of such a process. Furthermore, the extent to which such a process of democratization advances under an authoritarian regime can have important consequences for a future transition.

A useful typology of transition types is provided by Karl (1990) and is reproduced in Figure 2. This fourfold typology of transitions from authoritarian rule suggests that the transition itself poses a major challenge to the continuation of a democratizing process in civil society after the establishment of a new regime. The two outcomes associated with force, imposition and revolution, would only tend to erect severe impediments to the further democratization of civil society. If the transition results in the imposition of a "protected" democracy that places narrow limits on the participation of popular sectors and their representatives on the Left—what Garretón (1989a) has referred to as the "institutionalization" of the authoritarian regime—the potential for the further democratization of civil society will be tightly circumscribed by the very quality of the regime's exclusive nature. Conversely, if the collapse of the authoritarian regime ushers in a revolution, much will depend on the nature of the revolutionary state that succeeds the authoritarian regime. Historical experience, however, suggests that the result will be a less variegated and pluralistic civil society than that envisioned here, given the dominance of the revolutionary party and the centralized nature of the state.

Outcomes based on compromise would seem to be the most compatible with the development of a democratic civil society, although even with these outcomes there is not much room for optimism. The reform outcome is most likely to result in a transition that would further the processes of democratization in civil society. This is due to the role that the popular sectors themselves would play in bringing about such a transition and

Figure 2. Typology of transitions from authoritarian rule

		Strategies	
		Compromise	Force
Relative	Elite Ascendant	Pact	Imposition
Actor Strength	Mass Ascendant	Reform	Revolution

Source: Karl 1990: 9

suggests that important gains will be made in achieving greater equity and social justice after the transition to democracy. To some extent, it also implies that the process of democratizing civil society—or at least of organizing large segments of the popular sectors—is able to advance relatively far under the authoritarian regime.

Unfortunately, from the perspective of a democratic civil society, reform is also probably less likely to result in a successful transition to democracy. The same mass ascendancy that would lead to a transition characterized by reform could also elicit sufficient fear among important elite groups, especially on the political Right and in the armed forces, so as to result in the imposition of a very limited form of "protected" democracy, the adoption of highly exclusionary elite pacts as part of the transition process or, in the worst case, an authoritarian retrogression. Indeed, it is difficult to find any examples of reform characterized by mass ascendancy leading to a successful transition to democracy.

The final possible outcome, a transition characterized by elite pacts, provides more ambiguous possibilities for the development of a democratic civil society. Such pacts, or agreements among political elites, would presumably establish the "rules of the game" for the resultant democratic regime with the goal of institutionalizing a given distribution of power. This institutionalization would be accomplished by removing certain divisive issues from the democratic political agenda, such as the relationship between the church and the state, the roles of organized labor and the military in the new democracy, and issues concerning future prosecution for human rights violations under the authoritarian regime. Such a transition may create problems for the later consolidation of a democratic political regime, as well as for greater democratization (Karl 1986; O'Donnell and Schmitter 1986). This lack of consolidation, in turn, could place important limitations on a democratization process in civil society.

Yet, in contrast to a regime imposed by force, a democratic regime that is the result of elite pacts may provide more space for the further democratization of civil society. If important rights such as freedom of association and expression are respected under the new democracy, shantytown organizations can be expected to enjoy greater opportunities for growth and the realization of a variety of activities in comparison to the authoritarian regime under which they initially emerged.

While the continuation of a democratization process in civil society may eventually be forced to confront the constraints imposed on the democratic regime's own development by its founding pacts, it is impossible to predict when this will occur and how this confrontation will be resolved. Much will depend on the nature of the elites included in those pacts, the political parties that are capable of competing effectively for office and the course of events following the initial transition—including the further democratization of civil society. Perhaps the development of a democratic civil society could, over time, contribute to the erosion of the constraining features of the pacted democracy.

More generally, the transition to democracy (regardless of its type) is a watershed event in the evolution of popular-sector organizational activity. Translating organizational experiences accumulated under an authoritarian regime to a democratic one is always problematic, given the fundamental role the authoritarian experience itself played in conditioning popular-sector organizational activity. With the establishment of rule of law and the easing of repression, the locus of political activity shifts back to traditional arenas. Political parties, in particular, come to predominate once elections are called and generally serve to demobilize the very social movements whose activities were often critical for ensuring that the authoritarian regime would accept such elections in the first place (O'Donnell and Schmitter 1986). Expectations may rise during the transition and result in frustration among the popular sectors due to the slow pace or perceived lack of change once a new civilian government takes office. Members of popular organizations must, in effect, relearn how to participate politically in order to take advantage of the opportunities that political democracy may create and adapt to the new roles that participation in democratic politics entails.

For popular organizations, the demise of the authoritarian regime implies the loss of an unambiguous "enemy" against which they could mobilize participation and overcome various sources of division. The closing of traditional channels of access to the state placed a premium on self-help and solidarity in the face of growing physical and economic repression. The reopening of those channels can undermine this as people again look to the state and political parties for solutions to their immediate problems. Symbolic resistance through the expression of general discontent and the maintenance of democratic organizational structures can be very effective for maintaining high levels of organizational participation in the darkest periods of authoritarian rule or during periods of rising expectations as the transition appears imminent. In order to influence democratic politics successfully, however, popular organizations must move beyond symbolic forms of participation and develop concrete alternatives that can serve as a basis for negotiations with other actors, including political parties. As a result of the new challenges that democratic regimes pose, the specific organizational forms associated with the authoritarian regime may not be the most appropriate for organizing popular-sector participation with a return to democracy. Alternative organizational forms may be necessary so that the positive organizational experiences associated with authoritarian rule will not be lost with the advent of democratic rule.

The likelihood that popular organizations will survive the transition is closely related to the level of institutionalization that they achieve during the period of authoritarian rule. It is also dependent on the relationship that popular organizations are able to establish with political parties, which is the second intervening variable for understanding the ways in which popular organizations can contribute to the democratization of civil society.

The Political-Party System

The emergence of base-level organizational activity in popular sectors throughout Latin America has focused much attention in recent years on the relations between these organizations, or "movements" (as they are often referred to in the literature), and political parties. In virtually every case, important conflicts seem to emerge between popular organizations at the base and intermediate levels and political parties as the former become more established (Oxhorn 1988 and 1986; Mainwaring 1987; Tovar 1986a; Baño 1985; Castells 1983).

A variety of factors have been suggested that might contribute to this tendency. The presence of multiple parties competing for popular-sector support tends to be divisive and fragments popular organizations. In this regard, the parties can become a major obstacle to the formation of a single coherent social movement that can persist over time.

There is also a clash between the participatory and democratic style of organization that is characteristic of the popular sectors at the base level and the more hierarchical style of political parties that places less emphasis on aspects of internal democracy and participation in favor of representation. This is reflected in the "process" orientation of many base-level popular organizations. These organizations often exist as a source of solidarity, friendship, and other collective values among their members, who tend to form a community, as compared to political parties, which are more result-oriented and frequently reorganize to be more efficacious in achieving results.

Political parties are also frequently viewed as a threat to the autonomy of the popular organizations as new, or at least distinct, social actors. The desire for autonomy on the part of popular organizations is frequently seen as a characteristic of the anti-institutional bias often attributed to these organizations and the social movements they may represent, which are portrayed as alternatives to more traditional forms of political activity that focus on the state and party structures. Where repression has resulted in the proscription of traditional political-party activity for long periods of time, this desire for autonomy on the part of popular organizations also reflects the fact that they have emerged largely independent of formal party structures.

An additional source of tension between political parties and popular organizations is that the members of popular organizations often view political parties and the political elites that represent them with a strong sense of suspicion. The politicians that represent the political parties are often viewed as "outsiders" and somehow different. An important element of class prejudice is also present because such elites tend to be relatively advantaged in comparison to the urban poor who form these groups. In countries where authoritarian regimes have been preceded by long periods of political democracy and relatively institutionalized party systems, such suspicions are often fed by a tendency to apportion at least part of the blame for the collapse of the previous regime on the irresponsibility of politicians, a tendency often encouraged by authoritarian regimes in order to discredit the political parties (or at least the old political parties) and "depoliticize" society in general.

At the same time, there are clear links between the parties and popular organizations, especially in terms of a certain overlap between the leadership of these organizations and party activists. These links are not yet fully understood and will have important consequences in terms of the capacity of popular organizations to affect the wider political system in general (Boschi 1984; Garretón 1989a, and 1989c). The new, or "renovated," Left in Latin America, for example, sees the popular sectors as an important potential social base. The New Left rejects the rigid classical Marxist-Leninist project, which is based on the primacy of the working class or proletariat. It finds inspiration for an alternative project—a more democratic and participatory society—in the organizational style associated with popular-sector organizations, even though this new project has yet to address satisfactorily the problems of translating the idea of democracy "from the bottom up" to the level of the political regime and society as a whole vis-à-vis party structures (Barros 1986).

The relations between base-level organizations and political parties clearly emerge as a central issue in Latin American politics. There appears to be an implicit recognition that if a process of democratization of civil society is to proceed, political parties can facilitate this by serving as an essential bridge between the level of civil society and the political regime. At minimum, the tensions between political parties and popular organizations that contribute to the fragmentation and weakening of popular-sector organizational activity and the problematique of organizational autonomy vis-à-vis political parties will have to be resolved.

Most analyses of these problems have generally ignored a fundamental aspect of these new popular organizations: their territorially defined basis. As the model for the resurrection of civil society under authoritarian regimes suggests, the tendency has been for these organizations to emerge on the basis of spatially defined communities. This spatial definition, in turn, raises problems of articulation between political parties as the main instrument of territorial representation at the level of the political regime and these organizations as territorially based units of direct democracy. Parties are not only "outsiders"; they also can represent competing sources of identity that may threaten the integrity of the community identity so essential to the formation and continued existence of many popular organizations.

Political parties are based on concepts of representation, participation, and the aggregation of interests that are antithetical to those on which popular organizations are founded. To the extent that this is the case, one would expect the relations between parties and functionally based popular organizations to be very different, and indeed this seems to be true when looking at the development of labor movements in most countries. The relations between functionally based organizations (especially those centered around the work group and issues related to production rather than consumption) and political parties are less problematic because the organizational foundations of functionally based organizations do not entail values and interests that appear to be at odds with those guiding the constitution of parties. Both types of organizations seek members on distinct criteria that are independent of any territorially circumscribed community. The notion of a labor movement, for example, transcends any given territorial identity and, indeed, is dependent on the widest possible aggregation of individual workers for its strength, even though workers may be spatially concentrated.

On another level, an organized labor movement that seeks to pursue its interests through transformations in the capitalist system of production is given the opportunity to do so through political democracy. Political parties that claim to represent workers' interests can be critical allies in the labor movement's attempt to win control over state policymaking through electoral competition with other social groups, including the capitalists who own the means of production. As Przeworski (1985) points out,

> Electoral politics constitutes the mechanism through which anyone can as a citizen express claims to goods and services. While as immediate producers workers have no institutional claim to the product, as citizens they can process such claims through the political system. Moreover, again as citizens as distinguished from immediate producers, they can intervene in the very organization of production and allocation of profit. Capitalists are able to seek the realization of their interests in the course of everyday activity within the system of production. . . . By contrast, workers can process their claims only collectively and only indirectly, through organizations which are embedded in systems of representation, principally trade-unions and political parties. (11)

Conversely, a social movement composed of shantytown organizations pursuing the interests of the urban poor related to their consumption opportunities and life chances would be more concerned with defining the nature and quality of citizenship rights. A social project that stresses the solidaristic and participatory values associated with popular organizations would be likely to bring problems related to the articulation of such a movement and political parties to the fore. Such problems of articulation are further compounded by the possibility that such a movement of the urban poor, unlike organized labor in a capitalist society (where capitalists own the means of production), might pursue its interests *directly* vis-à-vis the state without any party intermediation.

The above suggests that the scope and nature of demands that an organization pursues would also affect the relationship between political parties and popular-sector organizations. Whereas a social movement composed of urban shantytown organizations would be expected to face problems of articulation with political parties because of their competing organizational bases, individual shantytown organizations that are not organically tied to a broader movement and pursue only the immediate interests of their members would probably accept a patron-client relationship with political parties in exchange for the immediate satisfaction of certain consumption needs, while also continuing to pursue their interests either through their own means or through direct contact with external agents such as the church and the local level of government. Conversely, individual functionally based organizations at the base level might seek the sponsorship of political parties if they are only concerned with the pursuit of the immediate needs of their members, perhaps as a source of legitimacy in dealing with management, or for other resources that parties can offer. A broader labor movement that is more concerned with pursuing social change might view particular parties (such as Social Democratic or Labor parties) as potential allies in the pursuit of their interests through control of government policymaking.

In this way, the model developed for understanding the resurrection of civil society under an authoritarian regime suggests a hypothesis:

> *Hypothesis 1*: Different types of actors (territorial or functional) have a proclivity for a given type of relation with political parties, depending on the scope and nature of their demands.

This hypothesis forms the basis of a model of different modes of relations between political parties and functionally or territorially based actors. The model is illustrated schematically in Figure 3. It should be noted that while these types of relationships are expressed in ideal terms, the analysis above clearly suggests that the emerging relation between political parties and the types of territorially based shantytown organizations that are the object of this study is one of *competition*, as represented by the lower right-hand quadrant.

Hypothesis 1 suggests that the development of a democratic civil society will be severely constrained by the extent to which political parties come to dominate political activity, something that has generally happened as soon as "founding elections" are called during a transition process (O'Donnell and Schmitter 1986). Two sets of factors, however, help mitigate this tendency toward a competitive relationship between political parties and territorially based actors.

The first set of factors relates to the democratic nature of party structures themselves (Oxhorn 1986). In essence, to avoid confrontation, political

Figure 3. Relations between political parties and base level actors:
Scope and nature of demands of demands or interests

Actors	Satisfaction of Group's Immediate Needs		Transformation of Regime and Society
Functional/ Work Group	Sponsorship by Political Parties		Periodic Allies with Political Parties
Territorial	Clientelistic Penetration by Political Parties		Competitors with Political Parties

parties could adopt some of the participatory values represented by these organizations if they wish to interact with them. Party structures would have to be decentralized in order to allow for a maximum amount of participation by the party's grassroots members in the party's decision-making processes. Ideally, such decision-making processes would need to be characterized by a two-way flow of information and an interchange of ideas between different levels of the party. Democratic lines of accountability would be required to link the party's elite or national levels with local branches.[22] Rigid, hierarchically organized political-party structures, with an insulated national party elite that manages party affairs in a highly centralized fashion, are most likely to generate conflicts between parties and territorially based popular organizations.[23]

Moreover, and specifically in relation to territorially based organizations, parties would have to be willing to accept that such organizations maintain a certain level of autonomy from party structures. For a variety of reasons, including the heterogeneity of popular sectors (see Glossary), pluralism will

22. These ideas are similar to those which Macpherson discusses in relation to what he calls a "pyramidal model of participatory democracy." See Macpherson 1977.

23. Significantly, similar types of open, democratic party structures may also be the best suited for dealing with the problems of instability, change, and uncertainty that characterize most Latin American democracies today. More generally, democratic and participatory intra-party structures may help to strengthen representative democracy and democratic liberties that have been weakened by the growing centralization and economic role of the state in modern societies. See Poulantzas 1980.

often tend to characterize popular organizations; that is, their members will belong to a variety of political parties or no party at all. The surest way to exacerbate tensions between political parties and territorially based popular organizations would be for the political parties to attempt to "capture" these organizations and subordinate the organizations' interests to those of the parties. Instead, parties must attempt to work with, not control, these organizations.[24]

The second set of factors, which is somewhat related to the first, involves the prospects for decentralization after the transition. Highly centralized political systems are the least conducive to the emergence of a democratic civil society and have been a primary reason why the development of civil societies may have been impeded throughout Latin America. The inertia of the state, combined with the absence of the ethnic and linguistic factors that were important in successfully achieving decentralization in Europe, are major obstacles to extensive decentralization in postauthoritarian Latin America.[25] The principal empirical questions are whether there exist sufficiently powerful interests to ensure that decentralization remains on the agenda both during and after the transition in each country, and whether the issue of decentralization can form the basis for an alliance between political parties and territorially based organizations.

In sum, the argument developed here suggests that under certain circumstances, not only will civil society be resurrected under an authoritarian regime, it may even undergo a process of democratization. The extent to which this democratization is able to advance will depend on the institutionalization that territorially based popular organizations can achieve under the authoritarian regime, as well as the nature of the transition from authoritarian rule that the country undergoes and the relations between popular organizations and the political-party system. Schematically, this process of the democratization of civil society is illustrated in Figure 4.

24. This point will be returned to frequently in discussing the Chilean case. Little empirical evidence is available discussing the political tendencies of the members of territorially based popular-sector organizations, although they generally tend to be associated with leftist parties and progressive tendencies within centrist parties. See Oxhorn 1988 and 1986; Castells 1983.

25. In this regard, the efforts of President Alfonsín of Argentina to relocate the Argentine capital were very significant. Had he been successful, Argentina might have developed a second pole to counter the dominance of Buenos Aires, with important implications for the subsequent development of civil society in Argentina. The relationship between decentralization and the development of civil society is discussed at length in the Glossary.

Figure 4.   The democratization of civil society

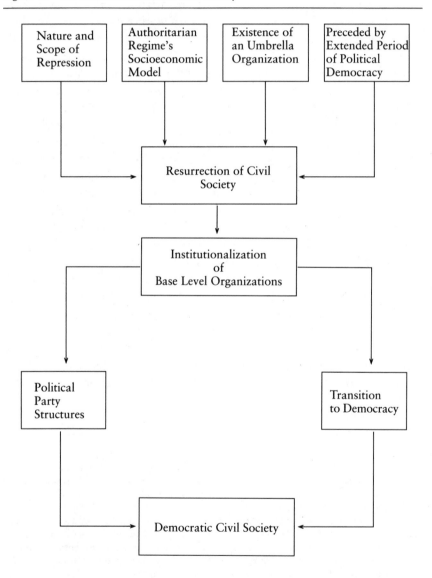

CONCLUSIONS: THE PROBLEMATIQUE OF "OLD" AND "NEW" ACTORS

In a fundamental way, the issues involved in the resurrection of civil society and its potential for democratization reflect the emergence of "new" actors (a myriad of territorially based popular organizations) and their juxtaposition with a variety of "old" actors (the traditional political elite and the parties they represent). The legacy of the authoritarian regime will affect both differently; as a result they may develop identities that are at odds with each other. The above discussion suggests that an important part of the identity of the new popular organizations may reflect a greater commitment to ideals associated with participatory democracy and greater distance from political parties. The identity of traditional political elites, on the other hand, is likely to reflect the institutional history of their respective parties and their own experiences under the previous democratic regime.

The recent history of base-level organizational activity in the shantytowns of Santiago, Chile, provides a unique case for attempting to examine the issues discussed here. The effervescence of these organizations through the mid-1980s, despite the fact that Chile had not yet begun a transition process; the unparalleled stability of its democratic regime until the 1973 military coup; Chile's long experience with a competitive political-party system; and the reemergence of the political-party sphere in 1983 after almost ten years of complete recess all suggest that the problems and possibilities associated with the resurrection of civil society and its democratization are very relevant to understanding Chile's political process.

Base-level organizational activity in Chilean shantytowns will be examined in terms of two distinct axes: the emergence of a new popular collective identity within popular organizations and the capacity of these organizations to engage in collective action through the formation of a new popular social movement. This approach will highlight not only the factors that favor the development and growth of popular organizations but, more important, focus attention on the specific and myriad factors that constrain that development.

I hope that such a nuanced approach will avoid the excessive optimism that has characterized a number of earlier studies of base-level organizational activity by accepting from the onset the true dimensions of the challenge facing popular organizations (cf. Perlman 1976; Evers 1985). My approach offers a more objective way for measuring and understanding the actual significance of base-level organizational activity by drawing attention to different levels of analysis for evaluating its development.

This study will therefore revolve around two questions. First, to what extent has a new popular collective identity emerged on the basis of shared dispositions among Santiago's urban poor? Second, if such a popular collective identity has in fact emerged, under what conditions would it be most likely to generate collective action in the form of a new social movement composed of the urban poor? The two questions are obviously related, but it is important to recognize that not all groups with shared dispositions are able or even willing to translate them into collective action capable of affecting society as a whole. Nor does such a popular identity need to be translated into a new social movement in order to influence Chilean politics. For example, as will be argued in the chapters that follow, one factor in explaining the Chilean opposition's apparent inability to retake and retain the political initiative prior to 1988 was the emergence of a cleavage between elite- and popular-sector identities concerning important issues such as the nature of democracy and democratic transitions.

But before turning to these questions directly, we must first examine the historical context within which base-level organizations emerged.

2

CHILE'S DEMOCRATIC HERITAGE AND AUTHORITARIAN EXPERIENCE

An Overview

Chile's political development represents an anomaly among Latin American countries. The "politicized state,"[1] which has been responsible for the high levels of political instability found throughout Latin America, simply did not develop in Chile. Instead, Chile enjoyed a level of political stability within increasingly democratic political institutions, which is remarkable even by European standards. From 1830 until 1973, Chile was governed by a succession of elected presidents with only two brief periods of exception.[2] Chile developed representative political institutions and a strong political-party system that became the hallmarks of Latin American democracy until their abrupt demise in 1973.

In this chapter I shall examine important aspects of the evolution of Chile's political institutions under the democratic regime in order to under-

1. The politicized state is characterized by the lack of an institutionalized political regime and political processes "in which at every crisis, and to some extent for every decision, the actors are called on to determine the way in which the system will operate." See Chalmers 1977, 25.

2. Democratic rule was first interrupted in 1891 after a brief civil war, and again during the turbulent period from 1924 through 1932 in which four presidents were pressured into resigning as Chile was racked by political and economic crises. During the entire 143-year period, Chile was ruled by some form of junta for a total of only 13 months (Valenzuela 1989).

stand the nature of popular-sector organizational activity and incorporation into the political process prior to the military coup. In general, the incorporation of the popular sectors into the democratic process was slow, uneven, and incomplete. The reasons for this can be found in the way political institutions developed. These same reasons are also important in explaining both the breakdown of Chilean democracy and the principal characteristics of the subsequent military regime.

I shall argue that the early institutionalization of the Chilean state and political-party system was largely responsible for Chile's prolonged democratic stability. The state became an arena for resolving social conflicts and demands, while political parties were able to manage access to the state peacefully for increasingly diverse segments of society. But these same characteristics of the political system also contained the seeds of democracy's demise. Specifically, the increasingly centralized nature of the state and the effects that this had on the development of the political-party system generated two distortions in the Chilean political process. First, the incorporation of new groups into the political process tended to outpace any corresponding change in the underlying economic structure that could support the redistribution of political power and satisfy the demands that these groups placed on the system. Second, the relative "overdevelopment" of the political system, in particular the political parties, caused the underdevelopment of civil society by stifling the emergence of autonomous organizations within society.[3] Both distortions became increasingly acute in the late 1960s and ultimately converged in the collapse of the democratic regime in 1973.

This chapter is divided into three sections. After examining certain key aspects of the democratic regime, I shall analyze the breakdown of Chilean democracy. I shall argue that the root causes of the breakdown were related to the two distortions mentioned above: the relative underdevelopment of the economic structure in comparison to the political structure, and the obstacles to the development of a civil society posed by the dominance of political parties. Finally, I shall explore the ultimate consequences of the breakdown of Chilean democracy in terms of some of the dominant characteristics of the military regime that replaced it.[4]

3. The term "civil society" will be used to denote the kind of variegated society composed of a number of self-constituted units and subunits associated with the corporate model of civil society discussed in the Glossary.

4. The final breakdown of the military regime, transition to democracy, and role played by the popular sectors will be discussed in Chapter 8.

THE CHILEAN DEMOCRATIC REGIME

A complete analysis of the development of the Chilean political process is beyond the scope of the present study.[5] Instead, I shall examine in this section several aspects of that process for their importance in understanding popular-sector organizational activity both before and after the military coup: the development of a centralized state, the predominance of political parties within society, the precarious incorporation of the popular sectors in the political process, the modalities of organizational activity in the *poblaciones*, and the breakdown of the democratic regime.

The Centralized State and Political Stability

The relatively early consolidation of the Chilean state under civilian authority between 1830 and 1860 served as the foundation for Chile's subsequent political stability (Pinto 1970; A. Valenzuela 1978; Loveman 1979; Gil 1966; Alvarado et al., 1973). Over time, the state became the arena for resolving social conflicts among groups competing for political power. Procedures and institutions were strengthened within the state for generating accommodation among elites who represented different constituencies. New groups were gradually incorporated into the political process as the state expanded. The state became the principal referent for social demands (Garretón 1989a). Power struggles were resolved through constitutional means, not the balance of military force.

The key to political stability in this early phase of Chilean history was a rough correspondence between the new institutions of the Chilean state and the political and economic power of the then dominant class, the large landowners. Pinto explains the relative uniqueness of the Chilean case in this regard:

> In effect, Diego Portales[6] consolidated a civilian authority that . . . established what other Latin American republics did not achieve: it

5. The best analysis of the Chilean political process beginning with the adoption of the 1925 constitution is Garretón 1989a. Detailed descriptions of the evolution of its various aspects from the founding of the republic are found in Gil 1966 and Loveman 1979. Pinto (1970) offers a very succinct and insightful analysis of the political economy of Chile from 1830 through the eve of the 1970 presidential election. For an interesting analysis of Chilean politics from the perspective of the role played by center parties, see Scully 1992.

6. Diego Portales is generally considered to be the father of the Chilean state, even though he never actually served as president.

defined the predominance of class that conformed to the objective realities of the moment. . . . He detected where effective power resided according to the economic structure and "rationalized" it politically. Other countries, in turn, did not formalize the objective tutelage of the large landowners in a "civilian" expression and had to live through a more or less prolonged stage of *caudillos* and dictators (Pinto 1970, 6)

Within the confines of a consolidated state, the ruling political coalition was gradually expanded (Scully 1992; Pinto 1970; Loveman 1979; Gil 1966). Although still confined to a small group until the 1920s, new commercial and industrial sectors tied to the export sector began to share political power with the large landowners.[7]

The War of the Pacific (1879), in which Chile defeated both Peru and Bolivia, was a turning point in Chile's political economy. As a result of its victory, Chile acquired the mineral-rich Atacama Desert. Nitrate, and later copper, exports from this region became the foundation for economic growth and development in Chile. The dominance of mineral exports in the Chilean economy has had many long-term effects on Chile's socioeconomic development, but two are particularly relevant to the current study: the expanded role of the state in Chilean society, and the relative underdevelopment of the economic structure in comparison to the political structure.[8]

The Expansion and Centralization of the Chilean State

Revenues from mineral exports reinforced the role of the state as the arena for resolving social conflicts and responding to social demands. The nitrate industry quickly came under the domination of foreign capital. As a result, Pinto notes, "*the government and not national owners of the export sector* is the agent which administers, spends and distributes a considerable fraction of the rent generated by external trade" (Pinto 1970, 10; emphasis in original). This export bonanza funded an important expansion of the state. Public services (particularly education) and public works projects

---

7. During this period, Chilean agriculture was also closely tied to the export sector and provided a significant source of foreign exchange. See Loveman 1979; Pinto 1970.

8. Other effects include dramatically increased vulnerability to fluctuations in international demand for Chile's principal commodity exports, the formation of a powerful labor movement, and the rise of the political left in Chile. The effects caused by the dominance of mineral exports in the Chilean economy are discussed in Loveman 1979; Gil 1966; Berquist 1986; Pinto 1970; and Cardoso and Faletto 1979.

(such as extending the railroad and telegraph networks) were expanded in the latter part of the nineteenth century as government revenues increased dramatically (Loveman 1979; Pinto 1970). Future Chilean socioeconomic development came to be characterized by the continued expansion of the state apparatus (Bitar 1986a).

The nitrate bonanza eventually came to an end with the discovery of synthetic forms of nitrate and the Great Depression of the 1930s (Loveman 1979). Copper exports gradually replaced nitrate exports, and foreign interests quickly dominated the new export sector in much the same way that they had controlled nitrate exports. The "rent" from copper exports continued to be channeled through the state.[9]

The Chilean state has played a pivotal role in Chile's industrialization (Stallings 1978; Bitar 1986a; Garretón 1989a). This was inevitable, given the investment resources that the state had at its disposal. It also reflected the "inward-looking" nature of its development model of import-substituting industrialization, adopted in the late 1930s. In contrast to the previous "export-led" pattern of economic development, the new development model required an expansion of the internal market and high levels of tariff protection for emergent industries.

By 1970, the economic role of the state in Chile was greater than in any other Latin American country, with the exception of Cuba (Bitar 1986a). In the late 1960s, the state was the sole or partial owner of many of the country's largest and most important industries. The state controlled 47 percent of the GDP in 1970 and in 1969 it supplied 75 percent of gross domestic investment in fixed capital. The state was also a major employer, with the public sector accounting for 40.6 percent of total employment in 1970 (Stallings 1978).

This expansion of state activities was accompanied by an increasing level of centralization (Gil 1966; A. Valenzuela 1977 and 1978; Garretón 1989a). The national parliament became a principal arena for the resolution of social conflicts and demands. The executive branch and numerous semi-autonomous public bodies, such as the State Development Corporation (CORFO), distributed large amounts of resources and attempted to find solutions for major social demands that were increasingly directed toward the state. Local governments experienced a progressive usurpation of their

9. The dominance of foreign capital in the copper industry generated increasing pressure for its nationalization. This was finally carried out by the Allende government in 1971. The history of the Chilean copper industry and its nationalization are analyzed in Moran 1974.

prerogatives and resources by the central government. As a result, local initiatives became increasingly dependent upon decisions made by the central government in Santiago.

The increasing centralization of the state was paralleled by the growing importance of Santiago, the nation's capital, in the political, economic, and cultural life of the nation. During the democratic period, Santiago was the largest and fastest-growing city in Chile. Its population grew from 952,000, or 18.9 percent of the total Chilean population, in 1940 to 2,662,000, or 30.1 percent of the total population, in 1970. Santiago's population was already three times that of Chile's second-largest urban area, Valparaíso-Viña del Mar, in 1940. By 1970, it was six times as large (Raczynski 1974).[10] Manufacturing was similarly concentrated in Santiago and Valparaíso. In 1973, Santiago's proportion of Chile's total industrial production was 49 percent, compared to 12 percent for Valparaíso. The city of Concepción accounted for the third-highest proportion of industrial production in 1973, amounting to just 11 percent (Gwynne 1986).

Political "Overdevelopment" and Economic Underdevelopment

The second long-term effect of the dominance of mineral exports in the Chilean economy is that it reinforced the tendency for political change to outpace changes in the structure of Chile's economy.[11] The expansion of the state, which began with a rise in nitrate revenues in the latter part of the nineteenth century, led to the emergence of new social groups that were dependent upon the public sector. The emerging middle-class groups, particularly in the urban centers, were dependent on employment opportunities being created by the expansion of state services, as well as those created by the growth in the service sector tied to the rise in the import-export trade. Two new political parties, the Radical and Democratic Parties, entered onto the political scene in the late nineteenth century to represent the interests of these new social groups.

These changes in the social structure were largely unrelated to corresponding changes in the underlying structure of the national economy. The new groups were dependent on the state, not the productive sector. As

10. The real level of concentration is even greater given that Valparaíso is the main port for Santiago and is located approximately seventy-five miles away from the capital.

11. This argument is drawn largely from the classic article by Aníbal Pinto, "Desarrollo económico y relaciones sociales" (Pinto 1970).

Pinto points out, "the channeling of a significant part of national income to the state created a structure of demand and employment very different from that which would have existed if these rents had gone into the hands of national owners [of the mining sector]" (Pinto 1970, 11). This process of political change culminated in the 1920s and early 1930s, after Arturo Alessandri was able to take advantage of convulsions in the export sector to win the 1920 presidential elections. Using the miners of the north "as electoral canon fodder" (Pinto 1970, 16), Alessandri was at the head of what Gil (1966) has described as a "revolt of the middle class." After eight years of relative political instability from 1924 through 1932, the oligarchy was forced to share its political tutelage with the middle classes under a new constitution enacted in 1925:[12] the "oligarchic state" had collapsed and was replaced by the "compromise state" (*Estado de Compromiso*) (Garretón 1989a).

The compromise state represented an important change in Chilean politics. The middle classes, through the political parties that represented them, now shared power with the old oligarchy. The way was paved for the increasing participation of the working class and its principal representatives, the Communist and Socialist Parties, in Chilean politics. Both parties participated in the Popular Front governing coalition with the middle-class Radical Party from 1938 through 1941, and the two parties of the Left together were able to win 32 percent of the popular vote in the 1941 parliamentary elections.[13]

12. As Pinto points out, Alessandri's electoral strength alone was not sufficient to overcome the oligarchy's opposition to sharing political power with the middle classes. The process had to be completed by "the dictator Ibáñez, who counteracted the resistance of the extreme Right by placing the army on the other side of the scale" (Pinto 1970, 16). During this rather chaotic period in Chilean history, marked by both economic and political crises, Chile was ruled by a number of military and civilian governments. For details on the period, see Loveman 1979, and Gil 1966. Also see Scully 1992.

13. The influence of the Left and working classes in Chile's democratic regime at this time should not be exaggerated. The Communist Party was outlawed from 1947 to 1958 and electoral participation never exceeded more than a third of the population until the 1960s (Garretón 1987c). Pinto best sums up the importance of the Popular Front experience for the lower classes: "In terms of social changes, it appears evident that the principal and most long-lasting of the experience was the opportunity that it established for the eruption and growth of representative organizations of the mass of workers, including the peasantry, that perhaps for the first time made their presence felt in the democratic dispute. . . . [T]he marxist Left achieved the control of almost a third of the official electorate [in 1941]. . . . But . . . that leftist wave scarcely altered the "system of power," at least in the sense of transferring to representatives of the popular mass some part of the effective influence in the management of the country" (Pinto 1970, 21–22). For more on this period, see Gil 1966 and Loveman 1979.

This alteration of the political balance of power in favor of the middle classes (and to a lesser extent the working class) was not accompanied by any significant corresponding change in Chile's economic structure. Pinto explains the importance—and uniqueness—of this lag between political and economic development:

> The second and most "modern" diversification of the social structure manifested itself and unfolded practically at the margin of corresponding changes in the economic structure of the country. . . . [I]n the inverse of the classic European model, the alleged transformation did not have its "natural" counterpart in a parallel change in the economic structure, which continued to be more or less the same. . . . While in the first case these basic stratums of modern society—and their political expressions, which are the middle- and working-classes—developed to the rhythm characteristic of the "industrial revolution," in Chile this happened without any substantive alteration in the productive system. . . . Given the above, it is possible to see the two outstanding incongruities in the Chilean reality of this time. . . . [The first is] the contradiction between an "underdeveloped" [economic] structure and an "advanced" sociopolitical organization. The second emerges as the contrast between this structure of the economic system and the level and composition of national demand, a contrast which the rector Molina summarized in his famous sentence "we are civilized in terms of consumption and primitive in terms of production." (Pinto 1970, 17)

Indeed, one of the pillars of the compromise state was the tacit agreement among elites not to disturb the antiquated system of agricultural relations on which the old oligarchy relied for its power and influence (Scully 1992; A. Valenzuela 1978; Garretón 1989a; Gil 1966; Loveman 1979).

It was not until the late 1930s under the Popular Front government that the implementation of a new development model based on import-substitution industrialization finally began to alter the structure of production in accordance with the political and social importance that the middle and working classes had acquired (Pinto 1970). The diversity found in Chile's social and political structure now had foundation in the growing complexity of Chile's economic structure. Chile began to industrialize and the modern sector of the economy grew. The internal capacity for meeting national demand correspondingly increased.

The increasing congruence between economic and sociopolitical structures that Chile's industrialization provided had its limits. As Garretón (1989b) points out, an important characteristic of the compromise state was the gradual incorporation of new groups into the political system in order to maintain political stability. Yet, as will be discussed in the subsection dealing with the breakdown of Chilean democracy, the development model itself, in the medium to long term, was incapable of altering the economic structure in line with the requirements imposed on it by the progressive political incorporation of the working class and, beginning in the 1960s, the peasantry and urban marginal sectors.

The Chilean political process was characterized, from the late 1930s onward, by a unique constellation of three interrelated processes (Garretón 1989a). Import-substituting industrialization advanced simultaneously with a process of "substantive" democratization, defined by the progressive incorporation of new sectors into the political system and improvements in their standards of living. Both, in turn, took place within the context of expanding voter suffrage under a democratic regime. Chile was unique in Latin America, where the process of substantive democratization generally had been associated with authoritarian regimes. Chile's industrialization process made substantive democratization compatible with political democracy, while the viability of the democratic political regime came to be dependent on the process of substantive democratization for its own viability and legitimacy. The limits of Chile's development model would not only threaten the process of substantive democratization, but the stability of the democratic regime itself. As Pinto points out,

> in the period that opened after the [1930s economic] crisis and especially after the breakout of the war, the productive structure was modified appreciably in the sense that it corresponded more closely to the social and political "diversification." But these variables and their inter-relationship must be understood in their dynamic reality. That is, if the first became more "modern," the complexity and "sophistication" of the social realm was also accentuated with the open rise of middle- and working-class groups and their political organizations. A "race" was thus posed between both planes that can be synthesized as a competition between the rhythm of economic development and "political development." (Pinto 1970, 31)

Political Parties and the Underdevelopment of Civil Society

The early development of the Chilean state was accompanied by the emergence of a modern political-party system in the late nineteenth and early twentieth centuries.[14] Political parties representing the full spectrum of political tendencies within Chilean society had already been formed at the time of the crisis of the oligarchic state in the 1920s. All of the principal political parties in Chile in the early 1970s, with the exception of the Revolutionary Left Movement (MIR), could trace their origins either directly or indirectly (as a result of their formation through schisms in older political parties) to the period preceding the formation of the "compromise state."

As a result of this early development of political parties, the political-party system was already well established before significant new social groups were incorporated into the political system. For example, the two principal political parties that represented the middle classes when they were fully incorporated into the political system in the 1920s, the Radical Party and Democratic Party, had been formed in 1861 and 1887, respectively. The working-class parties of the Left, the Communist Party and the Socialist Party, similarly trace their origins to radical workers' organizations that first emerged in northern mining communities in the latter part of the nineteenth century (Pinto 1970; Angell 1972; Berquist 1986). The incorporation of new social groups into the political process was thus facilitated by the prior existence of institutionalized mechanisms for representing the interests of those groups and channeling their participation. This helped to preserve general political stability and the stability of the party system, which itself was reinforced by the incorporation of new social groups (Garretón 1989a).

The centralized nature of the Chilean state generated a corresponding centralization of political-party structures (A. Valenzuela 1977; Garretón 1989a; Gil 1966). The central government distributed large amounts of resources and demands of various segments of society were addressed to the state for satisfaction. The state had also become the arena for resolving social conflicts and reaching accommodations among competing groups. National party structures were important because it was at the national

14. The development of the political-party system and its various implications for the Chilean political process are discussed in Garretón 1989a; Scully 1992; A. Valenzuela 1977 and 1978; Gil 1966; and Loveman 1979.

level of government that important decisions were made. Parties became increasingly centralized in order to compete more effectively for power within the centralized state, with each party aiming to ultimately gain control over it.

The effect of an increasingly centralized state on the centralization of party structures is most apparent in the relationship between the central and local levels of government. The expansion of national government authority caused a steady erosion of the power of local government. This meant that the effectiveness of local politicians became increasingly dependent upon their ability to extract resources and special favors from the national government. Highly centralized political parties became the mechanism for gaining access to the central state, tying local party officials to national party elites (A. Valenzuela 1977).

The combination of all these factors resulted in what Garretón (1989a) has called the "backbone" of Chilean society: the tight overlapping between political-party structures and social organizations. As a result of this overlap, virtually all spheres of Chilean society were highly politicized and penetrated by political parties. Political parties became the principal arena through which social actors were organized. The same parties then mediated the demands that organized sectors of society placed on the state. The development of a civil society (see Glossary) was stymied because emergent social organizations were weak and dependent on political parties.

In sum, the predominant influence of political parties within Chilean society (which is closely related to the centralized nature of the Chilean state) created a distortion in the Chilean political process. Chile came to be characterized by its "overdeveloped" political system, which dominated an "underdeveloped" civil society.[15] The effects of this imbalance on the viability of Chile's democratic political regime would become increasingly apparent toward the end of the 1960s, a point that will be discussed at length later.

The Incorporation of the Popular Sectors in the Democratic Political Process

The process of incorporating the popular sectors into the political process can be divided into three distinct phases. The first phase begins with the

15. The contrast with the Western European experience makes this clear. While its institutionalized party system and long period of democratic stability seemed more reminiscent of a

consolidation of the compromise state and the Popular Front government of 1938. The rise of the Christian Democratic Party (DC) in the late 1950s ushered in a second phase of popular-sector incorporation when Christian Democrat Eduardo Frei won the 1964 presidential election. The final phase begins with the radicalization of the politics of popular-sector incorporation in the late 1960s and ends with the 1973 military coup.

The Compromise State and the 1938 Popular Front Government

The consolidation of the compromise state in the 1930s first raised the possibility of incorporating the popular sectors into the Chilean political process. Although various intermittent efforts to organize the popular sectors around housing issues marked the early part of this century, they had few lasting effects (Espinoza 1988). Numerous renters' organizations were formed and several renters' strikes had been mobilized. But only partial responses to the movements' demands by the government had led to their demobilization. The political parties of the Left, particularly the Communist Party, had been closely associated with these early organizational activities, and conflicts began to emerge between the parties and the renters' organizations as the former focused their efforts on building a strong labor movement. Movements for renters' rights faded into history.

The organized labor movement became virtually the exclusive referent for popular-sector interests with the consolidation of the Compromise State. The labor movement was already relatively strong when unions were legalized in 1924 as part of the early reforms associated with the collapse of the oligarchic state. Various workers' organizations first began to appear in the late 1800s and by 1925 a total of more than 200,000 workers belonged to 214 different unions. The first major trade union federation, the Chilean Workers' Federation (FOCh), was officially formed in 1918 (Angell 1972).

Perhaps more important for organized labor's incorporation into the political process, the Chilean Left (particularly the Communist Party) played a key role in the development of the labor movement from its inception (Berquist 1986; Angell 1972). The Left increasingly devoted its

---

Western European country than a Latin American one, Chile's civil society was very different. The limited autonomy of social organizations meant that the type of strong civil society that also characterizes Western European polities did not emerge in Chile.

attention to organizing workers in the workplace, and this redirection was a principal factor in the early demise of the renters' rights movements in the 1920s (Espinoza 1988). The parties of the Left considered the popular sectors' consumption-oriented demands part of a "secondary structural contradiction" (Alvarado et al. 1973). Organized labor became the social foundation for the growing strength of the Left in Chilean politics. Through the strength of its organizations and its privileged relationship to the political Left, the working class came to dominate the politics of the popular sectors under the compromise state.

The dominant position of organized labor tended to serve the interests of only a small segment of the popular sectors. At its peak in 1972, total union membership was 632,485 and accounted for 22.24 percent of the work force (Baraona 1974). The strength of their organizations allowed unionized workers, particularly those in the modern industrial and mining sectors of the economy, to gain clear advantages over workers in smaller firms and the unorganized. This "privileged group within the popular classes" (Faletto and Ruiz 1970, 234) was able to negotiate higher wages and maintain a generally higher standard of living than the other segments of the popular sectors. Moreover, it was able to maintain its relative position both during inflationary periods—which its own negotiated wage increases contributed to—and subsequent downturns induced by restrictive monetary and fiscal policies designed to curb inflationary spirals (Pinto 1970; Faletto and Ruiz 1970; Bitar 1986a; Stallings 1978).

When organizations of *pobladores* (shantytown dwellers) began to emerge, they had only indirect contacts with the labor movement through political parties (Equipo de Estudios Poblacionales de CIDU 1972; Faletto and Ruiz 1970). The labor movement did not seek to assert a leadership role over the popular sectors as a whole. Instead, it sought to reinforce its own privileged position. Faletto and Ruiz make this clear:

> [T]here exists—it is undeniable—a great number of popular sectors which are not organized, but this is not the case for sectors of industrial workers or miners. But the latter [two groups] can achieve leadership over the popular groups as a whole, supporting them with their own organizational capacity, only with difficulty. It is their own character as a "relatively privileged" group that prevents this and their tendency is to establish alliances which allow precisely for the maintenance of their relative privilege. (Faletto and Ruiz 1970: 236)

Electoral participation offered only a limited means for popular-sector incorporation into the political system (Loveman 1979; Valenzuela 1978; Gil 1966). As seen in Table 1, voter registration remained extremely low throughout most of this century. The percentage of people registered to vote shows a marked jump for the 1952 elections, reflecting the 1949 electoral reform granting women the right to vote. Voter registration continued to increase thereafter as a result of electoral reforms in 1958 and 1962 that provided for secret ballots, made election fraud more difficult, simplified the registration process, and increased the penalties for not registering or voting. Finally, in 1970, the voting age was lowered from 21 to 18 and illiterates were granted the right to vote.

The Popular Sectors and Frei's "Revolution in Liberty"

The incorporation of the popular sectors into Chile's political process was accelerated dramatically by the rise of the Christian Democratic Party (DC) in the late 1950s and the unprecedented electoral victory of the Christian Democratic candidate Eduardo Frei in 1964. The DC represented a new phenomenon in Chilean politics: an ideological Center party that sought to provide an alternative to both the Right and the Marxist Left through a program based on a series of socioeconomic and political reforms. It viewed the urban poor as an important potential base of support for the Frei government's "Revolution in Liberty" and became the first political party to actively organize *pobladores* in the *poblaciones* (shanty-

Table 1.   Voter participation in presidential elections, 1925–1970

Year	Total Votes Cast	Voters Registered	Percent of Population Registered to Vote	Total Population
1925	260,895	302,212	7.4	4,073,000
1927	233,103	302,142	7.2	4,188,000
1931	285,810	388,959	8.8	4,429,000
1932	343,892	429,772	9.0	4,495,000
1938	443,898	503,871	10.2	4,914,000
1942	466,507	581,486	11.1	5,244,000
1946	479,019	631,527	11.2	5,643,000
1952	955,102	1,105,029	17.6	6,303,000
1958	1,250,437	1,521,272	20.8	7,316,000
1964	2,530,697	2,915,121	34.3	8,503,000
1970	2,954,799	3,539,747	37.0	9,566,000

Source: Loveman 1979, 260.

towns) on the basis of their consumption needs, particularly the need for adequate housing.[16]

The mobilization and organization of *pobladores* was pivotal in the Christian Democrats' plans for two reasons. First, the *pobladores* offered a large and generally untapped potential source of votes and the DC hoped to counter the Left's dominance in organized labor by building a large constituency in the *poblaciones* (Garretón 1989a; Espinoza 1988). This new Christian Democratic constituency would form a core element in a solid electoral majority that the Christian Democrats hoped to forge among the peasantry, the middle class, a modern national bourgeoisie closely associated with the state, and the urban poor (Garretón 1989a; Loveman 1979; Bitar 1986a; Castells 1973; Alvarado et al. 1973). The DC hoped that such an electoral majority would allow for "thirty years of unbroken Christian Democratic rule" (Fleet 1985, 80 n).

The urban poor were also seen as crucial to the success of the DC's objective of providing a peaceful alternative to violent revolution. For the Christian Democrats, the *pobladores* represented traditional segments of society that were not being assimilated into the modern economy and urban life in general. Their lack of socioeconomic integration was the source of their poverty. Over time, their poverty, when combined with the urban poor's lack of political participation, would generate frustration, and ultimately revolutionary violence. The DC hoped to channel the accumulating social pressures that urban poverty engendered through a series of reformist policies designed to attack both the urban poor's low standard of living and their lack of political participation.[17]

The Christian Democrats argued that extensive state intervention was essential for dealing with the problems of the urban poor. *Pobladores* were characterized as apathetic and incapable of overcoming their condition of marginality without external help. *Poblaciones* were seen as suffering from

16. The goals and policies of the Christian Democratic Party and the Christian Democratic government of Eduardo Frei (1964–1970) are discussed in Scully 1992; Fleet 1985; Loveman 1979; and Garretón 1989a. The policies of the Frei government dealing specifically with the *poblaciones* are discussed in Espinoza 1988.

17. Espinoza 1988. The Christian Democratic Party's policies regarding the urban poor were heavily influenced by the work of the Belgian priest Roger Vekemans and the DESAL research institute, which he headed. Their work on the so-called theory of marginality supplied most of the assumptions behind the DC program with respect to the *poblaciones*. Espinoza (1988) outlines the basic assumptions contained in the theory of marginality and demonstrates how they generally did not hold true in Chile during the 1960s. A similar critique of this theory can be found in Janice Perlman's study of Brazilian *favelas*. See Perlman 1976.

"internal disintegration, expressed in the absence of organizations, the lack of family cohesion or limited solidarity" (Espinoza 1988, 332). The central government therefore had to assume the primary responsibility for organizing the urban poor in the *poblaciones* and for providing them with other forms of assistance so that the situation of urban marginality could eventually be eliminated.

The Frei government sought to attack the problem of marginality by instituting a vast program of "Popular Promotion" (*Promoción Popular*). A network of base organizations, including neighborhood councils (*juntas de vecinos*), mothers' centers (*centros de madres*), youth centers (*centros juveniles*) and sports clubs (*clubes deportivos*), were legally institutionalized and erected by the Christian Democratic government in *poblaciones* and other communities throughout Chile. By 1970, there were just under 22,000 such organizations, including 3,487 neighborhood councils. Nine thousand mothers' centers were functioning with the participation of 450,000 women. The government also offered a variety of courses to the most active participants in these organizations. From 1964 through 1969, some 666,316 people attended the 17,435 courses for which attendance records were kept, which is more than the total number of registered union members in 1970 (Martínez and Tironi 1985; Rodríguez 1984). Large amounts of material assistance were channeled into the *poblaciones* for projects including the self-construction of houses (*Operación sitio*), the provision of basic urban services (potable water, electricity, sewage systems, etc.) and to support the various activities associated with the new organizations (Loveman 1979).

The Popular Promotion program also served as a mechanism for attempting to increase DC support in the *poblaciones* through the establishment of patron-client relationships (Espinoza 1988; Loveman 1979; Castells 1973; Alvarado et al. 1973; Equipo de Estudios Poblacionales de CIDU 1972). The programs associated with Popular Promotion "created a vast network of patronage and spoils, tying bureaucrats, party hacks, slum dwellers, and campesinos to government pursestrings" (Loveman 1979, 321). The DC used its close ties to the Catholic Church to transform church-sponsored organizations in the *poblaciones* into party organizations (Scully 1992). Courses offered by the government for participants in the newly created organizations were used to transmit the party's ideology into the *poblaciones*. The paternalism implicit in direct state assistance to these organizations "tended to reinforce the passivity which [the government] sought to eradicate. . . . [T]he paternalistic bias of the action in great measure limited the self-confidence of the organizations, which many times constituted themselves as channels for receiving and distributing material assistance" (Espinoza 1988, 333).

The Christian Democratic plans for the *pobladores* ultimately fell victim to the DC's own well-publicized goals. Structural limitations, and special-interest opposition to the Frei administration's housing programs, prevented the DC from reaching the goals it had set for itself (Castells 1983; Espinoza 1988; Pinto 1970). For example, *Operación sitio*, the government's principal housing program, was only able to meet the needs of 10 percent of the applicants in its first two years of operation (Espinoza 1988). The housing deficit, estimated at 406,000 units in 1960, grew to 585,000 in 1970 (Castells 1973). The Frei government fell short on other goals with a direct impact on the *pobladores*, as shown in Table 2.

There was still a disjuncture between Chile's economic structure and the social and political participation goals embedded in Frei's "Revolution in Liberty." As Pinto summed up:

> However one views the extent of this phenomena of "massification" [of social pressures], there is no doubt that it was not accompanied by a proportional expansion of the productive system. . . . [I]n essence, it is the course of external trade—essentially beyond any national will or decision—that allows for a precarious counterweight to the greater social pressure, [seen] above all through greater public expenditures. . . . The old problem is maintained, but the terms in which it is now planted appear to have changed considerably with the "massification" of the social process and the reiterated difficulty in establishing a more active growth [process]. (Pinto 1970, 47–48)

Table 2. Comparison of policy objectives and performance of the Frei government

Policy Objectives	Time Frame	Targeted Increase	Actual Increase
Retail prices	1965	25%	29%
Retail prices	1966	15%	23%
Retail prices	1967	10%	18%
New housing units	1964–70	360,000	260,000
Real GDP	1965–70	31%	18%
Per capita real GDP	1965–70	20%	5%
Gross investment	1965–70	70%	22% (through 1969)
New farm ownerships	1964–70	100,000	28,000

Source: Loveman 1979, 317.

The Left was initially caught off guard by the Christian Democratic initiative towards the *poblaciones* and was forced to take a reactive stance (Espinoza 1988; Duque and Pastrana 1971; Equipo de Estudios Poblacionales de CIDU 1972). The inability of the Christian Democrats to meet their own goals, and the popular-sector expectations that those goals had given rise to, gave the Left a potent weapon to use against the Christian Democrats. The Left denounced the excessive "reformism" of the Christian Democrats and appealed to the urban poor's growing needs. As the 1970 presidential elections approached, the organizations that the DC had created as part of its effort to build a solid electoral majority became the arena for an intensifying political competition between various political parties for control over the *pobladores*' movement and their votes (Espinoza 1988; Castells 1983 and 1973; Rodríguez 1984; Equipo de Estudios Poblacionales de CIDU 1972; Alvarado et al. 1973).

This political dynamic became most apparent with the acceleration of illegal urban land seizures by the homeless in 1969 (see Table 3). By November 1970, when Salvador Allende assumed the presidency, 300,000 people were living in shantytowns that had been erected through illegal land seizures in Santiago alone (Castells 1983). Although illegal land seizures are not uncommon in Latin America, Chile is unique in the degree to which political parties directed them and controlled subsequent activities in the resultant shantytowns (Equipo de Estudios Poblacionales de CIDU 1972; Alvarado et al. 1973; Castells 1983 and 1973; Rodríguez 1984).[18] Taking advantage of the *pobladores*' expectations and the worsening hous-

Table 3.   Illegal urban land invasions, 1966–1972

	1966	1967	1968	1969	1970	1971	Sept. 1971–31 May 1972	Jan. 1972–31 May 1972
Santiago	0	13	4	35	103	n.a.	88	n.a.
Chile (including Santiago)	n.a.	n.a.	8	23	220	560	n.a.	148

Source: Castells 1983, 200.

18. Chile is also unique in that only a small percentage of the urban poor are recent migrants to Santiago. Studies done in 1966 showed that migrants to Santiago were evenly distributed throughout the city and were not concentrated in *poblaciones* (Espinoza 1988). Moreover, of those people migrating to Santiago, just 13 percent were of a rural origin (Raczynski 1974).

ing situation, political parties successfully mobilized hundreds of thousands of people around this issue in the pursuit of a future electoral constituency. The *pobladores* were (usually) only interested in acquiring a place to live. After a land seizure, the political parties would help seek assistance from the state for legalizing the squatters' situation, obtaining materials for building homes and the provision of basic urban services.

The Popular Sectors and Allende's "Peaceful Road to Socialism"

Land seizures continued to escalate under Salvador Allende's Popular Unity (UP) government. By the end of 1972, 400,000 people in Santiago were living in shantytowns created by land seizures (Castells 1983). Mobilizing *pobladores* in land seizures and to pressure the state for material assistance had proved an effective strategy for political parties. Through it, parties sought to build electoral constituencies, pressure the political parties then in government, and generally demonstrate their "strength" vis-à-vis other political parties. The Left was first able to take advantage of this mobilizational tactic when the Christian Democratic government was in power. The DC generally chose not to repress such actions because violence directed against the *pobladores* could prejudice its own chances in the upcoming presidential elections.[19] When power shifted to the Popular Unity coalition, the DC adopted the same tactic that the Left had used against it in opposition to government policies. Moreover, various parties in the governing coalition competed amongst themselves to influence government policy and found that mobilizing *pobladores* was an effective tactic for improving their position within the coalition.

The Revolutionary Left Movement (MIR), which was not part of the UP coalition, had also been organizing urban land seizures and mobilizing *pobladores* since the late 1960s. The MIR hoped to pressure the UP government into adopting a more extreme position. It was also attempting to build a social base in the *poblaciones* for recruitment into the party's military apparatus by helping to extract resources for the *pobladores* from the state (Castells 1983; Alvarado et al. 1973; Duque and Pastrana 1971; Espinoza 1988).

19. Exceptions were few, such as an incident in Puerto Montt in March 1969 in which several people were killed. The leftist press took advantage of such cases by indignantly publicizing them. See Loveman 1979.

The struggle for control over an emerging *pobladores'* movement intensified during the Popular Unity period as the nation became increasingly politicized and polarized. This struggle was largely carried out in the same institutions created by the Frei government. Relatively few new types of organizations were created. Those that were often emerged because of the state's inability to meet certain pressing needs (such as the provision of police services in squatter settlements). Other organizations, such as the supply and price committees[20] and health committees, only emerged toward the end of the UP government as a reflection of the intensifying polarization and political crisis in Chile (Castells 1983; Morales and Rojas 1986; Rodríguez, 1984).

The basic modalities for organizing *pobladores* did not change significantly under Allende's "peaceful road to socialism." Organizational activities were still stimulated by the dynamics of interparty competition for votes. Competing parties mobilized *pobladores* on the basis of their basic needs in order to improve the relative position of the party vis-à-vis other parties. The type of relationship established between the parties and the members of these organizations was largely a patron-client one. Members of organizations in the *poblaciones*, including the participants in land seizures, were still primarily concerned with obtaining resources from the state. (Duque and Pastrana 1971; Castells 1983 and 1973; Alvarado et al. 1973).

The heterogeneous nature of the popular sectors and the inability of the UP coalition parties to completely control the activities of the *pobladores* caused the UP government to view the *pobladores* with apprehension and distrust. In fact, the dominant position within the Allende government was to limit the *pobladores'* movement to their most immediate demands and *not* introduce a perspective of attempting to change social relations. As one UP leader explained: "In the squatter settlements as they are organized, we never had a soup kitchen because the idea was that the family group must continue the same daily life. Our slogan was 'win housing and do not live by begging.' "[21] There is a certain irony in the UP's attitude toward the *pobladores*, as Castells explains:

> The *pobladores* were probably the sector which the Popular Unity Government views with the most distrust, despite that the great majority [of *pobladores*] supported it. The policy of the UP on this front is characterized by its oscillation, its pragmatism, alternating

20. *Juntas de Abastecimientos y Precios.* These groups were established to distribute increasingly scarce basic commodities within *poblaciones*.
21. Juan Aray, quoted in Castells 1973, 31.

between the fear of "ultraleft infiltration" and a certain new type of *asistencialismo* [which seeks to relieve the symptoms of poverty without attacking their causes]. (Castells 1973, 26)

Modalities of Organizational Activity in the *Poblaciones* under the Democratic Regime

Organizational activity in the *poblaciones* followed the same general pattern of organizational activity in Chilean society as a whole during the democratic period, but in an exaggerated form. *Pobladores* as a social category were among the last, along with the peasantry, to be incorporated into the Chilean political system and that incorporation remained incomplete. Their incorporation also coincided with the growing politicization and polarization of Chilean society. These factors, plus the disadvantaged nature of the social category itself—poor, generally unorganized, lower levels of education, and so forth—made the urban poor particularly susceptible to domination by political parties and dependence on the state for meeting their needs. The principal modalities of organizational activity in the *poblaciones* are summarized in Table 4.

As Castells (1983) points out, political parties essentially created the *pobladores'* movement in Chile. Prior to the coup, organizational activity in the *poblaciones* was determined by the general tendency in Chile for a highly ideological political-party elite to be linked through patron-client relations to a social base with largely particularistic demands. There was little sense of a collective identity as *poblador* on which to base more

Table 4. Modalities of organizational activity in the *poblaciones*, 1960–1973

Nature of demands	Particularistic. Little or no interest in systemic change and alternative forms of social organization.
	Lack of a sense of collective identity.
Organizational dynamic	Interparty competition for electoral support.
	Absence of self-help initiatives.
Relationship to external actors	State is the sole referent for seeking responses to demands.
	Client relations with political parties upon which they are dependent for access to the state.
	Limited organizational autonomy.

general demands and alternative social relations (Castells 1983; Espinoza 1988). The state was the focus of activities through which resources could be obtained and there was only a limited notion of "self-help" in the *poblaciones*. Even land seizures, according to Espinoza (1988), were largely intended to force the bureaucracy to act on housing issues.

These various characteristics of organizational activity in the *poblaciones* are best summarized with reference to the model of relations between political parties and base-level actors developed in Chapter 1 (see Figure 3). Prior to the military coup, such organizational activity provided a clear example of "clientelistic penetration by political parties." The people who participated in the myriad of territorial organizations were concerned predominantly with satisfying their immediate material needs. Political parties presented themselves as the most effective means for doing so, exchanging access to state resources for the partisan allegiance of the group's members. While the political atmosphere was becoming increasingly charged ideologically, there was a noticeable lack of concern among most of the participants in the *poblaciones* for systemic change. Their organizational activities were extremely vulnerable to the strategic calculations of the parties that mobilized them.[22]

Still, the relatively brief period of organizational activity among *pobladores* suggested a great deal of potential. But this potential was ultimately undermined by the same political parties that were responsible for the limited incorporation that the *pobladores* did achieve. Castells concludes:

> The squatter movement in Chile was potentially a decisive element in the revolutionary transformation of society, because it could have achieved an alliance of the organized working class with the unorganized and unconscious proletarian sectors, as well as with the petty bourgeoisie in crisis. For the first time in Latin America, the left understood the potential of urban movements, and battled with populist ideology on its own ground. But the form taken by this political initiative, the overpoliticization from the beginning, and the organizational profile of each political party within the movement, undermined its unity and made the autonomous definition of its goals impossible. Instead of being an instrument for reconstructing

22. In terms of the same typology, it is worth noting that organized labor during this period was a crucial ally of political parties, particularly leftist ones.

people's unity, the *pobladores'* movement became an amplifier of ideological divisions. (Castells 1983, 209)

The Breakdown of the Chilean Democratic Regime

The relative underdevelopment of both the Chilean economy and civil society in relation to its political development are important factors in the breakdown of Chilean democracy.[23] The destabilizing consequences of these two distortions increasingly converged in the early 1970s as Chile's political crisis became more acute. The stability of the Chilean political system under the compromise state was dependent upon accommodation, negotiation, and gradualism in implementing any reform measures (A. Valenzuela 1978 and 1989; Garretón 1989a). Legislative and constitutional reforms, however, steadily eroded the institutional arenas for reaching accommodation and negotiation among political elites. Presidential power was progressively enhanced, beginning with the 1959 reforms, which transferred control over the budgetary process to the executive branch. This freed the president from many of the constraints imposed by a need to seek agreements with opposition parties in parliament. Parliament, on the other hand, had been the principal arena for accommodation and negotiation among the political elites. As the authority of the executive was increased, the parliament suffered a concomitant reduction of its authority and prerogatives. This process culminated in the 1970 constitutional reforms, which greatly diminished congressional sources of patronage and logrolling (A. Valenzuela 1978 and 1989).

The above tendencies were exacerbated when the ideological Christian Democratic Party displaced the more pragmatic Radical Party in the center of the political spectrum in Chile.[24] The Radical Party had served as a

23. A complete discussion of all of the factors contributing to the breakdown of Chilean democracy is beyond the scope of this chapter. The following discussion is schematic and focuses only on those factors that are most relevant to understanding popular-sector organizational activities under the authoritarian regime. More comprehensive discussions of the breakdown can be found in Garretón 1987c and 1989a; A. Valenzuela 1978 and 1989; and Bitar 1986a. Also see Garretón and Moulian 1983; Gil, Lagos, and Landsberger 1979; Roxborough, O'Brien, and Roddick 1977; and Sigmond 1977. Useful reviews of the literature include Oppenheim 1989 and Nef 1983.

24. The following discussion is drawn from A. Valenzuela 1978 and 1989; and Garretón 1987c and 1989a. Also see Scully 1992, who reaches similar conclusions.

moderating influence in Chilean politics by forming alliances with both the Right and Left, depending on the political circumstances. This "pendular" behavior avoided excessive polarization within the political system and allowed the Radical Party to control the presidency from 1938 through 1952.

The Christian Democratic Party rejected traditional coalition politics. It did not wish to compromise its ideological project—Frei's "revolution in liberty"—by continuing the Radicals' pragmatic policy of coalition-building.[25] The DC sought to implement its policies when it won the presidency in 1964 with a minimum amount of cooperation from other political parties. The DC alienated other political parties, particularly the Radical Party, by rejecting any overtures of collaboration. This rejection was reinforced by Frei's unprecedented electoral margin in the 1964 elections and the DC's success in the 1965 parliamentary elections. The Christian Democrats felt that their "third way" between the Marxist Left and the Right would allow them to build a stable electoral majority. This further antagonized the Left, which perceived a genuine electoral threat in this new centrist force.

The Frei government was committed to land reform as a part of its "revolution in liberty" and as a way to incorporate the peasantry into its electoral base. This clashed head-on with a key pillar of the "rules of the game" underlying the compromise state: the traditional oligarchy's stronghold in the highly unequal rural land-tenure system would remain untouched. The Christian Democrats instituted an aggressive land-reform program that, although falling far behind in its initial goals for land redistribution (see Table 2), antagonized the Right and caused them to run their own candidate in the 1970 presidential elections.[26]

All of these factors, including a very close presidential election in 1958 in

25. This pragmatic policy had its costs. It undermined the Radical Party's credibility, leading to widespread perceptions of excessive opportunism. See Scully 1992.

26. Fearing a possible leftist victory in 1964, the Right chose to support the Christian Democratic candidate and thereby contributed significantly to Frei's overwhelming victory. The decision of the Right not to support the Christian Democratic candidate, Radomiro Tomic, in the 1970 election was decisive in Allende's winning by a narrow margin. Allende won the 1970 election with only a 36.2 percent plurality. The Right's candidate, the same Arturo Alessandri who had been president from 1958 through 1964, received 34.9 percent of the vote, and Tomic placed third by receiving 27.8 percent of the vote. The percentage of the electorate that voted for Allende in 1970 was actually less than the 38.6 percent of the vote he received in 1964, when Frei won with a clear majority of 55.7 percent. In comparison, Alessandri had won the presidential elections in 1958 with only 31.2 percent of the vote. See A. Valenzuela 1978.

which the Right narrowly defeated the Left, contributed to increasing polarization among Chilean political elites. A final factor contributing to this polarization in the 1960s was the increased radicalization of the Left. The Cuban Revolution and the accentuation of the cold war in Latin America, combined with the initiation of the United States' Alliance for Progress program in the early 1960s, had a major impact on the Chilean Left, especially the Socialist Party. The Left increasingly was committing itself to a Marxist-Leninist project for social change. This radicalization process culminated in the formation of the Popular Unity coalition, based on an ill-defined Marxist-Leninist platform for socioeconomic transformation, involving extensive nationalization of the means of production and raising the standard of living of the popular sectors (Garretón 1987c and 1989a; Bitar 1986a).

The Popular Unity government's efforts to implement its program for social change were met with increasing opposition. The Right had opposed the UP's efforts from the start and conspired, with U.S. support, to prevent Allende from taking office. The DC refused to cooperate in this effort and Allende was allowed to assume office (A. Valenzuela, 1978). But internal divisions within both the DC and the UP prevented further cooperation between the Center and the Left. The DC moved slowly toward the Right, fearing that it would lose control over the opposition if it did not. Facing increasing opposition within parliament, Allende was forced to resort to more and more executive actions to implement important reforms and pursue the nationalization policy. While legal, this further eroded the principles of accommodation and gradual change, redounding in increased obstructionism on the part of the opposition (Garretón 1989b; Bitar 1986a; A. Valenzuela 1978).

Elite polarization was increasingly amplified throughout Chilean society because of the dependence of social organizations on political parties and the general underdevelopment of a Chilean civil society. Elite polarization manifested itself in the continued mobilization of different segments of Chilean society as the parties in each portion of the party spectrum—the Right, Center, and Left—attempted to improve their relative positions vis-à-vis other political parties. This interparty competition was particularly acute among the parties within the Popular Unity coalition, as well as between the UP parties as a group and both the DC and the extremist MIR.

The mobilization of different groups within society by political parties was initially intended to strengthen the parties' relative electoral strength. As the polarization continued, mobilizations were used to demonstrate the relative "strength" of political parties outside of normal institutional channels (A. Valenzuela 1978 and 1989; Garretón 1987c and 1989a; Bitar 1986a). Bitar explains how increasing polarization forced these mobilizations into noninstitutional channels:

> As a response to the Right-inspired agitations of the *gremios* (trade associations), the UP encouraged even more direct participation by workers in the tasks of the government. At this point a new stage in the process was begun: the direct, unmediated involvement of the masses in political action. Given the obstruction of the legal-institutional framework and its growing uselessness in channeling political conflict, the opposed social forces began to come into open conflict with each other in the larger political arena, outside the sphere of formal governmental institutions and procedures. (Bitar 1986a, 97)

As A. Valenzuela (1978 and 1989) correctly points out, it was not the mobilization per se that ultimately proved to be so destabilizing, but the way in which different groups were mobilized. Mobilizations outside of formal governmental institutions and procedures contributed to the delegitimation of the democratic regime. This delegitimization had been a primary objective of the Right since Allende took office, because only then could sufficient support for a military coup be assured (Garretón 1987c and 1989a).

Just as important, this mobilization reflected the basic characteristics of the "backbone" of the Chilean political process. Elites mobilized social groups through a highly ideological discourse on the basis of the immediate material demands of the different groups[27] (Garretón 1989a; A. Valenzuela 1978 and 1989; Bitar 1986a). Political-party competition resulted in a spiral of demands in a highly politicized context. The early successes that the UP achieved in terms of raising the standard of living for the popular

27. A good example of how the DC was able to manipulate popular-sector demands to its own advantage—what Bitar (1986a) labels the DC's "populist tactics"—was its reaction to the Allende administration's proposed policy for wage adjustments in early 1973. The government had proposed that cost-of-living adjustments be implemented on a graduated scale favoring low-income groups. Through its control of the parliament, the Christian Democrats were able to expand the cost-of-living increases to cover all workers equally. They then blocked tax increases that were intended to pay for the higher wage in the public sector on the grounds that the proposed taxes discriminated against the middle class. The government's fiscal deficit was increased and its anti-inflation policies critically undermined. See Bitar 1986a.

sectors also raised these groups' expectations for continued improvements. Unfortunately, these same "successes" also unleashed an inflationary spiral that the Allende government found increasingly difficult to control (Bitar 1986a).

The Left, in particular, found itself in a difficult position. As opposition from the middle and upper classes intensified, the UP could not afford to prejudice the position of workers through government policies intended to correct a deteriorating economic situation. The UP came under increasing pressure from both the DC to its right and the MIR to its left as they continued to agitate their bases within the popular sectors to press for more demands. These pressures were multiplied by the efforts of the various parties within the UP to improve their relative position within the coalition (Bitar 1986a). Moreover, because the Left had itself engaged in these same types of practices for so long, it was extremely difficult to change when moderation became essential. As Bitar notes,

> The Left parties had always expressed mass grievances, and this tradition could not be altered abruptly. The electoral context, as well as the consequent competition within the UP and between the UP and [DC] accentuated these populist tendencies. . . . These problems could only be solved if the parties demonstrated sufficient consciousness, political maturity and organizational capacity to subordinate their immediate interests to strategic objectives. (Bitar 1986a, 227)

The relative weakness of Chilean civil society in comparison to the political party system exacerbated the political elite's polarization by allowing it to be channeled into a rising spiral of demands that undermined the economy and further eroded the democratic regime's legitimacy. The organizations of civil society could not moderate the centrifugal tendencies at the level of the central government. Their relative lack of autonomy allowed political parties to mobilize large numbers of people on the basis of particularistic demands in order to pursue short-run party interests, with little regard for its deleterious effect on Chile's democratic institutions.

The political parties did not, however, "create" the demands that served as the basis for mobilizing the popular sectors. While the parties may be responsible for raising expectations and a lack of political moderation on the part of the popular sectors, the popular sectors' demands reflected very real needs that were the result of Chile's underdeveloped and unequal economic structure. Chile was an underdeveloped country with severe socioeconomic problems. As had been the case historically with other groups, the incorporation of the popular sectors into the political system preceded changes in the socioeconomic structure and exacerbated the disjuncture between Chile's level of economic and political development.

The Frei government attempted to address this disjuncture through economic reforms that would essentially modernize Chile's economic structure. By the late 1960s, the failure of these reforms was dramatically evident. Not only had the Frei government been unable to meet its own development objectives, the economic situation began to seriously deteriorate toward the middle of his presidency. The failure of reform meant that only two options remained for Chile at this juncture: Chile could adopt a new development model that would alter the capitalist system of production in favor of the popular sectors, intensifying the process of substantive democratization; or Chile could attempt to reinvigorate its traditional model of dependent capitalist development, regardless of the social costs, which would include the freezing or even reversal of the political and substantive democratization processes (Garretón 1989a; Pinto 1970). Allende's "peaceful road to socialism" represented the first alternative, and its failure paved the way for a violent effort to impose the second.[28]

The Chilean Military Regime, 1973–1986: Repression, Economic Transformation, and Opposition

The violence unleashed by the coup of September 1973[29] and the military regime's subsequent efforts to change not only the Chilean political system,

28. The above is not meant to imply that the military coup was in any sense inevitable. As Bitar (1986a), A. Valenzuela (1978 and 1989), and Garretón (1989a) insist, a variety of factors converged to make the coup increasingly inevitable as time passed and the options open to the principal actors were narrowed, but the ultimate failure of the UP was in no sense predetermined. In the accounts of all three authors, the political parties and their leaders made avoidable mistakes that all contributed to the ultimate demise of Chilean democracy. This does not deny, however, that the viability of Chilean democracy was to a large degree dependent on structural change. Rather, the argument that both Bitar and Garretón make is that it was possible to achieve the necessary structural changes within the context of Chile's democratic institutions when Allende won the presidency in 1970.

29. According to the Report of the National Commission for Truth and Reconciliation, which was appointed by President Aylwin to investigate the most serious cases of human

but the socioeconomic structure of society as well, represented an extreme authoritarian attempt to resolve the imbalance between Chile's high level of political development and its underdeveloped economy and civil society.[30] The military regime sought to achieve this through the "depoliticization" of Chilean society and the imposition of a new, neoconservative, development model. In this section I shall examine the military regime in terms of its *repressive* and *transformative* dimensions (cf. Garretón 1989a) and shall end with a brief review of the development of the opposition during the peak period of popular-sector mobilization, from 1983 through 1986.

The Repressive Dimension of the Military Regime

A primary objective of the military regime was the depoliticization of Chilean society through the elimination of the traditional party system and the disarticulation of all forms of collective behavior, especially on the part of the popular sectors (Garretón 1987c and 1989a; Frühling 1984; Valenzuela and Valenzuela, 1986a). Political-party activities were suspended immediately after the coup. Political and social leaders, especially those associated with the UP government, were singled out for repression.

The regime's use of repression passed through several distinct phases (Frühling 1984). The first phase began on the day of the coup and lasted until June 1974, when the regime's repressive apparatus was centralized under the direction of the National Intelligence Directorate (DINA). The repression during this phase was extremely intense. It was characterized by its arbitrary nature and lack of any moral or legal limitations. Opponents of the military regime were declared the enemies of the nation. The regime sought to crush the social and political forces that had backed the Allende regime.

Political militants, labor leaders, and intellectuals were specific targets of repression during this phase. But the arbitrary nature of the repression and

---

rights abuses committed between 11 September 1973 and 11 March 1990, some 2,115 people died as a result of the violation of their human rights during this period. This includes 957 people who disappeared after being abducted by security agents. See Comisión Nacional de Verdad y Reconciliación 1991.

30. At this point, I am concerned only with the context in which popular organizations first emerged and later began to interact with political parties. Subsequent events, including the transition to democracy, will be discussed in Chapter 8.

its massiveness provoked widespread fear not only among supporters of the deposed president, but among the popular sectors in general. This fear was exacerbated by the regime's determination to act against political and social organizations as well. Its objectives were first, "to discipline the labour force in order to lower labour costs; the second was to destroy the Left as a political and ideological alternative; the third was to grant the government the exclusive power of deciding which social actors and petitions should be considered legitimate; and the fourth was to restrict political and cultural thinking which could challenge the government" (Frühling 1984, 355). The activities of labor unions were severely restricted. Neighborhood councils and professional associations were also tightly controlled by the government.

DINA was created in June 1974 to centralize the regime's repressive policies under one specialized apparatus and ushered in the second phase of repression. The phase lasted until DINA's dissolution in late 1977. The new phase of repression coincided with the strengthening of Pinochet's authority within the governing military junta and Pinochet maintained day-to-day contact with the director of DINA. It also coincided with the emergence of the regime's transformative dimension. The resultant economic dislocations, which will be discussed in detail below, required the strengthening of the military's control over the country.

Repression during this phase was still intense, but it became more selective. The victims of repression were now all members of underground political parties, including (for the first time) members of the Christian Democratic Party. Those who had supported Allende were more secure, as long as they did not participate in politics in any way.

During the first phase, the regime's repressive activities were extremely visible. It was no secret that people were being detained and that detention camps existed. DINA, however, was increasingly secretive. People were held for questioning in secret prisons, many of whom subsequently "disappeared." This secrecy and the disappearances were intended to produce fear—"the intense fear of the unknown" (Frühling 1984, 362).

The secrecy surrounding the details of the regime's repression was also accompanied by a propaganda campaign in the government-controlled media that emphasized the importance of maintaining public order and justified the exclusion of important segments of the population from public life. The media continued to focus on the violence exercised against dissidents, but labeled them as terrorists without legal rights. Human rights organizations were accused of conspiring to destabilize the regime. This combination of increased secrecy concerning the details of repression and a media campaign stressing public order was designed to give a sense of normalcy to life under military rule. The military government hoped to achieve "the destruction of political parties opposed to the regime by producing intense fear among political opponents without the disruption of a sense of normality in everyday life" (Frühling 1984, 362).

The third phase of repression corresponded to the regime's efforts to institutionalize and legalize its coercive practices within the image of an authoritarian rule of law. DINA was replaced by a new central repressive apparatus, the National Intelligence Center (CNI) in August 1977. Legal limits were placed on the security apparatus. The principal objective of the regime's repressive policies would now be the containment of opposition. The intensity of repression would fluctuate in response to the mobilization of the opposition.

The regime had come under increasing international pressures in 1977 and 1978 because of its human rights record. In order to improve its international image, the regime instituted a number of measures that would allow for some internal dissent and provide the appearance of rule of law. The creation of the CNI reflected this effort to change the image of the regime by allegedly subjecting the repressive apparatus to more legal constraints.

The overall level and intensity of repression tended to decrease in this phase. There was also a dramatic reduction in the numbers of detained people who "disappeared." But legal restraints imposed on the security apparatus were often overstepped. The CNI continued to use many of the unofficial forms of punishment practiced by its predecessor, including the ill-treatment of prisoners, detention in secret prisons and mass-media character assassinations of "subversives." Frühling summarized the effects of the newly "legalized" repression: "[M]ore than any other repressive phase, the third was characterized by the co-existence of a resemblance of legality with arbitrariness. One was never certain what punishment could be expected or whether it should be expected at all for political opposition. The system once again worked to make uncertain the risks taken on himself by any person who wanted to get involved in political activity, even though the intensity of repression diminished" (Frühling 1984, 367).

The nature of the regime's repression had two effects important for understanding popular-sector organizational activity. Both will be discussed at length in later chapters. The first effect was that repression disrupted the system of relations between the political-party structure and the social base—the "backbone" of the Chilean political system under the democratic regime (Garretón 1987c and 1989a). Tentative and precarious efforts to reconstruct a new system of relations would characterize the interaction between political parties and social organizations in the latter years of the authoritarian regime.

The second effect of the regime's repression of political parties was the emergence of substitutive arenas for political activity. The church's role as a protective umbrella for such activity has been critical (Garretón 1987c and 1989a; Valenzuela and Valenzuela 1986a). Such substitutive arenas first emerged through the church's activities in defense of human rights (Frühling 1984 and 1985) and subsequently expanded to include other issues and areas of society.

The Transformative Dimension of the Military Regime: The Social Costs of Economic Adjustment

The military regime sought to undergird the effects of political repression with a project for transforming Chile's socioeconomic and political structure. This project, which amounted to a "radical conservative experiment" in neoconservative economics (Foxley 1983), was designed to undermine the social bases of the old democratic regime and political-party system. It ultimately sought to replace them with a new, more authoritarian, democratic regime that would give primacy to market forces in defining the direction of economic development and state policies.[31]

The regime's project was composed of three principal elements: (1) a drastic reduction in the role of the state, (2) an opening up of the economy to international trade and financial flows, and (3) free-market policies governing price determination and capital markets (Foxley 1983 and 1986). The project reached its culmination in the new 1980 constitution, which sought to institutionalize a highly restricted form of political democracy. Two effects of the regime's attempt to implement this project are particularly relevant to understanding popular-sector organizational activity: the

31. The military regime's transformative project was heavily influenced by the work of Milton Friedman and the Chicago School of Economics. The nature of the regime's policies, the goals behind them, and their impact are discussed in Foxley 1983 and 1986; Vergara 1984 and 1986; and Garretón 1987c and 1989a.

relative impoverishment of Chile through the mid-1980s due to structural changes in the economy and the dramatic reduction in the state's social welfare and redistributive programs.

After almost fifteen years of military rule, Chile had suffered a dramatic impoverishment as a result of the military regime's implementation of a neoconservative economic model. Although Chile was about to enter a period of unprecedented economic growth that would begin to reverse this,[32] the popular sectors still confronted a very bleak socioeconomic situation as late as 1986. These social costs associated with the regime's economic policies conditioned popular-sector organizational activity in important ways. For example, the average standard of living in Chile by the mid-1980s had improved (at best) only marginally compared to 1970.[33] As Table 5 demonstrates, real per capita GDP was just 2.5 percent greater in 1987 than in 1970. Fluctuating widely, real per capita GDP surpassed that of 1970 in only 5 of the 14 years, 1974–87. Other estimates placed 1987 per capita GDP at levels substantially below that of 1970 (Ffrench-Davis and Raczynski 1988; Cademartori 1988).

The effect of this stagnation in per capita GDP was dramatic. Unemployment from 1975 to 1981, including those employed in state minimal employment programs, averaged 18 percent—three times the average during the 1960s. After that, unemployment averaged 23 percent through 1987, reaching a high of 31.3 percent in 1983. Real wages in 1987 were just 84.7 percent of what they had been in 1970 (Ffrench-Davis and Raczynski 1988). In 1986, the World Health Organization found Chile's caloric food consumption so far below minimum standards that it was characterized as a country "with nutritional deficiency." Prior to the

32. See Chapter 8.

33. This, despite an average annual GDP growth rate of 2.7 percent during 1973–84. The reason for this apparent paradox is found in the depth of the two recessions that Chile had experienced since the coup. The recovery from the sharp drops in GDP experienced during the 1975–76 and 1982–83 recessions provided a high rate of growth, even though it would take years for the GDP to again reach the levels attained before the recession's onset. Calculations of annual per capita GDP growth rates based on official statistics will also vary widely, depending on which years are included in the calculations. For example, the annual growth rate for the period 1976–81 is 6.1 percent. But if the same calculation is made for the period 1974–81, including the negative impact on GDP of the 1975–76 recession, the growth rate is just 2.2 percent (Ffrench-Davis and Raczynski 1988). This economic volatility led the prominent Chilean economist Aníbal Pinto to describe economic performance under the military government as "an economy in permanent recovery," noting that "after incomparable sacrifices and effort, the average Chilean is no better off than he or she was at the beginning of the seventies" (quoted in Cademartori 1988, 2).

Table 5. Growth in real GDP per capita, 1970–1987

Year	GDP per capita (1970 = 100)
1970	100.0
1971	106.1
1972	104.1
1973	98.1
1974	101.6
1975	83.4
1976	85.6
1977	91.5
1978	95.8
1979	101.7
1980	106.0
1981	109.6
1982	92.6
1983	90.4
1984	94.5
1985	95.2
1986	98.9
1987	102.5

Source: Ffrench-Davis and Raczynski 1988, table A.4, 77.

coup, Chilean caloric food consumption had surpassed minimum standards (Cademartori 1988).

The popular sectors were affected disproportionately by Chile's general economic deterioration. Between 1969 and 1978 alone, the level of consumption of the poorest 20 percent of Chilean families fell by more than 30 percent. Income inequality is high. In 1983, the richest 20 percent of Chilean families received 61 percent of total national income, compared to the 3.3 percent that the poorest 20 percent of Chilean families received (Rodríguez 1985). The share of total national income received by the lowest 40 percent of households decreased from 12.2 percent in 1965–70 and 12.9 percent in 1971–73 to 9.8 percent in 1982–85 (Ffrench-Davis and Raczynski 1988). The unemployment rate for heads of households was three times higher among the poorest 20 percent of families compared to all other families (Ffrench-Davis and Raczynski 1988). A 1985 study found that half of the workers in the *poblaciones* of Santiago were in a situation of "exclusion": 25 percent were unemployed, 14 percent were in state minimal employment programs earning substantially less than the legal minimum wage,[34] and 11 percent were involved in marginal or domestic service (Campero 1987). In 1987, the legal minimum wage was 65 percent less in real terms than in 1981 (Cademartori 1988), even though the cost of living rose considerably faster for the poor than for other sectors of society (see Table 6). The 1988 minimum wage was calculated to be half the amount necessary to maintain an average family (Angell 1989). The result of these trends was a tripling of the number of Chileans living in extreme poverty, defined as the inability of a family's total income to cover the cost of meeting minimum dietary consumption needs. Studies based on a national sample of households in both 1983 and November 1985 found that 30 percent of all households were living in extreme poverty, up from just 10 percent in 1970. Other studies suggest that the situation was considerably worse in many *poblaciones* (Rodríguez 1985; Ffrench-Davis and Raczynski 1988; Campero 1987).

High levels of unemployment, growing income inequality, and rising

Table 6. Consumer price index weighted for the consumption patterns of the poor, 1974–1986

Year[a]	General CPI		CPI Based on Poor's Purchasing Basket	
	September 1974 = 100	12 Month Variation (%)	September 1974 = 100	12 Month Variation (%)
1974	100.0	—	100.0	—
1975	487.4	387.4	667.8	567.8
1976	1,441.7	195.5	1,840.7	175.6
1977	2,500.0	73.4	3,913.3	112.6
1978	3,414.7	36.6	5,561.2	42.1
1979	4,646.2	36.1	8,215.3	47.7
1980	6,057.2	30.4	10,438.1	27.1
1981	7,072.2	16.8	11,335.8	8.6
1982	7,875.5	11.4	13,557.7	19.6
1983	10,197.4	29.5	18,503.6	36.5
1984	11,815.8	15.9	23,266.6	25.7
1985	15,863.7	34.3	30,456.0	30.9
1986	18,603.7	17.3	34,600.4	13.6

Source: J. Ruiz Tagle, "Los ingresos de los pobres y la recuperación económica," *Mensaje*, no. 354 (November 1986), cited in Ffrench-Davis and Raczynski 1988.

[a]All statistics are for September of each year.

34. In 1982, the wage paid in the largest program, the Minimal Employment Program (PEM) was just 31.8 percent of the legal minimum wage (Morales 1987).

levels of poverty are not transitory problems that can be overcome in the short term. They reflect deep structural changes in the Chilean economy that were caused by the imposition of an extreme neoconservative model of economic development. One important consequence of the military government's market-oriented development model was the deindustrialization of Chile.[35] Economic austerity during the regime's first two years, a reduction of the general level of tariffs from an average of 94 percent in 1973 to 10 percent in 1979, and a basic disregard for industry in setting exchange-rate, anti-inflation, and monetary policies took their toll on Chile's industrial capacity. Industrial production declined approximately 11 percent between 1973 and 1983 (Gwynne 1986). Per capita manufacturing output in 1987 was just 78.8 percent of what it had been in 1970 (Ffrench-Davis and Raczynski 1988).

The effects of the new economic development model were even more severe on industrial employment. While industrial production declined 11 percent, a conservative estimate of the corresponding decline in manufacturing employment is 33 percent. Where growth did occur, it tended to rely on capital inputs rather than increased labor. In seven sectors that overall experienced an 81.7 percent increase in production between 1973 and 1980, employment actually declined 16 percent (Gwynne 1986).

As a direct result of these trends, the relative size of the industrial working class declined 8.3 percent as a percentage of the economically active population through 1980, implying "a displacement of approximately 103,000 manual workers from regular wage-earning employment to independent [informal] employment or open unemployment" (Martínez and Tironi 1985, 146). The capacity of the labor movement to act as an independent social actor without alliances with other social actors decreased as the "strategic weight" of the working class in the Chilean economy diminished (Martínez and Tironi 1985).

Organized labor was severely weakened under the authoritarian regime (Angell 1989; Barrera 1988; Barrera and Valenzuela 1986; Campero and Valenzuela 1984; and Martínez and Tironi 1985). In 1987, only 10.5 percent of the labor force was unionized (Angel 1989). Structural changes in the economy generated the highest levels of unemployment in the industrial and construction sectors, the former strongholds of union organization. In addition to high unemployment rates, union organizing was

35. The process of deindustrialization and its consequences are discussed in Gwynne 1986, and Martínez and Tironi 1985.

made more difficult by the growing size of the informal sector. The informal sector accounted for 37 percent of all employment in 1986 (Angel 1989). At the same time, the government's Labor Plan (*Plan Laboral*), introduced in 1978, severely limited union strength by encouraging fragmentation in the labor movement and placing tight constraints on collective bargaining in favor of employers (Ruiz Tagle 1985; Frühling 1984).

Given these structural changes in the Chilean economy, the long-term outlook for a substantial improvement in the economy's capacity to absorb labor and generate higher standards of living still remained very much in doubt in 1986. Even advocates of the military regime's development model acknowledged that with rapid economic growth, it would still take fifty years to reduce extreme poverty to a minimum (Cademartori 1988). At the same time that the popular sectors were bearing these costs of economic structural change, the state's social welfare apparatus was being progressively dismantled. National social expenditures experienced their first significant and long-term decline since the 1920s under the military regime. By 1985, they had still not regained their per capita level of 1970 (Arellano 1985), and in 1986, per capita national social expenditures were 15 percent less than their 1969–70 average (*Revista de CIEPLAN* 1987).

The military regime did implement a number of positive changes in state social welfare programs designed to channel resources directly to those sectors with the greatest need. But the overall effect of such efforts was insufficient to counteract the increased magnitude and intensity of poverty after 1973 (Ffrench-Davis and Raczynski 1988). Participants in state minimal employment programs received between 40 and 67 percent of the legal minimum income in 1986. Social security coverage, which had reached 76 percent of the labor force in 1970 and 79 percent in 1974, declined to approximately 63 percent of the labor force in 1983. This was a level similar to that of 1960. Pensions, in real terms, were still below their 1970 level in 1985.

Public-housing expenditure in 1981 was 35 percent lower than in 1970 and it declined still further during the 1982–83 recession. Although public-housing construction rose substantially during 1984–86, the housing shortage still rose to 1.2 million units, up from 500,000 in 1973 (Cademartori 1987; Ffrench-Davis and Raczynski 1988).

Impressive improvements were realized in the nutrition and death rates of children under five due to the military government's programs directed specifically at this age group. Other evidence, however, indicated an overall deterioration in the health of the poor and suggested that trends in health statistics for children under five were no longer an accurate measure of the health of the Chilean population as a whole. For example, the limited available information suggested that malnutrition among the school-age population had increased. The average number of daily portions distributed under the School Nutrition Program each year from 1974 to 1985 was less than during 1970–73, despite the obvious increase in need. Moreover, Chile experienced an increase in infectious and parasitic diseases, as well as mental disorders—all of which tend to affect the poor disproportionately. Public hospitals were characterized by waiting lists for nonurgent cases, shortages of basic supplies, food and medicine, and a deterioration in the quantity and quality of patient care provided (Ffrench-Davis and Raczynski 1988; Campero 1987).

These problems at the national level were exacerbated by changes at the local level of government. A variety of reforms instituted under the military regime, including a doubling of the number of city governments (*comunas*) that together composed the Santiago metropolitan area, increased the segregation and concentration of the urban poor within Santiago.[36]

New municipal boundaries tended to segregate high- and middle-income sectors of Santiago. The popular sectors were concentrated in a number of *comunas* with high population densities and very low levels of per capita resources. This pattern was reinforced by the government's program of "eradications," in which squatter settlements dating back to before the coup were leveled and their inhabitants relocated. Between 1979 and 1985, some 172,218 people—4 percent of the population of the Santiago metropolitan area—were affected by this program. Overwhelmingly, these people were relocated from the relatively most well-off *comunas* to *comunas* that already had the highest population densities and the lowest levels of per capita resources.

As a result of these policies, *pobladores* tended to live in areas characterized by very low levels of basic public services, including education and health care. These policies also erected effective administrative barriers to income redistribution at the local level. For example, the seven *comunas* in which the greatest number of *poblaciones* were concentrated accounted for 28.9 percent of the metropolitan region's population, but only 4.04 percent of local level expenditures. In comparison, 21.8 percent of the metropolitan

36. The military government's policies concerning the local level of government and its effects on the popular sectors are discussed in Morales, Pozo, and Rojas, 1988; Morales and Rojas 1986; Morales 1987; and Rodriguez 1984. The following discussion is based on these works.

region's population lived in three *comunas* that together accounted for 51 percent of local government expenditures (Campero 1987; Portes 1989).

Opposition to the Authoritarian Regime, May 1983–December 1986

The military regime's economic model collapsed in 1982, plunging Chile into a prolonged recession and ushering in a new phase of Chilean politics.[37] The military regime found itself facing recurrent crises as the opposition grew in strength. Its principal objectives became the stabilization of the socioeconomic transformations already achieved and its own survival in terms of the time frame for a controlled democratic transition imposed by the 1980 constitution (Garretón 1987c and 1989a).

Traditional political-party activity had virtually ceased in the aftermath of the military coup. Still, the political parties demonstrated a remarkable resiliency when they reemerged to dominate the national political scene in the wake of the first national protest in May 1983.

The collapse of the economic model severely eroded middle-class support for the military regime. This weakened the military's ability to use repression to curb dissent and was essential for ensuring that a protest by organized social sectors opposed to the regime would not end in a massacre.[38] The protests were initially led by the labor movement, but the political parties increasingly made themselves present. As the parties became increasingly prominent in the newly created public political space, two opposition blocs were formed. The Democratic Alliance (AD) was formed by eight parties from the center-right to a moderate faction of the Socialist Party and was dominated by the Christian Democratic Party.[39]

37. The following account is very schematic and only intended to serve as a general reference for developments to be discussed in more detail in subsequent chapters. For a more detailed description and analysis, see Garretón 1987c and Oxhorn 1986. A useful analysis of the early development of the opposition through the end of 1982 is provided by the various studies in Valenzuela and Valenzuela 1986a.

38. Garretón 1987c. The first protest began a "cycle of protests" that ended in November 1984 with the declaration of a state of siege. The national protests during this period are described and analyzed in: de la Maza and Garces, 1985; *Páginas Sindicales*, nos. 55–65, May 1983–November 1984; *Hechos Urbanos*, nos. 21–37, May 1983–November 1984; CLACSO-ILET 1986; and Garretón 1987c and 1989c. The protests and the role of the popular sectors in the opposition are dealt with extensively in Chapter 7.

39. In addition to the DC, the Democratic Alliance (*Alianza Democrática*) included the Republican Party, the Liberal Party, the Social Democratic Party, the Radical Party, the Popular Socialist Union, and the Nuñez faction of the Socialist Party.

This action was quickly followed by the formation of the Popular Democratic Movement (MDP), dominated by the Communist Party.[40] The military regime entered into a dialogue with the AD in 1983 that was ended by the declaration of a state of siege in November 1984 without achieving any concessions from the government.

The formation of political blocs only complicated the opposition's task of formulating a transition strategy with clear objectives. Such a strategy was necessary for creating a specific opposition alternative to the political regime embodied in the 1980 constitution. The opposition then could have mobilized society in support of this alternative to pressure the military into entering negotiations seeking to reconcile the opposition's alternative with the 1980 constitution. Instead, the opposition appeared to be guided by a common "myth" that mobilizations alone could lead to a situation of "ungovernability" that would force the military regime to fall. Proposals by one bloc or party were quickly met by counterproposals. Opposition initiatives came to be defined more by which parties and groups were included or excluded than by their substance (Garretón 1989a).

As a concrete proposal for a transition continued to elude the opposition, the mobilizations ended through attrition. The mobilizations had no intermediate objectives and lacked the resources for achieving the one goal assigned to them by the opposition: the toppling of the regime. Garretón summarized the opposition's failure: "In synthesis, the problems of preserving identities and leaderships and tactical calculations of alliances and exclusions were given priority over a coherent and consensual transition strategy" (Garretón 1987c, 213). The political initiative oscillated between the opposition and the regime during this period, which is perhaps best characterized as an overall political stalemate. The following is a brief outline of the major events that tended to shift the initiative from one side to the other over the period.

The opposition maintained the initiative during the first cycle of protests, but that was abruptly ended by the declaration of a state of siege in November 1984. The state of siege was lifted in mid-1985, but the opposition did not regain the initiative until August with the announcement of the National Accord for the Transition to Full Democracy. The document was signed by the parties of the Democratic Alliance, along with the National Party and the National Union Movement from the Right and a

---

40. The MDP (*Movimiento Democrático Popular*) was formed by the PC, the Almeyda faction of the Socialist Party, the MIR, and various smaller groups on the Left.

moderate socialist party, the Christian Left. The National Accord was signed under the auspices of the archbishop of Santiago and represented the opposition's first major step toward defining an alternative to the military regime and the 1980 constitution. Various mobilizations were organized in support of the National Accord and its list of "immediate measures," which the parties asked the government to implement in order to create an appropriate environment for political negotiations. These mobilizations culminated in November of that year, when all of the opposition parties cooperated in staging a massive demonstration in the Parque O'Higgins.

Even before the successful Parque O'Higgins demonstration, the opposition was beginning to lose momentum. The Left had been excluded from the formulation of the National Accord and only the Christian Left and the Nuñez faction of the Socialist Party actually signed it. Moreover, the parties that signed the National Accord began to publicly disagree over its interpretation. The right-wing National Union Movement in particular insisted on a very limited interpretation of the National Accord and resisted any efforts to reach out to the Left. Finally, Pinochet simply chose to ignore the National Accord and the pro-government media launched a propaganda campaign highlighting the National Accord's ambiguities and disagreements among its cosigners.

The opposition lost the political initiative after the Parque O'Higgins demonstration, when the Communist-dominated MDP sent a public letter to the Democratic Alliance calling for greater opposition coordination and cooperation. The AD was thrown into a crisis over how to respond to the Left's public initiative. This led to the first signs of a serious polarization within the opposition since the beginning of the national protest movement. The source of the polarization was the Communist Party's strategy of popular insurrection (adopted in 1980) and the refusal by the Christian Democrats to enter into any kind of public arrangements with the PC until it unequivocally renounced all forms of political violence.[41]

In early 1986, the opposition was again able to regain the political initiative. The parties of the Democratic Alliance resolved the AD's internal crisis by agreeing that each party was free to determine its own policy with regard to the Communists. A new organization, the Civic Assembly (*Asamblea de la Civilidad*), was formed in the first part of 1986 by representatives from eighteen social organizations and allowed the opposi-

41. This polarization is discussed at considerable length in Chapter 7.

tion to overcome its polarization temporarily. All of the major political parties supported the assembly. Most important, they could cooperate in support of the assembly's activities, hidden from the public eye behind the cover of the various social organizations that officially formed the organization. The Civic Assembly met in April to write the Demands of Chile (*Demanda de Chile*), which represented the sectoral interests of all the social organizations participating in the Civic Assembly. The Demands of Chile was officially presented to the military government, which was given a deadline for providing an adequate response.

A national protest and general strike was programmed for early July after the government refused to respond to the Demands of Chile. A high level of mobilization was achieved and much of Santiago was shut down. But on the first day of the protest, two young people were brutally burned alive by a military patrol and one subsequently died from his injuries.

The atrocity of the regime's violent actions during the protest opened a major debate within the opposition over the usefulness of mass mobilizations. This debate, in turn, caused polarizing tendencies within the opposition to reemerge around the Communist and Christian Democratic poles. The polarization became more acute when, in August 1986, large caches of smuggled arms were discovered in Chile's northern desert and tied to the PC. A guerilla training school was also located and linked to the PC. Then, in September of that year, the Manuel Rodríguez Patriotic Front came very close to assassinating Pinochet. The Communists were further isolated within the opposition due to their support of the front and the military government declared a state of siege once again.

As 1986 came to a close, the military government had clearly regained the political initiative. A divided opposition began the slow process of preparing for the 1988 presidential plebiscite in which the country would vote yes or no to the single candidate proposed by the military junta.

CONCLUSION

The imposition of authoritarian rule posed tremendous new challenges for the popular sectors. But these challenges, and the popular sectors' ability to respond to them, were conditioned by Chile's unique democratic heritage.

The military assumed power, intent on transforming Chile's socioeconomic and political systems. Ultimately, it sought to synchronize Chile's political and economic development forcibly, by introducing a new development model and political system. As traditional channels for political participation were cut off by the regime's repression, structural changes in the economy bore heavily on the popular sectors' already precarious situation. Simultaneously, the state itself was undergoing dramatic changes that curtailed its ability and willingness to respond to the growing levels of poverty and inequality. The state was no longer the principal referent for the popular sectors' demands, but had now become the major obstacle to realizing their aspirations.

Chile's democratic heritage provided an ambiguous legacy for the popular sectors in terms of their ability to respond to these challenges. For the vast majority of *pobladores*, their incorporation into the political system had come relatively recently. This incorporation was always incomplete and subjected the urban poor to the strategic calculations of the political parties that mobilized them in the pursuit of increasingly narrow partisan interests.

Still, this limited incorporation provided many *pobladores* with significant organizational experiences that helped spur alternative patterns of organization to help meet pressing needs under the military regime. Similarly, Allende's ill-fated efforts offered a dramatic lesson on the importance of organization for trying to resolve the various kinds of problems the popular sectors historically faced, albeit with renewed severity.

Ironically, the military regime's repressive policies would, at least temporarily, resolve the potential problems that might result from the popular sectors' checkered history of relations with political parties. As long as political parties could not organize in any public or open fashion, an unprecedented space would be opened up for autonomous popular-sector organizational activities in the *poblaciones*. Once political parties could again emerge, this legacy could potentially become a major complicating factor for any popular organizations that might have emerged in the meantime. Political parties could be expected to reassert their control over the popular sectors, while the popular sectors themselves would likely be concerned with guarding any organizational autonomy they might have achieved. New tensions between the popular-sector organizations and political parties that reflect both the authoritarian experience and Chile's democratic heritage thus seem to be a real possibility. This would be especially true if the members of such organizations attribute at least part of the responsibility for Chile's crisis to the political parties that were so central to events leading up to the 1973 military coup.

In what follows, the various implications that Chile's democratic heritage and authoritarian experience have had for popular-sector organizational activity will be analyzed. The evolution of such activity and its interactions with political parties will be examined, first under the military regime, and then during the transition to democracy and the current democratic regime.

3

SHANTYTOWN ORGANIZATIONS AFTER THE MILITARY COUP

The Resurrection of Civil Society

The violent imposition of authoritarian rule by the military in September 1973 created a whole new set of problems and issues for the popular sectors. Almost immediately, new territorially based organizations began to appear in the *poblaciones* of Santiago. These "popular organizations" emerged with the support of a variety of nongovernmental institutions, particularly the Catholic Church, and were able to draw on the organizational experiences and democratic practices that the popular sectors had accumulated under democratic rule (Razeto et al. 1986; Valdés 1987). By 1986, 220,000 people—16 percent of all *pobladores*—were participating in these organizations in Santiago (Valdés 1987).

The early emergence of these organizations during the military regime in Chile stands in marked contrast to the conclusions developed in one of the few comparative theoretical treatments of base-level organizational activity under authoritarian regimes (O'Donnell and Schmitter 1986). Although O'Donnell and Schmitter are explicitly referring to all base-level organizational activity, which they call "the resurrection of civil society," and not just to such activity in popular sectors, their basic conclusion is that such activity becomes extensive only *after* a transition process has already begun.

O'Donnell and Schmitter argue that important divisions within the authoritarian regime itself have generally been the prerequisite for a transition process to begin. This early phase of a transition is then usually characterized by a "liberalization" (the process by which certain rights protecting individuals and social groups from the arbitrary acts of the state and third parties are made effective). Only then, they argue, when the costs of collective action are actually lowered by the regime and some contestation is permitted, will self-organized and autonomously defined political spaces emerge. The authors seem to assume that prior to this liberalization, repression and the fear of repression suppress any significant organizational activity at the base level of society, or at least any such activity that may be construed as being in some sense "political" and autonomous from the regime. While recognizing the important role that base-level mobilization and organization play in transition processes, O'Donnell and Schmitter rule out the theoretical possibility that this so-called resurrection of civil society can actually take place *before* a regime transition (or even a regime policy change) has been initiated.

Popular-sector organizations in Chile are important to the process of resurrecting civil society. This process, however, began prior to and independently of a democratic transition, or even a significant liberalization of the regime's policies. Somewhat paradoxically, it will be argued that the key turning point in this process came in the late 1970s, when the principal actors involved in popular-sector organizational activity began to recognize that the military regime was not a transitory phenomenon and the problems that it had engendered for the popular sectors required a more permanent, long-term response.

In 1978, the Catholic Church began to encourage the increasing autonomy of popular organizations and undertook a variety of efforts to augment the capacity of the popular sectors to organize themselves. At the same time, popular organizations expanded their activities in order to address the whole of their members' needs arising out of their political, social, cultural, and economic exclusion. This led to a further separation between popular organizations and the Church. The activities of popular organizations began to clash with the more limited goals that the Church had for organizations that remained under its direct control. The result of these two complementary processes was that by the end of 1986, popular-sector organizations had achieved a certain level of institutionalization under the authoritarian regime.

This chapter is divided into three sections. In the first section, some general characteristics of the popular-sector organizations that emerged after 1973 will be examined. I shall then analyze four distinct phases of popular-sector organizational activity after the military coup, showing how the emergence and evolution of popular-sector organizational activity reflected both the nature of the authoritarian regime and important aspects of Chile's preauthoritarian heritage. Finally, I shall explore the issue of the institutionalization of popular-sector organizations under the military regime in terms of Huntington's model of institutionalization (outlined in Chapter 1).

POPULAR ORGANIZATIONS UNDER THE AUTHORITARIAN REGIME: THEIR BASIC TYPES AND CHARACTERISTICS

The combined effects of the military regime's repression and socioeconomic policies gradually led to a resurgence of organizational activity in the *poblaciones*. As shown in Chapter 2, the numbers of urban poor swelled and their quality of life deteriorated dramatically as the traditional arenas for resolving popular-sector problems—the state vis-à-vis connections with political parties and the labor movement—were dismantled. A new organizational space was created at the territorial level within the *poblaciones*. The new popular organizations were tolerated by the military regime to the extent that they remained isolated and atomized, although the threat of repression was constant (Rodríguez 1984).

Popular organizations generally fell into five categories according to the principal activities in which they were engaged: organizations that expressed collective identities; organizations that sought to pressure the state for the satisfaction of demands; organizations for self-defense and protection against repression; political organizations; and subsistence organizations.[1]

1. The categories in the following typology are taken from Hardy 1985, although the descriptions are in large part based on my own observations. As will be emphasized below, popular organizations typically engaged in a variety of activities and placing any particular popular organization in one or another category is somewhat arbitrary.

Organizations That Expressed Collective Identities

These organizations included cultural and artistic groups, Christian base communities, and youth and women's organizations. Such organizations were closely tied to the preservation and reinforcement of a *popular collective identity*, a theme that will be discussed in greater detail in Chapter 4.[2] Organizations that fell into this category attempted to resist the disintegration and atomization of shared identities caused by the military regime's use of repression and its neoconservative model for society.

These organizations typically engaged in a variety of activities that involved both their own members and the larger community within the *población*. For example, they might have organized a series of activities to celebrate International Women's Day, International Youth Week, and May Day. They also were frequently involved in organizing celebrations of important anniversaries (the founding of the *población*, the Nicaraguan and Cuban Revolutions, the assassination of the Salvadoran archbishop Oscar Romero, the murder of a prominent *poblador* by the security apparatus, etc.). Cultural and artistic groups, in particular, frequently organized cultural events such as presentations of popular theater (often in the street and written by *pobladores*), folk music, and mural painting. Finally, a number of these organizations printed regular news and information bulletins that were distributed within the *población*.

Organizations That Sought to Pressure the State for the Satisfaction of Demands

These organizations most closely resembled the kinds of organizations that characterized the democratic period. The most important of these were the

2. It should be noted that not all Christian base communities (CEBs) were concerned with a popular collective identity. A good example of this is found in Burdick 1992, which looks specifically at the case of Brazil. For this reason, CEBs do not figure predominantly in the present study (see Appendix 1). Moreover, as will be discussed shortly, the consolidation of popular organizations required that they assert a certain autonomy from the church in defining their interests. Given the fundamentally religious nature of CEBs, this would always be problematic at best, even for the most politicized CEBs. See Levine 1986. The lack of autonomy from the church, in turn, can place severe limits on the ability of CEBs to promote political, and perhaps even social, change. This can be seen in the case of Brazil, where popular organizations that emerged under the military regime generally were more dependent on the progressive wing of the Catholic Church.

committees of people seeking housing (*comités sin casa*) and various
"debtors'" committees—groups of people who were behind in paying
electricity and water bills or mortgage payments in state housing programs.
These organizations also included attempts to organize workers in state
minimal employment programs.

This type of organization became relatively important for a short period
toward the end of the 1970s. The military regime's refusal to deal with
them and the obvious exposure to repression that membership in such
groups would entail caused these organizations to decrease in importance
in later years. These organizations also tended to be somewhat unstable,
and any success in getting their demands satisfied frequently resulted in the
dissolution of the group (Campero 1987; *Hechos Urbanos* 1985; Hardy
1985; Razeto et al. 1986). Those organizations in this category that did
survive began to refocus their activities toward satisfying the immediate
needs of their members as the economic situation deteriorated dramatically
in 1981.

Organizations in this category typically attempted to deal directly with
local governments. Their activities involved delivering petitions on behalf
of the group's members to local authorities demanding, for example,
solutions to the housing situation, improved urban services, or the renegoti-
ation of debts. Such organizations have also been involved in urban
land-seizures.

Organizations for Self-Defense and Protection against Repression

The dominant type of organization in this category was the human rights
committee. These groups were among the first popular organizations to
emerge after the military coup. Human rights groups were actively involved
in the collection of information on human rights abuses. They also helped
the victims of repression and their families to obtain legal, medical, and
other kinds of assistance through the various human rights organizations
operating in Santiago. Finally, these groups frequently sponsored educational and consciousness-raising activities directed toward the wider community within the *población* concerning the definition and meaning of
human rights.

In the aftermath of the first national protests in 1983, a number of new organizations were formed. These included various self-defense groups. Such organizations were most active during the protests, erecting barricades, digging trenches in unpaved roads to block vehicles, and so forth. Health groups also emerged in many *poblaciones* as a way to administer first aid and help those injured during protests. The latter were frequently involved in various health-related activities in the *poblaciones* in between protests.

Political Organizations

These organizations generally attempted to coordinate activities among different organizations at various levels, ranging from territorial subdivisions within larger *poblaciones* to all of the *poblaciones* within a particular municipality in the Santiago metropolitan area. Political organizations were particularly active in the protest movement. Some political organizations focused their activities on political ends and proposals dealing with the specific problems of *poblaciones*, but did not adopt a partisan position. Others were erected to serve as referents for the activities of particular political parties in the *poblaciones*.

Participation in political organizations was limited and such organizations generally sought more direct ties with base-level popular organizations. Only the most active leaders in the *poblaciones* tended to participate in these organizations, and a disproportionate number of those who did were political party militants. Those organizations that were not referents for political parties in the *poblaciones* frequently served as arenas for reaching agreements among the competing political parties represented in them.

Subsistence Organizations

These organizations attempted to find solutions to the basic needs of the *pobladores* and formed the largest category of popular organizations. At least half of all popular organizations fell into this category. According to one study completed in July 1985, there were 1,103 subsistence organizations functioning in Santiago, benefitting approximately 110,000 people.[3]

3. These organizations are frequently referred to as "popular economic organizations" (*organizaciones económicas populares*). The discussion of subsistence organizations is based on a comprehensive study of such organizations conducted under the auspices of the Programa de Economía del Trabajo (PET). See Razeto et al. 1986.

Subsistence organizations were dedicated to different forms of economic self-help. In general, they engaged in four principal types of economic activities: the production and commercialization of goods and services, finding solutions for housing needs, securing employment for their members, and the provision of basic consumption needs. Examples of subsistence organizations included handicraft workshops, housing co-ops, debtors' groups,[4] groups of unemployed workers, soup kitchens and consumers' co-ops.

Attempts to classify popular organizations, however, obscure their fundamental similarities. The vast majority of popular organizations pursued a variety of activities that cannot be placed in any single category (Razeto et al. 1986; Hardy 1985; Campero 1987). This is also apparent in the results from forty-six interviews conducted for the present study between June 1986 and January 1987. Leaders from forty-one different popular organizations throughout Santiago were selected according to four criteria: where they lived in Santiago, their age (were they old enough to have meaningful memories or organizational experiences prior to the military coup?), gender, and party affiliation. Heightened repression in the *poblaciones* in response to the national protests (which were then in full swing) and a paucity of prior research on organizational activities in the *poblaciones* since 1973 ruled out the possibility of constructing a "scientific" sample of *pobladores* for the interviews. As a result, I decided to focus on leaders of popular organizations because they were more accustomed to talking with outsiders. I also felt that they would be more likely to provide useful information since these people were more directly involved in trying to construct both a popular collective identity and a future popular social movement. No claims can be made that the results necessarily represent the attitudes of less active members of popular organizations, much less all *pobladores* in general. Instead, they are strongly indicative of important tendencies among organized *pobladores*. These tendencies will have a direct impact on the

4. Debtors' organizations, as well as committees of people seeking housing, are included in both the category of subsistence organizations and organizations that sought to pressure the state for the satisfaction of demands. This duplication reflects the difficulties in classifying popular organizations. It also underscores a key distinction between popular organizations after the coup and those that existed during the democratic period. Whereas virtually all popular-sector organizational activity prior to the coup would have been placed in the category of organizations that sought to pressure the state for the satisfaction of demands, under the military regime, only a small percentage of organizations fell into this category, and those that did assumed new characteristics that reflected the changed political context.

political role that the popular sectors play in Chile. These people are also among the *pobladores* who are most likely to initiate and lead any social movement that might emerge.[5]

The multifaceted nature of popular-sector organizational activities can be seen in Appendix 1, which lists the principal activities of forty-one popular organizations to which people interviewed for the present study belonged. These organizations, which ran the full gamut of popular-sector organizations, typically pursued activities that dealt with the social, educational, political, and economic situations of their members as *pobladores*. Similarly, organizational meetings were only rarely limited to dealing with the business of running the organization. When asked why their organizations held meetings, only one person out of the forty-six people interviewed felt her organization met just to deal with the organization's business matters. While all people responding to the question agreed that business matters were an important reason for holding meetings, 91 percent also felt that their organizations met in order to allow members to socialize. Sixty-nine percent suggested meetings served educational purposes, and 71 percent said their organizations met to engage in various kinds of political activities (see Table 7).

More generally, this multiplicity of activities and objectives was one of the fundamental defining characteristics of popular organizations under the military regime. Popular organizations sought collective responses to all of the needs and aspirations of their members, who formed part of a disadvan-

Table 7.   Why does your organization hold meetings?

	Total
To deal with business matters	45
To socialize	41
For educational purposes	31
To engage in political[a] activities	32
Only to deal with business matters	1
n.a.	1

[a]The term *political* is used here to refer to activities in which the participants either explicitly express their opposition to the military regime and its policies, or discuss the political situation of the country or the positions of political parties.

5. The methodology and design of the interviews are discussed in greater detail in Appendix 2.

taged and marginalized group in society. These were "integral" organizations (Razeto et al. 1986). Despite the importance of economic self-help in most forms of popular-sector organizational activity, their logic could not be reduced merely to economic need. Razeto et al. (1986) illustrates this in the specific case of subsistence organizations:

> [T]hese organizations are characterized by the fact that the sociopolitical and ideological dimensions of popular [sector] life and experience are closely linked in their activities. Their dynamic and concrete actions do not respond ever to a purely economic logic, but rather the [*pobladores'*] motivations and aspirations for a better life at the family and communitarian level (involving aspects of health, education, housing conditions and the *población* habitat, etc.) are amalgamated in them, as well as the perspective of action that is inserted in a process of economic-political change and popular liberation. As a function of these extra-economic dimensions, the organizations frequently form special commissions for the realization of cultural, social, solidarity, recreational and other activities and functions. (19)

Popular organizations should be viewed as fundamentally a response to the economic, political, social, and cultural exclusion that military rule imposed on the popular sectors. The breadth and multiplicity of activities in the different types of popular organizations shared this common dynamic. Hardy (1986) makes this clear in concluding her typology of popular-sector organizations:

> In sum, if we analyze all of the models of collective behavior present in [popular organizations], we will see that these follow two diverse, but convergent directions: a) Orientations tied to the daily life of the popular sectors that, although they do not include [open] manifestations of conflict, are expressions of the daily confrontations of these sectors with the factors that determine their exclusion, especially in the areas of material and cultural subsistence or their own identity. b) Circumstantial mobilizations and struggles that openly express the conflict between these sectors and the dominant model, especially in the area of economic and political exclusion. (31)

THE EVOLUTION OF POPULAR ORGANIZATIONS UNDER THE MILITARY REGIME

The emergence of popular-sector organizational activity under the military regime was an evolutionary process that passed through distinct phases. Not only did the number of organizations and participants tend to grow over time, but organizational forms and styles also changed. Four factors in particular conditioned this evolutionary process: (1) the changing role of the state; (2) the existence of a variety of support institutions that worked with popular organizations (the most important of which were under the auspices of the Catholic Church); (3) Chile's democratic heritage, especially the large number of *pobladores* who had acquired actual organizational experience prior to the coup; and (4) the severe constraints placed on traditional political-party activities.

The Changing Role of the State

A fundamental factor influencing the evolution of popular-sector organiza-tional activity after the military coup was its *antagonistic* relationship to the state. As explained in Chapter 2, the state had been the principal referent for the satisfaction of popular-sector demands and aspirations for political and social integration. Under the military regime, the popular sectors were excluded from access to the state. The regime's neoconserva-tive policies led to a significant curtailment of the state's role in the provision of social welfare services, as well as a dramatic decline in the popular sectors' life chances and consumption possibilities. "The [popular] organizations of today are born out of the lack of resources and not out of access to them" as in the past (Hardy 1985, 26).

The military also accentuated the state's capacity for repression and social control. It viewed the popular sectors with a certain fear, treating them at least as a latent enemy of the social order envisioned by the military (Valdés 1987). The popular sectors had been an important source of electoral support for the Marxist Popular Unity government of Salvador Allende and the *poblaciones* were still seen as the principal source of support for the extreme Left. Repression was particularly intense in the *poblaciones*, especially after the outbreak of the first cycle of national protests in May 1983.

A variety of policies designed to increase the state's capacity to fragment and control popular-sector activities were implemented by the military government (Morales 1987; Sánchez 1987; Valdés 1987; Rodríguez 1984). The military government quickly intervened in the control of local governments and the base-level organizations established in the 1960s. Only popular-sector organizations that the military government could dominate were recognized. Municipal reforms were designed to concentrate the urban poor in clearly defined geographical areas and atomize any emergent social movement. New welfare policies aimed at those "in extreme poverty" consolidated centralized control over the state's remaining social welfare programs and contributed to the further atomization of the popular sectors by dealing with the problems of the urban poor only on a case-by-case basis.

The Existence of Support Institutions

Popular-sector organizational activity could not have developed to the extent that it did had it not been for the presence of a number of nongovernmental support institutions that were actively involved in the *poblaciones*. The Catholic Church was very important in this regard, particularly through the Vicaría de la Solidaridad, which it established in 1976. Many of the other institutions most closely associated with popular organizations also operated under the church's auspices.[6] Support institutions filled a number of different roles in relation to popular-sector organizational activity after the imposition of authoritarian rule. Changes in the relative importance of each of these roles were significant in determining the evolution of popular organizations.

The church always played a critical role in shielding popular organizations from repression, although this role became less important in later years as popular organizations grew in number and autonomy. More than half of the organizations to which people interviewed for this study belonged met in church facilities (see Appendix 2). The church was able to fulfill this role of "protective umbrella" because it enjoyed relative immu-

---

6. The most comprehensive study of the role of support institutions working with popular organizations is Sánchez 1987. That study included twenty-four support institutions that were functioning in Santiago at the end of 1981.

nity from repression due to the military regime's reluctance to challenge the church directly.[7] Moreover, the church had the necessary physical space to shelter many organizations, given its extensive parish network in the *poblaciones*.

The church was also important as a catalyst for popular organizations. The Catholic Church had a long history of working with the urban poor that allowed it to quickly adapt to the new situation in the *poblaciones* created by the imposition of authoritarian rule (Campero 1987; Espinoza 1988; Smith 1982, Vallier 1970). Church support for popular organizations gave them a legitimacy that helped people to overcome their initial fears of repression. Priests, nuns and Catholic layworkers were often instrumental in bringing people together for the first time to form groups and seek collective solutions to their problems. A growing group of "popular educators" and social workers also filled this role of catalyst (Garretón 1989a and 1989c).

Support institutions performed a third function through the provision of material resources and help in the production and commercialization of handicrafts. Material resources included various supplies for soup kitchens, flour for small-scale bread bakeries, materials for handicrafts production, and used clothes that popular organizations sold to *pobladores* to raise money. Support institutions also provided technical assistance and training in the production of various kinds of handicrafts, growing family vegetable gardens and other production-related activities. Finally, support institutions played an important role in the commercialization of handicrafts produced by members of popular organizations by sponsoring handicraft expositions, seeking out buyers (both within Chile and abroad) and even selling handicrafts directly to the public.

The last principal role played by support institutions was the generation of organizational capacity within the *poblaciones* (Sánchez 1987; Valdés 1987; Razeto et al. 1986; Espinoza 1983). As will be discussed below, the church and other support institutions in the late 1970s adopted a new strategy of encouraging *pobladores* to organize themselves in autonomous popular organizations.[8] *Pobladores* were taught leadership and personal

---

7. See Garretón 1989a and 1989c; Valenzuela and Valenzuela 1986b; and Smith 1982. The Catholic Church was not completely immune from repression, especially at the base level. The military regime also engaged in an extensive legal and propagandistic campaign against the church's human rights work and the Vicaría de la Solidaridad in particular. See Escobar 1986.

8. An example of how support institutions encouraged popular organizations to assume greater independence and autonomy is in Gallardo 1985.

interaction skills, as well as the importance of organizing and collective action in general. Support organizations also endeavored to respect the autonomy of popular organizations to decide on their own goals and activities.

Chile's Democratic Heritage

Chile's long period of political democracy facilitated the emergence of popular organizations under the military regime in two ways. First, a large number of people living in the *poblaciones* had gained invaluable organizational experience through their prior participation in political parties, the labor movement, and the base-level organizations established in the 1960s. These people were the first to participate in the new popular organizations and they were gradually able to disseminate their experiences to others who had no prior organizational experiences (Razeto et al. 1986; Campero 1987; Valdés 1987; Sánchez 1987).

Chile's democratic heritage also contributed to the emergence of popular organizations after the military coup because it had demonstrated to a significant number of people the efficacy of organization and collective action for improving life chances and consumption opportunities. The Allende experience in particular was important for raising the consciousness of the popular sectors concerning the possibilities of a more equitable and just society (Bitar 1986a).

Constraints On Traditional Political Party Activities

Finally, the evolution of popular-sector organizational activity was greatly influenced by the virtual cessation of traditional political-party activity. As explained in Chapter 2, political repression had the effect of shifting the locus of political activity to the base level, particularly the *poblaciones*. Party elites were essentially cut off from the grassroots level. Moreover, political parties were no longer necessary as mechanisms for gaining access to the state. This permitted popular organizations an unprecedented degree of autonomy from political parties. Although party militants were active in popular organizations, political parties lacked any comprehensive strategy for dealing with the *poblaciones* and militants acted with much greater independence. As Campero (1986) points out, "one was dealing with a party militant who, without abandoning [his party], now became above all a representative of his *población* in the party and stopped representing the party in the *población*" (17).

The evolution of these four factors caused the development of popular organizations to go through four distinct phases under the military regime. Each phase was characterized by changes in the dynamic and scope of popular-sector organizational activity as a result of changes in these factors.[9]

Phase 1: Survival from Repression

The first phase lasted roughly from September 1973 until the end of 1974. Repression was extremely high and arbitrary during this period, and popular-sector organizational activity focused on help for victims of repression and human rights violations. There were almost no autonomous popular organizations during this period. Several different churches formed the Committee of Cooperation for Peace in Chile (COPACHI) in October 1973 and the majority of organizational activity was under its auspices.

In addition to human rights groups, the first organizations intended to deal with the problems of hunger and unemployment were formed by various church groups during this phase. These organizations were basically run by the support institutions that founded them and funneled material resources to a limited number of people who were directly affected by the new regime's repressive polices. By the end of 1974, there were 22 *comedores infantiles*[10] handing out food to the young children of the victims of repression, as well as a number of *bolsas de cesantes* (groups of unemployed workers) and *talleres laborales* (handicraft workshops). Organizations during this phase were viewed as temporary responses to a situation of "emergency." There was no perspective beyond the immediate channeling of help directly to the victims of repression, or real effort to create

9. The following draws on the accounts provided in Valdés 1987; Razeto et al. 1986; and Sánchez 1987.

10. The Spanish name is used for the first organizations that emerged in the *poblaciones* in order to distinguish them from organizations that emerged later. *Comedores infantiles* were soup kitchens that handed out food to the young children of the victims of repression. In the next phase, the *comedores infantiles* usually evolved into *comedores populares*, handing out food to the entire family of the victims of repression. The *comedores* and other organizations that emerged during the first two phases were characterized by their lack of participation, little decision-making autonomy, and extreme dependence on support institutions, in contrast to the *ollas comunes* (which will be referred to as soup kitchens) and the myriad of other organizations that began to emerge in the late 1970s.

permanent or autonomous popular organizations. Aid was generally given in a paternalistic fashion.

Phase 2: Solidarity With the Victims of the Regime

There was a marked expansion in organizational activity in the *poblaciones* during this phase, which lasted roughly from 1975 through 1977. But the dynamic and style of popular-sector organizational activity remained basically unchanged from the previous period; the change was more quantitative than qualitative. In 1977, for example, 323 *comedores populares*—which had replaced the *comedores infantiles* of the previous phase—were distributing food to 30,000 people in the Santiago metropolitan area.

Repression, although still at a high level, had become more selective with the formation of the DINA in mid-1974. Only those directly involved in political-party activities were now targeted (Frühling 1984). The regime's economic policies began to take shape and Chile was plunged into a deep recession in 1975 as a result of the military government's "shock" program to curb inflation (Foxley 1983). Support institutions responded by creating more organizations to deal with problems of unemployment and hunger.[11]

Popular organizations were still viewed as transitory during this phase—as temporary responses to an emergency situation that could not last. More and more people were being helped, but those who were helped largely remained limited to people with prior ties to union, shantytown, political, and religious organizations dating back to before the military coup. Organizations in the *poblaciones* were not viewed as new organizational forms that would incorporate new groups of people. Instead, they were used to maintain links between people who already had organizational experience and block the regime's attempts to disarticulate any remaining organizational nuclei. In particular, these early organizations focused on preserving the old core of the labor movement in the hopes that when the "emergency" finally passed, it would again assume its vanguard role among the popular sectors (Campero 1987). This short-term perspective reinforced the dependent and paternalistic characteristics of the previous phase. Many

11. The Catholic Church was assuming an increasingly central role in popular-sector organizations, both directly and indirectly through other support institutions operating under its auspices. The Committee of Cooperation for Peace in Chile was disbanded as a result of intense government pressure in December 1975. The next month, the archbishop of Santiago created the Vicaría de la Solidaridad to continue the Committee's work. The Vicaría was closely tied to the Catholic Church hierarchy and under the control of Catholic bishops. See Smith 1982.

organizations were little more than channels for distributing material assistance—severely circumscribing the self-help potential of popular organizations.

Phase 3: Crisis and Transition

From 1978 until 1981, popular-sector organizational activity underwent a fundamental change, as both support institutions and popular organizations perceived that a longer-term perspective was necessary due to advances in the military regime's efforts to ensure its own institutionalization. *Pobladores* and support institutions recognized that more permanent solutions for popular-sector problems were necessary and that these solutions required increasing the popular sectors' own capacity for creating autonomous self-help organizations. Most of the original organizations that had emerged since the coup experienced a crisis and eventually stopped functioning.[12]

This important change in the dynamic of popular-sector organizational activity was the result of several convergent trends. The first was that the situation could no longer be considered as one of a transitory "emergency" because it was becoming increasingly clear that the military regime was achieving a certain level of institutionalization.

The military regime held a "national consultation" in January 1978 in order to claim domestic support for a series of institutional reforms the regime intended to implement as part of its neoconservative social project. Municipal reforms were later introduced that were designed to increase the regime's capacity for social control. As part of these reforms, responsibility for social welfare programs was transferred to the municipal level. The program of "eradicating" shantytowns in order to concentrate and segregate the urban poor within the Santiago metropolitan area had also begun.[13] The establishment of the National Intelligence Center in August 1977 marked the beginning of the regime's efforts to institutionalize and

12. The number of *comedores populares* operating decreased from 323, with 30,000 participants, in 1977, to 201, serving 15,284 people, in 1979 (Sánchez 1987). Only 121 still were functioning at the end of 1982, and by July 1985 there were just 30 *comedores populares*. The most comprehensive census of subsistence organizations did not register even a single *bolsa de cesantes* as of November 1982. See Razeto et al. 1986.

13. Some of the implications of these reforms and the eradication program are discussed in Chapter 2. It should be noted that one aim of the eradications was to disrupt all forms of collective identity and activity emerging within the shantytowns by dispersing the inhabitants of eradicated shantytowns among different *poblaciones*.

legalize its coercive practices under an authoritarian rule of law (Frühling 1984). Finally, hopes that the labor movement would soon resume its central role within the popular sectors were dashed with the decree of a new Labor Plan in 1978, which sharply circumscribed union strength and activities (Ruiz Tagle 1985; Frühling 1984). This institutionalization process culminated in 1980, when a new constitution was adopted by the military regime. The constitution established the framework for an eventual transition to a limited or restricted form of political democracy in 1989.

Support institutions also faced mounting financial pressures that contributed to a reorientation of their objectives with respect to popular organizations. The military regime's new economic model was adversely affecting increasing numbers of *pobladores*, straining the technical, administrative, and material resources of the support institutions. The *bolsas de cesantes* and the *talleres laborales* had failed to meet the needs of their members due to both poor planning and their excessive dependence on support institutions. When the support institutions were forced to cut back on their resources, many organizations disintegrated.[14] There was a growing recognition that permanent and self-sustaining solutions had to be found.

At the same time, the support institutions' own sources of funding began to question the purpose behind the current types of organizational activities in the *poblaciones*. The prolongation of the regime and its obvious advances toward institutionalization required rethinking the role of the popular organizations. Because they were structured as temporary responses to a situation of emergency, the existing organizations were clearly no longer adequate. Funding agencies were leery of continuing to funnel resources into projects for maintaining the organizations without any clear sense of what they were actually intended to achieve.

Support institutions responded to these challenges with policies aimed at increasing the capacity of the popular sectors to organize themselves and sustain their organizations with less reliance on external help. Assistance for organizations would continue, but at a lower level and as only one aspect—not the only aspect—of a broader strategy for helping the popular sectors to become active in Chilean politics and society. Education became

---

14. The excessive dependence of the early organizations meant that when their external assistance was cut back, the organizations often could not cope and fell apart. A member of one of the few surviving *bolsas de cesantes* explained that his particular organization survived because "it fought for its demands. It did not wait for the Church to give it things. Otherwise, it would have died," like the others when the church stopped providing resources (interview, Santiago 1986).

an increasingly important part of the support institutions' activities in the *poblaciones*. *Pobladores* were taught the importance of organizing and how to organize. People learned how to run their own organizations. Courses in leadership skills and interpersonal relations were provided and courses on human rights were expanded. Support institutions also encouraged participation and democratic decision-making in the organizations, stressing the importance of collective action and solidarity.

All of these efforts were aimed at increasing the autonomy of popular organizations. Support institutions sought to reinforce this by respecting the autonomous decision-making processes of the organizations. Dependence was avoided by encouraging a certain level of self-sufficiency and resources were never sufficient to satisfy the organizations' needs. Handicraft workshops and various other groups working with the unemployed took on a greater responsibility in managing their own affairs and seeking or creating their own economic opportunities. Soup kitchens were required to find ways of augmenting the gradually diminishing contributions received from support institutions, although those contributions always remained very important to the organization.

A similar change in perceptions concerning the appropriate role of popular organizations was taking place in the *poblaciones*. *Pobladores* were increasingly beginning to associate their problems with the need for some kind of political change. This politicization of significant segments of the *poblaciones* was associated with the rejection of the military regime's neoconservative, market-oriented model of society. This was the period of the Chilean economic "miracle"; inflation was more or less under control and the economy was recovering from the depths of the shock-induced recession. The domestic market was flooded with consumer goods as protective trade barriers were rapidly eliminated and a new consumerism dominated the regime's propaganda. In this context, many *pobladores* viewed popular organizations as mechanisms through which they could collectively seek their own solutions for overcoming marginality. Popular organizations became a locus for resistance and represented an alternative to the authoritarian and individualistic model for social relations being imposed by the military regime. Organizations that attempted to pressure the state for the satisfaction of popular demands, as discussed above, were particularly important during the early part of this phase.

Pobladores themselves began to appreciate the severe limitations of previous organizations that remained dependent on support institutions and did little more than distribute material assistance to their members. Many popular organizations sought to expand the scope of their activities and escape the ecclesiastical framework of the church organizations. The autonomy to define and defend their own interests became increasingly important to popular organizations. Perhaps just as important, support institutions were encouraging these tendencies and helping the *pobladores* to realize them.[15]

Phase 4: The Consolidation of Popular Organizations

This final phase in the evolution of popular organizations can be traced to the collapse of the regime's economic model around mid-1981. Unemployment skyrocketed and problems of hunger, inadequate housing, poor health care, and so forth, became correspondingly worse as Chile entered into an economic depression rivaling that of the 1930s. The characteristics of popular organizations as described in the first section of this chapter became more pronounced and popular organizations multiplied rapidly. The number of subsistence organizations increased almost threefold from the end of 1982 through 1986.[16]

It is important to note that this consolidation and expansion of popular organizations coincided with a marked increase in the level of repression in the *poblaciones*. The first cycle of national protests began in May 1983 and the military regime reacted violently. States of siege were in force from November 1984 through mid-1985, and again from September 1986 through early January 1987. The *pobladores'* geographical segregation and their socioeconomic position made them vulnerable to repression. The military regime also attempted to use the *pobladores'* participation in protests to create a climate of fear in order to rally support on the basis of the military's ability to restore law and order. As a result, the *pobladores* were subjected to levels of violence both in between and during protests that were reminiscent of the worst moments immediately after the military

15. Gallardo 1987 and 1985 analyzes this evolution in the case of soup kitchens. A more critical analysis of the new strategy of popular-sector organizing adopted by support institutions during this phase is found in Espinoza 1983.

16. The best available statistics only cover subsistence organizations, which accounted for approximately half of all popular organizations in 1986. In November 1982, there were 494 subsistence organizations. This increased to 702 as of March 1984 and reached 1,103 by June 1985 (Razeto et al. 1986). The total number of subsistence organizations was 1,386 in 1986 (Campero 1987).

coup. Yet popular organizations grew significantly during this period and continued to participate actively in the protests.[17]

Despite their close association, it is important to maintain a distinction between popular-sector organizational activity and popular-sector mobilization in the national protests. As Garretón (1987c, 1989a, and 1989c) correctly argues, this mobilization was important for creating new social identities and it contributed to the formation of new political and social actors. But these same processes were already taking place prior to the outbreak of the national protests and continued independently through the popular organizations themselves. The national protests may have accelerated these processes, but the eventual frustration to which the protests led and their failure to achieve substantive changes did not signal an end or even a slowdown in these processes at the level of popular organizations. On the contrary, the number of popular organizations continued to grow as repression increased and the protest movement was paralyzed by declarations of states of siege.

The importance of this distinction between mobilization for the protests and popular-sector organizational activity rests on two frequently ignored facts. First, the literature on social movements usually assumes that there is a democratic regime or looks at the revolutionary potential of a particular social movement in less-developed countries. But popular-sector organizational activity in Chile was taking place under a repressive authoritarian regime and, as will be argued in Chapter 5, was not revolutionary in either its potential or its goals. For a social movement to survive in such a context, its capacity to resist repression is critical and largely dependent on organization and the presence of a strong sense of collective identity that can inspire people to accept the very real personal danger that participation involves (Calhoun 1991).

Moreover, the mere existence of popular organizations under the authoritarian regime represents an important form of *symbolic* protest that mobilizes people. The symbolic importance of this type of protest activity has much less significance in a democratic regime where the right to organize is already recognized by the state.

Second, as will be argued throughout the subsequent chapters, popular organizations do not yet represent a social movement. An important

17. The issue of repression and popular organizations during this period is discussed at length in Chapter 7 and Appendix 3. I shall argue in Chapter 4 that one reason why people choose to accept the increased risk of repression associated with membership in popular organizations is the nature of the collective identity that these organizations often embody.

empirical question is the potential of these organizations to form a new social movement. Protest is an integral aspect of social movements, but, aside from there being different ways to protest, organizational activity may be more important in the formation of a new social movement than explicit and direct forms of protest, especially under an authoritarian regime. The potential for the popular sectors to form a new social movement is very much dependent on their ability to maintain and expand a network of autonomous organizations that represent popular-sector collective action on the basis of a popular collective identity.

ASSESSING THE INSTITUTIONALIZATION OF POPULAR ORGANIZATIONS

A process of the "resurrection of civil society" had clearly begun in Chile as a direct result of the authoritarian experience. This suggests a number of important questions that remain unanswered. How far can this process continue under the authoritarian regime? Is it able to influence—or even survive—a democratic transition? Can this process of the *resurrection* of civil society contribute to a larger process of *democratization* of civil society?

As discussed in Chapter 1, the factors that will determine the answers to the above questions are closely related to the level of institutionalization that popular organizations are able to achieve under the authoritarian regime. It should be recalled that the level of institutionalization of popular organizations can be analyzed in terms of four variables: their adaptability, complexity, autonomy, and coherence (Huntington 1968). What conclusions can be drawn on the basis of the above discussion?

First, popular organizations demonstrated a relatively high degree of adaptability. This was reflected both in the phases through which popular-sector organizational activity had passed and in the experiences of individual popular organizations. Changes in state policies, perceptions of the significance of the military regime, and the role of support institutions were reflected in new patterns of organizational activity. Moreover, organizational activity in the *poblaciones* successfully adapted to a dramatic deterioration in the economic situation of the *pobladores*, as well as a marked increase in repression beginning in May 1983.

At the level of the individual organizations examined in the present study, there were various indicators of a significant capacity for adaptation. The majority of these organizations were formed prior to the declaration of a state of siege in November 1984, and all of them continued functioning despite the increased repression for those living in *poblaciones*. When asked if their own organization had ever been close to disbanding, more than 30 percent of those responding to the question indicated that their organization had successfully overcome various crises that threatened their organization's continued existence.

More generally, 31 people—91 percent of those responding to the question—indicated that their organizations regularly engaged in collective self-criticism that generated efforts to improve the functioning of the organization. Similarly, the changes that the interviewees perceived in their organizations reflected this adaptive capacity. Ninety percent of the people responding to the question "How has your organization changed since its beginning?" felt that their organization had changed in some significant way.[18] The most commonly perceived changes, noted by 20 percent of the respondents in each case, were an expansion of the organization's objectives and activities, increased participation, and increased consciousness among members. Seventeen percent noted an increase in affective relations and solidarity.[19] These latter changes are important aspects of popular-sector organizational activity and will be discussed at length in Chapter 4.

A second conclusion is that popular organizations were complex. They undertook a variety of activities in the pursuit of multiple goals. They also frequently had a number of subunits corresponding to these activities and objectives. As argued above, this was one of the defining characteristics of popular organizations. Appendix 1 and Table 7 demonstrate that this was true for most of the organizations covered in the current study.

The issue of organizational autonomy is more complicated. Popular

18. Interviewees did not always answer every question included in the survey, generally because the question was inadvertently omitted. Only very rarely did people refuse to answer a specific question, even though they were clearly given this option. See Appendix 2.

19. It should be noted that many organizations did not experience changes in leadership—an important indicator of the organization's ability to adapt. Campero (1987) suggested that this phenomenon represented a limitation on the democratic quality of these organizations. In the cases studied here, as well as elsewhere (Razeto et al. 1986; Valdés 1987; Hardy 1986), any lack of leadership rotation tended to reflect satisfaction with existing leaders and, in some cases, the lack of other members' experience. Decision-making in almost all cases was still very democratic in that all members participated and efforts were made to reach a consensus. The issue of leadership selection within popular organizations was itself often of secondary importance to the *pobladores*.

organizations were clearly vulnerable to external influences. They often received important resources, both material and nonmaterial, from support institutions. Soup kitchens, in particular, were highly dependent upon the supplies they received from the Vicaría de la Solidaridad.

Yet the support institutions themselves endeavored to minimize this vulnerability by encouraging greater popular organization autonomy. A primary lesson from the experience of the late 1970s was the recognition by both support institutions and members of popular-sector organizations of the need for popular organizations to avoid excessive dependence. The organizations that survived this period reflected this. The organizations also resisted the military regime's repression remarkably well. Popular organizations continued to function and grow as the protests (which were the direct cause of the resurgence of the military regime's repressive dimension) ended in frustration and a general demobilization of the opposition.

Moreover, the external resources that any organization received were never sufficient to meet its needs. In order for the organization to survive, its members had to work continually to augment its resources through a variety of means—further contributing to the development and institutionalization of the organization in the process. It is not at all clear that organizations that had achieved some level of institutionalization in terms of adaptability and complexity would have disbanded if their external resources had been suddenly cut off.

Finally, the relationship between vulnerability to external influences and autonomy is further blurred because of the peculiar nature of popular organizations under the authoritarian regime (Oxhorn 1986 and 1988). These organizations were the result of the popular sectors' vulnerability to the changes introduced into Chilean society by the imposition of authoritarian rule. Their evolution reflected collective efforts to find alternatives to the popular sectors' increasing vulnerability in the face of the socioeconomic changes induced by the military regime's repression and neoconservative policies. In a sense, the limited alternatives open to the popular sectors conditioned the vulnerability of popular organizations to external influences.

Soup kitchens offered the clearest example of this. Soup kitchens were arguably the popular organizations most dependent on external assistance. Yet, if the soup kitchen stopped functioning, its members usually did not eat. Unlike the *comedores populares* that preceded them, the soup kitchens (or *ollas comunes*) that emerged in the late 1970s and 1980s were actively involved in augmenting the assistance which they did receive—assistance that tended to decrease for each organization in later years due to the multiplication of such organizations. It would be wrong to assume that soup kitchens would have stopped functioning *only* if their external resources were cut off. This was especially true if the organization served other functions, in addition to that of providing food for its members.

This ambiguity regarding vulnerability to external influences highlights a second aspect of organizational autonomy: the organization's ability to define its own interests independently from those of external groups. Both the efforts of support institutions to respect the decision-making autonomy of popular organizations and the organizations' own efforts to separate themselves from the direct tutelage of the church are good indicators that a certain level of autonomy had been achieved in this regard. This, too, was a direct reflection of the perceived vulnerability and excessive dependence of the first popular organizations.

A fourth general conclusion deals with the coherence of popular organizations. The general description of popular organizations presented above suggests that there was a growing level of coherence in the form of a clear organizational style common to all popular organizations.

In sum, popular organizations under the military regime demonstrated important levels of adaptability and complexity. The issue of autonomy was somewhat more ambiguous and complicated, although there is evidence to suggest that a certain level of organizational autonomy had been achieved. Similarly, there appeared to be an emerging organizational style that might have provided popular organizations with the organizational coherence required for their continued institutionalization. It seems plausible to conclude that popular organizations had achieved a certain level of institutionalization under the authoritarian regime. But would it be sufficient to ensure their survival during and after a democratic transition? Could popular organizations serve as a foundation for a new popular social movement?

In the following chapters I shall address these questions by focusing on the dual axes of identity formation and collective action.[20] Specifically, I

20. These two dimensions of popular-sector organizational activity are intimately related to the four variables for measuring organizational institutionalization. Organizations that embody a collective identity are more likely to have achieved a significant level of institutionalization. For example, a popular collective identity could serve as the basis for organizational coherence and for distinguishing the organization's interests from those of external actors, such as the Catholic Church. Moreover, organizations that embody such a collective identity tend to pursue a variety of objectives and distinct activities associated with various facets of

shall argue that popular organizations represented a new popular collective identity and shall explore some of the implications this has on popular-sector collective action and the role of the popular sectors in the current democratic regime.

---

that collective identity. Finally, the presence of a popular collective identity in popular organizations could help them to adapt to changing situations and various organizational challenges.

4

POPULAR ORGANIZATIONS AND THE EMERGENCE OF A NEW COLLECTIVE IDENTITY

Lo Popular

The evidence presented in Chapters 2 and 3 demonstrates how the military regime ushered in important changes to the structure of Chile's economy and the social organization of its society, with particularly adverse consequences for the popular sectors. A growing number of people responded to these changes collectively by forming and participating in a wide range of popular organizations in the communities where they lived.

The emergence of new kinds of popular organizations in the context of dramatic socioeconomic and political change raises some important theoretical issues (as discussed in Chapter 1). The Chilean experience clearly reflects the relationships described in the model developed for understanding popular-sector organizational activity. That model postulates a close relationship between the specific nature of the military regime's repression and socioeconomic policies, on the one hand, and the emergence of such organizations, on the other. Similarly, the model suggests that the support institutions that provide shelter and assistance to popular organizations, as well as Chile's particular democratic heritage, will condition the ways in which the popular-sectors respond to the new needs and issues generated by the military regime. But the evidence presented in Chapter 3 also suggests that these new organizations are taking a particular form—one that appears to be more than a simple response to the immediate needs created by political repression and a deteriorating economic situation.

As I argued in Chapter 1, we can begin to understand this additional dimension by examining popular organizations from the perspective of an emergent popular-sector collective identity. In other words, has popular-sector organizational activity contributed to the creation and reproduction of a new collective identity? Does such an identity provide the basis for new forms of popular-sector collective action? As noted in Chapter 1, such a collective identity is central to the ability of the popular sectors to define and represent their interests in the political realm effectively. It can also reinforce the institutionalization of popular organizations, and ultimately serve as the basis for a new popular social movement. Equally important, this perspective allows for a greater understanding of the specific ways in which repression, the regime's socioeconomic policies, support institutions, and Chile's democratic heritage affect the perceptions of *pobladores* who are actively engaged in this organizational activity. The nature of their demands will be clearer, and we will have a better sense of how these people view the political system and their own role in it. Such things as the sources of tension between political parties and popular organizations, for example, should become more apparent.

Finally, I suggested in Chapter 1 that such a collective identity would play a special role in the specific kinds of popular organizations likely to emerge under an authoritarian regime. These people's worsening economic situation and general lack of resources correspondingly imply a much more important normative basis for understanding their continued participation. A popular collective identity is one way of understanding that normative base. Similarly, the arguments developed in Chapter 1 suggest that the values emphasized in the collective identity will be fundamentally democratic and egalitarian in nature. All of this suggests that a focus on popular organizations from the perspective of an emergent collective identity can provide insight into the function (and limitations) of popular organizations.

In this chapter I shall argue that the growth and persistence of popular-sector organizations after the military coup was closely related to the emergence of a new collective identity among the members of popular organizations. The argument will be organized around an abstract model of this popular collective identity, which will be referred to as *lo popular*. The model is based on my experiences over approximately two years working with popular organizations throughout Chile as a participant observer. The perceptions and beliefs of the forty-six people interviewed between June 1986 and January 1987 will be used to illustrate the core values associated with this emergent collective identity.

On data interpretation, a word of caution is in order. A great deal of effort was made to ensure a certain "balance" in the interview sample. For example, in selecting people to interview, attention was paid to where they lived in order to include the experiences of *poblaciones* exhibiting varying levels of organizational activity in 1986. Similarly, the majority of those interviewed did not belong to any political party, and the rest were selected to represent the political parties that were most active in the *poblaciones* at the time.[1] Still, it is not possible to make any strong claims as to the "representativeness" of this group of individuals. The views and experiences discussed in this and in subsequent chapters do not necessarily represent the views and experiences of other leaders of popular organizations or less active members, much less the 85 percent of *pobladores* who did not participate in popular organizations. Their views and experiences are beyond the scope of the current study. The views and experiences presented here, however, can serve as a basis for designing appropriate studies for these larger populations. In this sense, the discussion of *lo popular* remains preliminary. At the same time, the consistency of the experiences, values, and priorities among leaders from a wide variety of organizations suggests that tendencies have been identified. This is supported by the findings of the larger, more comprehensive studies discussed in Chapter 3, which point to a number of common characteristics that popular organizations generally shared. The organized segment of the popular sectors is the most politically relevant group, especially under the authoritarian regime when alternative avenues for political participation were foreclosed.

Finally, it should be recognized at the onset that the following discussion of *lo popular* is intentionally expressed in ideal (some would even say "romantic") terms. The purpose of this chapter is not to document a clearly defined reality that was representative of all members of the popular sectors during the military regime, or even a majority of them. Instead, the model of *lo popular* is designed to highlight the values and priorities associated with a new popular collective identity founded on territorially circum-scribed base-level organizations from the perspective of people who were

---

1. The design of the interview questionnaire, the nature of the sample and how it was constructed, and the limits and advantages of this type of data are discussed in more detail in Appendix 2.

actually striving to forge such an identity. As such, the model of *lo popular* indicates the fundamental features that a popular project for social transformation based on *lo popular* might assume. It also offers a useful contrast with more prevalent studies of the values and priorities of political elites.

WHY PEOPLE PARTICIPATE: THE IMPORTANCE OF NONMATERIAL INCENTIVES

Beginning with Mancur Olson's seminal work, *The Logic of Collective Action* (Olson 1965), a great deal of scholarly attention has focused on a seemingly simple question: Why do individuals voluntarily choose to participate in group activities, given the implicit costs of such participation and the lack of discernable material benefits directly tied to the individual's decision to participate? This logic of rational choice suggests a special paradox in the case of participation in popular-sector organizations in Chile after the 1973 coup. Although most organizations were initially formed to address pressing immediate needs, people continued to participate when such needs were not met—even as the "costs" of participation were rising due to repression.

This paradox can be seen in the interview results. For example, Table 8 shows that 28 out of 46 interviewees, or 61 percent, stated that their organizations were created (at least in part) to address some specific material need such as the lack of employment opportunities or their members' inability to feed their families. Yet, as shown in Table 9, only 9 interviewees listed material need as a reason why they actually participated in their respective organizations. Moreover, just 3 of the 42 interviewees (7 percent) who responded to the question "What has your organization achieved?" included the satisfaction of some material need among their respective organizations' achievements (see Table 10). And when asked what benefits they received from participating in their organization (Table 11), only 13 percent of the 39 people who gave an answer to this question included some kind of material benefit. Perhaps more surprising, when asked what they felt the characteristics of a good organization were, only one person referred to the resolution of "problems," and no one spoke of

Table 8. Why was your organization formed?

	Total
Organizations with multiple objectives	30
Objectives included alleviating material needs	28
All objectives unrelated to meeting material needs	18
Nonmaterial objectives:	
To raise members' consciousness	19
The need to organize, pressure for demands	16
To learn and/or teach	14
Work with other groups, serve the *población*	12
To oppose the regime, work for change	11
Unity, collective action, to be in a group	9
To create some form of "space" (for youth, women, recreation, etc.)	9

Note: Totals will only occasionally add up to 46 because interviewees may offer more than one response to any particular question.

Table 9. Why do you participate in the organization?

	Total
To be in an organization	32
To work for change, denounce some injustice	13
Material need	9
To increase others' consciousness	7
To learn	3
To create space for women	2
n.a.	1

Table 10. What has your organization achieved?

	Total
Solidarity, community	18
Increased consciousness among members	14
Material resources (equipment, meeting place, supplies, etc.)	12
Level of community acceptance	10
Education	7
Personal growth of members	6
Participation	4
Met a material need	3
Increased capacity to organize (new leaders, legitimate the organ., etc.)	3
Struggle/denunciation	3
Little or nothing	3
Democratize the *Junta de Vecinos*	1
Other	2
n.a.	4

Table 11. What benefits have you received from your participation in the organization?

	Total
Increased solidarity	17
Education	15
Growth as a person	14
Increased consciousness	9
Being part of an organization	8
Material benefits	5
Being part of the struggle	3
Other	4
No benefits	6
n.a.	7

the organization's ability to provide material goods, whether it be food in a soup kitchen, jobs for organizations of the unemployed, resources for handicraft workshops, and so forth (see Table 12).

Indeed, the data presented here suggests that people generally did *not* participate in popular organizations because they gained in tangible ways from such participation. This finding is particularly significant, given that participation in such organizations was often perceived as entailing substantial risk. Popular organizations in Chile were generally illegal under the military regime. They were also functioning in an increasingly repressive

Table 12. What are the characteristics of a good organization?

	Total
Organizational capacity	26
Solidarity/unity	18
Participation	13
The members have a high consciousness	13
Members are respected	10
Good leaders	8
Representative of its constituency or class	6
Democratic	6
Pluralist, open	5
Provides political education	4
Projection beyond the overthrow of Pinochet	3
Creates leaders	3
Nonpartisan—"popular"	3
Projection beyond the group	2
Solves problems	1
n.a.	1

environment in the mid-1980s, as a result of the regime's reaction to the protest movement.[2]

Why then did these people participate in organizations, despite the perception of possible repression as an additional constraint? As Wilson (1973) points out, people join organizations for a variety of reasons other than material gain. In particular, he notes that "solidary" incentives and "purposive" incentives related to achieving some nonmaterial goal are often important factors for explaining why people choose to participate. A quick glance at the data presented in Tables 8 through 12 suggests that these types of incentives did indeed motivate individuals to join popular organizations. In the clear majority of cases, the people interviewed said they chose to participate in their respective organizations to help others, to work toward a better life, and/or simply just to participate.

In each table presented so far, there was a very strong tendency for the interviewees to associate their organizations' activities and their participation with notions of solidarity, collective action to achieve some important group objective, and a desire to work for general socioeconomic and political change. Similarly, when asked to describe their most memorable experiences in popular organizations, 20 of the 43 people who answered this question (47 percent) specifically referred to belonging to a group and working with the members of that group. The bulk of the other responses also referred to solidaristic and group-oriented experiences, such as participating with other organizations, and helping others. Moreover, when asked what they liked best about their organizations, by far the most common answer, given by 40 percent of the respondents, referred to the solidarity and affective relations among members. The second most common response, given by 14 percent of respondents, identified their increased political and social consciousness through participating in the organization.

In this sample, and consistent with other findings (Razeto et al. 1986; Campero 1987), participation in popular organizations has a significant dimension that transcends—but does not completely exclude—material interests. Pressing needs for food, housing, health care, and so forth, may motivate many of these people to participate in a popular organization

2. When asked why they thought more people did not participate in popular-sector organizations, the principal reason given by 55 percent of the interviewees was fear of repression. Unlike other situations in which rational-choice logic may be applied, the "costs" associated with participation in this case were perceived by a significant number of individuals to be far greater than the time and inconvenience involved.

initially. But once in the organization, their perspectives and reasons for participating often change.

Going beyond the rational-choice logic and Wilson's important critique, which itself still remains within the logic of interest-maximizing behavior, the data suggest the presence of a phenomenon that rational-choice theories cannot easily account for: the emergence of a new collective identity that changed the way individuals perceived their interests. The consistency in responses to questions dealing with why people participated and their expectations all suggest the emergence of a holistic worldview that, in turn, popular organizations helped produce and reinforce.

This new collective identity, *lo popular*, can be defined in terms of a model composed of four core elements, relating to the concept of *vecino*, consumption demands, life chances and the popular sectors' definition of rights. Figure 5 presents a schematic representation of this model. In what follows, the meaning of these four core elements within the popular collective identity will be discussed in some detail. Afterward the implications this identity has for the functions and limitation of popular organizations as they developed under the military regime will be analyzed.

LO POPULAR AND THE CONCEPT OF *VECINO*

The literal translation of the Spanish word *vecino* is "neighbor." But the concept of *vecino* implies much more than the mere physical proximity of residences among a group of people. In the shantytowns of Latin America, it implies important bonds of community, characterized by common experiences, values, and reciprocal ties of solidarity (cf. Tovar 1986a). As a form of social relations, the idea of *vecino* exists independently of any regime type, although the imposition of authoritarian rule can increase its relevance for many.

The concept of *vecino* was integral to popular-sector organizations under the military regime. Alternative bases for organization, such as partisanship and the workplace, were blocked by regime repression. Relations based on the concept of *vecino* offered a way to resist the atomization of society caused by the disintegration of the social fabric. Popular-sector organiza-

Figure 5. *Lo Popular*: Elements of a new collective identity

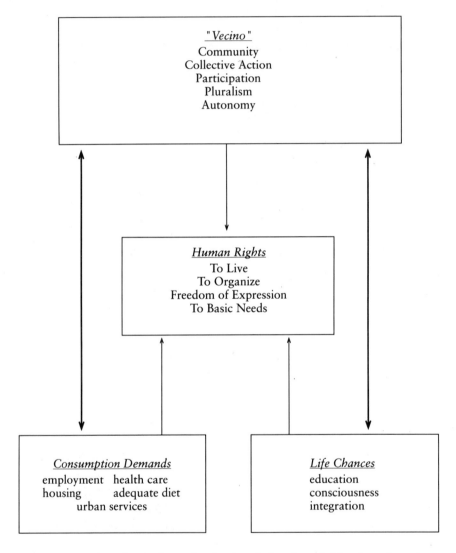

tions were often formed on the basis of the shared identity of *vecino*. Moreover, popular organizations reinforced this identity through their everyday activities. As one woman explained: "[The popular organization] deals with its members' problems, even the smallest: health, repression, children. There is greater '*convivencia*'[3] among them—they are better *vecinos* and work together to confront whatever problem." The identity of *vecino* encapsulated in popular organizations is itself multidimensional. As such, it is best understood in terms of a set of five interrelated ideals it encompassed: community, collective action, participation, pluralism, and autonomy.

Community

For members of popular-sector organizations, the idea of "community" was virtually synonymous with friendship and a sense of "belonging." When asked what they most liked about their particular organization, by far the largest number of responses referred to the affective relations among the organization's members and the feeling of belonging that membership provided.[4] The leader of a handicraft workshop, who was a member of the Communist Party before the coup and later joined the Christian Democratic Party, captured this general feeling when he described the benefits that members of his workshop as a whole enjoyed from their participation: "We are all friends, like brothers. We tell each other our problems. We feel sad when someone is arrested, is sick, or sent into internal exile.[5] We feel like members." A member of a women's group who lived alone with her mentally deficient daughter explained the friendships established through popular-sector organizations: "Knowing people is very valuable. It is something marvelous. It is important to have friends that try to value people for what they are and not what they have." This was echoed by a young woman who belonged to a soup kitchen: "[Through the soup kitchen] I know many people. Before [I joined], I did not. I am not the same person. Before I was ashamed, I talked with almost no one and had few friends. I am no longer embarrassed."

3. The Spanish word *convivencia* refers to people sharing their experiences and thoughts on a daily basis through face-to-face interactions. It is virtually synonymous with the concept of community, which will be discussed in detail shortly.

4. As mentioned above, this response was given by 40 percent of those who responded to the question. Only 14 percent of the respondents gave the second most frequent response, that their organizations increased the consciousness of the members.

5. The military regime frequently sent leaders of popular-sector organizations into "internal exile" in the remote southern and northern parts of the country as a way to disrupt the protest movement and disarticulate organizational activities in the *poblaciones*. See Serrano 1986 for a recounting of the experiences of one group of "exiles" and their families.

Being part of a community also implied certain obligations. It involved helping others. Just as important, there was also an obligation for members to learn from others, including how best to contribute to the group. The founder of a Christian base community, who was a member of the Communist Party and participated actively in a group that coordinated the activities of a number of popular organizations, made this clear when he defined what he felt "community" meant for the members of popular organizations in general and members of Christian base communities in particular: "In the [base] community one finds the truth among *vecinos* and comes to know oneself better. The community is an opportunity to serve something greater—to serve another and not only oneself. . . . I wanted to learn in order to help and teach others. This is community. One learns through knowing people."

The authoritarian regime eliminated the freedom of people to express themselves. The state no longer served as a referent for the realization of people's interests. Instead, it either seemed to ignore the popular sectors' demands and aspirations completely, or responded with force. The ideal of community embodied this sense of loss; it offered an alternative for organizing people's social relations under the military regime. A woman active in organizing women's groups stressed that "friends must listen and be listened to." Similarly, a woman who first became active in popular organizations by founding a women's group in 1985 explained that she enjoyed being in her particular organization because "everything is beautiful. I am one of the people who are happy [because of the group]. They listen to me talk. They're happy to hear me talk. They listen to me and they believe me. . . . I felt that I was vegetating in my house. I implored God for a place for . . . expressing oneself a little more freely."

Not surprisingly, repression had the somewhat paradoxical effect of reinforcing this sense of community as it was augmented. This can be seen in the way one man explained the changes over the past several years in the soup kitchen to which he belonged:

> There is now greater consciousness [among the members]. Our ideas are clearer, there is more *compañerismo*. I found a family. [The reason] is the situation itself, the regime itself—it is worse now than two years ago. There are no temporary jobs, only those of the POHJ.[6] There are more pressures—one no longer is owner of his

6. This was a state minimal employment program. Wages in this program were between 40 and 67 percent of the legal minimum wage in 1986 (Cademartori 1988).

home, of his person. Aside from there being no jobs, there is no type of freedom. The repression is worse. This all has made us unite more, share better. We are learning a lot from being in the soup kitchen.

This ideal of community was perhaps best summarized by a woman who helped found one of the first handicraft workshops for *pobladores* after the coup, even though she had no experience in organizations prior to 1973: "[In a good organization] everyone shares, everyone supports the organization, everyone participates. The organization achieves the participation of everyone. It achieves a real humanity."

The centrality of reciprocal ties of solidarity to the ideal of community must be emphasized. Leaders of popular organizations often recognized that the realization of this community ideal was not easy and its achievement was a principal goal of popular organizations. For example, as Table 10 shows, the most common response (given by 43 percent of the respondents) to the question "What has your organization achieved?" was solidarity and community. Similarly, the expression of solidarity by helping others was generally a principal objective of group activities. It often served as an underlying motivation for participation in popular organizations, as the data presented in Tables 8 through 12 suggest.

The obstacles to achieving solidarity included the military regime's own emphasis on personal consumption, individual self-help and responsibility as opposed to group or collective responsibility. Solidarity offers an alternative conception for organizing society in the face of growing hardship and exclusion. Solidarity becomes integral to achieving a better way of life. As such, it involves a rethinking of people's personal relations with others. This can cause people to have second thoughts about the desirability of social and political relations predating the military regime. A middle-aged mother of three who was active in women's organizations in the northern part of Santiago (which traditionally has been characterized by its low levels of popular-sector organization) illustrated this when she explained why solidarity was important to her: "People often like it when they are given things. But [then] those who give stop giving and there is nothing left. [With] knowledge you can help children, *vecinos*. I want to learn in order to help, not to keep it for myself. The majority of the people have not learned the value of education. I want to learn in order to be able to help, never to learn only for myself."

More generally, an elderly widow, who claimed never to have even thought about "politics" while her husband was alive because he made all of the decisions, and who then became a member of a women's organization and a health group, felt that "there are two kinds of poverty. One is when you cannot drink tea or warm your house. The other is of man: they think wrong, for themselves and nothing else. They are poor of spirit."

A particularly interesting (but not uncommon) example of the importance of the ideal of community to members of popular organizations was the "self-defense" group in a relatively well-organized *población* in the central zone of Santiago. The group was formed by teenagers in order to offer some means for protecting women and children in the *población* from arbitrary repression by security forces sent to the *población* on days of protest. Among other things, trenches would be dug in dirt roads and barricades built and set on fire to block main streets in an effort to keep the police and military outside of the *población* during protests. But going beyond this narrower objective, the group strove to remain active during periods when there were no protests. It did so by attempting to incorporate drug addicts and alcoholics—those most marginalized within the *población*—into the group, providing them with the "family" and friendship that they lacked. The group sought to help them to help themselves, teaching them new values, self-respect, and alternative ways to cope with their situation. As the twenty-year-old cofounder of the organization explained, the self-defense group was trying to "pull these people up." The organization's longer-term goals included the creation of a "popular library" for the whole *población* so that everyone could be better educated.

Solidarity and a sense of community had special significance for collective action because they provided an important basis for bringing together the different organizations in a *población*. This was most clearly illustrated by the increasingly common yearly celebrations for the founding of the *población*. Each organization planned how it would participate in what essentially amounted to a celebration of the *población* itself, which could last anywhere up to a week. Cultural groups presented street theater and sponsored poetry- and song-writing contests. Other groups planned and painted murals on the walls of buildings on the principal streets. A variety of competitive events were organized, ranging from soccer matches for little children to beauty contests, with individuals and teams competing first at the block level and moving up to the level of the entire shantytown. Food for visitors, including representatives from other *poblaciones*, was often provided by the shantytown's soup kitchen. Similar kinds of activities were also common for Christmas, major national holidays, and days with special international significance for *pobladores*, such as International Woman's Week and the anniversary of the Nicaraguan Revolution.

Solidarity frequently extended beyond the particular *población* in which an organization was located. This was accomplished by supporting the activities and demands of other groups through issuing public statements, visiting political prisoners in prison, sending representatives to meetings or marches in other parts of the city, refusing to eat for a specific number of days in support of hunger strikes by, for example, political prisoners facing the death penalty, and so forth. Organizational meetings often were called on to decide which groups the organization should engage in solidaristic types of activities with and how.

Collective Action

Lo popular as a collective identity was fundamentally antithetical to seeking individualistic solutions to the problems the popular sectors confronted because such solutions violated the ideals which it embodied. Popular organizations came to represent a belief that the problems each *poblador* faced were common problems that all *pobladores* should strive to overcome together—through their own organizations. Leaders of popular organizations frequently stressed that the only way these problems could be effectively overcome was through the integration of the popular sectors as a collective actor into society. An illustration of these ideas is found in how a sixty-year-old female Communist Party militant, active in the labor movement and the founder and president of one of the oldest and largest soup kitchens in Santiago, described a "good organization": "Union—if there is none, there is no organization. If there is no organization, the *población* would be lost. Everyone would go their different ways. The municipality, the police, they wouldn't respect us without organization."

The leaders of popular-sector organizations generally recognized the importance of organization. This is reflected in Table 9 which shows that 32 people, or more than 70 percent of those responding to the question and nearly three times the number of people giving the second most common response, said that they participated in order to be in an organization. The importance of organization, however, is not always apparent to *pobladores* when they first form. Members learn the value of organization by experience. Individual needs bring people together, but in the process people learn to adopt a broader, more collectivist attitude. For example, another woman, who founded a soup kitchen in a different *población* and was not a member of any political party, explained the not uncommon experience of her group: "We thought that the [soup kitchen would be needed] for a short time. We had meetings, we talked. [We realized] that we had the power to do something just, to get ahead together. Alone, one can do almost nothing."

Participation

The realization of the concept of *vecino* and the ideals it encompasses required the active participation of the members of popular-sector organizations. This criterion stood in sharp contrast to the model of society offered by the military regime, which denied the popular sectors any right to participation. In this context, participation—being a responsible member of the community—had become an end in itself. As a young woman who cofounded a human rights group explained: "It is necessary that man be responsible for the society in which he lives, that there be no paternalism. Together, mankind will solve problems. . . . As a human being, I have the obligation to participate in everything which determines the country's future and my own."

Of course, participation was not limited to just speaking in meetings. The importance of action, as opposed to merely discourse, for the members of popular-sector organizations needs to be emphasized. Being a member of a popular organization could frequently be quite demanding. Through participation, people's consciousness could be raised and organizational development enhanced. This can be seen in how a thirty-five-year-old female activist in the women's movement in the *poblaciones* and member of a small leftist party felt her organization had changed since its founding: "The people have an attitude of supporting the organization more, not criticizing just to criticize. They have acquired consciousness, which is a long process. They are friendlier. Consciousness must lead to practice: one cannot just talk, but must participate (in protests, for example). One cannot just criticize but must participate if he/she wants to criticize. This leads to practical consciousness."

Participation was still more than just an end in itself. It was seen by the leaders of popular organizations as an important means for realizing other values. For example, people *should* participate, according to the middle-aged mother of three quoted above, in order "to learn; each person helping others, to unite, to grow, to talk with each other." More generally, the young male president of a human rights organization who was a Christian Democratic Party member suggested that "through participation people will struggle for their social, political, and economic ideals. No one must cede to the representation of a million people if it is not in common, participative—representative. Through a democratic process the community can/must build organizations."

Given the importance of participation in the emergent popular collective identity—and the high level of commitment this required of the organization's members—the need to encourage higher levels of participation was a frequent problem for leaders of popular organizations to confront. For example, the young cofounder of the self-defense group quoted above noted that they "have tried to make members feel like they are part of the organization. This has been very good." Similarly, the quality of leaders' participation and how well they provided opportunities for others to participate in the organization was one of the factors used to evaluate leadership. For example, 32 percent of the respondents felt that encouraging participation was one of the roles of a leader in a popular organization. When asked to describe the characteristics of good leaders, 38 percent of the respondents emphasized participating with and encouraging others to participate.

To a certain degree, organizations were successful only insofar as they responded to the people's needs for participation. This can be seen in how a thirty-two-year-old female member of the Communist Party (who had played an important role in coordinating organizational activities at the level of her *población*) explained why more people did not participate in popular organizations:

> In general, it is a problem of the organizations. People do not participate in what they don't want to. [The problem] is a lack of clear policies in terms of what the people want—their needs, their worries, what they like. [Organizations] must give them channels for participation. People participate in activities rather than organizations [and] when they like the activities, the organization is full. [For example], the people want democratic *juntas de vecinos*. Organizations must help them to realize this. The people do not disregard organizations, but the organizations must be made more participative. Leaders must respond to the *población*.

Pluralism

The concept of *vecino* defines pluralism in the strictest sense: recognizing the legitimacy of distinct points of view. This definition of pluralism does not necessarily imply that people are willing to cooperate outside of the organization with those who hold distinct tactical or strategic points of view—an issue that will be dealt with in Chapter 5. Nonetheless, this ideal of pluralism stood in marked contrast to the policy of the military regime, which condemned all dissent as subversive. It also represented a departure from the increasing political polarization that characterized the 1960s and early 1970s.

The ideal of pluralism was derived from the notion of equality that was embedded in the ideal of community. Equality was not viewed by members of popular organizations in a limited or merely formal sense. Instead, equality was achieved through the effective integration of the individual into the community in which the popular organization was founded. "There is a concern for new members that they feel like part of a family," according to the member of a Christian base community quoted above. "We've worked hard for this. This is important because we are always finding more people." The female Communist Party militant, already quoted, who was active in coordinating organizational activities in her *población* added, "we cannot leave anyone outside [of the organization]. We want the people who only say 'yes' to try to be bold enough to talk."

A fundamental aspect of the ideal of pluralism in *lo popular* was that people had the right to express themselves and be listened to by others—a right most obviously denied them by the military regime. This can be seen in how the already-quoted leader of the shantytown women's movement described a good organization: "all of its members have the right to express what they feel. The base[7] is taken into account. The last person to arrive is taken into account." This emphasis on the right of all to express themselves leads to respect for different political parties and ideologies. Not surprisingly, in the interviews, a clear majority (92 percent of respondents) stated that their organizations were pluralistic and that this was important; no one said that their organization was not pluralistic or that it did not matter.[8] As an illustration, a young member of a human rights group who

7. In this context, the word "base" refers to the general membership of an organization as opposed to the people occupying leadership positions in the organization.
8. The other 8 percent included two people who responded that they did not know what pluralism was, and one who said that her organization was pluralist for the Left only. Eight people did not respond to the question.

was also a member of a moderate faction of the Socialist Party explained that "it is a right to think as one wants. If [a popular organization] is not pluralist, it is breaking an important right in the *carta fundamental*."[9] Similarly, although she said she did not know what the word "pluralist" meant, the woman who lived alone with her mentally deficient daughter did stress that "each person has the right to think how she wants. The group respects different opinions [and] this is important. We are all against the government, but many of us do not think the same. We have to respect this because each person has her own way of thinking."

Fundamentally, the importance of pluralism—and equality—in *lo popular* reflected the popular sectors' concern for the respect and dignity of all human beings. As the Christian Democratic president of a human rights organization eloquently stated: "Everyone who thinks differently should respect the opinions of others. If persons are in an organization that has leaders who are members of a political party, that does not mean that the organization belongs to that party. [The organizations exist to] struggle for the dignity of the poor class."

Pluralism was directly associated with democracy in *lo popular*, reflecting the democratic qualities associated with the concept of *vecino*. It also was a clear rejection of the authoritarian model represented by the military regime. For example, the people interviewed for this study overwhelmingly considered their organizations to be democratic (see Table 13). Moreover, they were virtually unanimous in agreeing that it was important that popular organizations be democratic. The thirty-one-year-old president of a legally recognized union of workers in the informal sector of the economy, who lived in a shantytown and belonged to the Christian Left Party, expressed sentiments shared by many: "Organizations must open up space [and] facilitate man's participation. Democracy is very complex. There are many visions. [Pluralism and democracy] cannot be separated. Everyone can participate equally, feel equal, with the same rights and obligations. There cannot be unequal conditions because this is not democratic. Democracy is therefore not isolated from the life of man—it cannot be separated from it. Popular organizations treat all people equally."

The democratic quality of popular-sector organizations was not reducible to holding regular elections for officers. Indeed, fifteen out of forty-two of the organizations covered in the interviews did not even have officers, elected or otherwise, and in four others leadership positions were rotated

9. The Universal Declaration of Human Rights.

Table 13.　Do you think that your organization is democratic?

	Total
Yes	
There is participation	13
There are elections	3
Other	23
Total	39
No	3[a]
n.a.	4
Is it important that the organization be democratic?	
Yes	
It is the objective of the struggle	7
Other	27
Total	34
Do Not Know	4
n.a.	8

[a]One respondent was a member of a state-sponsored sports club. He said the organization was not democratic because "no one participates in politics" in the club. The situation was recently rectified for a second respondent when the soup kitchen to which she belonged held elections for officers. She had felt that the soup kitchen was not democratic because of the predominant role the founder and president of the soup kitchen, a Communist Party militant, had played in its activities. (The president claimed that the soup kitchen had always been democratic.) The third respondent noted that the organization tried to be as democratic as possible but sometimes fell short because the members lacked experience. Officers in her soup kitchen had been elected every six months, and people rotated positions of responsibility to help remedy this, but the Vicaría de la Solidaridad said the soup kitchen could have elections only once a year if it wanted to continue to receive assistance.

among the members in order to maximize each individual member's own leadership experience. Thirteen respondents out of forty-two in Table 13 said specifically that their organizations were democratic because of their high levels of participation, and only three said that the election of officers determined their organization's democratic character.

More generally, such tendencies suggest that democracy was conceived of as a process in which people must be actively involved. This is consistent with the other values associated with the concept of *vecino*.[10] It is apparent in the way a forty-two-year-old man who cofounded a cultural center defined democracy: "Democracy is participation. [Participation] by sup-

10. It is interesting to point out that 22 out 37 interviewees stated that they felt democracy meant that everyone *must* participate. Only 8 people suggested that such an obligation would itself be undemocratic. The reason behind this sense of obligation seems to be rooted in the emphasis in *lo popular* on the intrinsic value of participation, and three people specifically said that one had to participate in order to be responsible.

porting it, constructing it, not waiting for it. With criticism, self-criticism and work." The twenty-year-old cofounder of the self-defense group quoted above added that democracy is "trying to get people to talk. There are problems with democracy if people don't talk. . . . Democracy is the greatest amount of participation. As collective as possible. Organizations must not be truncated because people cannot participate and make their own decisions."

Ultimately, popular organizations could not hope to encapsulate the concept of *vecino* if they were not pluralistic and democratic. Otherwise, individuals would be marginalized within their own organization, just as the military regime had marginalized them within Chilean society. As a young male youth-group leader explained: "Everyone has the right to speak and vote. Matters are discussed in the assembly, not in the hierarchy [of the organization]. Both minorities and majorities are respected. [This is important because] everyone feels they are part of the organization. They go to support the organization and not only be a number—they are supporting the shantytown social movement." Similarly, the leader of the shantytown women's movement quoted above concluded:

> [Organizations] must be open, pluralist, ample—if they are not, how many [members] will they have? Other points of view can be much better. If organizations are not this way, things can be done poorly because people only obey. . . . [Democracy means] the participation of everyone, respect for what others say. People make proposals and defend them. People do what is most appropriate for everyone. The best proposals are adopted to arrive at consensus. . . . [Everyone] is assuming responsibility, not one person.

In sum, the participative and integrative qualities of democracy in *lo popular* implied that responsibility, and power, should be shared among the members of popular organizations. They symbolized a rejection of the excessive (and often violent) centralization of authority under the military regime. This was one more facet of the importance of equality in the emergent popular collective identity. A middle-aged woman, active in popular organizations prior to the coup (but never a member of a political party) and a key figure in organizing soup kitchens throughout Santiago's eastern zone, was very clear in this regard:

> Nothing is achieved if agreements are not made by the majority. The organization is a ghost. . . . Democracy is "popular power." The

members decide and the members assume the responsibility. The group is a very small space for popular power. . . . Democracy means that everyone assumes responsibility. Everyone is conscious of what the organization does and wants. The members plan what is done and the majority participates. Members feel they are part of their own history. They are not alienated—they participate, discuss.

Autonomy

The realization of the ideals embodied in the concept of *vecino*—especially those of community, participation, and democracy—required that popular-sector organizations be autonomous from external actors in their capacity to define and pursue their own interests. Organizational autonomy was a prerequisite for being able to represent the interests of their members and the larger community. Only organizational autonomy in this sense could prevent the manipulation that members of the popular sectors have endured during both the military and democratic regimes in Chile. It would allow *pobladores* to assert their dignity as human beings.

Autonomy had to be preserved not only in the organizations' relations with the state, but from political parties and the Catholic Church as well. A middle-aged woman who became quite active in popular-sector organizations after the coup, but largely stayed in her home prior to 1973, captured this general feeling: "We solve our own problems here. We are people, not objects—autonomous, free. We place conditions on Missio[11] . . . because [we want Missio] to let the people grow. It is the right of the poor to make their own decisions. . . . [This is part of] the dignity of the person—to feel realized."

The insistence on the autonomy of popular organizations also reflected the importance of the common experiences and beliefs that underlay the ideals represented in *lo popular* in general and the concept of *vecino* in particular. It was an explicit recognition by members of popular organizations of a certain pride in what it meant to be part of the popular sectors. For example, the leader of a union of workers in the informal sector (previously quoted) argued: "We never, never accept people from outside the *población*, except to give talks. The popular sector must have its own

11. The Fundación Missio was a church organization that sponsored a variety of programs intended to promote popular-sector organizational activity in the northern zone of Santiago.

direction from its own perspective. It is a kind of 'university of the popular world (*mundo popular*).' [Popular organizations] must convert this experience into practice and theory. They cannot be dogmatic. They are a university where people work and learn."

While sacrificing organizational autonomy could result in immediate short-term material benefits, it also had its costs, according to the leaders of popular organizations. The union leader continued: "Independence is very important. It maintains organizations. [They need to become] more capable, learn to use and raise their resources, learn to confront [problems]. Paternalism is a bad approach. Chileans, we forget that nothing is for free. Everything has its cost—the cost of not participating, of not becoming more capable, of not creating incentives."

Basic self-respect also implied a clear rejection of paternalism. This is evidenced by the fact that twenty-seven interviewees, all of those who answered the question, agreed that paternalism was negative. When asked if their group had rejected or would reject external support, the vast majority (26 out of 38 respondents) said that their group would reject outside assistance that in some way threatened their group's autonomy. Seven respondents said that their groups had actually rejected such assistance in the past. The woman who became active in popular-sector organizations only after the coup explained their reasoning: "It is not our purpose to give things away. . . . No one benefits personally from donations. It is a question of their dignity: people feel more fulfilled if they pay five pesos [just over two U.S. cents] for [used clothes] than if they pay nothing."[12]

Given the popular sectors' past experiences with political parties, any

---

12. It is important to note that the Catholic Church was frequently criticized for its perceived paternalism by members of popular-sector organizations. The feelings of a middle-aged woman who was active in women's organizations in the northern zone of Santiago and belonged to no political party were typical: "The church protects an organization a lot. It feels like the parent of the organization. It does not let the organization grow because the people have everything that they need and will not grow. They are not capable of doing things to satisfy their needs. This is bad. Before, the church gave us a lot and the people became accustomed to it. It was paternalistic." A more telling example was provided by a fifty-year-old member of the MIR who had been released from prison several years earlier after being convicted for attempting to blow up an arms factory, and who was currently a member of a construction cooperative: "[Our cooperative] is independent, completely autonomous. It does not depend on any other organization, not even the church. It is independent to choose, to plan matters as it sees them. It is a hands-on experience. We think that the church restricts political activities and became paternalistic. Paternalism will ruin any organization. One reason the cooperative survived is because it is not under the church—none of the organizations under the church have survived."

offers of help from a political party was typically met with suspicion. A young woman who was a member of both a soup kitchen and a state-supported mothers' center explained how members of popular organizations generally viewed offers of assistance from political parties: "If a party offered [assistance, we would ask] for what purpose? If it offered it with conditions that we did not like or could not meet, we would reject it. If it is to work with us, share the needs of the people, okay."

The importance of being able to maintain the autonomy of popular organizations was so deeply rooted in the emergent popular collective identity that even the then semi-official rightwing Independent Democratic Union (UDI) party accepted it in its discourse. A UDI militant on the governing body of one of the two *campamentos* that were created as a result of land seizures in 1983 explained:[13] "UDI seeks solutions for problems through neighborhood mechanisms, etc. and the people recognize it for this. UDI has changed the mentality of the people because of this. I am their friend because they think I am the most just rather than only doing them favors. I don't ask them for anything."

The ideal of autonomy perhaps was best summarized in some examples given by the female Communist Party militant quoted above who was active in coordinating organizational activity in her *población*:

> Support is accepted when it is programmed at the level of the *población*, not the organization. An example is the milk program:[14] this affected all of us because of the context of the *población*. If it is in the service of the *población*, we will accept it. If we can plan what we like and don't like. We are always pursing the objective of service to the *población*. The poor also have a right to be leaders! We did not accept a project to build a medical clinic because it was paternal-

---

13. Because the land seizures took place shortly after the eruption of the national protest movement in May 1983 and had strong backing by the Catholic Church, the military government was unable to disband the *campamentos*, despite its resort to repression. After martial law was declared in November 1984, most of the members of the former governing body of this particular *campamento*, many of whom belonged to the Communist Party, were arrested and sent into internal exile. The UDI had already started organizing in the *campamentos* prior to this. The new governing body was controlled by the UDI and was able to maintain control of the *campamento* in large part because of resources the UDI could funnel into the *campamento* as a result of its ties to the Ministry of Housing.

14. The *población* had access to large quantities of powdered milk, which it distributed to individual families through a network organized by blocks.

istic and solved a problem of the regime. We wanted a medical clinic that is participative. . . . The organization must be through the initiative of those who want it. It was not an easy decision. We [later] obtained a project in which the poor people took it into their own hands—they prepared it and educated the people to take responsibility for the [project].

This insistence on organizational autonomy and the rejection of paternalism by members of popular-sector organizations was consistent with the criteria that the people interviewed used for evaluating leaders and the role of leaders in popular organizations. Significantly, no reference was made to the ability of leaders to provide material benefits to the members of popular organizations. Instead, the emphasis was placed on how leaders actually led organizations and allowed for the realization of the ideals that composed *lo popular* in the organization.

LO POPULAR AND THE CONSUMPTION DEMANDS OF THE POPULAR SECTORS

The existence of popular organizations was intimately tied to the consumption demands of the popular sectors because, as a sociological category, the popular sectors themselves were in part defined by their limited consumption possibilities with respect to the rest of society. These people were poor and had a number of immediate needs. Popular organizations, as has been demonstrated above, did not need to find short-term solutions to such needs in order to survive, but they could not ignore them either. This is clear in the way a twenty-two-year-old female cofounder of a human rights group described a "good" organization:

> Most important, the organization effectively represents the interests of the sector in which it functions—the *pobladores*. There are often organizations which struggle [against the military regime], such as "Democracy Now"[15] [when] the *pobladores* want them to do things

15. This was a 1986 opposition campaign to mobilize the population around the call for an immediate return to democracy.

> to resolve problems such as hunger, etc. Organizations should be born out of the necessities of the people. Do not create organizations just to create organizations. They have to help. . . . The Civic Assembly[16] has a good objective, but so what—*pobladores* don't identify with it. It achieved very little. [We need] social mobilization that emphasizes social concerns.

Table 14 lists what the interviewees felt were the most important popular-sector demands. By far, the most frequently mentioned demands were those that were closely associated with the popular sectors' limited consumption possibilities. The demands for decent employment, which generally referred to stable jobs with wages sufficient for supporting a family, and adequate housing, health care, and nutrition were all reflections of the limited consumption possibilities that are a defining characteristic of the popular sectors.[17] Other important demands, mentioned by far fewer people, generally tended to reflect other dimensions of *lo popular*.

Fundamentally, these demands represented the desire of the popular sectors to be able to meet their basic needs without undue sacrifice. This suggests that many leaders of popular organizations viewed society as having an obligation to provide the popular sectors with the opportunities required for them to live in dignity and overcome their marginalization. There were no demands for immediate social revolution. Indeed, one could point to the relative moderation of these demands given the circumstances in which these people found themselves living. Such moderation, it might be argued, reflected lowered expectations after so many years of repression and economic deterioration.

16. The Civic Assembly (*Asamblea de la Civilidad*) was an important opposition bloc that emerged in early 1986. Ostensibly organized by various organizations representing different social groups, particularly a number of middle-class professional bodies, it represented a broad opposition front that encompassed almost all the major opposition political parties and political tendencies from the Right to the Left. Its efforts culminated in a national strike in July 1986 in which there was a high adhesion and two young people were burned alive by a military patrol. Subsequent disagreements over appropriate opposition strategies (particularly over the value of social mobilizations), the role the Communist Party should play in the democratic opposition, repression of the Civic Assembly's leadership and the September 1986 assassination attempt against Pinochet all contributed to the Civic Assembly's diminishing importance as an axis of the opposition. For a more detailed discussion of the Civic Assembly's importance and the role played by the popular sectors in it, see Chapter 7.

17. The demand for education will be discussed in the following section as it related to the life chances of the popular sectors.

Table 14.   What are the most important demands of *pobladores?*

	Total
Decent employment	38
Adequate housing	24
Adequate health care	20
Education	17
Adequate nutrition	12
Affordable urban services (electricity, sewage, water, paved roads, etc.)	8
Peace, less repression	5
Participation	3
Freedom	2
Adequate clothing	2
End social diseases	2
Freedom of expression	1
Recreation	1
Culture	1
Ability to Organize	1
Democracy	1
Change the system	1
No longer be marginal	1
Family planning	1
Social laws	1
The right to struggle	1
Equal jobs and pay for women	1
n.a.	1

It is important to note that the concerns expressed in the principal demands listed in Table 14 reinforced the importance of understanding the popular sectors more in terms of where they lived rather than where they worked. The nature of the emergent popular collective identity was inextricably intertwined with the actual conditions in which these people lived, giving rise to shared interests. These interests were part of and emerged within the self-constituted identity of *lo popular.*

Finally, shared interests in employment, housing, health care, nutrition, and urban services will ultimately require solutions that are beyond the scope of any single popular organization to effectively implement. The nature of these interests requires that popular organizations interact with the state (directly or through political parties) at the local, regional and/or national levels in order to find effective long-term solutions to their most pressing problems. This interaction, in turn, could serve as an important impetus to coordinating popular-sector organizational activities at various levels. Such coordination (which would ultimately culminate in the formation of a popular social movement) would enable these organizations to mobilize resources and deal more effectively with external actors, including the state, political parties, aid organizations, and the Catholic Church.

LO POPULAR AND THE POPULAR SECTORS' LIMITED LIFE CHANCES

The emergent popular collective identity was shaped by more than just the immediate interests of the popular sectors. Their longer-term concerns for increased opportunities, social mobility, and an improved quality of life essentially reflected the popular sectors' desire for improved life chances. The demand for improved life chances is a historical one for the popular sectors, but the policies implemented by the military regime gave it new urgency. In the emergent popular collective identity, three related avenues for achieving such improvement held special importance: education, consciousness, and integration into society.

Education

Education was highly valued in *lo popular*. For example, members learning from and teaching each other, as well as learning from individuals with particular skills who are brought in by the organization, was an initial objective of 30 percent of the organizations covered in the interviews (see Table 8). As Table 11 suggests, these organizations were largely successful in achieving this objective. Education was the second most frequent response (38 percent of the respondents) when people were asked what benefits they had received from their participation in an organization. Finally, just over a third of the people interviewed said education was one of the principal demands of the popular sectors, behind the more pressing demands for employment, adequate housing, and adequate health care (Table 14).

Education was broadly defined in the emergent popular collective identity. Although there was an important popular-sector demand for equal access to public education for their children, *lo popular* also placed much emphasis on learning through participation in popular-sector organizations.

In particular, those who knew something, whether it be a skill or having a better understanding of national political events, for example, were encouraged to share their knowledge and teach others. This reinforced the values of solidarity and collective action within popular organizations.

In many popular organizations, people learned practical skills such as how to knit or bake bread. These kinds of skills allowed people to save money by being able to produce things for themselves that they otherwise would have to buy. The members of popular organizations also could use these skills to earn money by selling sweaters, handicrafts, prepared food, and so forth, to friends and neighbors. A number of groups also formed literacy workshops to help members who never learned to read and write.[18] In this fashion, education became an important mechanism for increasing organization autonomy.

Education in the emergent popular collective identity, however, represented more than merely acquiring practical skills. Education and knowledge were valued as resources and a means for achieving other ends. Education was a source of empowerment. Members of popular organizations sometimes even preferred that outside groups help the organization by teaching its members something rather than providing monetary or other material forms of assistance. The previously quoted woman who had played a key role in organizing a number of soup kitchens throughout the eastern zone of Santiago explained that she did not want money for her soup kitchens, but would prefer that external groups provide informative "videotapes, recreation, education. I don't see the importance of external groups providing money for food. That encourages paternalism. But if they provide help with personal growth and development, this helps the people to think things over and reflect. They will be able to contribute a lot more to their organization."[19] The widow who had only recently found herself

18. One handicraft workshop with which I have had a great deal of contact was particularly active in this area. Graduation ceremonies for those who successfully completed the course were major public events in the *población*. In attending one such graduation, one was immediately struck by the sense of pride exhibited not only by the people who were graduating, but also by their families, the other members of the organization, and the *población*. The workshop was so successful that it was able to publish its own manual, *"Aprendiendo Juntos: Leamos and escribamos nuestra realidad"* (Santiago: Taller de Acción Cultural, 1986) with the help of an outside group.

19. It is worth noting that this person was also involved in founding a literacy workshop. Like many people in the *poblaciones*, she had finished elementary school but had become functionally illiterate simply because of lack of practice in her daily life. She felt that her participation in the workshop helped others overcome their embarrassment at being unable to read, encouraging and helping others to learn based on her own experience.

thinking about politics for the first time was more to the point: "We must try to learn something rather than wait for something to be given to us—that is why the [women's] group is called 'promotion.' "[20]

By learning from other experiences, many leaders of popular organizations believed that one could come to appreciate the value of organization. The woman active in organizing soup kitchens in the eastern zone of Santiago felt that these organizations would benefit through "knowledge about other situations [and] other countries, what others achieve through their organizations. [People would learn that] nothing is in vain, anything can be achieved when there is organization."

Information was seen by the leaders of popular organizations as necessary for avoiding manipulation by others and full participation by *pobladores*. The founder of a union of workers in the informal sector explained why he felt access to knowledge was critical:

> The base must know what is happening at higher levels. It prepares the people to decide between alternatives. The old practice was to do thing without providing information, to manipulate the base. This led to a state of immobilization. People did not know what to do [and] they were immobilized as thinking beings. Growth of the person is key. . . . Communication avoids domination. With information one participates in politics. Without it, one cannot. . . . Communication must be both ways, not listening, [but] mutual relations, an interchange of knowledge and experience.

As such, equal access to knowledge and information became a prerequisite for democracy in *lo popular*. Another young man, who was active in youth organizations, pointed this out: "There will be democracy to the extent that everyone has the same information. If there are unequal levels of information, there cannot be democracy. Voting is not a solution to problems of consciousness and the ability to think abstractly. [This requires] the development of the knowledge each person possesses." Ultimately, knowledge was viewed by at least some members of popular organizations as the key to human freedom. The middle-aged woman who became active in popular-sector organizations only after the coup and was not a member

20. Another woman who became active in popular-sector organizations only after the coup addressed this issue specifically in terms of political parties: "Why don't they use their money to educate their people about things rather than give things [away]? This causes disunity between political parties and the people."

of any political party stated this clearly: "The people must have knowledge in order to be free as persons. Freedom is not only a democratic government. . . . How do the people make history if they are ignorant?"

Consciousness

Central to the kind of education that popular organizations endeavored to provide was consciousness-raising. Consciousness, in this sense, was broadly defined and most generally referred to an awareness that things *should* be better. People came to recognize that there was a need for some sort of socioeconomic and political change, and they themselves could play an important part in bringing such change about. The ideals encompassed within *lo popular*, in turn, provided the model for the necessary changes.

Raising the consciousness of people was behind the creation of many organizations. As Table 8 shows, this was the second most important reason (after the alleviation of material needs) given by respondents for the formation of their organizations. Moreover, a third of the respondents indicated that one of the achievements of their organizations was increased consciousness among the members (Table 10). Seven people interviewed, just over 15 percent of those responding to the question, also claimed that they participated in organizations in order to raise other people's consciousness (see Table 9). These efforts also met with at least some success. Nine out of thirty-nine respondents specifically referred to their increase in consciousness as a benefit from participating in a popular organization and most, if not all, of the other responses given suggested that popular organizations were indeed promulgating the central ideals associated with *lo popular* (see Table 11). When asked what they learned from their participation in popular organizations, respondents consistently made reference to various aspects of consciousness. Thirty-six out of 39 respondents (92 percent) said they learned solidarity and how to share, while 14 (36 percent) said they had grown as a person and 13 (33 percent) mentioned that they had acquired a higher level of consciousness.

Organizations encouraged people to participate for reasons other than their immediate needs. This was part of their integral nature, as discussed in Chapter 3. The Christian Democratic leader of a handicraft workshop explained that "people joined because of their needs. This is not helpful for their growth as people. [The organization should] give them other values. They should learn to be more dignified as humans." Another example was offered by the forty-two-year-old cofounder of a cultural organization, who did not belong to any political party. He explained that popular organizations allowed for the juxtaposition of "values"—"solidarity, participation, culture, human relations, freedom, and struggle"—with the "anti-values" of authoritarianism and individualism that they were bombarded with daily. An important objective of his organization had always been to "achieve the [individual's] personal development; the transformation of people into protagonists who can struggle for their freedom and help create a new society." A middle-aged woman who founded a soup kitchen and handicraft workshop, and who also did not belong to a political party, continued:

> There are almost no benefits [to participating in the soup kitchen]. I would be happy if everyone was conscious [of their situation]. If the organization does not create consciousness, it serves no purpose. The goal is that someday everyone will have consciousness. If not, it would be a waste of time. . . . Now the members have a certain level of consciousness. Before nothing could make them see [the reality]. Now they are interested in the organization. Yesterday they said they don't have to stay in the house, that they are at home too much!

The process of consciousness-raising frequently began with efforts to help members of popular-sector organizations understand that their presence in the organization reflected larger socioeconomic and political problems that they should work to resolve. As a young female member of a soup kitchen explained:

> I began to participate in order to raise people's consciousness by showing them why people are in the soup kitchen, by showing them the reality, for example, of children eating almost nothing because their father is in POHJ.[21] To show them how we are really living. . . . When the soup kitchen holds an assembly meeting, [it is] to make people understand a little better why we are in the soup kitchen, why we are going to deliver a letter [to the city government, for example]—why and for what end.

21. A state minimal employment program that paid wages substantially less than the legal minimum wage.

Essentially, as the woman who had organized a number of soup kitchens pointed out, such consciousness raising was directed at teaching people "that they must be *pobladores* capable of demanding their rights."

Members often acquired consciousness as their organization developed and matured. It was almost a spontaneous process. A twenty-one-year-old woman who helped found a women's organization several years earlier recounted the not uncommon experience of her group:

> [We have meetings] in part to create what one wants—a popular movement through an organization. In the beginning, [we met] to get out of the house. Later, it took on a greater meaning: to create a better society. What one learns in an organization can be applied to one's family. One can learn things there that can't be learned in other places: the power to participate, the power to say what is good and what is bad for the *población*. Learning things democratically.

Finally, because this consciousness was integral to the ideals embodied in *lo popular*, leaders of popular organizations felt that it was something that could be generated only by the people in the *poblaciones* themselves. The middle-aged woman who founded a soup kitchen and handicraft workshop explained why:

> I prefer "popular power" [i.e., popular organizations] to political parties for raising people's consciousness. Parties are concerned with the current political situation and nothing else. In order to provide more profound consciousness, organizations—popular power—are needed. It has to be taught from below. Politicians only give orders. Because of this, youths are killed—politicians give them orders without them understanding what they are doing. They manipulate rather than provide consciousness. . . . All politicians do it, the government too. The manipulation of the young.

In this regard, it is worth quoting some testimonials from participants themselves. For example, a young male Communist Party member took pride in the progress a group of teenagers had made in his cultural organization:

> The kids have matured a lot personally. One kid said that he learned that together we can confront problems [and] find alternatives. He

went beyond his individual problems [and recognized] the need to change the system. Now we can talk about mobilizations, etc., in meetings. Before, there were problems. [People would say] "I'm going because they are talking about politics." We have retrieved the value and legitimacy of participating in politics. It is a right. [And] the father of one girl is in the riot police!

A young mother whose husband had recently gone to Brazil in search of a job explained that through the soup kitchen, she learned why her husband was not working: "I thought it was because the guy was lazy. He did not go out looking for work. Now, after talking, etc., I realize that the problem isn't him, . . . it's that there are no jobs." Finally, a female member of one of the few democratically elected neighborhood councils (*juntas de vecinos*) in Santiago in 1986 explained what she learned: "I learned that together we can achieve many things, alone no. Before, one lived enclosed in her house, worried about her own things and nothing else. Now I know about others. I can feel better because I help others."

This emphasis on consciousness in the emergent popular collective identity assumes the need for social transformation. Such transformation transcends the immediate need to restore political democracy, although that is certainly necessary. As the female cofounder of one of the first handicraft organizations formed after the coup, when asked why she participated in popular organizations, explained: "I have to contribute everything I have learned—it is a duty. It is a duty to struggle for change in this society. It is not so important that Pinochet leaves power as that there is a change in the society. When he leaves, if there is no complete change, our situation will remain the same. I've known democratic governments and in reality there is a lot of hunger in democracies."

The popular organization itself, encapsulating as it does the emergent popular collective identity, often served as the model for that changed society. "In the organization you live the society that you want to construct. It is the starting point where you build society," to use the words of the young cofounder of a cultural group. He continued:

What one lives now [in the organization] is what one wants to live tomorrow—democracy, participation are lived within organizations. Criticisms are accepted, people accept their errors as knowledge— they take responsibility for them and learn from them. . . . The organization is for people to develop and grow, to search for new roads. It is liberating . . . in every sense, helping its members to liberate themselves.

This perception of the popular organization as a model for social change was recognized as being particularly important under the authoritarian regime. To be otherwise would be inconsistent with the values embodied in the emergent popular collective identity. The young cofounder of a self-defense organization pointed this out: "We are fighting for the real participation of the people in the decisions that involve them. We have to realize this [in our organizations]. . . . We are fighting for respect." Simply being in a popular organization was a form of symbolic resistance to the military regime.

Many members of popular organizations viewed their organizations as reservoirs of democracy. This was especially important for younger people, who really did not know what democracy was. The leader in the shanty-town women's movement explained why she felt this was important: "With a dictator, we live in a democratic space that we create . . . and in this way we will support democracy. We teach people to carry out democracy in practice." The woman already quoted who had been active in popular-sector organizations only after the military coup added:

> We respect democracy within the organization a lot because it is a way not to lose the custom of voting and [to show] that not everything is done through force. . . . Democracy is born within oneself as a person—[it is part of] his/her mentality. . . . People often talk of "democracy" but without creating democracy. [Democracy is] normal, democratic elections in which the people elect their own government, but much more: One must think it, live it, construct it again.

Integration Into Society

The goal of integration into society was pivotal to the emergent popular collective identity because, as the young cofounder of a self-defense group pointed out, "it's horrible to be marginalized." Essentially, integration was equated with participating in deciding Chile's future. It meant that "I am consulted, I am part of this country," to use the words of a thirty-one-year-old founder of a women's group. The older woman who had been active in popular-sector organizations for a number of years as a member of the Christian Democratic Party was more specific about how she understood integration: "[Our] hope is to be first-class citizens and not second-class citizens like we are now. We feel resented because we are isolated. We have lost our own identity."

Members of popular organizations viewed their organizations as an important mechanism through which to achieve integration. It was in part for this reason that the most important characteristic of a "good organization" for members of popular organizations, as shown in Table 12, was a high level of organizational capacity—the response given by 58 percent of the respondents. For the young cofounder of a self-defense group, popular organizations had an important role to play in a democracy: "[Popular organizations will] criticize the democracy. They will complain when things are not going well at a particular point in time. They will know how to denounce, how to reach the highest levels. Organizations are always in contact with the political situation—they are not marginalized from the political process." The middle-aged woman who founded a soup kitchen and handicraft workshop captured these ideas well when she explained how she became a leader of popular organizations:

> I saw that there was something that had to be done. Suddenly, all of us, the *pobladores*, have to do things. We are capable of doing things. The regime creates a great need to have organizations. We must be united. . . . I like "popular power" which is created through organizations. There things are formed. In organizations the people acquire power [and] values. There should be an organization on each block! I am a fanatic for organizations!

LO POPULAR AND HUMAN RIGHTS

The final core element of the emergent popular collective identity was how human rights were conceptualized in *lo popular*. This conception of rights is important for understanding the nature of *lo popular*, because it crystallized what the popular sectors might expect from society if they were given a choice. Not surprisingly, the nature of human rights for members of popular-sector organizations was closely tied to the other three core elements of the emergent popular collective identity—the concept of *vecino*, consumption demands, and life chances. The nature and scope of these rights also offer insight into the political behavior of the popular sectors that transcends both authoritarian and democratic regimes. These rights are, fundamentally, a large part of what members of popular organizations would struggle to achieve under any regime.

The notion of rights is also important because it provides a key nexus for understanding the relationship between collective identity and collective action based on that collective identity. Depending on their scope and nature, rights can require major transformations of society for their effective realization. As discussed in Chapter 1, this requirement has important implications for the kind of relationship likely to emerge between popular organizations and political parties. Rights also are intrinsically a type of "public good." Once such rights are acquired, they will be granted not only to all members of the popular sectors, regardless of whether they participate in popular organizations, but to all members of society as well. The struggle for rights is a logical basis for the creation of a popular social movement.

It is worth noting how the people interviewed defined human rights, as shown in Table 15. It is readily apparent that the principal rights were closely associated with the central aspects of the popular collective identity as elaborated in this chapter. Leaders of popular organizations were concerned with securing guarantees for their interests as determined by the concept of *vecino*, their consumption demands, and their life chances. Fundamentally, the realization of these rights would overcome the marginalization that characterized the popular sectors, not only under the military regime, but also during Chile's previous democratic regime as well.

The members of popular organizations sought integration into society, which entailed access to the basic necessities of life and the amenities of modern society. They sought this integration in the way that was most consistent with the overarching concept of *vecino* in *lo popular*. Thus, there was the clear emphasis on the rights of freedom of expression, respect for people, and opportunities for personal development. Even a young female member of a handicraft workshop, who claimed she was neither interested in nor understood politics, defined human rights as "defending the opinion of each person, each person is respected. People can also demand what they want." This emphasis can explain in part why rights relating to equality, participation, and freedom to organize were not specifically mentioned more frequently. They were generally subsumed under other rights, espe-

Table 15.   What do you think human rights are?

	Total
To live	19
Freedom of expression	19
Decent employment	12
Adequate housing	12
Respect as a person, respect for others	12
Health care	11
Education	11
Freedom	9
Adequate diet	6
Opportunities for personal development	5
Justice	4
To live in one's own country	4
The Universal Declaration of Human Rights	4
Equality	3
Recreation	3
To make demands	3
Elections	2
Participation	2
To organize	2
Democracy	2
Rights of children	2
Self-defense and to defend others	2
Private property	1
Requirements for subsistence	1
n.a.	2

cially the freedom of expression, in the minds of members of popular organizations. The former political prisoner who belonged to a construction cooperative and the MIR summarized all of this well in his definition of human rights: "Rights as people—to be heard, the right to equality, to be respected. [It is] the right to a fair trial, to education, a well-paid job, a house, recreation. To freely elect one's representative. . . . Without respect for human rights there is no democracy."

Members of popular organizations often recognized that the realization of these rights would require social transformation. As an example of what this kind of societal transformation might imply, the opinion of a female Communist Party militant who was active in coordinating organizational activities within her *población* is worth quoting: "The right to have an opinion and to have this opinion taken into account are legitimate rights. [The people] want to construct a country where they don't murder, where there is no hunger. Where you can speak freely and there is respect for human rights—for people's opinions. The opinion of everyone is valid. They deserve it as people."

LO POPULAR AND POPULAR ORGANIZATIONS AS AN ORGANIZATIONAL FORM

As an organizational form, popular organizations offered their members a collective avenue for overcoming the marginalization imposed upon them by the military regime. Popular organizations in fundamental respects were the antithesis of the most negative aspects of military rule in Chile. Whereas the military government centralized power, excluded all forms of political participation and endeavored to fragment Chilean society, popular organizations offered a source of empowerment to the popular sectors. Within popular organizations, participation was privileged and Chile's social fabric began to reconstitute itself. The repressive context of military rule and a deteriorating economic situation heightened the symbolic significance of *lo popular* and popular organizations as an alternative to the authoritarian pattern of social relations being imposed through the state. As more traditional bases for organization and channels for participation were foreclosed, popular organizations became a new locus for expressing dissent. Their mere existence dramatically demonstrated that there was another model for Chilean society.

Somewhat paradoxically, the very harshness of these conditions allowed (if not actually forced) a substantial number of *pobladores* to redefine their identity as *poblador* through their participation in popular organizations. Shared interests were highlighted by the severity of the dislocations felt in the *poblaciones* as a result of the military regime's policies. These interests reflected the assaults on what the popular sector felt were their basic human rights. These interests, however, were not "created" by the imposition of authoritarian rule. They also were characteristic—albeit to a lesser degree—of the popular sectors' subordinate and precarious incorporation into Chile's first democratic regime. In sum, the repression and dramatic economic situation during much of the military regime both conditioned and facilitated popular-sector organizational activity in the particular form that it took. But the interests defined by the members of these organizations, and even many of the problems they confronted, transcended regime types.

CONCLUSION

I have argued here that popular-sector organizations were able to survive (despite their inability to satisfy many of the urgent material needs of the urban poor) in large part because they fostered the emergence of a new popular collective identity. An abstract model of this identity, *lo popular*, is found in Figure 5. The model shows schematically how this new collective identity was formed by four interrelated core elements: *vecino*, consumption demands, life chances, and rights. As the arrows in the diagram suggest, the first three core elements were interwoven to form a holistic worldview that contributed to the popular sectors' own definition of human rights.

The presence of such a collective identity as the basis for popular-sector organizational activities provided a strong foundation for the institutionalization of these organizations. To the extent that these organizations demonstrated adaptability, complexity, autonomy, and cohesiveness—the four variables in the model of institutionalization discussed in both Chapters 1 and 3—this level of institutionalization was possible at least in part because successful popular organizations were not viewed by their members as short-term responses to immediate needs. Instead, they were seen as representing a vehicle for the realization and reproduction of the ideals and common interests represented by *lo popular*.

These arguments about the importance of a new collective identity for the development of popular-sector organizational activity place the rational-choice problematique and the classic problems of collective action (such as the free-rider problem and the costs of participation) in a new light. First, the preoccupation with the costs of participation in the rational-choice literature is shifted to the costs of *not* participating from the perspective of a new popular collective identity. The ideals embodied in *lo popular* provided a new rationality for guiding participation. Participation became both an end in itself and a means toward other, often intangible, ends in the new collective identity. It stressed the importance of collective interests over short-term personal advantage.

The above arguments also suggest that methodologies based on the logic of interest-maximizing behavior may offer unsatisfactory explanations of organizational activities involving processes of identity formation. The new popular collective identity may change how people actually perceive their interests. Assessing the relative costs and benefits of participation is necessarily subjective. The arguments presented concerning the emergence of a new collective identity within popular organizations suggest that the cost-benefit analysis of individuals participating in popular organizations is not a static process, but one that may take place in the context of the individual's changing values and goals for participation. For example, a person might join a soup kitchen in order to "maximize" her self-interest in maintaining a minimally sufficient diet, but continue to participate or increase her level of participation in order to "maximize" her self-interest in personal growth—or even the collective interest of improving the soup kitchen's capacity to pressure the municipal government to expand the school lunch program for all children living in the *población*.

There is a logical problem in trying to explain participation in popular organizations solely on the basis of interest calculations when the formula that individuals use for calculating their interests may change as a direct result of their participation. Continued participation becomes contingent on factors that are independent of an individual's efforts at interest-maximization. At best, the resultant explanation becomes unduly complicated; at worst, dynamic elements are overlooked or ignored in favor of oversimplistic explanations of complex social processes.

Given the emergence of a new popular collective identity in popular organizations, the question of the translation of that collective identity into effective self-constituted collective action arises. The empirical question does not concern the costs and benefits of participation per se, but rather the dilemmas of effective popular-sector collective action in general. In this case, it deals specifically with the articulation of the ideals embodied in *lo popular* and the elite worldviews represented in political parties. Did political parties attempt to co-opt or undermine self-constituted and autonomous popular-sector collective action? Or did they work with the popular sectors, accepting their autonomy in the definition of popular-sector interests? Or did political parties actually begin to absorb the popular collective identity by transforming themselves and making popular-sector collective action independent of political parties appear increasingly unnecessary?

5

DEMOCRACY, POLITICAL PARTIES, AND *LO POPULAR*

At least since Karl Marx's analysis of the role played by the *lumpenproletariat* in the 1848 French Revolution (Marx 1963), the danger to society posed by the organization of its disadvantaged "masses" has been an important issue in comparative politics. Huntington (1968), for example, argued in his seminal work that the mobilization of the lower classes represented a major challenge for democratic regimes in developing countries because of the tendency for their demands to outstrip the capacity of political institutions for channelling and moderating those demands. This issue has gained added urgency in Latin America today, as most countries attempt to consolidate still-fragile democratic regimes. Given the dramatic economic situation that virtually all of those countries face, we still do not know if they will ultimately be able to succeed.

In looking specifically at popular-sector organizational activity in Chile, I want to address several important theoretical issues that were elaborated on in Chapter 1. First, there may be an inherent tension between political democracy as a regime type and a democratic civil society composed of popular organizations. The centralization of power and the limited nature of participation necessary for the former may be incompatible with the latter's emphasis on direct participation and the dispersion of power throughout society. How does this tension influence popular-sector views of "democracy"? Is it likely to generate demands that will lead to the institutional overload Huntington predicted? What might be the priorities of the popular sectors in terms of political change?

Similarly, the relationship between popular organizations and political parties may be problematic. It should be recalled that this relationship will be determined by the scope and nature of popular-sector demands (see Fig. 3 and the related discussion in Chapter 1). From Chapter 4, we can conclude that the potential for tension is great. Given the wide scope of interests and demands associated with *lo popular*, popular organizations and political parties would likely be competitors for the allegiance of *pobladores*. How has this potential for competition influenced popular-sector perceptions of political parties and their role in a democratic regime?

In this chapter I shall examine the views of leaders of popular organizations during the military regime concerning a future democracy and the relations between political parties and popular organizations. I shall argue that *lo popular* as a collective identity contributed to a relative *moderation* of popular-sector demands, due to the centrality of the *procedural* aspects of political democracy in *lo popular*, as opposed to possible *substantive* policy outcomes that a democratic regime might make feasible. Moreover, political parties have an important role to play in representing popular-sector interests within a democratic regime from the perspective of *lo popular*. Tensions between political parties and popular organizations arise only when political parties are seen as trying to assert a larger role at the expense of the autonomy of popular organizations.

As a collective identity, *lo popular* was consistent with a procedural definition of political democracy. A future democracy was perceived as being the political regime best able to ensure the popular sectors a voice in setting national priorities, and guarantee that they would not have to shoulder a disproportionate part of the costs associated with overcoming the legacy of prolonged military rule. This perception, however, may have stemmed from an overidealistic (and perhaps unrealistic) notion of the proper relationship between political parties and popular organizations. It was also based on a conception of "democracy" that went beyond the changes brought about by Chile's subsequent transition to democracy. These views offer a good example of the theoretical tension between political democracy as a regime type and a democratic civil society.

The expectations and views that members of popular organizations expressed in 1986 reflected the fact that Chile had been ruled by a repressive military government for thirteen years and that a transition process had not yet begun. This was a period when the popular sectors were visibly and dramatically acting as protagonists in Chilean politics, as they increasingly came to dominate the protest movement. There was a natural optimism that this protagonism would continue as events unfolded.

As we shall see in Chapter 8, those expectations and views began to change in the late 1980s. These changes reflected both the nature of the transition process, which started in late 1988, as well as the form the new democratic regime took when it was finally installed in March 1990. The following will provide a useful baseline for interpreting changes in the expectations and views of the organized segment of the popular sectors in later periods. It can also provide insight into the sources of popular-sector frustrations in the aftermath of the transition.

Perhaps more important, the attitudes and views of leaders of popular organizations in 1986 offer unique approaches for resolving many of the theoretical issues raised in Chapter 1. The remoteness of democracy in Chile, the growing politicization of *pobladores* and their leaders in the *poblaciones*, and the still recent reemergence of political parties suggest that the tensions between popular organizations and political parties would be heightened. Both were seeking to maximize their influence over the unfolding and still very uncertain political process. Similarly, the potentially problematic relationship between political democracy and a democratic civil society would be highlighted by the circumstances of 1986. The views expressed by leaders of popular-sector organizations tend to reflect how they would like to see a political democracy and democratic civil society emerge at a time when later constraints (including the eventual demise of the protest movement) were not yet apparent. These people were much more likely to be "maximalists" in terms of their political views than in following years. If the fears of theorists as diverse as Marx and Huntington held true for Chile, it should have been clearest in 1986. By exploring the attitudes of leaders of popular organizations in the mid-1980s, we can learn much to guide further efforts aimed at integrating the popular sectors into Chile's current democratic regime.

I shall first explore here politics from the perspective of *lo popular*, including expectations concerning a future democratic regime and the role that popular organizations might play in it. I shall then explore some of the implications of *lo popular* as a collective identity for understanding the relationship between popular organizations and political parties.

POLITICS AND *LO POPULAR*

A useful starting point for this discussion is the threshold at which activities are characterized as being political in nature from the perspective of *lo popular*. A high threshold, it should be recalled (see Glossary), implies that activities are considered "political" only when they are aimed directly at influencing policies through political parties. Conversely, a low threshold recognizes a variety of activities as "political" that are unconnected to political parties, including symbolic forms of protest. A high threshold is consistent with the minimal procedural requisites for political democracy (i.e., free and competitive elections to select the most important officials). Nonparty institutions, particularly social movements and grassroots organizations, have no necessary political role or function. Such a political role would be consistent only with a much lower threshold for determining what is or is not "political."

The leaders of popular organizations interviewed as part of this study typically used a low threshold when defining political activity. When asked "What does it mean to engage in politics?" 73 percent of the respondents replied with a broad definition of politics that went beyond activities relating to political parties. Only 7 out of 45 (16 percent) of the respondents claimed that political activity was limited to the activities of political parties alone. An older woman, who was active in shantytown organizations prior to the military coup and was a member of the Christian Democratic Party, offered a good illustration of this. For her, political activity was "something very important. It is to teach people that they are capable of making decisions and defending their rights—not to be objects or puppets. It is done in an indirect way: when [a woman's] husband's salary is too small, [we tell her] it is because of the system. If there were more industries, he would earn more. They talk about this, but do not realize it is political. For them, politics is only parties. But everything is political in an indirect way." Given this broad definition of what is considered "political," it is not surprising that a similar percentage of respondents, just over 71 percent, felt that their own organizations were engaged in political activities. As a younger woman who belonged to the Communist Party noted, political activity was "looking for a solution in order to escape from your problems."[1]

This low threshold for political activity provided a broad general framework within which leaders of popular-sector organizations often viewed political participation and the role of political parties, at least under the military regime. Fighting for one's rights and one's basic needs through a variety of means and channels appeared to be at the core of this conception of politics. Participation in political parties and various other kinds of organizations, as well as symbolic protests and voting, were all considered to be legitimate forms of political activity.

The Popular Sectors and the Question of Social Class

Questions concerning the class perceptions of members of popular organizations revealed the possible relationship between the emergent collective popular identity and processes of class formation. This relationship has implications for how the popular sectors as a social category might be incorporated and represented within the Chilean political system. As Table 16 shows, the interviewees overwhelmingly viewed themselves as being members of the "lower" or "poor" class. This is how 60 percent of the respondents identified themselves when asked what social class they were members of. This compares to just 25 percent who felt they were members of the working class and 7.5 percent who either did not know or did not consider themselves as members of any class. The data presented in Table 16 also suggest that members of popular organizations conceived of society as being composed of social classes, but not in a traditional Marxist sense. For more than three-quarters of the respondents, the traditional working class appeared to be subsumed in the larger category of lower class.

---

1. The authoritarian regime contributed to this generally low threshold for political activity in *lo popular*. The regime itself characterized popular organizations as political and the risks associated with all political activity under the military regime became associated with participation in popular organizations. Popular-sector organizational activity was labeled subversive and popular organizations only rarely enjoyed legal recognition. If members of such organizations were not the direct targets of repression, there was a generalized perception that they might become so at any time. Rather than depoliticizing society as it was intended to do, repression had the unintended consequence of expanding the domain of politics beyond the activities of political parties for at least one significant segment of the population.

Table 16.   What social class are you a member of?

	Total
Lower or poor class	24
Working class	10
Middle class	3
No class	1
Does not know	2
n.a.	6
What are the different social classes?	
Upper, middle, and lower	21
Upper, middle, and working	6
Upper and lower—There no longer is a middle class	5
Upper and working—There no longer is a middle class	1
Other	1
n.a.	12
Is it good or bad that there are social classes?	
Good	0
Bad	25
There should be greater equality	1
They are unavoidable	4
n.a.	16

Moreover, six people suggested that the middle class in Chile had been virtually eliminated as a result of Chile's economic crisis.

Although no respondent chose to use the specific term "popular" in describing any particular segment of Chile's social structure, this perception of the social structure was consistent with the argument that a process similar to one of class formation was unfolding within the Chilean popular sectors (see Glossary). It clearly reflected the structural changes associated with the development model introduced by the military regime and detailed in Chapter 2. Moreover, it was very consistent with the dichotomy of the "haves" and "have-nots" that is fundamental to the conception of the popular sectors as a social category, as argued in the Glossary. Not surprisingly, none of the respondents felt that the existence of social classes was in some sense "good," and the vast majority of respondents indicated that it would be better if social classes did not exist.

Two implications emerge from these findings. First, the data suggest *how* the popular sectors felt they should be incorporated into the political system. Political appeals to the "working" class and political programs that seek to integrate the popular sectors and their demands into the political process—and, more generally, into Chilean society as a whole—exclusively through organizations connected with the labor movement would appear to be inadequate. At least for large portions of the organized popular sectors, appeals to *lo popular*, as the basis of a new collective identity, and popular organizations would be a more relevant starting point for their integration into the political process. As will be shown in Chapter 7, efforts by political parties to treat the popular sectors as part of the working class rather than as a distinct social actor were a major source of tension between political parties and popular organizations.

Second, the data in Table 16 suggest that the organized popular sectors did envision some form of social change. Consistent with *lo popular*, they appeared to desire a more equal society.[2] As will be argued below, another source of tension between political parties and popular organizations is the perception that political party leaders were from a different, more privileged, social class.

Political Democracy and Popular-Sector Expectations

The vast majority of Chileans desired a return to democracy in 1986 and the leaders of popular organizations interviewed for this study were no exception.[3] One reason for this support for political democracy undoubtedly was related to the poor's perceptions of the current economic situation. For example, when asked why there was poverty, 61 percent of the interviewees blamed the government directly—more than twice the number of people who identified other sources.

But support for political democracy was grounded on more than just economic concerns. There was often a feeling among the people interviewed that things would somehow be better if there were a return to democracy. As a young woman who was active in organizing women's groups explained, "I imagine it is wonderful to be able to say what I think without having to run and hide; to also work in democracy for what I want."

2. This should not be construed to mean that the organized popular sectors were seeking such social transformation through a revolution, or that non-Marxist political parties had little hope of establishing a significant social base in the popular sectors. This will be made clear throughout the remainder of the chapter.

3. Eighty-one percent of the respondents said they wanted a return to democracy, and only 10 percent said it did not matter. One person said she did not know, and the others said they only wanted a "real" democracy characterized by revolutionary social transformations.

Another women, who was somewhat older and also active in organizing women's groups, echoed this sentiment, although perhaps with a touch of cynicism: "I will feel more liberated, freer, more content—maybe even happier."

The people interviewed seemed to have had few illusions about democracy. As already noted in Chapter 4 (see Table 14), their demands were relatively moderate. Moreover, when specifically asked how they expected their demands to be dealt with under a future democratic regime, 73 percent of respondents felt that their demands would be satisfied only partially and/or slowly. Just three percent felt there would be no improvement in terms of having their demands met, while another three percent expected a dramatic improvement. A middle-aged male leader of a cultural group clearly explained the element of realism in the popular sector's expectations for democracy: "[Democracy] will not resolve [our problems], but it will help. I remember that I lived in a democracy. The problems were very similar but there was an opening, possibilities for dialogue [with the government]. Sometimes change was achieved. Tanks were not sent when there was a march in the street. There was some repression, but no deaths."

Table 17 lists the characteristics that the members of popular-sector organizations associated with a democratic regime. Very few people appeared to associate democracy with revolutionary change. Instead, they tended to associate it with more opportunities to express themselves (54

Table 17. What does "democracy" mean to you?

	Total
Opportunity to talk, be heard	25
Participation	19
More justice and less repression	8
Elections, majority rule	7
Basic needs are met	7
Freedom	5
Respect for human rights	4
Education	3
Freedom to travel	3
Greater equality	3
Ability to work	2
Greater opportunities	2
Possibility of representation	2
Socialism	2
Access to consumption goods	1
Means of communication at the service of the people	1
Other	4

percent of respondents) and participate (41 percent), as well as greater social justice. Their responses suggest a marked emphasis on the *procedural* aspects and guarantees associated with democracy. Relatively little attention was given to the possible policy outcomes that might result under a democratic regime.

This moderation and realism has several sources. An obvious one is the immediacy and harshness of the regime's repression in the *poblaciones*, which can be seen in how a young female leader of a cultural organization, described democracy: "Democracy is like a fantasy. Everyone is free, there are rights. We can go out into the street. It would be beautiful, precious. . . . Children would have the right to study, to improve their lives. . . . We can gather where we want. Democracy means that we all make decisions, we, the people. . . . We express what we want, what we need."

More fundamentally, these people viewed political democracy as a mechanism for incorporating the popular sectors into society—as a way for the popular sectors to be heard and to ensure that the social costs associated with future policies would be shared more equitably within Chilean society. In this way, democracy would provide the popular sectors with the possibility of reasserting the dignity denied to them by the military regime. Only a return to democracy would allow the popular sectors to assume the role of protagonist in Chilean society—a role they had so far been denied under both the military and democratic regimes. As a collective identity, *lo popular* symbolized this potential protagonism. As the young male Christian Democratic leader of a human rights group suggested, "[A democratic regime] is a state that is conscious of all of its people. It means that organizations will have a way to be heard on their points of view. We are all struggling to be heard." Similarly, a female leader of one of the few democratically elected *juntas de vecinos* in Chile at that time pointed out how democracy meant "freedom. One can express oneself, do what one wants. There is respect for human rights. We are all people and we are not manipulated as if we had no will of our own."

The specific responses listed in Table 17 highlight how the respondents' conception of democracy was closely related to the value commitments and ideals embodied in *lo popular*. The emphasis on participation and respect for people, in particular, was reminiscent of the core elements of *lo popular*. Just as people wanted to be listened to and respected in their organizations, they wanted to be listened to and respected by the national government. For example, the middle-aged leader of a cultural group explained that, "democracy is the power to decide what one really needs. It means that the government must listen to demands. *Pobladores* must have their right to protest and state their demands freely. [They must] also have the right to organize." Similarly, a young Communist male who formed a cultural organization for young people explained that "if [the government] does not respond to the voices of the people, there is no democracy. [Government] must respond to the people." And unlike the situation under the military regime, political democracy provided an obvious mechanism for resolving the problem of an unresponsive government. As a woman who was active in organizing people in her *población* pointed out, with democracy, "at least we can have more trust in the government than in a dictatorship. It is more feasible to remove it—every five or six years and not fifteen!"

This parallel between the values embodied in *lo popular* and how respondents viewed democracy was also clear in the importance of participation in both. The active participation of members in organizational activities was central to the meaning of *lo popular*. It was also a core element in the definition of democracy shared by many leaders of popular organizations. A good example is the following comment by the young Communist militant quoted above: "Democracy means participation. It means being a social subject that can contribute to society and provide economic and social opportunities through this system of government. [One can participate] at different levels . . . through social organizations, through political parties. Participation is not in individual terms. In order to influence the democratic process, it is necessary to unite, to unite around common interests."

The influence of *lo popular* on the respondents' political beliefs was also apparent when they were asked to describe what an ideal society would look like. Respondents generally expressed a desire for more equal, participatory, and just societies. Such a society would be structured through reciprocal ties of solidarity in which all people actively shared in determining the destiny of the country. This democratic vision was illustrated most clearly by two *pobladores*. The first was a middle-aged woman who had been active in organizing soup kitchens and coordinating their activities throughout the zone in which she lived. For her, an ideal society was "more than anything, the revolution—a country of equality, ample justice. Everyone has the right to give their opinion, decide where they will live, how they will live and raise their children, etc. Nothing is imposed— freedom in one's own life, one's own family. . . . We will feel capable." The second was a young male leader of youth groups. For him, the ideal society was, "socialism, à la Chile. Everyone would have the same rights, the equality of democracy—rights to health care, education, a proper diet. We [would] have a place to live. The two differences would decrease: Those at the bottom would rise and those at the top would come down. They would never reach the same point, but there would be fewer differences."[4]

The Role of Popular Organizations in a Democracy

The leaders of popular organizations interviewed generally envisioned important roles for popular organizations in a future democratic regime. More than 80 percent of respondents felt that popular organizations should be incorporated directly into the political system in a new regime. No one said that popular organizations would not be necessary in a democracy, a point of particular importance, given the direct relationship between the development of popular-sector organizations and the authoritarian regime. Popular organizations were seen as fulfilling roles that went beyond the struggle for a return to democratic rule, even though the absence of democracy was a major determinant of their initial emergence. Moreover, 85 percent of the people responding to the question felt that a democratic regime would actually make it easier for their organization to continue functioning.

People imagined a variety of roles for popular-sector organizations in a democracy. One role that was frequently mentioned was that of popular organizations as building blocks for the kind of society implied by *lo popular*. For example, a young male member of a human rights group explained: "For the development of any society, the second important element (the other is the family) is the organization. It is a pillar for constructing a good society, one that is pluralist, open to all and not individualistic. [A society] that is more collective."

Leaders of popular organizations often describe their organizations as basic units for participation. A thirty-one-year-old militant in the Christian Left Party who was the president of a workers' union in the informal sector

4. It should be noted that these expectations for democracy and demands were related to the respondents' perception that the current situation was intolerable. For example, when asked what was the worst society that they could imagine, just under 50 percent of the respondents indicated the present Chilean society under military rule.

pointed out that "organizations are a fundamental necessity. It is from here that man begins to participate in society. In socialist countries too!" Ultimately, participation in popular organizations was seen by many leaders of popular organizations as a way to allow the popular sectors some say in the setting of national policies and priorities. The young Communist Party member quoted above illustrated this belief well:

> Logically, organizations have to continue [after the military government], and with more reason because of the tasks of reconstructing the country. People in organizations have more consciousness than people who are not in organizations. They must be the vanguard. They must see to it that problems are being resolved. . . . The government will not be able to solve all of the problems in one day. There must be priorities. This is the role of the organizations. This is what their leaders are thinking about. The organizations are a channel [between] the state and the people. In Chile, the great majority is unorganized. There will always be problems of unemployment, education, health care. There will be no solution in even 50 more years. [The organizations] are a power within the state—the power of the poor.

The Popular Sectors and Local Levels of Government

The willingness of popular-sector organizations to work with local levels of government is critical for their ability to integrate into any democratic system. As discussed in Chapter 1, local levels of government are important for overcoming any tensions between a democratic political regime and processes of democratization in civil society. In Chile, this would require organizations to work with municipal governments and, most probably, official neighborhood organizations called *juntas de vecinos*.[5] Under the military regime, popular-sector organizations had only minimal contact with both. For example, of the forty-six people interviewed, only four felt that current municipal governments could be trusted or were making positive contributions to the local situation. The rest felt that the municipal governments supported the military regime. Only one person's organization

5. See Chapter 8 for the importance of *juntas de vecinos* for base-level participation.

had any regular contacts with the municipal government, and this was because she was a member of one of the few democratically elected *juntas de vecinos* in Santiago at that time.[6]

Similarly, *juntas de vecinos* were also viewed with extreme caution, in part because they had been connected with efforts by the state security apparatus to infiltrate *poblaciones* and identify political and social leaders. Only three of the 45 people responding to the question felt that the *junta de vecinos* in their area made any positive contributions to the community. The organizations to which four people belonged did have ties to their *juntas de vecinos*, but this included the woman who was a member of a democratically elected *junta de vecinos* and another woman who lived in an area where the *junta de vecinos* had also been elected. Two other respondents said that their organizations had unsuccessfully tried to establish a relationship with their respective *juntas de vecinos*.

When asked about their expectations for local levels of government under a democratic regime, all of the respondents expressed their belief that once democratically elected, the municipal government would be important for seeking solutions to their needs and for making their concerns known. The municipality and the *juntas de vecinos* were generally recognized as the principal levels of government for participating in a democracy.[7] A thirty-two-year-old female Communist militant, for example, explained that what was needed was "democratic, participative [local] government so that people could participate and be heard." The young male Christian Democratic member of a human rights group quoted above added that "organizations are important for the participation of the base in the construction of society. Like *juntas de vecinos*, which were very important [when] they channeled all of the *pobladores'* demands and were democratically elected."

6. The municipal government only reluctantly accepted the de facto existence of this particular *junta de vecinos*. The previous *junta*, which the municipal government had organized, was disbanded after one of its leaders stole all of the *junta*'s funds. The municipality did not know what to do about the missing money and when the residents of the neighborhood nominated a new *junta*, the official in charge of all of the *juntas de vecinos* under the municipality's jurisdiction said the *junta* should continue functioning while it awaited an official response. After three months of waiting, no response had yet arrived. The respondent also pointed out that the *junta* would like to form organizations for the unemployed and people who were suffering from severe overcrowding. But they would have to hide such activities because the municipality considered them to be "political," and the members of the *junta* were afraid.

7. As will be discussed in Chapters 8 and 9, both are critical to understanding the dynamic of popular-sector organizational activity under the current democratic regime.

A POPULAR-SECTOR VIEW OF POLITICAL PARTIES

Public opinion surveys in Chile have demonstrated that Chileans generally had a better understanding of the existence of political parties prior to the first elections after periods of authoritarian rule than people in other countries (Huneeus, 1988). The results of one national poll and the responses from people interviewed in the present study are shown in Tables 18 and 19, respectively.

A comparison of the two tables suggests that the leaders of popular-sector organizations interviewed as part of the present study were also fairly knowledgeable about political parties.[8] Interestingly, while both

Table 18. Level of knowledge of Chilean political parties in 1986

	%
Christian Democratic Party (DC)	46.3
Communist Party (PC)	35.1
Socialist Party (PS)	28.0
National Party (PN)	25.0
Radical Party (PR)	22.6
Independent Democratic Union (UDI)	10.2
National Action Movement (MAN)	8.4
Unitary Popular Action Movement (MAPU)	8.4
Revolutionary Left Movement (MIR)	6.7
Christian Left (IC)	5.6
National Union Movement (MUN)	5.0
Social Democratic Party (PSD)	4.5
Liberal Party (PL)	4.3
Radical Democracy (DR)	2.6
National Advancement (AN)	1.9
Humanist Party (PH)	1.9

Source: Carlos Huneeus, "El sistema de partidos políticos en Chile: Cambio y continuidad," *Opciones,* no. 13 (1988): 164.

Note: People polled were asked to list all the political parties they believed existed in Chile. The number given refers to the percentage of people naming the corresponding political party.

8. It should be noted that the national poll asked people to list all of the parties that they knew of, while the responses in Table 19 reflected people's judgments about which parties were the most important. Most interviewees, however, named all of the parties they thought existed. Those interviewed as part of the current study also made some obvious errors. The MDP, or the Popular Democratic Movement, was a coalition of leftist parties and the Civic Assembly was formed by a large number of social organizations rather than political parties (see Chapter 2). MOC was an offshoot of MAPU.

Table 19. What are the most important political parties in Chile today?

	Total
DC	33
PC	31
PS	22
MIR	10
IC	8
MAPU	8
The Right or PN	7
MDP	3
MOC	2
UDI	2
Radical	1
Social Democrat	1
MAN	1
Civic Assembly	1
None exist	1
Do not know	2
n.a.	2

groups seemed to be in rough agreement concerning the significance of the DC, PC, and PS, leaders of popular-sector organizations appeared to give more weight to the MIR and IC, a radical left and moderate socialist party, respectively, than the national sample suggests was the case. The national sample, on the other hand, apportioned much more importance to the Right in general, particularly the extreme Right (UDI and MAN), which had very close ties to the military regime and questionable adhesion to democratic values.

This difference between the national survey and the opinions of the leaders of popular organizations questioned for this study is in large part explained by the relative presence of different political parties in the *poblaciones*. For example, when asked which parties were most important in their own *población*, interviewees' responses suggested that the Communist Party was by far the most important political party in the *poblaciones*, followed by the PS and MIR. The IC and DC were mentioned by an equal number of respondents. In contrast to both the national public opinion polls and the respondents' own views of national-level politics, the Left generally had a much stronger presence in the *poblaciones* than the centrist Christian Democrats, and the Right appeared to be almost nonexistent.

It is worth noting that the people interviewed demonstrated an ambivalent attitude toward politicians in 1986. For example, when asked if they trusted politicians, only 43 percent of those responding to the question said they did. Thirty-two percent said they did not and an additional 18 percent of the respondents indicated that they had confidence in only a segment of the political elite. This suggests certain tensions in the relations between political parties and popular-sector organizations. It is not, however, the result of a general rejection of political parties by members of popular-sector organizations. Consistent with *lo popular*, respondents recognized that political parties had roles to play in the opposition to the authoritarian regime and a future democracy. The source of tension between political parties and popular organizations was found in the common perception among members of the latter that the parties did not fill their appropriate role and overstepped the boundaries of legitimate party activities.

Political Parties and the Ideals of *Lo Popular*

Leaders of popular-sector organizations generally believed that political parties had two roles to play. The more important role was that of representing and fighting for a project or vision of society that people identified with. This was reflected in the responses given by 67 percent of those who had an opinion when asked what they thought was good about political parties. Similarly, when asked what roles should political parties play in a democracy, the most frequent responses referred to ideas about representation.

The second role was furthering education. This role is related very closely to the first, in that parties were seen as sources of ideas (and even interests) beyond the individual experiences of *pobladores*. Through education, parties also contributed in raising people's consciousness—another central aspect of *lo popular*. The views of a young man active in youth organizations were typical in this regard: "At times the [perceived] interests of the *pobladores* are minimal in comparison to those the parties [represent]. The parties must be capable of providing interests, of opening and elevating the discussion. They must raise the real demands of the sector. They must educate about demands—what they mean. For example, what is democracy?" In a more critical tone, the young cofounder of a *población* self-defense group expressed similar ideas: "The parties must involve the base. The majority are in the *poblaciones* and the parties must be present. It is key that they always work on education. That is what we lack most. . . .

We need educational activities: courses on Marxism, historical materialism
[etc.]."[9]

It should be emphasized that both roles reflect the ideals embodied in *lo
popular* and are consistent with what political parties are normally expected
to do in democratic regimes. Political parties are viewed as having an
important and active role in the political incorporation of the popular
sectors. But this cannot supplant an equally important and active role for
the popular sector's own autonomous organizations. While parties can
clearly help *pobladores* define and interpret their interests, parties should
not impose their own partisan interests on the popular sectors. The popular
sectors must be allowed to make meaningful choices and influence how
parties define and interpret their projects for society.

Similarly, the people interviewed generally stressed the importance of
respecting party pluralism, thus reflecting the centrality of pluralism and
respect for different ideas within *lo popular*. When asked if there were any
political parties that did not have a role in a democracy, well over 50
percent of the respondents said there were none, and 16 percent would
place restrictions only on the extreme Right and/or Left. This is particularly
significant in the Chilean case. The history of extreme party polarization
and the prolonged existence of a military dictatorship had pushed the issue
of excluding Marxist parties from the political system to the forefront
of the national political debate. Moreover, a substantial percentage of
respondents indicated that they would personally be willing to work with
members of any political party. More than twice as many respondents, 69
percent, said they would be willing to work with people of all political
parties as compared to those (26 percent) who said they would not work
with parties representing distinct parts of the political spectrum.

The Relationship between Political Parties and Popular Organizations

The organizations to which the people who were interviewed belonged
generally did not have any formal organizational ties to political parties.

---

9. As will be discussed shortly, this educational role was closely tied to popular-sector
assessments of the problems that led to the breakdown of Chilean democracy.

The forty-six people interviewed were members of a total of forty-one organizations, out of which only two had any clear ties to a political party.[10]

Leaders of popular-sector organizations generally felt that popular-sector organizations should not be controlled by any single political party. For example, more than 90 percent of the respondents were quite clear in their insistence on the need to maintain organizational autonomy vis-à-vis political parties. Only four people felt popular organizations should be controlled by political parties, and one person said she did not know.

Most of the people interviewed, however, were willing to accept help from political parties if no conditions were attached. The member of the democratically elected *junta de vecinos* was typical in her views when she said that parties "can help, but not control." Or, as a middle-aged member of a woman's group explained, parties should "serve rather than use organizations." Any other type of relationship with political parties would threaten the organization's democratic practices and respect for pluralism. A good illustration of this belief was offered by a middle-aged woman active in organizing women's groups: "Each member can choose her own party, but the life [of the organization] must be harmonious. Organizations should be independent of political parties because there will always be

10. Both organizations were connected to the UDI, an extreme right-wing party with close ties to the military government. The people who were interviewed were chosen because of their organization's affiliation with the UDI in order to contrast their beliefs with those of other members of popular-sector organizations. One of the organizations, from which two people were interviewed, was the governing body for a shantytown that was created by one of the two successful massive land invasions in 1983. The current leadership group was installed after the previous leaders of the shantytown were sent into internal exile by the military government shortly after martial law was imposed in November 1984. The second organization, from which one person was interviewed, was set up by the UDI to help people gain title to plots of land. At the time of the interview, only a few people had received a minimal level of assistance through the group. The woman interviewed was also a member of a housing cooperative that was raising funds to buy construction materials for homes for its members—in the hope that she would get a plot of land through the UDI. The latter group was much more successful in terms of raising resources and had no ties to any political parties. Its members, including the woman herself, would clearly identify themselves with the opposition.

One person claimed that the PC controlled her soup kitchen due to the predominance of the PC in the *población* and the fact that the founder and president of the soup kitchen was a Communist. However, the links were indirect or nonexistent, and the organization received substantial assistance through contacts with the local priest. Political-party infighting divided one organization in two and the woman interviewed from that organization was associated with the side that was striving to keep political-party influences outside of the organization. She was not a member of any political party. Finally, a young man who founded a *población* self-defense organization noted that, at that time, the organization had no ties with any party, but would consider seeking affiliation with the MIR once the political division within the party was overcome.

different ideas among the members and they will not accept one party. For this reason, it is not democratic if one party is the owner of the organization."

This insistence on maintaining organizational autonomy was also stressed by the respondents who actually did belong to a political party. For example, a middle-aged member of the Christian Democratic Party (who used to belong to the Communist Party until after the coup) explained that "the party should support but not infiltrate [social organizations]. Politics should not be introduced. [The party] should lend militants who work [for the organization] with consciousness and not deceit. If there are material resources, okay, but without conditions because there are people with distinct ideas, religions, and parties."

The president of the union for workers in the informal sector, who was a member of the Christian Left Party, similarly emphasized that popular organizations should be "as pluralist as possible. We do not like to use organizations for political ends. Parties cannot feed on the problems that the popular world suffers." Popular organizations and political parties had complementary, but distinct, roles from the perspective of *lo popular*. A female member of the Communist Party described this relationship in the following manner: "Organizations should be very separate from parties. If they are not, it is a mistake. The function of the party is to give guidance. The *pobladores* look for solutions, alternatives and proposals for solving the problems. No party can replace the organizations." Another Communist Party member, the young man who founded a cultural center for young people quoted above, added:

> [Organizational] autonomy exists—parties do not define everything. We have learned that social organizations have a high level of autonomy. They are people with interests. Some are the same as ours, others no. If [party militants] do not understand this, they are bad politicians, bad militants. There are no naive people, people who allow themselves to be fooled. The organization is a vehicle through which we can achieve changes. . . . Therefore there is no need for the party to use them. Parties grow through social organizations, but that is not the only reason for creating organizations. . . . [Social organizations] have their own demands that often have nothing to do with those of the party.

The desire for a relationship between popular organizations and political parties that preserved the independence of popular organizations can also be seen in the role that respondents felt party militants should play within popular organizations. Because party militants allegedly received some training and political education from their parties, they were seen as natural leaders and sources of the kind of education political parties ideally should provide popular organizations. This was the general response given by more than two-thirds of the respondents. Surprisingly, only 5 percent of the respondents said that militants should serve as a link between the organization and their party. This is half the number who felt that party militants were sent by the political parties to manipulate popular organizations.

It is important to emphasize that, as members of popular organizations, militants were expected to pursue the interests of their organizations and not the interests of their respective political parties. This was stressed by most leaders of popular organizations. For example, a middle-aged woman who became quite active in popular organizations after the coup and who had no party affiliations felt that "[party militants] must center themselves around what the popular organization is and not give them orders because they are given orders by their parties. They do not have to be partisan—they are fighting for [the *poblador*'s] demands. If the parties understood this, the popular organizations would be much stronger. . . . The parties would be in the service of the organizations instead of the organization being in the service of the parties." Similarly, a middle-aged woman who belonged to the Unitary Popular Action Movement—Worker Peasant (MOC) noted that a militant "must put the party line aside for the good of the grassroots, the organization. Never worry about who someone is. The key is to work there as a social leader rather than a political one—there is no party line. Explain that the parties don't manipulate. We all choose for ourselves and express ourselves."

For the members of popular organizations, the appropriate relationship between parties and popular organizations is fundamentally a matter of mutual respect. Particularly in the context of an authoritarian regime (which they felt had denied most *pobladores* any respect), this general demand for respect was a major motivating force behind the emergence of *lo popular*. The female Communist militant already quoted illustrated this sentiment quite clearly:

> Independently of one's militancy, one has to respect the interests of the organization. The party should provide orientation for the organization's demands and the militant is the mechanism for doing this. It is not because [the *pobladores*] have the problem that they

have to look for the solution; it is mutual respect, both the parties as well as the organizations and vice versa. The militants should be in the organization, respecting its activities. . . . The people have the capacity to decide which way they will go.

Popular-Sector Disillusionment with Political Parties

While *lo popular* legitimated roles for political parties in the Chilean political process, there was also a certain disillusionment with political parties and party elites among many leaders of popular organizations. This disillusionment resulted from a variety of causes. An obvious one in 1986 was the lack of any progress toward unseating the military regime. Ironically, this appearance of inefficacy was only reinforced by the military regime's own propaganda, which for twelve years had portrayed political parties and party elites as self-interested and incapable of resolving Chile's most pressing problems, but likely to make them worse if they were returned to power. In the following I shall focus on three specific sets of factors contributing to this disillusionment: the popular sectors' interpretation of the breakdown of the Chilean democratic regime, their actual experiences with political parties in popular organizations, and the perceived social distance that separated *pobladores* and political-party leaders.

One source of popular-sector disillusionment with political parties related to the popular sectors' understanding of the breakdown of Chilean democracy and the lessons that should be learned from that experience. As Table 20 indicates, a substantial proportion of respondents (36 percent) specifically blamed political parties for the military coup. The political parties of the Right, in particular, were discredited insofar as 50 percent of respondents assigned responsibility for the coup to the Right and bourgeoisie. Similarly, political parties shared in the responsibility assigned to the Popular Unity Government by 11 percent of the interviewees, the fourth most common answer given.[11]

Leaders of popular-sector organizations drew a variety of lessons from

11. It is interesting to note the relatively high number of interviewees who identified a significant American role in the breakdown of Chilean democracy. This was largely attributable to the influence of the Left in the *poblaciones* and the documented fact that the United States government and several U.S. corporations did play active roles in trying to bring down the Allende government. See Senate Intelligence Committee 1975 and Hersh 1983.

Table 20.   Who was responsible for the military coup in 1973?

	Total
The Right, the bourgeoisie	22
The political parties	16
The U.S., imperialism	15
The Popular Unity government	5
The people lacked education, consciousness, etc.	4
Everyone	2
Other	2
Do not know	3
n.a.	2
What lessons should be learned from the coup?	
Must educate the people	12
Must support the elected government	10
Unity is necessary	8
Keep the military out of politics	8
The limits of democratic institutions	6
Need an alternative military force	4
Ban the opposition	2
Strengthen social organizations	2
Parties must behave differently	2
Do not repeat the same experience again	2
Other	3
n.a.	11
Have politicians learned these lessons?	
Yes	11
I hope so	5
No	9
A qualified no	3
n.a.	18

this experience, as shown in Table 20. Surprisingly, only eight people felt that one of the lessons to be learned was that the military should stay out of politics. More important, the members of popular organizations tended to feel that the Allende government did not succeed because of two related factors: a general lack of awareness of what was at stake and excessive partisan fighting. Both factors gave way to abuses by all sides, and eventually led to the polarization of the country that resulted in the loss of democracy in Chile. This explains why 34 percent of those asked to suggest which lessons should be learned from the military coup said that people must be educated, the most common response given. Political parties, as pointed out above, have a special role to play in this educational effort. Parties specifically were seen as being responsible for the fact that the general population did not fully appreciate what was involved in the struggles of the early 1970s. Similarly, the next two most common responses, the need to support the government and the need for unity, reflected a common notion that partisan and sectoral interests were placed before the greater national interests of preserving Chilean democracy.

When asked if they felt politicians had learned these lessons (Table 20), a clear majority of those responding were skeptical. Such skepticism is readily apparent in how leaders of popular organizations perceived political party behavior in 1986, thirteen years after the coup. When asked what they felt were the negative aspects of political parties, by far the most common response was their lack of unity and excessive partisan behavior. This was the response given by almost half of the respondents, more than four times as many as those giving any other answer. Ever since the formation of the Democratic Alliance and the Popular Democratic Movement in 1983, parties often seemed to focus more energy on the pursuit of narrow partisan interests than on working toward the creation of a consensual alternative to the military regime (see Chapter 2). For many, political parties appeared to be committing many of the same errors that had resulted so disastrously in the 1973 military coup. A good example of this perception was offered by a middle-aged woman who organized a number of popular organizations in her *población* when she lamented that "politicians are worried about ousting Pinochet. This is primary for them. But they know that the Allende government was lost because of them—the people were not prepared and could not support it in any way. Therefore I do not understand why they do not work on this. For politicians, politics is a tool—they use it when they need to. They must educate, raise consciousness—educate about politics, what it is. . . . People see politics as dangerous because they do not understand it." Similarly, a middle-aged woman, who became active in popular-sector organizations for the first time just after the coup when she helped form one of the first handicraft workshops in Santiago, was frustrated because politicians were not working to "create a true democracy. Each one with his own plan of government instead of fighting amongst themselves as they did under Allende. I understand that parties are necessary, but when they fight amongst themselves they are the enemy of what they want to do and help."

A second source of disillusionment stemmed from the actual experiences of leaders of popular-sector organizations with political-party activity in the *poblaciones*. As pointed out above, almost all of the organizations to which interviewees belonged had no formal ties to any political party. The emphasis on pluralism and internal democracy associated with *lo popular* generally precluded such links, and most successful organizations that were able to survive for any length of time engaged in specifically nonpartisan activities. This did not, however, prevent political parties from trying to gain influence in organizations, although such efforts frequently created tensions and risked destroying the organization.

As Chapter 3 (and the preceding discussion concerning the type of relationship that leaders of popular organizations wanted to establish with political parties) made clear, organizational autonomy was of singular importance. Yet there was a general perception that parties represented the primary threat to such autonomy.[12] Eighty-eight percent of the respondents reported instances of manipulative and disruptive behavior by political parties with respect to popular organizations. For example, the young female cofounder of a human rights group noted that "the idea of the parties is to do many things that the people [in the organizations] do not have the capacity to do. They do not respect the agreements and the positions taken among the people. They do not respect the ideas of others, the independence of the organization. For example, the Jota[13] called for a march because the party leadership told them to and no one participated. It made no sense."

The behavior of political parties in popular organizations was frequently deemed disruptive. Respondents perceived partisan politics to be the most divisive influence within their organizations. Of those who indicated that their organizations had suffered divisions among members at various times, 39 percent said those divisions were the result of people disagreeing over partisan positions in the group. Most of the other sources of division were minor in nature or dealt with personality clashes among different members, as would be expected in any group of people.[14] Similarly, the primary

12. The reasons for this kind of behavior by political parties are related to the effects of repression. Parties had to re-create their links to society after they were severely weakened, if not actually severed, by the military regime. This will be discussed at length in Chapter 7.

13. The youth branch of the Communist Party.

14. Fears of parties manipulating popular organizations in pursuit of their own interests were sometimes taken to extremes. For example, one of the cofounders of a cultural organization withdrew from the group after being accused of trying to sway the organization towards the Christian Left Party, even though this particular person was not a member of any party and firmly believed that "social" leaders should not join political parties. His brother, a lawyer, offered to teach a workshop on legal matters for the cultural organization and his brother-in-law, a journalist, offered to help the group to publish its monthly newsletter. Both were members of the Christian Left Party and the cofounder of the organization was assumed also to be a member of the IC because his relatives were. Even though the organization was

source of conflict among different popular-sector organizations, according to the respondents, also related to partisan politics. Typically, the clash was between an organization that was controlled by one party and other nonpartisan and pluralist organizations.[15]

These sources of disillusionment were reinforced by a sense of social distance between political parties and popular organizations. A significant number of respondents felt that parties were too elitist and nondemocratic in their internal activities. When specifically asked if they felt political leaders represented their interests as *pobladores*, almost 50 percent of those responding to the question said no or very little.

There were several reasons for this perceived social distance. One was the feeling that political leaders were uninterested in the problems of the urban poor and were more concerned with their own interests. This was consistent with how people compared the parties' behavior in 1986 to the early 1970s. It also was apparent in the answers people gave when they were asked about the circumstances under which political elites visited the *poblaciones*. By far, the most common feeling was that they did not come at all (30 percent), or they came only when there was some personal and/or party advantage in doing so (20 percent).

A related factor stemmed from perceived distinctions of social class between party leaders and *pobladores*. For example, a young woman who belonged to a soup kitchen explained that "our problems are not important to them. The people with the most money are the tightest. They do not help the poor." Even people who had been or were at present members of political parties often shared similar feelings. Another young woman, who was active in women's organizations and had recently resigned from the Christian Left Party, pointed out that parties did not represent her interests as a *poblador* because "they are all people at the very top [elites] and they

---

interested in offering a variety of workshops for community residents and was concerned about improving the quality of its newsletter, the offers of help were rejected because other members of the organization feared the ulterior motives of party militants and accused the cofounder of trying to take advantage of the organization for partisan reasons.

15. I came across a number of "phantom" or "ghost" organizations, to use the term *pobladores* have adopted for organizations that exist in name only. Such organizations were "created" by political parties in order to gain a presence for their militants in various coordinating bodies. These organizations rarely, if ever, met and their "membership" was limited to several party militants who then asserted their right to be represented in different coordinating bodies where the party would then gain a vote. Also see Baño 1985. The divisions often arose over challenges to the legitimacy of the organization's claim to representation in the coordinating body and efforts by the responsible political party or parties to influence the majority in the coordinating body improperly.

represent another social class. It is very difficult for a *poblador* to reach the highest levels [in political parties] and not forget their social class origins." Another woman, who was also active in women's groups and was a member of MOC,[16] responded to the same question by noting that "I do not know up to what point [they represent my interests]. I do not think that they are poor people and they are not going to feel that the necessities of the *poblaciones* are their own. . . . We are the ones who are suffering. They hardly even suffer. They are worried, yes, but they are not suffering. . . . We are the ones who are bringing the problems to them.[17]

CONCLUSION

Although living under a military regime, many leaders of popular organizations did not view a future political democracy as a panacea that would solve all of their needs. Nor were they seeking revolutionary social change with the fall of the military regime. Instead, political democracy appeared to be valued for the procedural guarantees that only a democratic regime could provide and that the authoritarian regime had conspicuously eliminated. Members of popular organizations wanted to be incorporated into the political process in order to help set national priorities and ensure that their interests would not be subordinated to those of other sectors of society.

These findings offer a useful starting point for understanding popular-sector organizational activity in Chile as it continued to evolve from the mid-1980s to the installation of a new democratic government in 1990. First, they illustrate the theoretical problems discussed in Chapter 1, which described political parties and popular organizations as two alternative forms of territorial representation. During the period of opposition to military rule, the interviews suggest a strong tendency to envision a complementary relationship between political parties and popular organizations.

16. *MAPU Obrero-Campesino* was a small splinter group of the MAPU Party. It was in the political coalition dominated by the Communist Party, the Popular Democratic Movement (MDP).

17. The military regime often reinforced such impressions through selective repression. For example, police would sometimes openly let opposition leaders leave rallies or political meetings, while less prominent participants were arrested. The message was clear: those who were not arrested were in some sense "privileged" and different.

In terms of the model offered in Chapter 1 (Fig. 3), popular organizations viewed political parties as *potential* "allies" in the pursuit of popular-sector interests (as defined by *lo popular*). At the same time, these people expressed an important skepticism regarding the willingness of political parties to accept popular organizations as potential allies. Instead, parties were viewed as favoring a relationship closer to one of "sponsorship" (Fig. 3). Did the members of popular organizations expect political parties to treat popular organizations with an unreasonable degree of disinterestedness and altruism? Was such a relationship between political parties and popular organizations even desirable, given the importance of political parties in channelling and ultimately moderating popular-sector demands under a democratic regime? (O'Donnell and Schmitter 1986; Schmitter 1981; Huntington 1968)

Paradoxically, the data presented here also suggest that leaders of popular organizations were capable of comprehending the magnitude of the economic problems that Chile confronted in the mid-1980s. But their insistence that the popular sectors be integrated into Chilean society on equal terms with other social groups seemed to imply changes that are much greater than those actually realized during the transition in the late 1980s. This could affect popular-sector perceptions of the current democratic regime and their role in it. Given the dominant role that political parties played in the transition, this gap between the expectations of leaders of popular organizations and the subsequent course of events could also exacerbate already existing tensions between popular organizations and political parties. More generally, these findings might indicate a fundamental incompatibility between processes of democratization in civil society and a transition to political democracy, or at least the kind of transition that was feasible in Chile. Although segments of Chile's urban poor exhibited a certain realism regarding Chile's economic situation, their political demands could generate potentially destabilizing pressures for the new democratic regime.

This potential will be explored by looking at the role of the popular sectors in the transition and their participation under the current democratic regime. But before doing so, we shall examine first the views of the major political parties and political elite regarding popular organizations in the mid-1980s.

6

POLITICAL PARTIES AND THE POPULAR SECTORS

The Perspective of the Political Elite
in the Mid-1980s

The relationship between political parties and popular organizations established under the military regime affected the emergence of a popular social movement in fundamental ways. First, as will be discussed in Chapter 7, this relationship had the effect of undermining efforts to create such a movement in 1986. The weakness of political parties in the repressive context of the mid-1980s created narrow partisan interests that were inimical to the emergence of such a movement. In the subsequent period leading up to and including the transition to democracy, this same relationship continued to subordinate popular-sector interests in creating a social movement. In contrast to 1986, however, this was accomplished by a new opposition coalition that faced the daunting task of defeating the military and its allies in the upcoming plebiscite so that a transition to democracy could finally begin. Political parties blocked renewed efforts to create a popular movement out of the very real fear that such a movement would only complicate their already difficult task. By 1990, the evolution of the relationship between parties and popular organizations seemed to determine how the popular sectors would be incorporated into Chile's new democratic regime. Rather than assuming the role of an autonomous political actor, the popular sectors appeared destined to become a mass of relatively underprivileged people in need of society's generosity and the important swing votes in future elections.

Was this evolution in the relations between political parties and popular-sector organizational activity inevitable? Is it likely to continue on the same path now that democracy has been restored in Chile? As suggested in Chapter 5, leaders of popular organizations could envision an alternative relationship in which political parties and popular organizations complemented one another in the political arena. This chapter will suggest that the views political parties held of the popular sectors and their organizations in the mid-1980s similarly envisioned a more propitious environment for the continued development of popular-sector organizational activity. This potential could be seen in the politicians' recognition that problems existed in the relations between political parties and the popular sectors, as well as their perceptions of important changes in Chilean society since 1973. This potential was also a consequence of the learning process that political parties went through following the military coup. It involved a reassessment of previous political styles and behavior, leading to a set of proposed reforms for a new democratic regime that held the promise of allowing for the continued evolution of a popular social movement in Chile based on *lo popular.*

There were a very large number of political parties and political-party factions in 1986, as the incomplete lists presented in Tables 18 and 19 in Chapter 5 show. These parties and assorted party factions generally fell into one of four principal tendencies: The Right, the Center, the Renovated Left, and the Traditional Left.[1] This study focuses on six political parties representative of these tendencies.

Representing the Right, one national party leader was interviewed from both the National Union Movement (MUN)[2] and the Independent Democratic Union (UDI). A number of small parties with questionable political

---

1. See Garretón 1987c and 1989a. As Garretón points out, it was not yet clear in 1986 that the Renovated Left tendency would crystallize into a genuine fourth pole in Chilean politics. This tendency was quite strong in a number of smaller parties and different branches of the Socialist Party. Moreover, at least one of the parties placed in this category, the Christian Left, was very active in the popular sectors in 1986. By placing parties in the same category, it is not meant to imply that there was complete agreement between them on all important issues. For example, within the Right, there were substantial disagreements between the two parties covered in this study, including the degree to which the UDI was actually committed to liberal democracy. Where such disagreements are relevant to the argument being made here, they will be pointed out.

2. This would later be renamed the National Renovation Party (RN).

significance clustered around the Christian Democratic Party (DC) in the Center, but only members of the latter were interviewed for centrist tendencies. In recognition of the dominance of the Christian Democratic Party in both the politics of the Center and in the opposition in general, I interviewed five national leaders from the DC. An effort was made to distribute these interviews among leaders representing the more progressive and more moderate wings of the party in order to get a balanced appreciation of the party's perceptions of popular-sector organizations. The Renovated Left was represented by the most important moderate faction of the Socialist Party, the Nuñez branch (PS[N]) and the Christian Left Party (IC).[3] Two national leaders from both parties were interviewed.

The Renovated Left encompassed a variety of parties and party factions within the socialist orbit, as well as a number of "independent" socialists. These parties and individuals were attempting to "renovate" socialist thought in light of changes in modern societies (the political significance of the middle class, the creation of professional militaries, etc.) and an interpretation of the problems in Chilean socialism before the military coup. It was also intended to distinguish socialist politics from the politics of the Communist Party in order to create a fourth or socialist pole in Chilean politics that would overcome the traditional "three thirds" polarization discussed in Chapter 2.

As the people involved in this effort were quick to admit, the renovation process was still far from complete, and the contours of a new socialism in Chile are still not clear in the 1990s. However, several characteristics distinguished this tendency from the Traditional Left. The Renovated Left was firmly committed to political democracy as a regime type that was integrally tied to a socialist project for the economy and society. This socialist project strove to supersede the capitalist model of socioeconomic relations; in this way, the tendency sought to distinguish itself from European social democracy. Moreover, the Renovated Left rejected the basic tenets of Leninism and any conception of a vanguard party or class. Although the role of the proletariat was considered to be very important, there was an explicit recognition of the heterogeneity of the Renovated Left's potential social base. Because of its firm commitment to political democracy, there was an acceptance of party pluralism, the uncertainty of

3. Almost all of the IC's most prominent leaders left the party after 1988 to join other parties within the Renovated Left. As a result, the party's future is very much in doubt and it now has little political importance.

elections, and the reversibility of socialist reforms as a result of the electoral process. This, in turn, implied the need to build stable majorities and electoral "blocks for change."[4]

The Traditional Left represented the Marxist-Leninist political parties in Chile. The revolutionary potential of the proletariat as a class was emphasized by the Traditional Left and the vanguard role of the party was privileged. Any attachment to political democracy was instrumental insofar as political democracy served to further the cause of social revolution and the eventual imposition of a dictatorship of the proletariat. Two individuals with close ties to the national-level leadership of the Communist Party (PC) and a national leader of the more radical Almeyda branch of the Socialist Party (PS[A]) were interviewed as representatives of this tendency.

THE NEED TO RE-CREATE A SENSE OF "NATION"

As discussed in Chapter 2, Chile underwent a dramatic increase in social stratification after the imposition of military rule. The political parties in 1986 were very much aware of the important social changes that Chile had experienced, even if they were unsure of their exact dimensions and political consequences.

When interviewed, political elites were asked how they felt Chilean society had changed since 1973. The clearest trend in the responses was a recognition of the increased distance between social classes, with a concomitant increase in the relative size of the lower classes. All of the political parties largely coincided in this view, with the exception of the two parties on the Right. As one leader of the Christian Left explained, "we have lost a sense of nation. Chile is very segmented. People do not feel that they are part of the same nation."

There also appeared to be recognition of the decline of the traditional working class and working-class organizations. Again, with the notable exception of the Right, individuals from the other three tendencies made

4. The literature on renovated socialism is quite large. Some of the most important and best works include: Garretón 1987c; *La Renovación Socialista* 1987; Arrate 1985; Arrate et al. 1986; and Vodanovic 1988. Also see Walker 1990.

various references to this structural change in Chile and its relation to increased poverty and inequality.

Not surprisingly, recognition of these changes in Chilean society made improving the situation of Chile's poor the priority for all political parties. Even the Right agreed on this priority. Virtually all major political-party documents that addressed broad concerns for the future talked specifically about this problem.[5] One of the DC leaders interviewed expressed a common concern shared by most political parties when he explained that his major preoccupation for the post-Pinochet era was with the "capacity of democracy for social cooperation in which it will be genuinely possible to avoid that benefits do not go to those who most need them—the poorest. The maximum priority are those who are poorest." As part of this awareness and commitment to social reform, the respondents suggested that most political parties regularly discussed the situation in the *poblaciones*. Moreover, the people interviewed noted that political parties were concerned with having contacts with *pobladores* and a direct presence in the *poblaciones*.

This concern with party presence in the *poblaciones* also reflected a recognition that there were problems in the relations between the political parties and the popular sectors. Table 21 suggests that all of the political parties perceived some sort of distance or tension in their relations with the popular sectors, even though they did not all necessarily confront the same types of problems.

Clandestineness and repression under the military regime were the principal causes of these problems in party relations with the popular sectors, according to members of both the Center and Traditional Left tendencies. Interestingly, the parties of the Renovated Left did not feel that clandestinity and repression created problems in this sense. The representative of one of the parties on the Right felt that his party also faced persecution in the

5. This was clearest in the agreements reached by opposition parties during the 1985–86 period. See the National Accord for the Transition to a Full Democracy, and Bases for Sustaining a Democratic Regime: Further Elaboration of the National Accord for the Transition to a Full Democracy, both signed by important parties of the Right, Center, and Renovated Left; the Chilean Left to the Country: Our Proposal for Opposition Cooperation in the Struggle for Democracy, signed by most of the major political parties of the Renovated Left and the Traditional Left; and the Demands of Chile, which was written with input from most major parties and later ratified by all major political parties of the opposition. Even the Right acknowledged the need to address the problem of extreme poverty on a priority basis, although the Right generally gave the military government high marks in this area. For example, see Riesco 1985; Unión Democrática Independiente 1986 and 1983.

Table 21. What are the negative aspects of your party's relations with marginal sectors?

	Total	Right	Center	Renovated Left	Traditional Left
Clandestiny, repression	4	0	2	0	2
Misery generating extremism	2	0	2	0	0
Their fear of being used	1	0	0	1	0
Politicians are incapable of ousting Pinochet	1	0	0	1	0
Tensions between the base and the party leadership	1	0	0	1	0
Passivity of popular sectors	1	0	0	1	0
Popular-sector heterogeneity	1	0	0	0	1
Organizational problems	1	0	0	0	1
Inexperienced militants	1	0	0	0	1
National-level organizations are too ideological	1	0	0	0	1
Persecution by Marxists	1	1	0	0	0
The poor's marginality	1	0	1	0	0
Party too concerned with winning elections	1	0	1	0	0
Failure to take advantage of space opened by the church	1	0	1	0	0
Center's problem: avoid being for the status quo	1	0	1	0	0
Poor political formation, low education generating extremism	1	0	0	1	0
n.a.	1	1	0	0	0

poblaciones, but by Marxists. The Renovated Left appeared to be most aware of the problems in the relations between parties and popular organizations (discussed in Chapter 5) from the perspective of leaders of popular-sector organizations. At least, this was the impression given by their responses in Table 21 which referred to fear of being used and the suspicion of party leaders by the urban poor. For the Center, it is worth noting that there was some preoccupation for a tendency toward the radicalization of the popular sectors as a result of their poverty.

Within the DC, there was a particular awareness of the relationship between current tensions and the experiences leading up to the military coup in 1973 (Ortega 1985). The intense interparty competition that led parties in the past to assert their control over social organizations in order to further party interests was not easily forgotten. Moreover, as one of the DC leaders interviewed pointed out, past antagonisms among party militants from the popular sectors helped to generate a climate of distrust that undermined cooperation among militants from different political parties in popular organizations.[6] One influential DC policymaker even went so far as to imply that one of the primary threats to the consolidation of a future democratic regime was the resurrection of these same divisive practices that had already destroyed democracy in Chile once (Foxley 1987 and 1984).

HOW THE PAST CONDITIONS THE FUTURE: POLITICAL LEARNING AND EMERGING AREAS OF CONSENSUS

Significant areas of consensus were emerging within Chile's political class in 1986, based on its members' respective analyses of the breakdown of Chilean democracy and expectations concerning the risks a future democratic regime would face (Flisfisch 1987). These areas of consensus were not necessarily programmatic or substantive, and certainly were not ideological. They formed the basis for convergent (or potentially convergent) patterns of political behavior and strategy for a future democratic regime.[7] Three of these emergent areas of consensus were very relevant to the possibilities for a popular social movement to emerge in Chile. They suggested that the political parties would be receptive, or at least not overtly antagonistic, to such a popular social movement. These areas of convergence reflected the recognition by political parties of (1) the need for greater unity among political parties and the necessity of coalition governments, (2) the need for greater flexibility and pragmatism by political parties, and (3) the importance of autonomous social organizations in civil society.[8]

6. This was particularly apparent in the efforts by various intermediary bodies to establish some sort of popular social movement. These efforts will be discussed in Chapter 7.

7. As will be discussed in Chapter 8, this convergence crystallized in 1988 with the formation of the Command for the No (Concertación por el No).

8. In addition to the interviews, these three emergent areas of consensus were evident in a number of party documents and statements by party leaders. For the Right, see Riesco 1985; Yrarrázabal 1985; and Correa 1985. The UDI was not part of the opposition and saw itself as the natural inheritor of the military regime's legacy. It did not envision itself as being part

The Need for Greater Unity and Coalition Governments

An important lesson that most political parties had learned from the experiences of the previous twenty years was that effective governments needed to have the solid support of a majority of the population and could not exclude the interests of any major segment of society in the design and implementation of government programs. Governments needed to be truly national in scope and this required, given Chile's multiparty system, coalition governments and greater cooperation among political parties in general.

The Christian Democratic government of Eduardo Frei (1964–70) was viewed by many party leaders to have ushered in a new and inherently unstable political era in Chile with its single-party strategy for governance. Unlike previous national governments (in which people from different political parties shared power) the Christian Democrats were seen as having deliberately sought to govern alone, effectively locking other political parties out of any possible power-sharing arrangements. Moreover, its

---

of a coalition with the political parties then in the opposition. Aside from the area of coalition governments, UDI policy statements were remarkably consistent with the broad outlines of the other emerging areas of consensus presented here. See Unión Democrática Independiente, 1986 and 1983. For the Center, see Martínez 1985; Ortega 1985; Arriagada 1985a and 1985b; Foxley 1987 and 1984; Boeninger 1985, 1984a, and 1984b; *Proyecto Alternativo* 1984, vols. 1–3; Zaldivar 1986; and Secretaría Tecnica, Comisión de Municipalización 1984. For the Renovated Left, see Garretón 1987a, 1987b, and 1987c; Nuñez 1985, 1986a, 1986b, and 1987; Lagos 1985a and 1985b; *La Renovación Socialista* 1987; Vodanovic 1988; Drago 1986; Arrate 1985; Ottone 1986; Benavente 1985; Maira 1986a, 1986b, and 1986c; Gonzales 1986; Bitar 1986b; and Izquierda Christiana 1986. For the Traditional Left, see *Carta abierta* 1986; Furci 1984; *Izquierda Chilena al país* 1986; Central Committee, Partido Comunista de Chile 1985; *El Siglo* November 1986, February 1984, June 1983, and November 1983; *Movimiento Democrático Popular* 1985; *Cincuenta preguntas al Partido Comunista de Chile*, 1984; *Principios* January–March 1984 and September 1983; Gómez 1986; Corvalán 1983; *Es tiempo de unir y luchar* 1984; and *Venceremos* August 1986.

The major interparty agreements reached in the 1984–86 period and cited in note 5 also emphasized many of these areas of consensus. Finally, the work by the Grupo de Estudios Constitucionales (or Grupo de los 24) supports the argument that these areas of consensus had emerged. The Grupo was formed in 1978 to develop an alternative constitution and institutional model for Chile. Political parties from across the political spectrum participated in the group's activities. See Cumplido 1984.

In addition to the above, the analysis that follows (in this chapter as well as Chapter 7) also draws on a number of more informal discussions with political-party leaders during my stay in Chile over the period 1984–86. It is intentionally schematic and deals only with those aspects of the political parties' learning process that related specifically to party relationships with a new popular social movement.

reformist "Revolution in Liberty" program, which combined agrarian reform with efforts to incorporate the urban poor into the political system, was seen as directly threatening the interests of the political Right. This direct threat reinforced the exclusionary nature of the government and contributed to the alienation of both the Right and Left from the Christian Democratic Party. The DC's growing isolation only contributed to tendencies toward polarization within the political system.

Similarly, a significant critique of the government of Salvador Allende (1970–73) was that it was a minority government that attempted to govern in the interests of just one segment of Chilean society. Not only did Allende take office with a narrow plurality of votes, the policies adopted by the government were explicitly designed to further the interests of one class: the proletariat. A major shortcoming of the regime (especially in the critique of the Renovated Left) was that Allende failed to offer a genuinely national project for Chile after he took office and therefore was unable to build a solid base of support that included the majority of the country.

The military government of Augusto Pinochet was seen as the culmination of this process of rule by and for increasingly smaller minorities. The personalization of the regime by Pinochet and the dramatic changes in Chilean society resulting from the regime's neoliberal project were seen as the almost logical conclusion to trends that had surfaced in Chilean politics in the 1960s.

In order to focus directly on the question of political learning, the political elites were asked what specific lessons they felt their parties had learned over the last twenty years. Their responses are listed in Table 22. Recognition of the need for national consensus and coalition governments, the two most common responses given, came out most clearly among the representatives of the Center. This was not surprising, given the experience of the previous Christian Democratic government. To a large degree, the Christian Democrats felt that they had to convince other opposition parties that they in fact "learned their lesson." This was one of the principal motivations in the formation of the Democratic Alliance in 1983. Christian Democratic plans for a future democratic government included constructing a "grand coalition" that would include parties from the democratic Right to the more moderate parties of the Left. Such a coalition was the cornerstone of the DC's strategy for reconstructing Chile in the post-Pinochet era. According to one of the vice presidents of the DC, the task of building this coalition required "overcoming in a genuinely disinterested way calculations of interest, short term calculations of political costs, patrimonial

Table 22. What are the principal lessons that your party has learned from its experiences over the last twenty years?

	Total	Right	Center	Renovated Left	Traditional Left
The need for unity and a national consensus	5	0	3	1	1
The need for coalition governments	3	0	3	0	0
The need for realistic policies and less ideology	3	0	2	1	0
The importance of participative social organizations	3	0	2	1	0
The need for the real participation of people	2	0	1	0	1
The need to consider the military option	2	0	0	0	2
The value of democracy	2	0	0	2	0
The need to integrate the military into society	1	0	0	1	0
The need for an alliance with the middle classes	1	0	0	0	1
The reactionary nature of the military and judiciary	1	0	0	0	1
The need for roots in the population to survive	1	0	0	0	1
Need to adapt to changing situations	1	0	0	0	1
Need for a modern political organization with a message	1	1	0	0	0
The new right is not the same as the economic right; it has an ideology	1	1	0	0	0
The need to defend human rights	1	0	1	0	0
Parties should serve the people vs. use them	1	0	1	0	0
Need for unity of the Left	1	0	0	1	0
Do not underestimate the Right	1	0	0	1	0
The Socialist Party must regain its autonomy	1	0	0	1	0

egoisms, lesser problems of misunderstood identities and so many other attitudes that belittle the behavior of political actors in the face of such a great challenge" (Martínez 1985, 63).[9]

The Renovated Left also placed great emphasis on the need for building a stable majority behind a "bloc for change." It drew on the experiences of the Allende years in concluding that social change within a democratic regime requires majority support. Moreover, the Renovated Left saw such social change as necessary for a viable democracy in Chile, given the country's unequal and segmented social structure. The pace and specific form of these changes would be defined through the electoral process. The Renovated Left would be pivotal in this process, forming coalitions with both the Christian Democrats and the Traditional Left as the circumstances dictated.

The Right placed less emphasis on the issue of coalitions—in part because it was divided on the issue. For those parties that leaned toward the opposition in pressing for a transition to democracy in 1986, the coalitional strategy was very important. For the pro-government UDI, it was understood that it would not seek any coalitional relations with opposition parties. Instead, it sought to unite the Right in order that the legacy of the military regime could be more effectively protected.[10]

The Traditional Left was ambiguous in its support for unity and coalition governments. This position is hardly surprising, given that the Traditional Left was marked more by continuity with past practices than by change. But as Table 22 shows, one member of the Communist Party felt that his party had learned the importance of unity. Moreover, the parties of the Traditional Left, especially the PC, had consistently called for a united

9. Ironically, the DC's emphasis on building a grand coalition created significant tensions within the Alliance between the DC and other parties, especially the Nuñez branch of the Socialist Party, which itself was a cofounder of the Alliance. The DC viewed the Democratic Alliance as the basis for such a grand coalition in the first democratic government. The PS(N) rejected this view of the Democratic Alliance and insisted that it was only a temporary alliance for opposing the military regime, not a future governing coalition. The PS(N) finally, and somewhat abruptly, withdrew from the Democratic Alliance largely as a result of this difference in late 1986. These differences, however, were largely overcome by 1988.

10. One common element in the Right that related directly to this issue was its emphasis on the need for a future democratic regime to protect the interests of minorities. In both the Frei and Allende periods, the Right, as well as increasingly large segments of society in general, perceived that their fundamental interests were being threatened by government policies. Whatever the mechanism, the Right converged with the opposition in its insistence on the need for truly "national" governments that did not infringe on the interests of any significant segment of society.

opposition and a provisional government to replace the military regime that would represent all democratic parties. This provisional government would then convene a constituent assembly to write a new constitution and hold elections. The ambiguity in the position of the Traditional Left was more the result of their vision of what a post-Pinochet political regime would actually look like (a point that will be addressed in some detail in Chapter 7).

The Need for Greater Party Flexibility and Pragmatism

Most political parties felt that they must become more programmatic, and less ideological, in their orientation. This was seen as necessary for successful party coalitions and greater interparty cooperation. It reflected what the parties viewed as the excessive influence of ideology in Chilean politics prior to 1973, and the role that this played in the demise of Chile's democratic regime. From the perspective of political parties in 1986, political differences by the early 1970s had been reduced to irreconcilable disagreements about what an ideal society should be. Politicians lost sight of what was actually feasible or realistic in Chile and political parties came to see themselves as representing a particular future for Chile that could not be compromised.

Political parties generally concurred that the high ideological content of the proposals they had put forth in the past was an expression of each party's belief that it embodied the best possible future for Chile. This was seen as inevitably leading to a kind of political reductionism, in which the national interest became equated, in the minds of political leaders, with the fate of their own party—that the country could have interests that were above partisan politics or that were not linked to a given party's ideological utopia for Chile was frequently forgotten. As one of the leaders of the Nuñez branch of the Socialist Party pointed out, "many politicians forget that the end for which the party was constituted is the nation and not the party. The party is a means for an end."

According to the political parties, a fundamental change took place in Chilean politics when the ideological Christian Democratic party displaced the more pragmatic Radical Party as the principal expression of the political Center in the 1950s. Seeing itself as representing a "third way" in contrast to the Right and Left, the DC attempted to offer a new model of social relations based on the values of Christian humanism. This model was the basis for Frei's "Revolution in Liberty" and justified the single-party strategy followed by the DC. The ideological content of the DC's project for social change made negotiation and compromise difficult, if not impossible. It contributed to the polarization of Chilean politics, making the ideological content of the Left's own project for society even more destabilizing when Allende came to power in 1970.

This concern for pragmatism and flexibility can be seen in Table 22. More generally, it emerged in the tone of political-party documents and the works of many prominent politicians. For example, the technical aspects of economic and development policies were emphasized. Assurances were given concerning rights to private property. Only more general and less contentious values such as political democracy, respect for basic human rights, and the need to fight poverty were referred to in order to avoid precipitating divisions within the opposition.

This was particularly true in the important interparty agreements reached in 1985 and 1986, such as the National Accord for the Transition to a Full Democracy and the Bases for Sustaining a Democratic Regime: Further Elaboration on the National Accord for the Transition to a full Democracy, which were signed by important parties of the Right, Center, and Renovated Left, and the Chilean Left to the Country: Our Proposal for Opposition Cooperation in the Struggle for Democracy, which was signed by most of the major parties of the Renovated and Traditional Left. Another important example was the Demands of Chile. Although far from realistic in terms of the likelihood that the military government would respond favorably, it was a very pragmatic effort designed to gain the widest amount of support by including the demands of the principal segments of Chilean society.

The emphasis on pragmatism and realism was very strong among the parties of the Right. It coincided with the military regime's deliberate efforts to delegitimize party politics and ideology in favor of technocratic solutions to social problems. Although neoliberalism was closely associated with the Right (as one of the respondents from the Right in Table 22 pointed out), it was an ideology compatible with the emerging area of consensus on political activity since it postulated a very limited realm for politics in society.

Not surprisingly, the Traditional Left was farthest away from this area of consensus. As Table 22 suggests, the Traditional Left may have become even more ideological as a result of the authoritarian experience. This rigidity was implied in the response given by the two representatives of the Communist Party, who referred to the need for the Left to consider the military option. One of the characteristics of the Traditional Left in Chile before the military coup had been the high ideological content of its project, although the Chilean Communist Party was considered to be more moderate and pragmatic than the Socialist Party. The degree and ways in which the Traditional Left had changed in this regard was a major topic of debate and source of division within the opposition. This change will be discussed at some length in Chapter 7, as it relates to the issue of social mobilization and political violence.

Both of these emerging areas of consensus—recognition of the need for coalition governments and more pragmatic policies—could favor the emergence of a popular social movement. The excessive polarization of Chilean politics and the tendency of political parties to put party interests ahead of all else contributed to a stifling of most autonomous organizational activity in Chilean society prior to the coup, as seen in Chapter 2. To the extent that political parties demonstrate a greater openness toward different and even competing points of view, it will be easier for a future social movement to deal with all political parties and resist efforts by any single party to capture such a movement.

If political parties deal with each other constructively at the national level, political divisions may become less important at the local level where the basis for a social movement is found. There may also be less pressure on political parties to capture emerging social movements if politics becomes more conciliatory in nature. The reality of coalitional politics can foster pluralism within social movements because exclusive relations with any single party may no longer suffice for gaining access to governmental resources and policymakers. In sum, there may be greater possibilities for new and diverse types of political relations between parties and civil society that bodes well for the emergence of a new social movement of any sort.

Recognition of the Importance of Autonomous Social Organizations

Perhaps the most significant and clearest area of consensus among political parties was on the general importance of autonomous social movements, particularly autonomous popular organizations. This consensus reflected party analyses of the pre-coup period, which highlighted the relative weakness of civil society that excessive party control over social organizations caused. It also reflected the parties' recognition of the de facto existence of a number of popular organizations that enjoyed a relatively high degree of autonomy from political parties.

Table 22 confirms that for the Center, Renovated Left, and Traditional Left, there was an increased awareness of the importance of social organizations and greater participation in a future democratic regime. Popular organizations would play an important role in increasing both, and all four political tendencies encouraged their further development. As Table 23 demonstrates, nearly all party leaders responded in ways that suggested that political parties valued the roles that such organizations played. Only the representatives of the Right expressed any ambivalence regarding the role played by popular organizations. This reflected their tendency to view such organizations as a source of opposition support.

The political parties of the Center, Renovated Left, and Traditional Left generally believed that a democratic transition would have positive consequences for popular organizations. Moreover, there was a clear consensus on the latter's importance as vehicles for participation in a future democracy (see Table 24). Significantly, social organizations were mentioned twice as often as a mechanism for participating in a democracy than were elections and traditional political institutions such as political parties and Congress. Only one party leader from the UDI felt that participation

Table 23.   What is the attitude of your party toward popular organizations?

	Total	Right	Center	Renovated Left	Traditional Left
Must stimulate organizations	5	0	3	1	1
They are important	4	0	1	2	1
Must respect their autonomy	1	0	0	0	1
Importance for local democracy and participation	1	0	0	0	1
Nonpolitical organizations are good	1	1	0	0	0
Goal is national organization like the labor movement	1	0	0	1	0
They are a de facto reality	1	1	0	0	0
n.a.	1	0	1	0	0

Table 24. How should people participate in a future democracy?

	Total	Right	Center	Renovated Left	Traditional Left
In organizations	10	0	4	3	3
In elections and traditional political institutions	5	0	3	1	1
Only through parties	1	1	0	0	0
At all levels of society	2	1	0	1	0
n.a.	1	0	1	0	0

should be limited to political parties. This emphasis on organization reflected a commonly shared view that political parties had played too dominant a role in the previous democratic regime.

According to the elites interviewed, party strategies with respect to the *poblaciones* emphasized organizing *pobladores*. The two most frequent responses given referred to the strengthening of popular organizations and the mobilization of *pobladores*, and these were given by people from all four tendencies. The parties offered a variety of complementary reasons for the importance of promoting popular organizations. One reason was that Chilean society had changed and the existence of popular organizations made it difficult for political parties to return to the same kinds of relationships that they had had with the popular sectors prior to the coup. One of the two leaders interviewed from the Nuñez branch of the Socialist Party (which was associated with the Renovated Left) expressed what many politicians had come to believe by suggesting that "democracy cannot be exhausted in an electoral exercise every so often. There has to be a rich social fabric of organizations." The much younger representative from the Almeyda branch of the Socialist Party (which was part of the Traditional Left) made this contrast with past practices clearer when he argued that "there will be no return to the electoral relationship [which predominated prior to the military coup], never. For example, I never voted in a political election and I am a high-level official. We either continue as we are [under the dictatorship] or we have a participative society, one that worries about hunger, etc."

Opposition political parties recognized that participation was especially important in Chile, given the scarcity of resources. As one writer representing the Renovated Left explained: "Paradoxically, to not contemplate the existing participative potential is . . . to limit the viability of an alternative democratic proposal in this country that, as we know, must reconstruct itself with severe restrictions and dramatic situations of life for an immense popular majority. Participation is, in our conception, not only the expression of real democracy, but, fundamentally, a necessary condition for making it possible" (Ortíz 1985, 185). One of the Christian Left leaders who was interviewed continued: "In countries with poor economies and a lot of economic and political concentration, the only way for progress is through an increase in mechanisms for participation—participatory democracy. Systems of decentralized power must be structured for specific themes, from the national level on down."

Popular organizations were viewed as being integral to creating this participatory society, in part, because of the need to overcome the authoritarian legacy. The leader of the Christian Left quoted above explained why: "The process of the dictatorship is a process of the degradation of social organizations and crushing of individuals. The only way to fight this is through collective organization, reunion, common sense, a sense of being part of a whole. This will lead to the recuperation of a lot of force [and] self-respect. This is very important for democracy. The long dictatorship has changed the [national] psyche. People feel very incapable, weak, impotent. That they do not have power for creation, for participation."

For many, popular organizations offered a mechanism for increasing the efficiency with which resources were used by channeling them directly toward specific problems at the local level. Interestingly, the Christian Democratic Party and the Nuñez branch of the Socialist Party often emphasized the important role that popular organizations played in augmenting national savings, promoting local economic development, and resolving chronic unemployment problems in the *poblaciones*.[11]

More important perhaps, popular organizations were seen as a source of strength for a future democratic regime. The relationship between popular organizations and a viable democratic regime tended to be viewed in two distinct ways by political party leaders. For many in the Christian Democratic Party, the tendency was to focus on popular organizations as a mechanism for ensuring democratic stability. Because of their sheer size, the popular sectors were seen as a potential threat to the democratic regime. It was feared that parties of the Left would contribute to their radicalization by playing upon the immensity of the popular sectors' problems. By

11. See Foxley 1987; *Proyecto Alternativo* 1984, vol. 1; and Secretaría Técnica, Comisión de Municipalización 1984 for the Christian Democrats. For the PS(N), see Nuñez 1986a and Drago 1986.

resolving the conflicts associated with the marginal sectors at the local level (rather than through politics at the national level) and by integrating the poor into the democratic system, many hoped to defuse these problems before they became destabilizing (Martínez 1985). But for this integration to be successful, it would have to allow the popular sectors to express and defend their own interests. Alejandro Foxley, an influential policymaker within the DC, explained:

> The impatience because of the accumulated deficits and the years of abandonment can only be regulated through the organized participation of the *pobladores* in the solution of these problems: through an adequate appreciation of their ideas, for their work; through their effective incorporation in public mechanisms which must deal with the solutions and, above all, through an appeal to their own responsibility for confronting, with their efforts, their future. This is possible if they are organized as part of a national task which is respectful of the *pobladores* and their necessities [so that they are] not made instruments for sectarian political projects. (Foxley 1987, 217)

Both the Renovated and Traditional Left placed a greater emphasis on strengthening civil society in order to resist future authoritarian impositions. Popular organizations were part of the necessary task of "democratizing society in the face of the [authoritarian] system to make it more difficult for the dictator to succeed," according to one of the leaders of the Socialist Party's Nuñez branch. The young leader of the Almeyda Socialists echoed the opinion of many when he stated that "if there had been real participation by the people, there would have been no military coup." Finally, one of the Communist Party leaders interviewed added: "If democracy is not made effectively participative so that it is lived day by day and not only when there are elections, it will be very weak and cannot resist fascist coups. It is indispensable for assuring a sufficiently healthy climate. The people must understand that they are governing themselves."

If popular organizations were to fill these roles, however, the political parties agreed that they would have to enjoy a higher level of autonomy from parties than such organizations had enjoyed in the past. This was very clear in the interviewees' responses listed in Table 25, even though there appeared to be considerable disagreement as to whether popular organiza-

Table 25.   Are popular organizations autonomous?

	Total	Right	Center	Renovated Left	Traditional Left
Yes	2	0	0	1	1
At the base level only	1	0	0	1	0
The most representative only	1	0	0	0	1
Autonomy is incomplete	3	0	1	2	0
There is little or no autonomy	4	1	2	0	1
n.a.	3	1	2	0	0
Is autonomy important?					
Yes	12	2	3	4	3
No	0	0	0	0	0
n.a.	2	0	2	0	0

tions were currently autonomous.[12] The political elites interviewed were unanimous in insisting on the need to maintain popular organization autonomy. One of the leaders of the Nuñez Socialists explained:

> A positive fact in the world of the *poblaciones* is that they have their own organizations. The party wants to respect the autonomy of the world of the *poblaciones*, accept the organizations that they create. . . . This is a lesson from the past. Politicians tended to penetrate everything. The party does not want to impose its reality on the world of the *poblaciones*. It privileges their own reality. . . . There should be reciprocity [in the relations between political parties and popular organizations]: the political party has a policy toward the world of the *poblaciones* and the popular organizations have to be capable of influencing the leaderships of political parties.

The problem of organizational autonomy was fundamentally one of respecting pluralism within popular-sector organizations. The popular sectors were heterogeneous and no single party could hope to claim hegemony over them. Efforts by political parties to control popular organizations only led to the manipulation of the organizations. As one of the leaders of the Christian Left explained,

---

12. This disagreement and its causes will be discussed in some detail in Chapter 7 as one factor contributing to the emergence of tensions between political parties and popular organizations.

[Pluralism] allows for the expression of everyone. If the organization is not pluralist, it becomes a space for political parties to maneuver— [popular organizations] are more clients than protagonists. . . . [T]he reality is that the world of the *poblaciones* is diverse. . . . It is not a homogeneous world.

Pluralism was deemed essential if the popular sectors were to maximize their ability to influence the political system. Respondents were again unanimous in agreeing that popular organizations should be pluralist, even if they currently were not. When popular organizations are not pluralist, according to the leader of the Almeyda Socialists who was interviewed, "they are restricted. This decreases their power to generate change, to pressure." A leader of the Christian Democratic Party added that "the problems which *pobladores* experience affect everyone equally. [Their organizations] are more efficient and forceful in making demands if they are pluralist. Ideology becomes less relevant. It loses its force because ideologies are already made compatible in the organization. When the organization is not pluralist, politics is more important than the problems."

Finally, the interviews suggested that political parties were favorably disposed toward efforts to create intermediate organizations of *pobladores*, as shown in Table 26. Important disagreements revolved around percep-tions of which political parties or tendencies would be most favored by the creation of such intermediate organizations. The Left generally favored the

Table 26. What is your opinion about efforts to create organizations such as the Unitary Command for Pobladores, which claims to be a legitimate representative of the marginal sectors?

	Total	Right	Center	Renovated Left	Traditional Left
Must be unitary and created by the *pobladores*	3	0	0	1	2
Should be more than one and created by the *pobladores*	2	0	2	0	0
Must be democratic	3	0	1	2	0
Party's goal is the creation of such an organization	1	0	0	1	0
Opposed because the PC will always control	2	1	1	0	0
Must be apolitical	1	1	0	0	0
n.a.	2	0	1	0	1

formation of a single intermediate organization for the popular sectors that would be more or less analogous to the experience of the Chilean labor movement prior to the military coup. The Center and Right, however, were much more concerned that a single intermediate organization representing *pobladores* would be dominated by the Left, and in particular by the Communist Party. Leaders from these tendencies either insisted that there be multiple intermediate organizations representing the popular sectors, allowing for the presence of various parties and tendencies, or rejected such efforts entirely because they saw Communist control over them as inevitable.

This fear that the Left would dominate popular organizations was especially strong among the Right, who insisted that popular organizations be apolitical. In practice, this would necessarily result in organizations that either did not admit party militants; or, as is more likely, did not discriminate on the basis of party militancy but instead insisted on a clear separation between partisan politics and the activities of the organizations. In both cases, the Right insisted on the autonomy of popular organizations from political parties.

The above views concerning political activity and styles of political behavior suggest that political parties viewed such popular social movements more or less favorably and that they would not deliberately seek to undermine efforts to create such a movement. Going beyond the professed changes in how political parties viewed popular organizations, parties must also be willing to create the necessary institutional space for autonomous popular organizations to continue developing.

THE INSTITUTIONAL SPACE FOR POPULAR ORGANIZATIONS

The existence of institutional space for the emergence of a popular social movement (as discussed in Chapter 1) involves both the decentralization of state power and the democratization of internal political-party structures. Decentralization of state power is essential for reinforcing a popular social movement at the base level. It would allow popular organizations to represent the popular sectors before local authorities with the capacity to respond effectively to popular demands. In Chile in 1986, this "space" referred to the likely shape that a future democratic regime would take. Internal party democracy, however, is equally relevant to the emergence of a popular social movement. It allows for the reciprocal kinds of relations between parties and popular movements discussed above, and it is an essential safeguard against political parties' seeking to undermine efforts to create a popular movement.

The Chilean political parties' commitment to both the decentralization of state power and internal democracy indicated the degree to which changed perceptions were likely to influence actual party policy proposals and behavior. Moreover, if the state were to be effectively decentralized, or if political parties created truly democratic and participatory structures, the resultant institutional space might contribute to the emergence of a popular movement regardless of the explicit goals of party elites.

Decentralization of the State

One of the most unique features of the Chilean military regime from a comparative perspective was its commitment to decentralizing the state by delegating administrative and decision-making authority to the regional and local levels, a commitment that dated back to as early as 1974. Local municipal governments, in particular, were strengthened through the transfer of key programs such as health care and education to their jurisdictions by the national government (Morales, Pozo, and Rojas 1988).

The military had several motives for attempting to decentralize state authority. One was purely strategic: the overcentralized Chilean state was too easy and tempting a target for the Chilean Left. By winning only the presidency, a Marxist government had gained immense control over the Chilean economy and society through power that was concentrated in the executive branch. Decentralization was viewed as one more barrier to future attempts by the Left to impose a totalitarian regime because it would make the task of "taking power" that much more difficult: there would be simply too many levels to control and each lower level could, in turn, resist such efforts by the Left at the national level.

A second motive was much more tactical in nature and related to the implementation of decentralization. Mayors and local officials were appointed by Pinochet and their behavior was closely controlled. Local governments were used as a means for increasing the capacity of the military regime to repress opposition at the grassroots level. It also served as a conduit for dispersing patronage and establishing patron-client relations through the disbursement of social welfare benefits.[13]

Despite these abuses, opposition political parties in 1986 generally viewed the military government's decentralization programs as the only changes introduced by the military regime that were "salvageable" for a future democratic regime, albeit with important modifications.[14] Opposition political parties, for the most part, concurred with the military government's assessment of the state as being excessively centralized[15] and offered proposals for its decentralization. Such proposals generally involved democratizing the military regime's own efforts at decentralization. They also attempted to ensure that power would be effectively transferred to local and regional levels of government by widening the decision-making powers of local authorities and providing sufficient fiscal resources to provide greater independence from the central government.[16]

Ironically, opposition parties agreed with the military regime's strategic assessment that an overcentralized state was vulnerable to extremist efforts to seize control. Rather than constraining a future Marxist regime from implementing programs for social change, however, much of the opposition saw decentralization as the key to preventing future military coups. One of the leaders of the Nuñez branch of the Socialist Party explained the dominant opposition view: "The municipalities are central to a very strong and solid democratic structure for the participation of the popular sectors. This will provide a guarantee for future democratic stability by providing for greater distribution of power. This will make a coup more difficult. [The concentration of power] was a great political error of the Popular Unity [government]." More generally, the parties envisioned that stronger local levels of government would allow for greater citizen participation and a stronger civil society that could resist totalitarian impulses at the national level of government from either the Right or the Left. Decentralization "is a real form of participation and for limiting the possibilities of an omnipotent state," according to Andres Zaldivar, a prominent Christian Democrat (Zaldivar 1986, 4).

Many in the opposition, especially those associated with the Center ten-

13. Pinochet would later use the mayors whom he appointed to rally support for the regime and in preparation for his candidacy for president in the October 1988 plebiscite.

14. This very limited acceptance of changes introduced by the military government would change dramatically as the date for the 1988 plebiscite approached. See Chapter 8.

15. For example, in the interviews, only two respondents from the Renovated Left disagreed.

16. For example, see Secretaría Técnica, Comisión de Municipalización 1984; *Proyecto Alternativo*, vols. 1–2, 1984; Foxley 1987; Nuñez 1986a; Drago 1986; and Cumplido 1984.

dency, also viewed decentralization of the state as necessary for ensuring democratic stability. In an argument reminiscent of the work of Samuel Huntington (1968), institutions that could channel political conflict and neutralize it before it became threatening to the political system's stability were seen as necessary to safeguard a new democratic regime. In this view, local government acted as an institutional mechanism to isolate conflict at a level where consensus could be reached more easily, or at least contained without threatening to polarize the entire political system (Martínez 1985; Foxley 1987; and Zaldivar 1986). A similar line of reasoning had a strong echo in the thinking of the Right. This was apparent in comments made by the representative from the pro-government UDI, who also expressed views on participation very similar to those discussed above by representatives from the opposition: "The state must decrease the level of concentration [of power] and decentralize. It must open areas for participation in city government. . . . There must be the ability to decide priorities and the way in which people will participate. They must at least feel that their demands are being considered. . . . This will create consensus on priorities. Not everyone can be satisfied. Participation is a mechanism for self-discipline in society."

Decentralization at the local level was also seen as a means to encourage Chile's economic development and overcome the economic crisis confronting Chile in the mid-1980s. Local and regional government were to play a role in directing economic planning to best meet the particular needs and resources of their jurisdictions (Secretaría Técnica, Comisión de Municipalización 1984; Foxley 1987; and Martínez 1985). Similarly, the efficiency of local levels of government for allocating scarce resources was an excellent argument for decentralization. One of the leaders of the Christian Left who was interviewed expressed this most clearly: "Decentralized methods for managing the decisions and resources of the state mean that those who are affected must participate in the determination of programs and the assignation of resources. This leads to a better utilization of resources. The history of Chile is proof that this is optimal and leads to greater inclusiveness [in government programs]. Examples are the coordination of state actions with local government in the areas of health care and education."

The Democratization and Decentralization of Political Parties

The space available for the emergence of a popular social movement may be severely circumscribed by the relationship between popular organizations and political parties. Democratization and decentralization of political parties is very important in this regard. The effective participation of a party's grassroots membership, particularly members from *poblaciones*, in its decision-making processes can ease the tension between popular organizations and political parties by minimizing fears of party manipulation. It can also help ensure that political parties are more representative of the ideals associated with the emergent popular collective identity.

The political leaders who were interviewed generally agreed that Chilean political parties had been too centralized and hierarchical in the past, with the notable exception of the PC.[17] Similarly, they tended to believe that their parties were working (within the limits imposed by political repression) to correct this problem through greater internal democracy and the decentralization of party decision-making structures. Most of those interviewed felt that their parties were now democratic or becoming more democratic than they had been in 1973, although the representatives of the Traditional Left and one person associated with the Renovated Left felt that clandestineness made their parties less democratic than before the military coup.

Given the ambiguity caused by the illegality of all political parties in Chile in 1986, a more revealing indication of the commitment of political parties to internal democracy and the decentralization of party structures is the ideal conception that the politicians had of political parties. There was an overwhelming consensus on the importance of democratic and participatory political parties. Significantly, one leader each from the Right, Center, and Renovated Left saw the highly participatory, open, and decentralized political parties of the United States as an ideal model for what political parties should be. Again, the exception was the PC, which still clung to the Leninist tradition of democratic centralism. Moreover, this issue of party democracy was prominent in many party documents and the writings by prominent politicians.

The reasoning behind the emergence of this consensus revolved around two related factors. The first was a reevaluation of the importance of political democracy as an end in itself. The rediscovery of the importance of political democracy by most opposition parties led to a reevaluation of past political practices that were clearly not democratic. Political parties were more conscious of being consistent in their belief in democratic practices. A prominent Christian Democrat made this quite explicit: "A

17. Both representatives of the PC emphasized that their party was structured according to the principle of "democratic centralism."

primary responsibility falls on the parties, who must transform themselves into the agents of this renovated democratic political culture. . . . If the content of the democratic message is the necessity of cooperation, of unity, of tolerance and mutual respect, of agreement and responsible participation by the people, the symbols and testimonies that the parties present cannot be contradictory with this message." In order to avoid polarization and the possibilities of future military coups, political parties agreed that they must recognize social diversity rather than attempt to ignore it. The democratization of political parties was seen as contributing to this by recognizing social diversity within the party itself (Garretón 1987c).

Two exceptions to this general consensus deserve highlighting. The first was the importance of "democratic centralism" to the Traditional Left, principally the PC. Both representatives of the Communist Party emphasized the importance of maintaining discipline among militants. They suggested that major decisions were reached through debate involving all levels of the party, even though the final decisions were always taken by the party's Central Committee. As an ideal, they emphasized that the democratic legitimacy of the process was predominantly an internal matter that justified the censuring of individuals who chose to carry on this participatory process in a more public light. While there was clearly a strong hierarchical tendency in the PC (due to its Marxist-Leninist heritage), the authoritarian nature of the party tended to be reinforced by the necessities imposed on it by political repression.[18] The Almeyda branch of the Socialist Party, however, took a very different position by explicitly promoting democratic party structures. As the representative of the Almeyda Socialists explained, in a "normal" situation, "democracy must be the priority over efficiency [in the party]. There must be a maximum level of democracy, without disregarding minimum levels of centralization and efficiency. We always believe that everyone can get his two cents' worth in."

The second exception was the UDI. As the person who was interviewed made clear, the party never should cede excessive authority to the party's general membership. The most capable should control party decision-making, a position consistent with the party's technocratic approach to politics in general.

---

18. As will be discussed in Chapter 8, this issue became an important source of division within the PC after the transition. It contributed to an internal crisis in the early 1990s that threatened the party's very existence.

CONCLUSION

Political-party perceptions of the Chilean political process were affected by prolonged military rule in ways that suggest a propitious environment for the continued development of popular-sector organizational activity. Parties from across the political spectrum expressed a commitment to addressing the needs of the poor, while affirming the importance of pluralism, political pragmatism, and autonomous social organizations. In terms of the model of relations between political parties and base-level actors developed in Chapter 1, the findings presented here suggest that political parties favored a relationship with popular organizations in which they were considered potential allies. There was an explicit and consistent rejection of patron-client relations, as well as recognition that popular organizations should maintain their autonomy rather than be sponsored by political parties. There was little indication that political parties saw popular organizations as competing with them for the allegiance of the popular sectors.

Moreover, political parties favored institutional changes that would reinforce this mutually supportive relationship between political parties and popular organizations, providing space for the emergence of a new popular social movement. There was a general recognition of the need to continue with the military regime's project for decentralizing the state, particularly through the democratization of lower levels of government. Similarly, there appeared to be a genuine commitment to decentralizing and democratizing political-party structures. Both would help disperse power within the political system in ways consistent with the ideals associated with *lo popular*. These changes promised to open up unprecedented opportunities for popular-sector influence in the Chilean political system.

We see thus a convergence between political-party and popular-sector outlooks. As discussed in Chapter 5, many leaders of popular organizations held views consistent with *lo popular* that paralleled the dominant views of the political elite. Both groups envisioned a positive role for popular organizations and a possible popular social movement in Chilean politics. Such a role was not mutually exclusive with strong political parties, but suggested a more equal relationship between the two. Political parties and popular organizations had their respective roles to play within the political process, and these roles suggested that they would be periodic allies working toward similar goals.

Yet, despite these trends within the political-party system, the actual relationship between popular organizations and political parties has tended to be fairly antagonistic. Political parties, in particular, have often viewed autonomous popular organizations as potential competitors. This was most clear in the parties' reaction to various attempts by the leaders of popular organizations to construct a new social movement between 1986 and 1988. Political-party opposition caused such efforts to have only very limited success, with the ultimate result being the effective demobilization of the popular sectors as a political actor under the current democratic regime. To understand how this happened, in Chapters 7 and 8, we shall look at the specific obstacles to greater levels of self-constituted and autonomous collective action on the part of the popular sectors.

7

THE DILEMMAS OF
COLLECTIVE ACTION

"Old" and "New" Political Actors
Under an Authoritarian Regime

The centrality of an emerging popular collective identity, *lo popular*, in popular-sector organizational activity during the military regime showed, at the very least, the possibility that the popular sectors would be able to engage in self-generated collective action on the basis of this collective identity. Such collective action could, ultimately, lead to the emergence of a popular social movement that sought to transform society according to the value commitments and ideals embodied in the popular collective identity. Moreover, as shown in Chapter 6, there was considerable potential for a positive relationship to emerge between political parties and popular organizations that could help provide the necessary political space for the emergence of such a popular social movement.

These apparently favorable circumstances belied important constraints on the continued development of popular-sector organizational activity in Chile. These constraints varied in relative importance according to the changing political context and included the increasingly central role political parties were assuming in Chile's political process. Further constraints reflected the opposition's difficulties in securing a transition to democracy in the face of the military regime's intransigence, as well as the way in which popular-sector organizational activity itself had been conditioned by

the military regime's repressive environment. As a result of these constraints, collective action by *pobladores* beyond the level of individual
community-based groups was increasingly limited from 1986 on. Ultimately, they led to the political demobilization of the popular sectors under
the present democratic regime.

In this chapter I shall look specifically at efforts of self-constituted
collective action on the part of popular-sector organizations under the
authoritarian regime. I shall argue that strong impulses for such collective
action were present and resulted in important attempts to construct a
popular social movement. Such efforts were nevertheless undermined by
the attempts of political parties to capture any incipient social movement
formed by popular-sector organizations. I shall then, in Chapter 8, examine
how the dynamics of the transition exacerbated constraints on popular-
sector organizational activity, contributing to the almost complete political
marginalization of the popular sectors as a collective actor.

Under the military regime, self-constituted collective action by the popular sectors involved overcoming the atomization and fragmentation of
popular organizations caused by political repression. Efforts to coordinate
activities among popular organizations, even within the same *población*,
were relatively visible by their very nature, and consequently more vulnerable to the government's security apparatus than were activities limited to
an isolated organization. This was particularly true given the military
regime's explicit efforts to disarticulate all forms of collective behavior
within Chilean society that could not be controlled or were inconsistent
with a neoliberal model of society.

The atomization of popular-sector organizational activity may also have
been a reflection of the very nature of the popular collective identity itself.
The values and ideals embodied in *lo popular* were integrally related to the
community bonds associated with the concept of *vecino* and the territorially
circumscribed nature of popular organizations. The ability of popular
organizations to go beyond the narrow communities on which they were
based was problematic at best, and still remains an important empirical
question. Ironically, the exclusionary and repressive nature of the military
regime may have facilitated popular-sector organizational activity that went
beyond the community level. The lack of alternatives and the presence of a
clear, unambiguous "enemy" helped popular-sector leaders overcome the
territorial limitations of popular organizations as part of the struggle
against the dictatorship—a point to which I shall return in Chapter 8.

The evidence presented below, however, suggests that political parties were the principal obstacle to self-constituted collective action by the popular sectors under the military regime. As shown in Chapter 2, a dominant characteristic of the Chilean political system during the democratic period had been the centrality of political parties, an important factor in the breakdown of Chilean democracy in the early 1970s. Similarly, it should be recalled that in the mid-1980s, after nearly ten years of complete recess, political parties reemerged as major political actors in opposition to the military government. Both of these factors—the centrality of political parties prior to 1973 and their reemergence as political actors in 1983— were key to understanding the uneasy relationship that evolved between popular-sector organizations and political parties during the military regime. Political parties needed to reestablish their identities and ties to social bases in a society that was markedly different from the one they had known prior to the military coup. The exigencies of this task often created tensions between the immediate interests of political parties and those of an emergent popular social movement.

This chapter is divided into three sections. In the first section I examine some of the sources of tension in the relations between the political parties and popular organizations under the military regime. I shall argue that these tensions were the result of how political parties viewed both the problems of the popular sectors and of party identity under authoritarian rule. Some of the consequences of these tensions are then explored, including the progressive marginalization of the popular sectors within the opposition, which was closely tied to the debate among opposition parties over the relationship between social mobilization and political violence. Finally, a case study of the 1986 Unitary Congress of Pobladores highlights how political parties effectively stifled the emergence of an incipient popular movement through political party infighting for control over the movement.

SOURCES OF TENSION IN PARTY RELATIONS WITH POPULAR ORGANIZATIONS

Despite the discourse of political parties and their proposals for a future democratic regime, the relations between the political parties and popular organizations were marked by tension under the military regime. This tension had two principal sources. The first related to how political parties understood the problems associated with the popular sectors. Rather than defining these in terms of the need to integrate the popular sectors into the political system (as emphasized in *lo popular*), political parties focused on the working class in general, and on organized labor in particular. Their policies often represented an explicit effort to help the popular sectors because they were viewed as the "victims" of the authoritarian regime's economic model and a potential threat to future democratic stability. The second source of tension was the need of political parties to reinforce their political identities after nearly thirteen years during which normal processes for measuring their representativity were repressed.

Political-Party Approaches to the Problems of the Popular Sectors

The members of popular organizations generally understood the problems of the urban poor in ways that frequently clashed with the approach of political parties to these same problems. Moreover, this clash of perspectives highlighted a significant shortcoming in the policy formulations of the major political parties: a marked lack of attention to the mechanisms that could actually incorporate the popular sectors into the political process.

Political parties generally considered organized labor to be the principal representative of the popular sectors (Baño 1985; Pozo 1986). The Chilean political class was unwilling and/or unable to adapt itself to a changing social reality in which organized labor, and the traditional "working class" (or proletariat) as a whole, were much less important than in the past. Parties also tended to treat the *pobladores* with reticence because they could not completely control them and because *pobladores* could produce unpredictable changes in the political system (Pozo 1986). Party elites were accustomed to working with organized labor, which had traditionally been an important social actor in Chile with a long history of successful relations with political parties (Angell 1972). Moreover, many labor leaders were party militants. Through them, political parties were able to assert an active presence in the labor movement after a prolonged period in which most traditional political-party activity effectively came to a halt (Campero and Cortázar 1985). In the absence of elections or other objective measures of political-party strength, union elections became an important arena for interparty competition.

It is hardly surprising to find this bias among the parties of the Traditional Left, especially the Communist Party, since it is consistent with an orthodox interpretation of Marxist theory. *Pobladores* were considered to be a "semi-proletariat" (Central Committee, Partido Comunista de Chile 1985), or, according to one of the members of the PC who was interviewed, the "ejected working class." There was a high level of Communist Party presence in the *poblaciones*, but this was due in part to the blacklisting of former Communist labor leaders who, unable to work, turned to organizing in the shantytowns (Oxhorn 1988 and 1986). It also reflected the active role that the *pobladores* had assumed in social mobilizations since 1983. In a certain sense, members of popular-sector organizations had "earned" the attention of the Communist Party. As one of the PC members explained,

> It is the workers' movement, the organized class, that has had a principal role [for the Communist Party], but the *población* or marginal sectors have demonstrated in practice a capacity for struggle, for organizing themselves in order to satisfy their demands, and for representing party ideologies in these organizations. They have become class organizations rather than just organizations seeking the satisfaction of immediate demands. They recognize the national problem. . . . It is not that the *pobladores* are the vanguard class, but they have played and will continue playing an important role.

The other member of the PC who was interviewed noted the "inconvenience" of having to work with *pobladores* in the *poblaciones* because "the mixture of ideologies, etc. [in the *poblaciones*] leads to multiple phenomena that make the *población* struggle less efficient than what the industrial struggle could be." In *Principios*, the official journal of the Communist Party, the party recognized that the

> activity in the *poblaciones* has helped a great deal, but it cannot replace what belongs to the working class as such. Resolving the matter of the presence and strength of the Chilean labor movement [in the protests] is of the greatest urgency. . . . The class organizations must assume their role of vanguard and play the role of orientation and struggle that they have adopted historically. (*Principios* September 1983, 67–68)

Finally, the Central Committee of the Communist Party made it quite clear that in deepening and amplifying the struggle, the most important role must be played by the working class and we must make greater efforts to incorporate the other stratums and classes of the population around them . . . [such as] the semi-proletariat sectors. (Central Committee, Partido Comunista de Chile 1985, 11)

It was somewhat more surprising, however, to find a similar attitude in the Center. As argued in Chapter 2, the Christian Democrats had much to do with organizing the popular sectors in the 1960s as part of the Frei Government's "Revolution in Liberty." The DC's ability after 1973 to improve its strength in the labor movement relative to the Left may have been one factor explaining this bias (Campero and Cortázar 1985). The Christian Democrats stressed the importance of tripartite negotiations among organized labor, employer groups, and the state to overcome the economic crisis and rebuild Chile's economy (See *Proyecto Alternativo* 1984, vols. 1–3; 1984, Foxley 1987; Boeninger 1984a).[1] Parallels were drawn with the successful operation of similar kinds of corporatist arrangements in Western Europe, especially in the immediate postwar reconstruction period.

Pobladores, on the other hand, were typically viewed as the principal "victims" of the authoritarian regime (Baño 1985), as the disadvantaged masses. They were not seen as an actual or potential social actor like the working class. Their organizational activities, especially in the protests, were viewed more as spontaneous reactions than the beginnings of something more permanent and proactive. Society, therefore, had a moral obligation to help the poor.[2] This moral obligation also stemmed from the Catholic Church hierarchy's "option for the poor." Both the Christian Democrats and the Christian Left segment of the Renovated Left expressed this moral concern.

At the core of this bias in the Center was the Christian Democrats' preoccupation with the threat that marginal sectors posed to future democratic stability. As Alejandro Foxley explained, an important explanation for the ability of the military regime to maintain itself in power for so long

1. Tripartite negotiations became a core element in the Aylwin government's economic policies, and actually began shortly after it took office. The importance of this for workers, however, has been relatively limited. See Epstein 1992.

2. The similarities between the position expressed by the DC in the mid-1980s and the basic tenets of the theory of marginality that guided DC policies in the 1960s during the Frei government (Chapter 2) should be noted.

was the "diffuse but real fear of the masses which [had] been impoverished as a consequence of the regime's own policies" (Foxley 1987, 32). Throughout the interviews of Christian Democratic leaders, there were indications of this fear that the extreme poverty of the poor would lead to their political radicalization. This is one reason why, when asked about their greatest preoccupation for the post-Pinochet period, by far the most common response expressed a concern for the stability of any democratic regime.[3]

Party perceptions of the principal demands of the popular sectors were revealing in this regard, as shown in Table 27. First on the list of demands, according to the political leaders interviewed, was the demand for jobs, followed by a series of other demands for an improved quality of life. This coincided quite closely with the principal demands expressed by the *pobladores* themselves (see Table 14). What was lacking in the perspective of the political Center, however, was any appreciation of factors that might moderate the demands of the popular sectors, such as their desire for

Table 27. What are the principal demands of the *pobladores?*

	Total	Right	Center	Renovated Left	Traditional Left
Employment (Number indicating it is their primary	12	2	5	3	2
demand)	9	2	4	2	1
Education	9	0	4	2	3
Health care	8	0	3	3	2
Housing	7	0	1	3	3
Participation, freedom to organize	6	0	2	2	2
Recreation	4	0	1	0	3
Public order, security	4	1	1	2	0
Freedom	2	0	1	0	1
Food	2	0	0	1	1
Democracy	2	0	2	0	0
To vote	1	0	0	0	1
Respect	1	1	0	0	0
Respect for human rights	1	0	1	0	0
Satisfaction of basic needs	1	0	1	0	0
Urban services	1	0	0	1	0

3. As will be seen in Chapter 8, these fears proved largely unfounded once Aylwin assumed office. But they shaped the DC's policies toward the popular sectors during the military regime and continued to be influential in the first democratic government.

effective participation and their relatively low expectations. Instead, many politicians in the DC emphasized the dangers posed by the inability of a democracy to allow for rapid economic recovery (Martínez 1985). The then general secretary of the Christian Democratic Party, Eugenio Ortega, warned in 1985:

> Not only has the maintenance of life lost meaning [under the authoritarian regime], but so has the quality of life in the marginal world. The level of future social conflicts could be marked by the extension of this problem, transformed into hopelessness in vast national sectors, especially among the young. They have lived not only without opportunities, but have suffered a devaluing of their dignity and of their personal development. Up until now no one can imagine the levels of aggressiveness that can be growing in the popular world experiencing such a long process of objective oppression. Its current lack of expression in the face of the fear of the [government's] power does not indicate that it does not exist. It can only indicate its expected emergence in conditions of freedom.

An interview of one of the Christian Democratic Party leaders highlighted the dilemmas and problems the DC feared a future democracy would face with regard to the popular sectors:

> There is no capacity to solve all of the problems generated in thirteen years—the extreme poverty, historic levels of unemployment. Priorities must therefore be set and this will create tensions with those [whose demands] are postponed. There is a tension between the moral obligation to the poor and the labor movement, which has power to pressure because it is well organized. The key is how to incorporate both groups without affecting [the regime's] stability. The solution requires political engineering: there must be a balance between the pressures of the labor movement, the needs of the *pobladores* and other needs. . . . It is a process full of conflicts in which the least bad solution must be sought.

Just how the popular sectors might fare in this balancing process was not at all clear in 1986. The same DC leader pointed out that the popular sectors had no power to mobilize pressure:

The dictator did not allow it in the construction of organizations [in the *poblaciones*]. They will need one or two years [after a transition] to achieve this. The power of the *pobladores* is moral and the obviousness of the problem. . . . The first year or two is the time to implement policies that will allow for their integration and convert them into factors for stability rather than instability. This is the ideal, but studies show that it is difficult to have stability with a sector of poverty.

The position of the Renovated Left was somewhat more ambiguous. For this tendency, a popular social movement based in the *poblaciones* could have equal or greater importance compared to the labor movement. Yet little interest was expressed in developing a level of politicization in the *poblaciones* that would have allowed *pobladores* to build a popular social movement with a national presence (Baño 1985). The preference for viewing *pobladores* as victims within the Christian Left has already been noted, and other segments of the Renovated Left assumed a similar position through their association with the Christian Democratic Party in the Democratic Alliance opposition bloc (Espinoza 1986).

On the other hand, there was still a certain amount of ideological inertia within this tendency that was reminiscent of the Traditional Left. For example, one theorist of the Renovated Left argued that the working class would occupy the central position in defining a future alternative hegemonic power bloc formed by a variety of political parties with different ideological outlooks (Ottone 1986). Another example was provided in an interview with a Nuñez Socialist who explained how his party "defined itself as a party of the working class broadly defined, of which the marginal sectors are a part."

This bias in favor of the working class and traditional working-class organizations generated tensions between political parties and popular organizations in several ways. First, it clashed directly with important elements of the emerging popular collective identity. The members of popular-sector organizations tended to identify more closely with the idea of a "poor" or "lower" class than with the working class (see Table 16), thus reinforcing the perception of the political class as distant and nonrepresentative of the popular sectors.

A bias in favor of the labor movement also clashed directly with the demands of members of popular organizations for respect and integration into the political system. Political parties showed little or no interest in helping the popular sectors create a genuine popular social movement. Instead, parties of the Traditional Left and some elements of the Renovated Left viewed popular organizations as an alternative to a temporarily weakened labor movement. This view led to a sense of being used to further interests that may or may not have coincided with those of the popular sectors as a whole, with little regard for what the popular sectors might actually have been seeking.

The moralism expressed by the Center, as well as some elements of the Renovated Left, painted a portrait of the poor as "victims" and contained a strong element of paternalism that clashed with the core ideals of *lo popular*. In particular, it denied the members of popular organizations the respect they sought, and generated suspicion and fear of manipulation through dependence. These problems were further compounded by a focus on stability, which implied control and subordination of the popular sectors as a potential social actor.

As shown in Chapter 2, the problems of extreme social inequity were structural in nature and had no easy or rapid solutions. These structural changes in the Chilean economy and society created a situation in which organized labor was both weak and unrepresentative of large portions of the popular sectors. Union membership in 1987 was just 10.5 percent of the labor force (Angell 1989), and high levels of unemployment still made effective collective action by workers much more difficult. This reality would suggest that tripartite negotiations, while still very important, were insufficient. Even if the extreme imbalance between organized labor and employers could somehow be lessened through institutional mechanisms and political guarantees,[4] tripartite agreements would cover only a limited portion of the labor market, 30 to 40 percent of which was in the informal sector of the economy (Lagos 1985a).

Problems of Party Identities under an Authoritarian Regime

Political repression and the absence of normal mechanisms for measuring support for political parties created a situation in which parties sought to

---

4. One of the Aylwin government's first priorities was the reform of the military regime's labor laws, although the reforms only marginally improved the legal situation of workers. See Epstein 1992 and Ruiz Tagle 1992.

reinforce their identities continuously and reestablish links with civil society (Garretón 1987c; Foxley 1987). This need to reestablish party identities and the lack of adequate mechanisms for doing so created a fundamental source of tension in the relations between political parties and popular organizations, as they themselves were involved in a process of establishing a new collective identity.

Political parties were unable to act openly in Chile until the eruption of the national protest movement in May 1983. But even following that, their actions were still severely circumscribed by political repression and the denial of access to effective means of mass communication (Valenzuela and Valenzuela 1986; Garretón 1989a and 1987c). The political class had been largely unable to reproduce itself during most of the period of military rule, and most political elites in the latter half of the 1980s had been prominent politicians prior to the coup. There was, in the words of one of these elites, "a lost generation of political leaders" that could not be formed due to the cessation of normal party recruitment and socialization processes (interview, Santiago, 1984). The effective cessation of political-party activity for so many years resulted in a gap between the changing sensibilities of the mass public and a political class that was preoccupied with problems of ideology and party organization (Garretón, 1987c). This distancing between the political class and Chilean society was pronounced with respect to the popular sectors (Oxhorn 1986 and 1988).

The problem of re-creating political identities was also exacerbated by the formation of a number of political party alliances beginning in 1983 (see Chapter 2). The existence of political blocs such as the Democratic Alliance (AD) and the Popular Democratic Movement (MDP) focused the political debate around questions regarding which parties had or had not been included in any given bloc or agreement. Proposals by one bloc were met with counterproposals by other blocs and a spiral ensued that highlighted differences rather than similarities in order to create (or preserve) distinct political identities. Smaller political parties felt threatened by the dominance of alliance partners, leading them to engage in strategies designed to highlight their own uniqueness, which further contributed to fragmentation within the opposition. A single opposition alternative for a democratic transition became an increasingly elusive goal (Garretón 1987c), until the military regime itself caused the parties to alter their strategies in 1987 by starting a political liberalization process that would culminate in the 1988 plebiscite.

Political-party infighting and the lack of party unity within the opposition only exacerbated the tensions between political parties and the popular sectors. As discussed in Chapters 4 and 5, pluralism and unity were central to the emerging popular collective identity. Their apparent absence within the opposition contributed to the distrust that members of popular organizations exhibited toward politicians and political parties. Moreover, the image of excessive partisanship and tendencies toward exclusionary tactics on the part of different political parties or blocs were reminiscent of the activities that members of popular organizations believed helped cause the breakdown of Chilean democracy in the 1970s.

Perhaps more important, political parties often tried to use popular organizations to reinforce their identities vis-à-vis one another. For political parties that had lost contact with their social bases, popular organizations were often seen as vehicles for quickly reestablishing those bases in the popular sectors—if the party could gain control of them (Oxhorn 1988 and 1986). This need led to attempts by different political parties to capture independent and autonomous organizations. Interparty conflicts among members of the same organization often ensued, as parties competed for control.

Social Change and Lost Party Bases

The changes in Chile's socioeconomic structure and the prolonged period of political repression had different implications for the Center, the Renovated Left, and the Traditional Left. They affected party strategies with respect to the popular sectors, and were an important source of tension between political parties and popular organizations as different parties attempted to increase their presence in the *poblaciones* or further buttress their dominant position there.

A critical change in the politics of the popular sectors after the military coup was the perception among political parties that the Traditional Left had gained in relative strength at the expense of both the Renovated Left and the Center. All three representatives of the Traditional Left felt that relations had improved between their respective parties and the popular sectors, as compared to the other two tendencies whose representatives felt that their parties had distanced themselves from the *poblaciones*. The only partial exception to this was the Christian Left, whose representatives disagreed as to whether their party's presence had increased in the *poblaciones*, or remained unchanged.

This distancing was evident in the politicians' opinions concerning their parties' actual presence in the *poblaciones*. Both representatives of the PC considered that their party was quite active in the *poblaciones*, as did one of the members of the Christian Left. The representative of the Almeyda branch of the Socialist Party felt his party was fairly active, but less so than the Communist Party. For the Center and the rest of the Renovated Left, they considered their respective parties' presence in the *poblaciones* to be weak or uneven.

Finally, the representatives from each of the three opposition tendencies characterized the actual relations between their parties and the popular sectors differently. The two Communist Party members who were interviewed insisted that their party enjoyed good relations with the popular sectors. The Christian Democrats were divided on this question, with the majority describing the relationship as weak. Only the two representatives of the Christian Left felt that their party had good relations with the popular sectors, while one representative of the Nuñez branch of the Socialist Party believed that "socialism"—but not necessarily his party— had a wide following in the *poblaciones*.

The implications of these findings were different for each tendency. The *poblaciones* had become a principal and the most secure social base for the Communist Party under the military regime. Its traditional social base in the labor movement, especially in heavy industries, had been severely eroded by the military regime's economic model and many former labor leaders were now leaders of popular organizations. The Communist Party had to turn to the *poblaciones* in order to maintain its importance as a political actor by claiming to represent a significant segment of Chilean society. For the Communist Party, the task of reestablishing its political identity and its ties with civil society was closely tied to its ability to successfully organize in the *poblaciones*.

The credibility of the Communist Party's claim to represent significant segments of the Chilean popular sectors was especially important in 1986. At that time, the party feared that it might be excluded from future negotiations leading to a democratic transition, and even banned from participating in a new democratic regime. The 1980 constitution formally declared unconstitutional all organizations and political parties that "propagate[d] doctrines . . . of a totalitarian character or which [were] founded in the struggle of classes" (Constitución política de la República de Chile, Article 8). The Communist Party's future was closely tied to opposition willingness to secure at least minimal changes to the 1980 constitution that would allow the party to fully participate in politics.

Many leaders of the Christian Democratic Party felt their party was being squeezed out of the popular sectors due to both their own neglect and the growing radicalization of *pobladores*. One of the DC leaders interviewed pointed out that many Christian Democratic Party officials stopped working in *poblaciones* after the coup because of the threat that political activity posed to the people with whom they worked. But she also noted that work in the *poblaciones* was "difficult and offered few returns for traditional politicians. There are a lot of traditional politicians in the DC. If there had been elections, there would be many [Christian Democrats] working there because there are votes. Now it is not profitable." For another official of the DC, the popular sectors represented "our greatest weakness as a party." The problem was in part one of lost opportunities: "There is space [in the *poblaciones*] for the DC, but it has not yet entered." He went on to lament the party's lack of interest in taking advantage of the space the Catholic Church had opened up in the *poblaciones*, largely because of the presence of leftist party militants.

By the mid-1980s, the Christian Democratic Party was attempting to reassert itself among the popular sectors, largely to avoid the radicalization of the popular sectors by the Left, and particularly by the Communists. The female party leader quoted above explained:

> Both the DC and the PC are in the *poblaciones*. Being able to organize people is a great challenge. First, so as not to leave them to the violence—to succeed in making the people understand that there are other routes to a solution to the current situation, that violence serves no purpose. This is a great challenge because violence is the natural alternative given the circumstances in which the *pobladores* live—to take by force what they are denied. For example, they see everything in the supermarkets while people are dying of hunger. It is a bomb that can explode at any time.

The other DC official just quoted added that "The objective problem is that hopelessness [and] misery lead to a greater receptivity toward extremist messages. . . . The DC has not been able to find a middle ground between the message of the Left and a government that gives things away."

Both dynamics (trying to secure a significant social base within the *poblaciones* as a way of ensuring incorporation into the political system and seeking to rectify past mistakes before the situation in the *poblaciones* became too radicalized) were present within the Renovated Left in the mid-1980s. For the Nuñez socialists, the problem involved regaining a presence that may have been lost: "Although it is certain that in the party there has not existed—at least collectively—in recent years any preoccupation for the world of the *poblaciones*, we aspire to define concrete policies that will allow us to insert the party life in this fundamental segment of Chilean society" (Departmento Nacional de Pobladores Partido Socialista (Nuñez), n.d., 1).

The PS(N) saw itself as facing a situation very similar to the one the Christian Democrats faced with respect to the extremism of the Communist Party. One of the leaders of the Nuñez socialists complained that "the presence [of our party in *poblaciones*] is very difficult. There is a very active and radicalized percentage [of *pobladores*] that is small and works for the PC. Our discourse on peaceful struggle, a political solution, [and] no confrontation therefore is difficult in the *poblaciones*."

The Nuñez socialists also felt that the Christian Democrats as well as the Communists caused them problems in trying to organize in the *poblaciones*. Because of their experiences with these two parties, members of popular-sector organizations simply did not believe the Nuñez socialists when they promised to respect the autonomy of popular organizations. The same person from the PS(N) continued: "The principal tension [between our party and popular organizations] is the product of the perception that popular organizations have that they are being used and manipulated by political parties. This is their experience with the DC and the PC—a very powerful experience. They find our discourse strange with respect to their autonomy—they doubt it."

Although the Christian Left leaders who were interviewed mentioned a certain preoccupation with a more generalized radicalization in the *poblaciones*, they also viewed the popular sectors as offering an opportunity for expanding the social base of their party. As one of the leaders of the IC who was interviewed pointed out, the Christian Left was a relatively new political party that lacked the historical ties to society that the older parties enjoyed—making the fate of the IC much more uncertain in the event of a return to democracy.[5] The party was formed in 1971 as the result of a split

---

5. In fact, the IC appears to be one of the first casualties among major political parties in the aftermath of the transition.

within the Christian Democratic Party. The IC did not have the opportunity to solidify a large and stable base of support prior to the political turmoil and breakdown of Chilean democracy in the early 1970s. It hoped to take advantage of the impact that progressive church doctrines such as liberation theology and the work of Christian base communities had had in the *poblaciones* and exploit the "space" that some members of the DC felt had been neglected. The popular sectors were a high priority for the IC. In the words of one of the IC leaders interviewed:

> [The Christian Left] is a party that defines its position on the side of the poor—"the Christians of the Left." It follows the Catholic Church's option for the poor. The party defines itself as socialist—in the service of the poor. The *poblaciones* are an important base for the IC. . . . It is the political option that the Christians in the *poblaciones* take.

Another IC leader who was interviewed hinted at how the fate of the popular sectors as a social actor and the IC were intertwined. Referring to other cases of recent transitions to democracy, this person pointed out that "all of the [social actors] that had autonomy in the struggle against the dictator have lost space afterward. The Christian Left is trying to prevent this in Chile."

In sum, the imposition of authoritarian rule in Chile abruptly closed the political space in which political parties had been able to establish their political identities and social bases. The partial reopening of this space in the latter half of 1983 created a new dynamic for relations between political parties and popular organizations. Political parties were seeking to reestablish their political identities and bases within a markedly different society compared to that of 1973. It was a process of recuperation and adaptation, and the stakes for the political parties were perceived to be quite high. The relative success of each party would partly determine its role in the subsequent transition process and its ability to influence that process in ways that would further its political interests in a future democratic regime. In some cases, a party's success or failure might even decide its ultimate political fate.

The popular-sector organizations were vulnerable to this process. Popular organizations were beginning to forge a new social identity and social movement at a time when political parties were most concerned with preserving and reinforcing their own political identities. Political parties had to adapt to the socioeconomic changes that Chile experienced during the period of military rule; while popular organizations represented an important response by the popular sectors to these changes. Popular organizations were, in essence, new (or potentially new) social actors confronting much more experienced and powerful "old" actors that were trying to reassert themselves. The inherently unequal nature of these relations can be seen in a frank comment by a member of the Communist Party: "The structure of the party should not be confused with those of the organizations. There are periods under repression when the parties must use the organizations so that they can be present [in the *poblaciones*]. This is not our conception of what the relations between the party and organizations should be, but it is the conditions in which we live. . . . It will be overcome in a democracy."

Two important political phenomena during the military regime illustrated many of the problems discussed above. These were the progressive marginalization of the popular sectors within the opposition in the mid-1980s and the Unitary Congress of Pobladores held in April 1986.

SOCIAL MOBILIZATION AND POLITICAL VIOLENCE: THE MARGINALIZATION OF THE POPULAR SECTORS WITHIN THE OPPOSITION

Chilean politics entered into a new phase with the first national protest in May 1983. Throughout Santiago, in both middle-class and popular-sector neighborhoods, large numbers of people openly expressed their opposition to the military regime. In subsequent months, the protest movement extended itself to other cities throughout Chile and a new public political space was created. Political parties reemerged onto the national scene as important political actors for the first time since 1973.[6] The military regime responded to the protests and social mobilizations with increased levels of repression. Dozens of people were killed, hundreds wounded, and thou-

6. The national protests during this period are described and analyzed in de la Maza and Garces 1985; *Páginas Sindicales* May 1983–November 1984, nos. 55–65; *Hechos Urbanos* May 1983–November 1984, nos. 21–37; CLACSO-ILET 1986; and Garretón 1987c and 1989c; Schneider 1991.

sands arrested as the regime sought to contain outbursts of social discontent.

The popular sectors bore the brunt of this repression.[7] Most of the deaths and injuries involved *pobladores*. The regime used the protest movement as a pretext for massive *allanamientos* in the *poblaciones* before and after declared days of protest. These were combined police-military operations in which entire *poblaciones* were sealed off and all the men were at least temporarily detained while their papers were checked and their houses searched. Away from crowded downtown areas and physically segregated from upper- and middle-class neighborhoods, the government showed a complete disregard for even the minimal rights of the urban poor in order to create a climate of fear among the middle and upper classes—not to mention among the *pobladores* themselves. This contributed to the isolation of the popular sectors, who (along with university students) became the principal participants in the protests, as the middle class withdrew its active support. As one analyst argued:

> The violence of the *pobladores* is, definitely, nothing more than a myth. . . . The persecution of the *pobladores* by the military regime after the protests, in effect, made them the victim that the regime needed in order to coalesce the rest of society around its authority. This [persecution] was stronger, in the long term, than any cry for a political opening, transition to democracy or social harmony. (Tironi 1987, 32)

The popular sectors were isolated not only geographically as a focus for government repression, but also within the organized opposition, which refused to recognize the popular sectors as an autonomous social actor (Oxhorn 1986; Espinoza 1986; Garretón 1987c; Baño 1985; and Pozo 1986). The popular sectors played only a minor role in the formation of major opposition initiatives, despite their dominant role in the social mobilizations. For example, *pobladores* were not accepted into the opposition's Protest Command which was set up in June 1983 to coordinate national protest activities. The National Workers' Command (a broad-based union organization formed in 1983 to mobilize organized labor for the protests) similarly refused to reach any agreements with the popular-sector organizations representing the *poblaciones* (Espinoza 1986).

---

7. See Appendix 3 for a clearer picture of the dynamics involved in popular-sector protests.

The 1985 National Accord for the Transition to Full Democracy (National Accord) represented the first major breakthrough in the goal of unifying the opposition behind a single alternative to the military regime. Organized under the auspices of the Catholic Church, the majority of left-wing parties with a significant presence among the popular sectors were excluded during the National Accord's formulation. Instead, the National Accord was written and signed by a group of political elites who had been prominent politicians prior to the 1973 military coup.

The Civic Assembly, formed by representatives of eighteen different social organizations (including the newly created *Unitary Pobladores' Command* (CUP), which will be discussed in detail below), was the focal point for opposition activities during the first half of 1986. It enjoyed the active support of all opposition parties. Many of the demands raised by the CUP were even incorporated into the Assembly document, Demands of Chile, which served as the basis for a series of social mobilizations culminating in the July 1986 national protest and general strike. Yet even here, the popular sectors as an autonomous social actor tended to be marginalized from the process.

The Assembly favored those sectors with the highest and most representative level of organization. The popular sectors were at a disadvantage compared to other sectors of society, whose organizations had a long history and at the time were going through a process of democratization in their leadership and decision-making processes. The CUP was the newest organization participating in the Civic Assembly. As will be argued below, it also was among the least representative of any of the participating organizations, in large part due to the role that political parties played in its formation. Regardless of these handicaps, the CUP was only one organization out of eighteen, and middle-class organizations were able to dominate the Assembly.

It is not surprising that neither the National Accord nor the Civic Assembly had a very wide following among the members of the popular sectors. The vast majority of popular-organization leaders interviewed either felt the National Accord did not represent their interests as *pobladores* (48 percent) or knew nothing about it (36 percent). Only four people—barely 10 percent of those responding to the question—felt represented by the National Accord. The Civic Assembly, in large part due to the activities of the CUP, fared much better. Still, only 48 percent of those responding to the question felt that their interests were fully represented by the Civic Assembly and 17 percent said they knew little or nothing about it. A middle-aged woman, who was active in organizing soup kitchens in her sector of Santiago and did not belong to any political party, explained the feelings of a sizeable portion of the members of popular organizations with respect to the Civic Assembly:

> It is a large body in which everyone has influence—the Right, the Left, social organizations, political organizations. There are no exclusions. We all have to support it. It is a little weak, though. There is a fear of dealing with real things. The people are for a stronger struggle than the Assembly. [The people] are suffering the problems. Their insistence on nonviolence hurts me. They do not know the repression, the deaths, because they are in the rich neighborhoods. We are trying to avoid so many deaths and injuries with barricades, etc. The people are seeking their own methods of self-defense. It bothers me a little because they talk of nonviolence, but not in a country where there is a military government that only uses arms! They do not suffer hunger—their situation is good. They do not have malnourished children. We have to get accustomed to all of the problems, the *allanamientos*. There is no opportunity for the people in the *poblaciones* to change their life. The poor stay poor, their kids will be poor, without a profession. They talk in the name of the people but do not know what is happening.

Party Identities and the Problem of Violence

The above quote struck at the heart of one of the most divisive issues within the Chilean opposition from 1985 through 1986: the relationship between social mobilizations and political violence. It was an issue that dramatically encapsulated the tensions between political parties concerned with reconstructing their social bases and popular-sector organizations. For the political parties, the debate over political violence was reduced to the question of whether or not the more moderate parties of the Center and Renovated Left should enter into political discussions with the parties of the Traditional Left, and the Communist Party in particular. The two more moderate tendencies explicitly endorsed only nonviolent forms of protest, while the Communist Party considered "all forms of struggle" to be equally legitimate against the dictatorship. At issue was whether the two positions were so incompatible as to preclude even a minimal dialogue between the "democratic" opposition and the Traditional Left.

The military government had always used even the possibility of such discussions to divide the opposition and discredit political parties by portraying them as the unsuspecting prey of Communists intent on installing a dictatorship of the proletariat. But the question of political discussions with the PC took on special importance in late 1985, when the Communist Party raised the issue publicly. In November 1985, the opposition held a surprisingly successful political demonstration in Parque O'Higgins. As a result of the tacit cooperation between the Popular Democratic Movement (MDP) (which was dominated by the PC) and the Democratic Alliance (AD) (in which the DC was the largest party and the PS[N] was the DC's most important ally), hundreds of thousands of people showed up for a mass demonstration without repression or other forms of political violence. The MDP issued a public letter to the AD, suggesting that the opposition take full advantage of the political initiative it had acquired by formalizing channels for political cooperation between the two blocs.

The immediate effect of the letter on the Democratic Alliance was dramatic. The AD appeared to be on the verge of disintegrating for several months, as the parties that formed the alliance failed to reach a consensus on the appropriate AD response. Ultimately, the parties of the Democratic Alliance "agreed to disagree" and each party was free to formulate its own policy regarding talks with the MDP. Both the Radical Party and the Nuñez branch of the Socialist Party subsequently entered into a formal dialogue with the MDP, while the Christian Democrats defended their right to talk with whomever they saw fit and in any manner they chose—in public or in private. The practical results of the latter's position were that the DC continued the informal contacts it had always maintained with the Traditional Left, but now it had to defend publicly its right to continue a nonpublic dialogue. The progovernment press took full advantage of the Christian Democrats' position; its headlines for several weeks ran allegations that these informal contacts were a facade for a series of secret negotiations and pacts between the DC and the Communist Party.[8]

The Communist Party Strategy of "Popular Rebellion"

The Communist Party pursued a strategy based on the formation of what it referred to as broad "antifascist" fronts from the time of the 1973 coup

---

8. As a prominent official of the DC confided at the time, the impact of the MDP's letter and the resultant controversy was "a type of nonsense," elevating an "infantile matter into a grand matter in Chilean politics" (personal interview, Santiago 1986).

until 1980. At that time, the party formally adopted a new strategy based on "popular rebellion," which recognized the legitimacy of all forms of struggle, both nonviolent and violent, to bring about the fall of the military regime. For the first time, the Communist Party was openly advocating armed confrontation with the military as part of its new strategy.

The reason for the dramatic change in the Communists' strategy was twofold. The military regime had successfully held a national plebiscite in 1980 that ratified a new constitution. The 1980 constitution was intended to provide for continued military rule through 1989 and the installation of a restricted democratic regime thereafter. Authoritarian rule appeared to have been institutionalized and the PC felt that the possibility for a peaceful change of power was remote. Moreover, the strategy of antifascist fronts had failed, in large part because the DC refused to enter into any kind of alliance with the Communist Party. Under these circumstances, the party perceived its options to be extremely limited (*Cincuenta preguntas al Partido Comunista de Chile* 1984; Furci 1984; Varas 1987).

The problematique of this strategy of "popular rebellion" is best understood in terms of its very ambiguity. Although the new strategy was announced in 1980, its practical effects were quite limited until *after* the first cycle of national protests had begun in May 1983. The new strategy did not take on a clear form until the formation of the paramilitary Manuel Rodríguez Patriotic Front (FPMR) on 14 December 1983 (Frente Patriótico Manuel Rodríguez, n.d.), and various self-defense groups based in the *poblaciones*, such as the Rodriguista Milicia, even later.[9]

The strategy of "popular rebellion" was aimed at generating a state of ungovernability in Chile. Mass mobilizations involving the entire population were to paralyze the country and force the military government to allow the opposition to establish a provisional government. The new government then would call for a constituent assembly and, later, democratic elections. The mass struggle would be complemented by military operations carried out by the FPMR against strategic targets in order to weaken the military's resolve and divert security forces away from the mass mobilizations. The various (largely unarmed) self-defense groups would

9. The PC officially claimed that the FPMR was an independent and autonomous organization whose activities, however, it wholeheartedly supported. While the exact nature of the relationship between the two is not known, the Communist Party has stated publicly that it had contributed to the development of the FPMR (Paulsen 1988). The principal leaders of the FPMR were important officials within the Communist Party and the majority of the members of the FPMR also were members of the PC.

attempt to protect the protesters by erecting barricades, stoning police, and so forth, and would serve as recruiting grounds for the FPMR. Once the dictatorship had fallen, the FPMR claimed that it would dissolve.[10]

The ambiguity in the Communist Party's position involved questions of ends and means. First, the Communist Party had insisted that popular rebellion could lead to a more "advanced" form of popular democracy as the result of the military regime's collapse. The Communist Party refused to take an unambiguous position in support of political democracy and continuously raised the specter of another Cuba or Nicaragua in Chile. Related to this question of what kind of regime the PC was actually trying to achieve through its strategy of popular rebellion was the role of armed struggle itself. Again, the PC refused to take an unambiguous position on what it felt were the limits to the use of military force by the opposition. As the rest of the opposition rightly pointed out, armed struggle was unlikely to result in a return to political democracy. The PC's continued endorsement of armed activities (like those of the FPMR) brought into question its more immediate goals for the post-Pinochet period and, more important, cast doubt on the PC's future commitment to political democracy in the most likely event of a democratic transition in Chile.

The Communist Party Identity and the Question of Its Future Survival

The change in Communist Party strategy came at a time when the perceived threat to its very existence was most acute. The military regime, which had made the PC the principal target of unprecedented levels of political repression, appeared to be stronger than ever. At the same time, the PC was isolated within the opposition because its repeated calls for the formation of an "anti-fascist front" had consistently been rejected. Moreover, the

10. The FPMR largely followed through on this promise. It adopted a more moderate line in the late 1980s, pledging to refrain from any paramilitary activities in support of both the Campaign for the No in the 1988 plebiscite and the Aylwin presidential candidacy. This led a small hardline faction to break from the FPMR and form the FPMR-Autónomo. In 1991, the FPMR formally renounced any paramilitary pretensions, transforming itself into what it described as a social moment that would represent those segments of society without other channels for expressing their interests. For the basic elements of the PC's strategy of popular rebellion, see Gómez 1986; Central Committee, Partido Comunista de Chile 1985; *Cincuenta preguntas al Partido Comunista de Chile* 1984; Frente Patriótico Manuel Rodríguez, n.d.; and Furci 1984.

composition and social base of the party had changed. Much of its old leadership, accustomed to working within a democratic regime, were either dead or in exile. The party's base in the labor movement had been undermined by repression and a new economic model, gradually forcing the party to move toward the *poblaciones*. Younger people, who had no experience with democracy, and poorer people from the *poblaciones* began to assume increasingly important positions within the party. Some change in strategy would appear to have been almost inevitable.

The ambiguities inherent in its policy of "popular rebellion" allowed the Communist Party to reestablish its political identity and social base in the new circumstances of the 1980s. While the military was still in power, the leadership of the PC felt that this strategy would best ensure the party's political survival.[11]

The Communist Party argued that the regime was the ultimate source of violence in Chile. It appealed to the right of all people to resist tyranny and defend themselves against an oppressive government. For example, an editorial in the official Communist Party publication *Principios* stated:

> What the Communists, together with the Popular Democratic Movement, are claiming as a right is not so much the use of violence in the abstract, as an end in itself, but rather the legitimate right of the people to defend themselves in the face of the institutionalized violence of the regime, in the face of the *allanamientos* in the *poblaciones*, the daily slaughter and torture, the permanent repressive terror (*Principios* January–March 1984, 14).

The editorial went on to point out the hypocrisy in opposition calls for social mobilization without allowing the people to defend themselves against the repression. There was even a deliberate effort to appeal to Chile's Catholic heritage: "In terms of violence, we must remember that, beyond any philosophical or ideological definitions, the Christian ethic that culturally nurtures our people has never equated the violence of those who rebel against injustice and oppression with the violence of the powerful" (*Carta abierta al pueblo de Chile* 1986, 1).

11. This is not meant to imply that other possible strategies would not have been so effective or even more so. Nor is it intended to suggest that the strategy of popular rebellion was equally effective for ensuring the party's survival after 1986, when it became increasingly clear that the only alternative open to the opposition was to attempt to defeat Pinochet in the plebiscite scheduled for 1988. These issues will be discussed in more detail in Chapter 8.

Fundamentally, the Communist Party was appealing directly to the frustration and desperation of both militants and the *pobladores* who were directly suffering the high costs of repression. In one sense, the strategy of popular rebellion was a call for doing anything that could end the massive suffering.

In another sense, the significance of both the strategy of popular rebellion and its very ambiguity is found in its relation to a myth of "the resistance" and heroism. Whatever the eventual outcome might be—political democracy or socialist revolution—the Communist Party was seeking to portray itself as being beyond reproach in its determination to end the dictatorship. For example, one Communist Party leader (normally part of a more moderate faction) argued that if the PC were to abandon its strategy of popular rebellion while the military government was still in power, the Communist Party would cease to exist. Its members would desert the party either for more radical parties or for parties associated with the Renovated Left. Under those circumstances, being a "Communist" would lose all meaning (personal interview, Santiago, 1985).[12]

Similarly, the importance of the popular rebellion strategy for the PC can be seen in the same *Principios* editorial quoted above:

> The ample and massive popular support for the MDP is explained by its clear and consequential attitude of struggle against the dictatorship, rejecting all conciliation or maneuvers with it, fully interpreting the spirit and combative disposition of the popular masses which have lost their fear of repression and are disposed to "die fighting [rather than from doing nothing]." (*Principios* January–March 1984, 5)[13]

In its own defense, the Communist Party pointed out that the repression and lack of unity in the opposition were no worse than during the 1973–80 period (*Cincuenta preguntas al Partido Comunista de Chile* 1984). The PC also distinguished its strategy of popular rebellion from the strategy of armed revolution that the far Left had adhered to in Chile since the mid-

---

12. In fact, many *pobladores* did leave the party when it moderated its policies to support the opposition's efforts to win electoral victories in the 1988 plebiscite and 1989 elections for president and a new legislature. The reasons for this exodus, however, are more complicated and will be discussed in Chapter 8.

13. The exact phrase, "morir luchando, de hambre ni cagando," escapes any literal translation. It became a rallying cry for the popular sectors during protests.

1960s (*Es tiempo de unir y luchar* 1984). Finally, the party repeatedly stated that it was willing to accept a liberal democratic regime, as long as the military was removed from power.[14]

The rest of the opposition, according to the Communist Party, was applying a double standard. Many parties associated with the opposition, especially the Christian Democrats, were slow to condemn the violence unleashed by the military coup—the Communists being among its principal victims—and had been willing to enter into discussions with the far more violent military regime (*Principios* January–March 1984). With regard to opposition efforts to enter into political alliances with the Right, the Communists claimed that the real threat to democracy had never been from the Left, but from the Right:

> The Left's support of democracy in Chile has sustained and vitalized our national being. . . . The great achievements of the Chilean democratic society were associated with the activities of the popular political parties. On the contrary . . . the political problem in Chile and in Latin America is that the dominant forces in the political right are not democratic and, more often than not, their interests are not national interests. (*Carta abierta al pueblo de Chile* 1986, 2)

The Communist Party felt that its isolation from other opposition political parties only strengthened the military regime. It served as a justification for further repression of the Party, and even of non-Communists who were accused of being "Communists" by the regime (*Principios* January–March 1984; Central Committee, Partido, Comunista de Chile, 1985). The practice of exclusion was "a political error that some democratic sectors have permanently resorted to in the definition of their alliance policies"; in effect they were "accepting the dictator himself as a censor" of such policies (*Carta abierta al pueblo de Chile* 1986, 1).

The Christian Democratic Position

The Christian Democratic Party consistently rejected any public overtures by the Communist Party to enter into a formal dialogue. Since the Commu-

---

14. See Corvalán 1983; Central Committee, Partido Comunista de Chile 1985; *El Siglo* November 1986; *Cincuenta preguntas al Partido Comunista de Chile* 1984; Gómez 1986; *Izquierda chilena al país* 1986; and *Carta abierta al pueblo de Chile* 1986.

nist Party adopted a strategy of popular rebellion in 1980, the DC based its intransigence on the Communist Party's refusal to reject unequivocally all forms of political violence. This refusal did not, as pointed out above, prevent the DC from maintaining informal contacts with the Communists, as long as such contacts were not made public.

The Christian Democrats defended their position on two basic grounds.[15] First, they argued that the strategy of popular rebellion, with its military component, was inherently undemocratic. The DC contended that the only goal behind the strategy was a socialist revolution along the lines of Cuba or Nicaragua. Moreover, in the Communist strategy, the final outcome would not be decided democratically, but instead by a correlation of forces in which military power would prevail.

Second, the Christian Democrats argued that the Communist position was counterproductive. It placed the confrontation between the regime and the opposition on a military plane, where the government enjoyed an overwhelming advantage. By advocating violence, the Christian Democrats also argued that the PC was alienating the middle and upper classes from the opposition, thereby strengthening the regime that these classes viewed as guaranteeing law and order. Finally, many Christian Democrats argued that the PC strategy actually decreased the effectiveness of social mobilization because the middle classes refused to participate, and their participation was essential for forcing the government into negotiations with the opposition.

The Christian Democrats assigned the full responsibility for divisions within the opposition to the Communist Party, because of its decision to adopt a strategy of popular rebellion (Arriagada 1985b and 1986b; Foxley 1987; Valdés 1986). The DC would enter into formal discussions with the PC only when the PC unequivocally renounced the use of violence. For the Christian Democrats, the reasoning was clear. As Eugenio Ortega, then general secretary of the Christian Democratic Party, explained, "the Communist Party compromises those groups that rub shoulders with it or ally with it" (Ortega 1985, 81).

The intransigence of the Christian Democratic position cannot be fully understood unless one examines the DC's own problems of identity and its need to reestablish links with its social bases. After the perceived chaos of

15. The various elements in the Christian Democratic Party's position can be found in the following: Arriagada 1985b, 1986a, and 1986b; Cortázar 1987; Boeninger 1986; Foxley 1987; Ortega 1985; and Valdés 1986.

the Allende period and years of government propaganda intended to discredit political parties in the eyes of the middle class, the Christian Democrats could not take the allegiance of the middle class for granted. Entering into a public dialogue with the Communists was something they could not risk. Moreover, the Christian Democrats found themselves in the situation of having to recuperate their position within the *poblaciones*. They sought to do so through a firm stand on the issue of violence and a complete disassociation between themselves and the PC, which was the most active political party in the *poblaciones*, especially in popular organizations. In a simplistic way, the Christian Democrats attempted to establish their presence in the popular sectors in part by assuming a highly antagonistic position vis-à-vis the Communists.[16]

Political Violence and the Emerging Popular Collective Identity

The positions of both the Christian Democratic Party and the Communist Party appeared fundamentally unrealistic to members of popular organizations. These people generally did not support violent revolutionary change, but they also would not rule out the use of political violence in opposition to the military regime. A middle-aged man who cofounded a cultural group and was generally suspicious of all politicians best explained the predominant feeling among the members of popular organizations with regard to the issue of violence: "There are cases when yes [violence is legitimate]. As the church itself says, when a tyrant does not permit a people to live in dignity. Revolution is not gratuitous violence—it makes a lot of sense. For this reason the violence of the young is sometimes justified—it is close to revolutionary violence."

Protests in the *poblaciones* inevitably resulted in much violence. Yet, 35 out of the 46 people interviewed (more than three quarters) participated in protests. Thirty-eight people (83 percent) felt that the protests were legitimate even though they were illegal. This includes five respondents (11 percent) who specified that the protests must be nonviolent. Only four

---

16. The parties of the Renovated Left generally supported nonviolent means of protest, but rejected efforts to isolate the Communist Party within the opposition. See Garretón 1987a and 1987b; Lagos 1985a; Arrate 1985; *Liberación* March–April 1986; *Liberación* November 1986; *Carta abierta al pueblo de Chile* 1986; and *La izquierda chilena al país* 1986.

people (9 percent) felt the protests were illegitimate. A middle-aged woman who was the leader of a woman's group explained why barricades, rock-throwing, and so forth, were necessary in Chile:

> It is a right—we all have the right to be heard. If the authorities do not listen through good means, they will hear through bad means. It is the only way to express our disagreements and ideals. . . . With democracy, we can do this through marches, newspapers, etc. It is different, there are other alternatives. If, for example, I don't like something, we will have a march and no one will attack us. . . . Now it is illegal, but there are no alternatives.

Members of popular organizations generally linked the violence associated with protests to government repression and the need for self-defense. This was very clear in the interviews, where only six people (13 percent) attributed the violence to the Left. Seventy-three percent, however, specifically blamed government provocation for the violence associated with the protests. An additional 13 percent of the respondents attributed such violence to more general problems created by the military regime, such as injustice and the need for self-defense. When asked specifically if it was possible to justify this violence, only 26 percent of those responding to the question said no. One person suggested that the government could legitimately exercise force against the protesters, but only if the opposition was involved in acts of destruction. The rest of the respondents felt that in the present circumstances, opposition violence was in fact legitimate.

Interviewees also were asked for their opinion about popular armed groups such as the Manuel Rodríguez Patriotic Front. More than 60 percent of the people responding to the question felt that such groups were legitimate, but only under specific circumstances (Table 28). By far, most of the support would appear to be based on the ability of these organizations to defend the population against repression. Moreover, four people suggested that such groups were illegitimate only because they were ineffective, lacked majority support, or were no match for the Chilean military. When asked if such groups should continue their activities after Pinochet left power, eight people said yes; twice as many people (sixteen) said no. Of the remaining respondents, five felt the groups did not even exist in Chile and the others generally preferred to withhold their judgment until it was clear what kind of regime would actually follow Pinochet—whether a political democracy or another authoritarian regime.

Table 28.   Are popular armed groups legitimate?

	Total
Yes	
For self-defense	19
If they have a purpose	5
When they do not kill people	1
No	11
No because the majority rejects them	2
Not at this time	2
n.a.	6
Should they continue after Pinochet?	
No	16
Yes	8
The people will decide	2
If there is a tyrant	1
If they serve a purpose	2
They do not exist now	5
n.a.	12

What emerges is neither a blanket endorsement of political violence by armed groups opposed to the military regime, nor an unequivocal rejection of all forms of violence associated with political resistance and self-defense. It is a realistic position, one that recognizes the frustration and impotence felt by most *pobladores* in the face of an intransigent authoritarian regime. As before, the words of the *pobladores* were most revealing. Surprisingly, it was a young male member of the Christian Democratic Party who most clearly articulated the sentiments of the majority of the members of popular organizations:

> I do not agree with [popular armed groups], but I recognize that they have a great heart. They have the valor to defend the weakest. They should not exist, but now they exist out of necessity. I have talked with people who belong to the [Manuel Rodríguez Patriotic] Front. They say that when the dictator goes, so will they. Their role is to defend. . . . If it were not for them, how many people would have died? They are building a little life by taking up arms against the state.

An important aspect of the protests was their symbolic content (Garretón 1987c and 1989c). They allowed people to express their rejection of the authoritarian regime. Within the world of the *poblaciones* where poverty, physical violence, and a generalized hopelessness were widespread, part of that symbolism related to acts of "heroism" and being part of "the resistance." The barricades, the self-defense groups, even the FPMR, were all part of this (see Appendix 3). The Communist Party was attempting to tap into this symbolism, and to a certain extent it was successful.[17]

Yet, there were limits to this symbolism, especially with regards to paramilitary groups such as the FPMR. Two examples are quite illustrative of this and both involve the protest of September 1986.

Support for the FPMR had been quite high among members of popular organizations in two different *poblaciones* where the FPMR had been fairly active for some time. FPMR activities within *poblaciones* typically involved residents of the *población* and better-trained members who lived elsewhere. One of the two *poblaciones* was situated near high-tension power lines delivering electricity to much of Santiago. The FPMR had planned to sabotage the towers on the day of the protest and cause a power blackout. It had been storing the necessary materials in a house within the *población* and several local young *pobladores* were assigned the task of watching the house. Just prior to the protest, the house was discovered by the police and the young *pobladores*, both male and female, were arrested and charged under the antiterrorist law. In the other *población*, the FPMR was involved in an armed confrontation with the police on the day of the protest and the only casualty was the death of one of the FPMR's young local recruits.

Support for the FPMR subsequently plummeted in both *poblaciones*. The FPMR was blamed for taking advantage of young *pobladores* who were improperly trained and did not know what they were getting involved in. In both cases, the allegedly better trained and older members of the FPMR—who did not live in the *poblaciones*—escaped unscathed. The symbolism of the valiant warriors defending the *población* evaporated when reality and symbols clashed with dramatic results. Members of popular organizations would support the FPMR as long as the effects of its actions did not touch them directly.

Old and New Actors and the Problems of Defining Competing Identities

Chile was far from becoming another El Salvador, or even another Peru, under the military regime. The popular sectors, which would have had to

17. Not surprisingly, when the political context began to change in 1987 and the appeal to acts of heroism and resistance was no longer very effective or practical, many *pobladores* who had joined the PC during the height of the protest movement left the party. This is discussed at length in Chapter 8.

serve as the backbone for any significant insurrection or revolutionary struggle in Chile's highly urbanized society, were simply not prepared to support such actions. The Communist Party's strategy of popular rebellion against a very repressive military regime found much resonance among members of popular organizations, but so did many of the arguments of the Christian Democrats who appeared to be more concerned with a future democracy. The symbolism of the resistance and the right to self-defense were strongly felt in the *poblaciones*, yet there was relatively little desire to contemplate the immense human costs of any serious effort to defeat the armed forces militarily or carry through a social revolution.

Despite this, the issue of political violence became an important and divisive issue within the Chilean opposition in the mid-1980s. The issue of political violence became so important in large part because political parties had to face the problems of reconstructing their identities and ties to society after a prolonged period of authoritarian rule. Both the PC and the DC took firm stands on opposite sides of the issue, and neither side felt it could compromise on its position without losing substantial societal support.

The only clear winner in the debate over political violence in the opposition was the military regime, which never stopped resorting to violence to achieve its ends. In effect, the military government chose the issue for the opposition. The divisions within the opposition that then emerged allowed the government to raise the specter of a return to the chaotic situation of 1973 and further discredit all opposition parties. Many of the opposition's most notable advances, such as the first cycle of protests, the 1985 demonstration in Parque O'Higgins and the Civic Assembly, were achieved when the issue of violence was simply ignored. Yet throughout it all, the poor continued to be those who suffered most under the regime.

THE UNITARY CONGRESS OF POBLADORES

The integration of the popular sectors into the opposition required some form of institutional mechanism. If that integration was to take place on the basis of an emergent popular collective identity, the popular sectors would have needed to form some sort of intermediate representative body that could serve as an interlocutor with other segments of the opposition. This body, in turn, would have served as the basis for a popular social movement.

The tensions between political parties and popular organizations under the military regime became most acute when *pobladores* attempted to construct such a popular social movement. The struggles of political parties over their own political identities and the reestablishment of social bases directly undermined such efforts, preventing the full development of popular collective action based on *lo popular*. The Unitary Congress of Pobladores, held in April 1986, illustrated very clearly how the interests of a potential popular-sector social actor were generally subordinated to the political interests of parties.[18]

Four ideological and political umbrella organizations, or "referents," had been working in the *poblaciones* of Santiago for a number of years under the military regime: the Movimiento Poblacional Solidaridad, the Movimiento Poblacional Dignidad, the Coordinadora Metropolitana de Pobladores (METRO) and the Coordinadora de Agrupaciones Poblacionales (COAPO).[19] These four groups explicitly worked to help promote the spread of popular-sector organizations to all *poblaciones* by providing advisers and teaching *pobladores* how to organize, develop leadership skills, and so forth. The referents also served as catalysts for forming new groups by bringing people together to form a particular organization, arranging meetings, finding meeting places, and so forth. They did not, however, represent networks of popular organizations and had very few organic ties to the *poblaciones*. Their efforts to promote the coordination of popular-sector organizational activity among different *poblaciones* were aimed at forging a new social actor or popular social movement that would serve as the legitimate interlocutor for popular sectors in the Chilean political process.

Each referent allegedly represented a different ideological focus for dealing with the problems faced by *pobladores*. Although they claimed to be independent of political parties, each referent had in fact been formed by a particular party or parties and they all maintained very close relations with those same parties through their members, who were almost all active party militants. The work of the referents, in practice, became closely associated with building bases in the *poblaciones* for the political parties they represented. *Solidaridad* was created by the Christian Democratic party; *Dignidad* was dominated by the Christian Left; the Communist

18. The following is based largely on personal interviews I conducted with various leaders involved in the Congress and my own observations at the Congress, which I attended as a "fraternal delegate." See Oxhorn 1991.

19. On the development of these referents, see Campero 1987 and Espinoza 1986.

Party controlled METRO; and COAPO represented the Revolutionary Left Movement (MIR).

Despite their obvious partisan biases, the three referents of the Left, *Dignidad*, METRO, and COAPO, had been working since 1984 on the formation of a pluralist and autonomous popular social movement that would serve as interlocutor for the popular sectors in dealings with the political parties and the state.[20] Such a movement was envisioned as being more than simply an intermediate organization created by *pobladores*. As Espinoza explained: "The way in which the unitary process was conceived, beyond its organizational aspect, manifested the desire of *pobladores* to become an actor, based on a definition of identity that did not exhaust itself in general ideological definitions, but rather one based on the organizations themselves which the *pobladores* had developed" (Espinoza 1986, 47).

The Congress was intended to be the culmination of this process, which had begun in early 1984. Its timing was largely influenced by the announcement in March 1986 that a "Civic Assembly," composed of the most important social organizations in Chile, was being formed by the opposition. At the Congress, a comprehensive list of popular-sector demands was to be elaborated and a Unitary Command for Pobladores (CUP) would be elected. *Dignidad*, METRO, and COAPO were to be absorbed by the CUP into a single pluralistic organization democratically constituted through the direct participation of *pobladores* representing distinct *poblaciones* throughout Santiago. The CUP would then become the sole legitimate representative of the *pobladores* and be incorporated into the Civic Assembly.

Questions about the representativeness of the Congress and interparty competition for control over the CUP prevented it from assuming the leadership of a genuine popular social movement with strong roots in the *poblaciones*. To some extent, the problems of the Congress's representativeness reflected the difficulties involved in organizing any large-scale political activity in Chile at that time, especially one involving *pobladores*, given the high levels of fear and repression in the *poblaciones*. But these difficulties should not excuse the fact that in many respects, the Congress failed to

20. Conversations in this regard began in early 1984. *Solidaridad* withdrew from the conversations after the second meeting (Espinoza 1986) and declined to participate in the Congress because it felt that at that particular time, it was inappropriate to think in terms of a single representative body representing all *pobladores* (*Hechos Urbanos* July 1986). In effect, the Christian Democratic Party had chosen not to cooperate with the Left and instead sought to create its own social base in the *poblaciones* through *Solidaridad*.

achieve its objectives. Instead, it brought deep political divisions to the fore and highlighted the deliberate attempts of political parties to use the incipient popular movement to their own advantage.

The problems associated with the Congress first surfaced in the various assemblies held throughout Santiago to select delegates. A race had begun early on to ensure that a maximum number of each party's militants would be delegates. In the end, more than 90 percent of delegates to the Congress were party militants, with the PC and the IC respectively having the first- and second-largest blocks of delegates.[21] "Ghost" organizations were created by the political parties in order to send representatives to the Congress and inflate each party's presence. The majority of organized *pobladores*, who were not members of any party, were systematically excluded from participating in the Congress. There was also a marked overrepresentation of those areas in Santiago where the political parties were strongest. Areas with weak party presence were either deliberately excluded, or simply did not know about the pre-Congress assemblies.

At the Congress, the election of the CUP was reduced to a blatant demonstration of political-party infighting. The PC rejected a compromise proposal offered by the IC and MIR to recognize the nonrepresentative nature of the Congress by declaring it transitory and electing only an executive governing body without officers. This temporary body would then work toward the goal of holding a representative congress and electing a permanent CUP in December of that year. Instead, the PC insisted on having elections for officers within a permanent governing council. Behind closed doors, the approximately 25 percent of delegates with voting rights elected COAPO's candidate as president, and gave the office of vice president to the METRO's candidate. The IC and MIR had agreed to combine forces in order to block the PC's attempt to win control of the CUP through its presidency. The "compromise" candidate chosen to thwart the PC was a member of the most politically extreme and least representative party present at the Congress.

Consensus was finally achieved after the near crisis that resulted when the METRO withdrew from the CUP immediately after losing the election. The next day, with no official explanation, the elections of the previous

21. In reality, the majority of party militants in Santiago's *poblaciones* in early 1986 were Communist. This was in part due to both the PC's greater experience in organizing clandestinely and, as mentioned earlier, the repression of the labor movement. The IC, on the other hand, was a relative newcomer to the world of grassroots organizing in the *poblaciones*. But its presence had grown significantly over the previous two years.

night were conveniently forgotten and a transitory CUP governing body (without elected officers) was presented before the full Congress. This transitory body was given the task of organizing a more representative congress to be held in December 1986, when a permanent CUP would be elected—essentially the same compromise that the PC leadership had initially rejected.

The Congress represented a clear example of the problems party elites had created in attempting to establish organizational links with the *poblaciones*. The extreme level of party control exercised over the delegates led party militants to recognize how unrepresentative the Congress actually was. The Congress had been transformed into a sort of political convention, with backroom bargaining and negotiations intended to influence the distribution of power within the incipient popular social movement. Political infighting led to embarrassing divisions that exposed the weaknesses of popular-sector organizations, rather than creating even the facade of a new democratically constituted organization with legitimate claims to be the sole interlocutor for Chile's popular sectors in the political process.

The Congress's shortcomings become all the more apparent when viewed from the perspective of the members of popular organizations themselves. Ninety percent of those interviewed felt that coordination among popular organizations was important. Similarly, large percentages of the people interviewed also felt that such coordination already existed at the grassroots level and that the primary responsibility for such coordination fell on the *pobladores* themselves. But when asked specifically about the Congress, 50 percent of those responding did not know anything about it. Most of those who knew something about the Congress (16 out of 20 interviewees) felt that it did not represent them.

The general feeling among those who were aware of the Unitary Congress of Pobladores was one of disappointment. This is clear in the statements of two women who had attended the Congress from different *poblaciones*. Both women were accustomed to working with party militants, even though neither belonged to any party. Yet, in this instance they were clearly frustrated:

> [The referents] approached the Congress like parties. . . . It was ideological. Party X had to be at the head, saying the others were more misleading, we are less, that kind of thing. They did not worry whether the leaders there represented bases with [their own]

concerns, that they represented groups and were not just individu-als—that they were representative. They could be [party] militants, but they had to represent a base—what the people behind in their loan payments, the unemployed, the people without houses thought. The CUP should have done this. If [the CUP] is not fixed, it serves only for causing divisions. It refused to recognize leaders elected by the base because they were not members of a particular party. This was not respect for the interests of the people. (woman active in organizing soup kitchens)

I was invited to a congress of *pobladores* and I found it to be a fight among political parties. I thought I would see many *pobladores* from different areas and that it would be democratic. What I found was a joke. But I like it because it was a lesson [about political parties]. I always got confused when it came to political parties. For this it was good, but what happened served no purpose. (woman cofounder of a handicrafts organization)

The Congress also highlighted another important problem in party relations with the popular sectors under the military regime: the radicaliza-tion of party militants in the *poblaciones* compared with the party elite. The alliance between the radical MIR and the moderate socialist IC was more than just a tactical measure for pursuing the parties' immediate interests. It also reflected a clear rejection of the PC's allegedly excessive moderation in seeking some form of dialogue with the DC. At the national level, the fear was that the PC had become too radical and had opted for the same revolutionary strategy that the MIR supported. In the *poblaciones*, the PC was viewed as being too moderate by party militants because of its overtures to open a public dialogue with the Christian Democrats. While at the national level the IC had kept its distance from the more radical positions of the Communist-dominated Movimiento Democrático Popular (MDP), IC militants from the *poblaciones* were entering into open alliances with the MDP's most extreme component.

The experience of the Congress shows how the military regime had severed normal channels of communication between party elites, party militants at the grassroots level, and members of popular organizations who did not belong to any political party. The task of repairing these lines of contact, essential for the successful operation of democratic political institutions, would be a hard one.

CONCLUSION

That the imposition of authoritarian rule in 1973 and its subsequent history was traumatic for Chile goes without saying. What needs to be emphasized (and this is perhaps the most intriguing paradox of Chile's recent history) is that the experience of military rule appears to have generated converging learning processes at the elite and base levels of society. This may ultimately provide space for a new popular social movement in the Chilean political system, but problems of party identity and the reconstitution of party social bases seem to have stifled efforts by the popular sectors to fill that space under the military regime.

Political parties were seriously weakened by the authoritarian regime, despite the obvious resilience they demonstrated by their return to a position of dominance in the opposition after 1983. These weakened parties had to adapt to important and long-term changes in Chile's socioeconomic structure. They were "old" actors seeking to reaffirm their position in Chile's changed political process.

One of the changes to which parties had to adapt was the increased significance of the popular sectors and organized labor's diminished importance. The popular sectors remained the largest social category in Chile. They had new needs and demands that were the product of their violent exclusion from the political system and their economic impoverishment under the military regime. During the military regime, the foundations for a "new" social actor that could represent the popular sectors may have been laid in popular organizations encapsulating the emergent collective identity, *lo popular*.

Studies of democratic transitions have shown that political parties typically dominate these processes and that the importance of social movements tends to decline once transition processes are under way (O'Donnell, Schmitter, and Whitehead 1986). These studies frequently fail to explore the implications of such macroprocesses for the future political fortunes of individual parties. These involve the distribution of power, and in some cases, they can threaten the very survival of certain political parties. The processes through which political parties seek to reestablish their political identities and social bases are central to understanding the role that social movements may (or may not) play in transitions to democracy. Such processes do not bode well for the emergence of new popular social movements. The same conditions that contributed to the emergence of a new popular collective identity in Chile, weakened both the ability and the willingness of the political actors who had dominated Chilean politics prior to the coup to reach an accommodation with this potentially new social actor. Political parties may simply have perceived the stakes involved in reaching such an accommodation to have been too high.

This perception is consistent with the model of relations between political parties and base-level organizations developed in Chapter 1 (see Fig. 3 and related discussion). This model suggested that the nature of that relationship would be determined by the scope of the demands or interests expressed by popular organizations. Efforts to create a popular social movement reflected an expansion in the scope of popular-sector interests conditioned by lo popular as a collective identity. This brought the incipient social movement into direct conflict with the political parties most closely associated with efforts to create such a movement, namely the Renovated and Traditional Left. The relationship was clearly one of competition, in which popular organizations ultimately lost. These parties sought to dominate popular-sector politics and refused to share representational space with popular organizations as an autonomous actor. Similarly, the Center (which was not present at the Congress), and to a lesser extent the Renovated Left, sought to limit the scope of demands expressed by popular organizations. This would enable the parties to penetrate popular organizations through the establishment of patron-client relations with them.

It should be emphasized that these problems were not merely the result of self-interested political-party behavior. They were exacerbated—if not made inevitable—by the constraints imposed upon political parties by an entrenched military regime that resisted even minimal steps toward political liberalization in 1986.

Beginning with the collapse of its economic model in the early 1980s, the regime entered into a phase of "crisis management" in which its principal objectives were the stabilization of socioeconomic transformations that had already been achieved, and its own survival in terms of the time frame for a controlled transition as laid out in the 1980 constitution (Garretón 1989a). The period from mid-1983 to mid-1986 was essentially one of stalemate between the military regime and the opposition. The latter had to maintain an extremely difficult balance. At a minimum, the opposition needed to generate a level of mobilization sufficient to ensure that the military would respect its own time frame for a transition. At best, the opposition still hoped that such mobilization could force the regime into making genuine concessions in terms of a transition to democracy. But it had to achieve this mobilization without instigating a repressive backlash by military hardliners that the middle class might support as necessary to safeguard "law and order." As already noted, the Pinochet government recognized the opposition's dilemma and responded to the protest movement by augmenting the level of repression in the *poblaciones* in order to generate a climate of fear among the middle and upper classes.

The opposition was very aware of this dilemma. The Christian Democrats, in particular, were concerned that the middle classes would be alienated by opposition mobilizations that appeared to be centered on the *poblaciones* and focused attention on diluting the increasingly "popular" character that the protests were assuming. The Communists, on the other hand, were more concerned with increasing the pressure on the military regime, regardless of the possibility that this would lead to an even more violent response from the government and the desertion of the middle classes to the government camp. This required that the *poblaciones* (where the PC enjoyed the strongest political presence) continue to play a central role in the protests and that "all forms of struggle" be accepted as legitimate.

These problems in the Chilean case underscore the uncertain and contingent nature of most transition processes (cf. O'Donnell and Schmitter 1986). More important, they emphasize the disadvantages that popular sectors must overcome if they are to influence such processes in a positive way. It needs to be stressed, however, that the findings presented in this study demonstrate that at least some of that uncertainty (with the resultant marginalization of the popular sectors within the opposition) was due to the weakening of party ties to civil society as a result of the authoritarian experience itself.

The problematic relationship between popular-sector organizational activity and political parties became more apparent as Chilean politics entered into a new phase in 1987, highlighting the ways in which the authoritarian experience itself conditioned popular-sector organizational activity. The problems popular organizations faced in their relations with political parties in the mid-1980s not only continued, but were exacerbated by the circumstances under which Chile's transition to democracy unfolded. Narrow partisan interests became less important for determining party relations with popular organizations as a consensual strategy for confronting the military regime emerged among opposition parties. This created a new dynamic whose effects on popular-sector organizational activity were even more negative in terms of the immediate prospects for the emergence of a popular social movement. It is to an examination of this latter period, roughly from 1987 through the first year of the new civilian government, that we now turn.

8

THE POPULAR SECTORS AND THE RETURN OF DEMOCRACY

After more than fourteen years of authoritarian rule, the pace of political change in Chile picked up markedly in 1987. For the first time since the 1973 coup, political parties were legalized and eligible adults again registered to vote. The opposition achieved a sufficient degree of unity to ensure the transition to a democratic regime, which began with Pinochet's defeat in the 1988 plebiscite and ended when the opposition's candidate, Patricio Aylwin, assumed the office of the presidency in March 1990. All these events—particularly the return to democratic rule—created new challenges and opportunities for popular-sector organizational activity. The speed at which the political situation was evolving brought into relief many of the factors that had conditioned popular-sector organizational activity under the military regime, offering new insights into the potential—and limits—of popular organizations for defining and representing the interests of the popular sectors as a new social actor.

Popular organizations have had to adapt to rapidly changing circumstances, while at the same time they continue to confront some of the military regime's most enduring legacies much more directly than other segments of Chilean society. The challenge facing the popular sectors is to ensure their own integration into the institutions of the new democratic regime, adapting their experiences from the authoritarian period to the possibilities for popular-sector collective action engendered by the return to democracy.

As the previous chapters have stressed, *lo popular* and popular-sector organizational activity under the military regime have been fundamentally shaped by the authoritarian experience itself. The easing of repression and the opening up of new channels for participation had the immediate effect of removing those factors that initially gave rise to popular organizations and the emergence of *lo popular* as a new collective identity. How would this affect the continued evolution of *lo popular* and popular-sector organizational activity more generally?

Moreover, certain limits to popular-sector organizational activity were already apparent under the military regime. In particular, as such organizational activity sought to go beyond individual, territorially circumscribed communities, it came into increasing conflict with political parties. Would a return to democracy also result in a return to old patterns of organizational activity in the *poblaciones* dominated by political parties? Or would *lo popular* continue to evolve and serve as an alternative basis for popular-sector collective action? If the latter is the case, would such collective action necessarily take the same forms as it had under the military regime? Or would alternative organizational forms prove more appropriate to the changed circumstances?

I suggested in Chapter 1 that three factors would determine the answers to these questions: the level of institutionalization achieved by popular organizations under the military regime, political-party structures, and the transition to democracy. In Chapter 3, I argued that popular organizations had already achieved a certain level of institutionalization by the mid-1980s. As we shall see, this is confirmed by the continued growth in popular organizations from 1988 on. But the number of popular organizations and their continued functioning is only part of the picture. The relationship between political parties and popular organizations during the transition and afterwards is also critical, especially given the problematic nature of that relationship under the authoritarian regime. More generally, the amount and nature of the political space for continued popular-sector organizational activity which was created by the transition will be of fundamental importance for understanding the future role of the popular sectors in Chile's political process.

This chapter is divided into two parts. In the first part I shall demonstrate how the transition and the events immediately preceding it were dominated by elite actors who actively sought to limit social mobilization and channel political activity into exclusively electoral forms. The relationship between popular organizations and political parties changed to reflect the dynamics of the transition process, but it was still a competitive relationship to the extent that popular-sector leaders endeavored to create a new popular social movement. In this new context of political democratization, the result was an effective demobilization of the popular sectors as a collective actor in Chilean politics. Several factors that contributed to the demobilization of the popular sectors are analyzed, including the constraints on the transition, the preponderant role played by political parties, and confusion within the popular sectors. Once again, the experience of the Unitary Pobladores' Command (CUP) is used as an illustration.

In the second part I look at the current democratic regime and the role the popular sectors play in it. It will be argued that fundamental changes to the Chilean state, political-party system, and civil society during the military regime have potentially opened up significant new avenues for popular-sector participation in postauthoritarian Chile. Whether or not these avenues are followed will depend, in large part, on the ability of the popular sectors to adapt their experiences under the military regime to the new opportunities provided by a democracy. The various obstacles the popular sectors face in attempting to do so will be discussed. I conclude by examining some of the fundamental limitations of popular organizations as revealed by the return to a democratic regime.

THE TRANSITION FROM ABOVE AND THE RETURN TO ELECTORAL POLITICS

Although the transition process would not actually begin until Pinochet's bid for another term as president was defeated in the October 1988 plebiscite, the form that an eventual transition would have to take and the opposition strategy required to achieve it were becoming increasingly clear in 1987: A transition to democracy would be feasible only if it took place within the general framework provided by the 1980 constitution. The opposition would have to accept implicitly the 1980 constitution's de facto legitimacy (something it had previously refused to do) and adhere to the military regime's own plans for a relatively controlled transition to civilian rule. At the same time, the opposition would have to press the military for guarantees ensuring the fairness of the electoral process. It could then use the limited political space that would be opened up (freedom to organize and campaign publicly, access to the mass media, including television) to block Pinochet's personal ambition to remain in power, win concessions from the military on subsequent constitutional reform and, ultimately, assume the presidency in 1990.[1]

1986 proved decisive in demonstrating the futility of the opposition's continued reliance on mass mobilizations to force the military regime into making concessions on the pace and nature of the transition. Particularly after the relatively successful July protest and national strike, when two young protesters were deliberately burned alive by a military patrol, all of the principal opposition parties—with the notable exception of the PC—gradually came to the conclusion that the protests could not achieve their stated goals without a very high cost in terms of the violence that the regime was prepared to unleash and the growing disaffection of the middle class. All subsequent opposition efforts would focus on electoral issues, beginning with an unsuccessful effort to mobilize people to press the demand for immediate presidential elections in 1987.

Protests aimed at destabilizing the regime in order to force the military to make concessions were increasingly seen by the opposition as counterproductive. The violence surrounding the mass protests created a climate of uncertainty and fear, particularly among the middle class, which only helped strengthen the military regime. The military regime was afforded a certain legitimacy in attempting to restore "law and order," even though the state security apparatus was responsible for the bulk of the violence. At the same time, middle-class suspicions of excessive popular influence in the opposition were encouraged.

The problem of political violence also accentuated another problem in the opposition: the lack of a consensual alternative to the military regime that could serve as the basis for negotiating the regime's termination. As already discussed, divisions within the opposition (including those regarding the role of the protests themselves) had prevented a united opposition from developing a concrete alternative to the military regime and the 1980 constitution that would provide the basis for initiating a genuine transition

1. Good general accounts of the plebiscite and transition processes are found in Angell and Pollack 1990; International Commission 1989; and Garretón 1989b. The unfolding of events from 1987 on is analyzed from the perspective of the popular sectors in a very useful series of publications by ECO *Taller de Análisis Movimientos Sociales y Coyuntura.* See various issues.

process. The lack of an opposition consensus only exacerbated uncertainties and fears concerning what would happen if the opposition were to assume power.

Ironically, acceptance of the institutions and economic model established by the military regime became the central core of an opposition consensus. As the deadline neared for a constitutionally mandated plebiscite in which voters would either accept or reject the military junta's candidate for an eight-year term as president, the issue of political violence lost much of its polarizing potential after the atrocity of the July protest.[2] The opposition's options narrowed as the military government began to establish the institutional infrastructure that would govern the pending electoral process. In particular, laws were passed covering voter registration and the legalization of political parties in 1987. The opposition now faced two alternatives: it could either continue to reject even the de facto legitimacy of the military regime by boycotting the plebiscite and then challenging the validity of the inevitable victory of the junta's candidate, or it could unite to oppose the junta's candidate and take advantage of the opportunities that the military's efforts to secure its political legacy opened up.[3] This latter option would necessarily entail the parties' active involvement in registering voters and their incorporation into the regime's process for legalizing political parties. Once legally recognized, the parties would be given the right to organize and campaign publicly, as well as to observe both voting and vote-counting processes to ensure against fraud. They would also enjoy at least limited access to television and other mass media. Moreover, the process of registering voters and collecting the signatures required for their legalization would allow political parties to further penetrate society and reestablish their social bases in an orderly fashion.[4]

The military's success in advancing the institutionalization of the 1980 constitution made an opposition consensus necessary and feasible. Whereas

2. Tolerance of political violence within the opposition also declined in the aftermath of the attempted assassination of Pinochet in September 1986 by the Manuel Rodríguez Patriotic Front, a paramilitary organization with close ties to the PC. A state of siege was declared and repression increased, including the assassination of prominent opposition figures in what appeared to be the security forces' revenge for the deaths of several of Pinochet's escorts in the Front's attack.

3. It should be noted that during the first half of 1987 a group of political leaders attempted to organize a campaign for competitive elections as an alternative to the plebiscite called for in the 1980 constitution. People were often urged to register in order to prepare for either possibility. As Garretón (1989b) correctly points out, however, the campaign had almost no possibility of succeeding.

4. A party had to collect 30,000 signatures across Chile to be legalized.

past efforts to forge a united opposition (such as the 1985 National Accord) had broken down in large part due to disagreements over the time frame and appropriate method for securing a transition to democracy,[5] these issues had now been effectively resolved by the military. The constitution set a deadline of 11 December 1988 for holding the plebiscite. As that deadline approached, the opposition's best hope was in defeating the junta's candidate by as resounding a margin as possible in order to win concessions in modifying the 1980 constitution prior to the presidential elections that would have to be held in 1989. The opposition could take advantage of the mechanisms provided by the 1980 constitution to push the liberalization process further than originally envisioned by its framers. This could only improve the prospects for an eventual return to a relatively unrestricted democratic regime.

While the outcome of such a strategy was far from certain and depended on the opposition's ability to overcome substantial disadvantages (including widespread doubts as to the willingness of Pinochet to accept an opposition victory), the military would also run substantial risks if it attempted to subvert the free expression of popular will in the plebiscite. For the military, the 1980 constitution had come to symbolize the legacy of its rule. Any failure on their part to respect the letter and intent of the constitution's provisions would undermine this legacy and invite serious dissension within the military's ranks. The 1980 constitution thus imposed significant constraints on the military's freedom of action, particularly Pinochet's personal ambition to remain in power (Oxhorn 1986). These constraints presented the opposition with important opportunities—provided it accepted the de facto legitimacy of the constitution and the legislation promulgated to implement it.

5. While it is true that Pinochet chose to ignore the National Accord and publicly declared it irrelevant, divisions among the accord's signatories over its interpretation and the problems created by the radical Left publicly adhering to the accord effectively undermined its credibility as a viable alternative through which to negotiate a transition to democracy with the military. The divisions within the opposition weakened the National Accord to the extent that Pinochet could marginalize it from the national political process relatively easily. Only a unified opposition with much higher levels of public backing could have forced the military regime to make concessions it otherwise was reluctant to concede. While the Civic Assembly also ultimately failed to win any significant concessions from the military, the considerable level of opposition consensus behind it and its much higher level of support among the general public meant that the military could not simply ignore it the way it had ignored the National Accord. For example, the Civil Assembly's leadership was openly harassed in an unsuccessful effort to undermine its campaign building up to the July 1986 national protest.

The opposition's decision to abide by the military's own framework for the transition meant that its only chance to gain control of the process lay in the electoral arena. Electoral strength was essential to increasing the opposition's bargaining power, first with the military regime prior to the 1989 presidential elections, and later with the Right once democracy was restored in March 1990. All opposition efforts would have to be directed toward maximizing voter turnout, especially among the popular sectors whose vote would be pivotal given their large numbers. The opposition had to accomplish this without alienating the important middle-class vote or undermining the confidence of the business community in a return to civilian rule. If the opposition failed on either count, it risked losing the electoral competition and jeopardizing the military's willingness to accept an opposition victory.

The opposition's new electoral strategy accentuated many of the trends already apparent in 1986 concerning the growing political marginalization of popular organizations, even while the individual votes of *pobladores* remained crucial. Now, however, this marginalization was not so much the result of the narrow partisan interests of political parties, but of the constraints imposed on political activity by the nature of the transition process. Once a commitment was made to challenge the military regime in the 1988 plebiscite, political parties came to dominate citizens' participation in politics. This virtual political-party monopoly on participation was subsequently reinforced by the opposition's victory in the plebiscite and the resultant elections for president and parliamentarians in which political parties on the Right also played a predominant role. Chile's political-party elites were once again at the forefront of Chilean politics. In contrast to the early 1970s, they were now endeavoring to portray an image of moderation, conciliation, and pragmatism that could be seriously undermined by apparently uncontrollable social mobilization demanding redress for Chile's multiple social problems. Earlier opposition concerns about the growing radicalization of the popular sectors continued to persist. They were exacerbated by Pinochet's own campaign strategy, which focused on the uncertainty and potential havoc that an opposition victory would entail by drawing graphic links between the opposition and the social upheaval of the early 1970s. As in 1986, the relatively moderate nature of the aspirations and demands expressed by popular-organization leaders did not support such fears. But the weakness of political-party links with civil society and the constraints on political activity still maintained by the military government meant that political parties either did not understand the moderate nature of popular-sector expectations, or could not convey an image of such moderation to other segments of Chilean society.

This is similar to the pattern found in most recent transitions to democracy in Latin America (O'Donnell and Schmitter 1986).[6] In Chile, however, it gave the entire transition process a distinctly elitist character that stands in sharp contrast to the effervescence exhibited by civil society in preceding years. Although citizen participation was still quite high throughout the period 1987–89, it was largely restricted to registering to vote, the signing of petitions required for the legalization of political parties, and voting in the plebiscite and subsequent elections.

In February 1988, the Command for the No (*Concertación por el No*) was formed by thirteen opposition political parties, and it eventually grew to include seventeen by the end of 1988. It was dominated by the Christian Democrats (as the largest party in the coalition), the Nuñez branch of the Socialist Party, and the newly formed Party for Democracy (*Partido por la Democracia*, or PPD).[7] Other parties included the Christian Left, the Almeyda branch of the Socialist Party, as well as a number of smaller parties from the Right, Center, and Renovated Left. These same parties would later form the *Concertación de los Partidos por la Democracia* (*Concertación*).

Maintaining the opposition's newfound unity was no simple task, despite the underlying consensus that theirs was the only viable opposition strategy. It required accentuating what had typically been the central role of political elites in other recent transitions to democracy. The interests and concerns

6. The Chilean case does differ in several respects. First, the "electoral moment" emerged *before* the transition process actually began and was seen as the only alternative for ensuring that such a transition actually took place. Second, political parties did play an important, but clearly not exclusive, role in earlier mobilizations leading up to the decision to participate in the plebiscite. Mobilizations were an explicit part of opposition-party strategies for confronting the military regime, and the new consensus reflected the parties' belief that their strategy for mobilizing opposition had failed.

7. The PPD was created to allow parties from the Renovated Left to bypass the 1980 constitution's prohibition against political parties professing a Marxist ideology. Initially viewed as an "instrumental party" that would no longer be necessary once the constitution could be amended, the PPD's impressive popularity among the electorate, which will be discussed in greater detail below, led many of its founders to abandon their original aim; and the PPD is currently one of the major political forces in Chile. A similar instrumental party was created for the Traditional Left, the *Partido Amplio de Izquierda Socialista* (PAIS). Divisions within the Traditional Left and the defeat of virtually all of PAIS's candidates in the 1989 elections led to its dissolution in 1990.

of the coalition's disparate members had to be accommodated and deliberate efforts were made to counterbalance the inevitable tendency for the command to be dominated by what was clearly its largest member, the DC. All important decisions had to be made through negotiations between the leaders of the various parties—essential if the opposition was to portray itself as a viable alternative to the military regime and Pinochet's continued rule.

The task was further complicated by the absence of any objective indicators of each party's capacity to represent significant segments of Chilean society, since the last national elections were held in 1973. While the relative strength of the DC and PS(N) were clear, all parties had suffered from the cessation of normal political-party activity for fifteen years and the capacity of any particular party to mobilize potential voters was not clear. Even during the height of the national protests, individual political parties invariably failed when they tried to mobilize people without the cooperation of other parties; the success of the protests was contingent on the support of all of Chile's principal political parties. No political party appeared too small or unimportant to be ignored and the opposition could ill afford giving the progovernment media an opportunity to exploit fears of excessive party factionalism and dissension within the opposition ranks.[8]

If effective mechanisms had existed to allow for greater direct input by mass actors into the opposition's political decision-making processes, it would have been very risky to use them. The outcome would always threaten to raise issues over which an opposition consensus did not exist. Moreover, events were progressing at a rapid pace. After so many years with virtually no institutionalized opening for the opposition, it had now just over a year and a half to organize a campaign to defeat an entrenched military dictator bent on retaining power. Finally, the uncertainty and the haunting specter of the events of the early 1970s meant that the opposition had to appear to be placing national interests ahead of more narrow party interests. Any effort to mobilize mass support behind the position of a particular political party in order to influence negotiations would only raise concerns that political elites were again resorting to the same kinds of narrow partisan tactics that had contributed so disastrously to the September 1973 coup.

8. The results of the 1989 national elections changed this and, not surprisingly, there has been a gradual decrease in the influence of smaller parties within Aylwin's coalition government. For example, see *Análisis* 14 (29 April–5 May 1991): 10.

Political participation was thus subordinated to the necessity of maintaining previous agreements reached among a relatively small number of political elites. This limited input was further exacerbated by the nature of the electoral process established by the military regime, with little input from the opposition. The country was divided into a series of electoral districts for selecting members of both houses of Congress. Each district was allocated either two Senate seats or two seats in the lower house, but voters could only vote for one deputy or senator in each district. Parties could form alliances and present lists of two candidates for each district. For both candidates on a given list to win, their combined total vote count had to be more than twice that won by the list receiving the second highest total vote count. For example, in a district with just two lists, the winning list would have to receive two thirds plus one of the district's total vote in order for both of its candidates to be seated. If the combined total was less than that, the candidate receiving the most votes on the second list would automatically receive the second seat in the district.[9] This meant that the Right would only have to win at most one third of the votes in any given electoral district in order to win one seat, necessitating an even higher level of coordination between opposition parties so that they could overcome this obvious electoral bias. Candidacies had to be carefully apportioned to maximize each list's vote-getting potential. Most important, the parties of the Concertación had to agree to present only one list in each district because multiple opposition lists would only help the Right to capture more seats in the Congress.

The importance of elite agreements for determining the nature of political participation was reinforced (and expanded to include representatives of the political Right) by subsequent developments, including the actual outcome of the 1989 elections. To begin with, the opposition had accomplished what many had considered impossible just a few years earlier:

9. The results from one of Santiago's two senatorial districts provide a good illustration. The two candidates on the Concertación's list were Andres Zaldívar, of the DC, who received 29.8 percent of the vote, and Ricardo Lagos, of the PPD, who received 29.2 percent of the vote. Jaime Guzmán, of the UDI, received 16.4 percent of the vote and Miguel Otero, of the National Renovation Party (RN), received 14.6 percent of the vote on a list representing the Right. (A third list captured 5.3 percent of the vote.) Because the combined total of the two opposition candidates was less than double that received by the second-place list (58.9 percent to 30.9 percent), Guzmán, and not Lagos, was awarded the district's senatorial second seat. Overall, the Right won nine Senate seats, out of a total 38 contested seats, in districts where Concertación candidates came in first and second. For the lower house, this happened thirteen times, although two of PAIS's candidates also won in this way. See Angell and Pollack 1990.

Pinochet's efforts to retain the presidency for an additional eight years were thwarted; Patricio Aylwin was to assume the office of the presidency after winning just over 55 percent of votes cast and the Concertación had won a majority of the elected seats in both houses of Congress. The obvious efficacy of the opposition's strategy based on elite accommodation could only help to legitimize, if not institutionalize, the same pattern of circumscribed political participation during Aylwin's subsequent term in office. Aylwin was also committed to forming a coalition government, even though Chile was not a parliamentary system. What better way could there be to manage the delicate task of maintaining an alliance of approximately a dozen disparate political parties eager to ensure their own role in Chile's new democracy and maximize their chances in future electoral competitions?

Moreover, the Concertación's principal legislative initiatives (from those dealing with the situation of political prisoners and human rights abuses under the military regime to constitutional reforms concerning local government, the composition of the Senate, and the judiciary) would be stymied unless the Aylwin government could reach an accommodation with the Right. Although the parties of the Concertación had won 72 out of 120 seats in the lower house[10] and 22 of the 38 elected seats in the Senate, the Right effectively controlled the Senate due to the presence of nine senators who were appointed by Pinochet. Any legislative act required at least some support from the Right in order to avoid a Senate veto. Substantive reforms of the constitution and other institutions established by the military regime would require larger majorities. These ranged from 27 senators and 68 deputies for laws governing the party and electoral systems, to 31 senators and 80 deputies for reforms of the constitutional amendment process itself and civil-military relations (Angell and Pollack 1990).

Efforts by the Aylwin government to further the democratization process and eliminate the "authoritarian enclaves" embedded in the 1980 constitution would require intense negotiation among the parties of the Concerta-

10. It should be pointed out that two of those seats went to candidates representing PAIS, one from IC and the other from the Almeyda branch of the Socialist Party, but in reality both can be treated as part of the Concertación. After the elections, the PS announced its long-awaited reunification. The IC was also in the Concertación, and its future as a major political party also is in doubt. It was able to elect only one candidate to the Chamber of Deputies and even its then president, Luis Maira, failed in his bid to win a Senate seat. With the subsequent reunification of the PS, a number of prominent IC leaders, including Maira, left the party, taking a sizeable portion of the party's popular base with them. These changes in the political spectrum will be discussed at greater length below.

ción and the Right in order to reach a compromise acceptable to all the principal political parties. Such negotiations actually achieved their first success with the constitutional amendments enacted in mid-1989,[11] and they intensified after the elections of that year, in anticipation of the reopening of the Chilean Congress in 1990. Chile's new democratic regime quickly became popularly known as the "democracy by agreements" (*la democracia de los acuerdos*) because of the central role played by party elites who were responsible for reaching a consensus on virtually all major political decisions before submitting them to public judgment.[12]

An important exception to these trends has been the PC, and the Traditional Left in general. Both have been marginalized from the growing centralization of political decision-making at the elite level. Several factors have contributed to this marginalization, and the PC's concomitant political isolation. The principal causes, however, involved the PC's refusal to unequivocally disavow the legitimacy of political violence and constraints imposed by the nature of the transition process itself.

The division between the DC and PC became more pronounced in 1987, as a new opposition consensus emerged and the PC rejected its essential premise. The PC made a tremendous tactical error when it initially called for a boycott of the voter registration process and condemned the plebiscite

11. Negotiations were held between representatives of the Concertación, the Right, and the military regime in mid-1989 and resulted in several modifications of the 1980 constitution. Procedures for amending the constitution were made marginally easier, the influence of the military in the future democratic regime was reduced through reforms of the National Security Council, the constitutional ban on "subversive" ideologies was removed, civilian control over the armed forces was expanded, and the total number of senators was increased to reduce the relative influence of the designated senators. Negotiations also resulted, two weeks before the elections, in the appointment to the executive body of the Central Bank two members approved by the opposition, two members approved by the military government, and a mutually agreed upon independent president. See Angell and Pollack 1990.

12. See *Análisis* 14 (6–12 May 1991): 8–10. A partial exception to this general pattern concerned changes to the military regime's system of labor relations in which representatives of trade unions and businessmen were directly incorporated into the negotiation process through a series of tripartite agreements between the government, organized labor, and employer groups. But these negotiations were also carried out at the elite level, with almost no opportunity for rank-and-file participation. See Epstein 1992 and Ruiz Tagle 1992.

The above is not meant to imply that the current Chilean regime is in any sense "undemocratic." As Edgardo Boeninger, minister–secretary general of the presidency and a principal architect of Chile's democracy by agreements, explains, these elite agreements are nothing more than "an expression of representative democracy" (*Análisis* 14 [13–19 May 1991]: 5). They do, however, imply only a limited role for popular mobilization and reduce the opportunities for social movements or any nonparty actors to influence governmental policy directly—a theme I shall return to below.

as illegitimate. The PC was still clinging to a policy of refusing to recognize even the de facto legitimacy of the institutions established by the military regime, while other principal opposition parties publicly recognized the futility of this position. Then the PC suddenly reversed its position, supporting not only the opposition's voter registration drive, but the "No" campaign and Aylwin's eventual bid for the presidency.

The abrupt policy reversal was too little, too late; the PC was racked by confusion, uncertainty, and dissension at all levels of the party. The Concertación still would not incorporate it into the political negotiation process, due at least in part to the military's insistence on excluding the PC and the powerful propaganda tool that reaching any compromise with the PC would give Pinochet. Moreover, while it pledged to support the new democratic regime and formally ruled out resorting to political violence under the current circumstances, the PC refused to condemn the use of political violence as inherently undemocratic and explicitly left open the possibility of returning to its policy of supporting "all forms of struggle" should the circumstances so warrant. It even suggested that someday violence might be necessary to protect Chile's democratic regime from attacks by the Right.

A number of considerations have influenced PC strategy since 1987. The decision in 1980 to adopt a strategy of popular rebellion was taken at a time when the PC perceived the military regime to be at the height of its power after its new constitution had been ratified in a national plebiscite. Seven years later, it appeared that Pinochet would actually succeed in institutionalizing a very restrictive democratic regime and personally retain power well into the 1990s as a result of another national plebiscite. Moreover, just as in 1980, the DC was refusing to ally itself openly with the PC to oppose Pinochet.[13] The PC was clearly entering a new crossroads in terms of its political future, and it initially adopted an essentially conservative strategy.

Regardless of its efficacy for undermining the military regime, the popular rebellion strategy and the PC's refusal to compromise with the military regime allowed the PC to not only survive, but grow. The PC had adapted to the shift in its social base from the labor movement to the *poblaciones* and maintained an image of having consistently rejected the legitimacy of

13. It should be pointed out that in 1987, the DC was on much stronger ground in doing so, given the FPMR's attempted assassination of Pinochet in September 1986 and the discovery of secret arms caches and guerrilla training schools linked to the PC in August 1986.

the military regime and its political institutions. Given the widespread uncertainty, if not incredulity, concerning the likelihood that Pinochet would actually accept a defeat in the upcoming plebiscite, the PC chose not to change its strategy. From the PC's perspective, if the opposition failed in its effort to initiate a transition by using the political space provided by the plebiscite, the position of the PC would only be strengthened; if the opposition did succeed, the PC could ill afford to alienate itself from its new social base if it hoped to remain a significant player in the new democratic regime.

Ironically, the radical position the PC had adopted in 1980 had become part of its own legacy, and it was constrained in much the same way that the Chilean military was by the 1980 constitution. The PC could not disown its previous policies without bringing into question everything that it had come to represent. In many fundamental respects, the strategy of popular rebellion represented a compromise whose very ambiguity (see Chapter 7) allowed different factions within the party to coexist until the eventual outcome of the party's strategy was determined by events that were often beyond the party's control. The PC's gradual abandonment of a strategy of protest mobilizations and its abrupt reversal regarding voter registration and the plebiscite contributed to a significant decrease in Communist militants in the *poblaciones*, as many young people who had joined the party at the height of the national protests in the mid-eighties now found it unattractive. These same issues would later contribute to what the PC itself would describe as its own internal "crisis" after the return to democratic rule (I shall discuss this below).

The PC's predicament also reflected the effects of years of intense repression on its internal party structures and practice of democratic centralism. Physical security necessitated a more fragmented and atomized party structure. This slowed down traditional mechanisms for consensus-building and augmented the importance of the party's central decision-making apparatus for determining party strategy more or less unilaterally. However internally "democratic" the party may have been in the past, its strategy for surviving under the military rule was explicitly Leninist and internal unity was seen as indispensable, at whatever cost. This did not imply that the PC could not dramatically change its policies, but that such changes had to be gradual. It took the party seven years to adopt a strategy of popular rebellion and an additional three years to begin to implement it with the formation of the FPMR. After just three more years, it was already evident that the new policy had largely failed, but the party found it difficult to adapt rapidly to the new opportunities of 1987. This was compounded by the determination of the Right (and much of the Center) to exclude the PC from as many of those opportunities as possible. Moreover, the very uncertainty as to whether the opposition's new strategy would succeed contributed to the PC's indecisiveness.[14]

Yet the PC did adapt in the end—albeit with great difficulty. It supported the voter registration drive and the "No" campaign. It participated in the 1989 elections, supporting Aylwin's presidential bid and (unsuccessfully) running candidates for both houses of Congress. The party has also formally distanced itself from activities associated with political violence, and has even legalized itself under legislation enacted by the military regime.[15]

The elitist nature of the transition and Chile's "democracy by agreements" required that the demands of all segments of Chilean society be moderated and their political participation managed by political elites within the carefully circumscribed parameters of the electoral process. While the popular sectors were not the only group to be affected by these trends, they had a special significance for them. This was due to the particular position of the popular sectors within Chilean society, the predominant role they played in the national protest movement of the mid-1980s, and a general tendency to associate the popular sectors' political activities with the extreme Left, and the PC in particular.

THE TRANSITION FROM THE PERSPECTIVE OF POPULAR ORGANIZATIONS

The period just prior to the 1988 plebiscite and transition entailed significant changes in popular-sector collective action. On the one hand, the progressive marginalization of the popular sectors as an autonomous actor within the opposition was accentuated by a return to electoral politics. On

14. This uncertainty literally lasted up until the military government officially recognized its defeat after considerable delay and hesitation. See International Commission 1989.

15. It should be noted that the strategy the DC had been developing since the mid-1980s was quite suited to the circumstances that had emerged in early 1987, and in this sense must be considered a success. Its leadership of the opposition was basically uncontested, and the DC was in a position to carry the votes of the all-important middle class in challenging the military on the military's own terms.

the other hand, *pobladores* were mobilized to register and then vote in both the plebiscite and the 1989 elections. The *poblaciones* were still a center of political activity, but now the opposition was worried about electoral gains among the popular sectors by the military regime's supporters. Firmly in control of municipal governments, the Right would use the considerable resources this put at their disposal to set up patron-client networks for winning the votes of individual *pobladores.*

At a minimum, the requirements of successfully implementing the opposition strategy for achieving a transition to democracy meant that activities not directly connected with the electoral process would be of secondary importance, including those of popular organizations. Traditional forms of political participation predominated over the alternative embodied in popular organizations. "Everything was for the elections, including the best leaders, which led to a decrease in" popular-sector organizational activity, according to one woman who was active in organizing soup kitchens (personal interview, Santiago, August 1990). Political-party militants were reassigned to voter registration and campaign-related activities. Members of popular organizations who did not belong to any particular party often volunteered to help as well.

Confusion within the popular sectors also contributed to the subordination of autonomous popular-sector organizational activity to the perceived requirements of the transition process (ECO, various issues). Electoral politics was a completely new experience for many of the leaders of popular organizations, either because they were too young to have participated in Chile's previous democratic regime, or they had simply avoided politics until they became involved in popular organizations after the military coup. Moreover, there was no precedent for an autonomous role for the popular sectors in any kind of democratic process in Chile, and the protest movement in which they had actively participated was now considered a failure. The leaders of popular organizations were no longer in a position to innovate alternative forms of political participation in a rapidly changing political context dominated by political parties intent upon restoring traditional modes of participation.

This confusion was compounded by the tactical errors of the PC and much of the Traditional Left. After refusing to compromise themselves by recognizing institutions established by the military regime for a transfer of power to civilian rule, the PC suddenly announced its adherence to the Command for the No's campaign—even though it would not be integrated into the Command for the No. This further underscored the ambiguity of the PC's position within the opposition. A significant segment of the leadership that had emerged within the popular sectors was unsure how to act in the face of what appeared to be the PC's repudiation of its previous uncompromising position, and the party's now uncertain future.

The imperatives of trying to win both the plebiscite and subsequent elections made it difficult—if not impossible—for political parties to accept the emergence of an autonomous popular social movement that could represent the popular sectors in dealings with either the state or political parties. Once again, the experience of the Unitary Command for Pobladores (CUP) illustrates the problematic nature of relations between political parties and popular organizations. It should be recalled that the CUP was created at the Unitary Congress of Pobladores held in April 1986. As explained in Chapter 7, interference by political parties undermined the representativity of the CUP and a decision was taken to convene a new congress in order to elect a new set of permanent officers for the CUP at the end of that year. The subsequent course of events prevented that congress from being held, but the CUP enjoyed a brief resurgence in 1987.

As opposition parties began to redefine their own strategies in 1987, the *pobladores* who had organized the CUP enjoyed considerable freedom of action in attempting to create an autonomous popular social movement. As one of the original leaders of the CUP, who at the time belonged to the more radical Almeyda branch of the Socialist Party, explained: "After the Congress, we realized that political fighting did not lead anywhere. We generated our own discourse, abandoning party interests. It was very complicated for all the *población* leaders. It led to unity among the leaders in order to maintain the movement" (personal interview, Santiago, July 1990). *Pobladores* who were members of the DC now participated in the CUP,[16] which began to reinvigorate its organizational activities in the *poblaciones*. These efforts culminated in the moderately successful First March Against Hunger held in June 1987.

As a consensus emerged within the opposition on a strategy for challenging Pinochet in the upcoming plebiscite, the relative freedom of action enjoyed by the CUP's leadership was increasingly constrained. The tensions between the emergent popular social movement and political parties reached a peak in June 1988, when the CUP's leadership disobeyed the parties and organized a second March Against Hunger. The same CUP

16. The DC did not participate earlier due to fears that the CUP was being used by the far Left.

leader concluded: "The political parties removed all of the leaders of the CUP in June–July. Political leaders were put in their place. The logic of the operation was that of the Command for the No. Social leaders were put into [local] Commands for the No. The social organization was disarticulated because it lost its best leaders. . . . The CUP lasted [another] six months. Out of 40 leaders, only [one] remained" (personal interview, Santiago, July 1990).[17]

The search for elite consensus and the institutions of the military regime imposed constraints on the political process that led to the dismantling of popular-sector organizational structures that reached beyond individual *poblaciones*. These were the same structures that could potentially have served as the basis for creating an autonomous popular social movement. While no longer motivated predominantly by narrow partisan interests, the effects of decisions made by political elites on popular-sector organizational activity had many more far-reaching implications than in 1986. Even more clearly than the earlier Congress, the demise of the CUP in 1988 underscored the dependence of popular organizations functioning at an intermediate level and their ultimate vulnerability to political processes beyond their control. The ease with which the political parties successfully dismantled the nascent movement against the wishes of its founders suggests that the popular sectors will have to overcome major impediments before they can directly affect national politics in an organized and autonomous fashion.

Despite the potential that appeared to emerge in 1986 and again in 1987, the influence of the popular sectors as a collective actor was quite limited during the transition and the period immediately preceding it. *Pobladores* did participate in massive numbers, in both registering to vote and actually voting. But no popular-sector actor was capable of mobilizing large numbers of the urban poor on the basis of distinct popular-sector interests and values. Instead, the initiative for popular-sector mobilization came almost exclusively from political parties on the basis of general appeals to the

---

17. When asked how the parties were able to accomplish this, the person interviewed explained that the parties "took away their authority absolutely. They were dispersed. . . . Money and projects were cut off." It should be pointed out that the CUP was also weakened by the initial rejection of the Command for the No's strategy by the PC and other elements of the Traditional Left. The CUP's inability to define its own posture regarding this fundamental issue independently of the principal political parties represented in it highlighted the organization's lack of autonomy as a political force. See ECO, August 1988.

desirability of a return to democracy.[18] While most *pobladores* perceived the transition as being in their general interest, they were unable to influence its course in ways that may have better served their specific interests as part of a political exchange with other actors.[19]

CONTINUITY AND CHANGE IN CHILE'S NEW DEMOCRATIC REGIME

Given the popular sectors' experience during the transition, the future emergence of a new popular social movement would seem problematic at best. Moreover, the contribution that the popular sectors can make to the further democratization of civil society appears to be relatively limited. Yet there *has* been a regime change, possibly opening up new opportunities or political "space" for the development of the popular sectors into an autonomous social actor. In the short term, much will depend on the specific policies that the Aylwin government adopts in dealing with the popular sectors and their organizations. More fundamentally, changes in the political-party system and the state, as well as the ability of popular organizations to adapt their experiences under the military regime to the opportunities that a return to democracy provides, will set the parameters within which popular-sector organizational activity can continue to develop.

The Concertación and the Popular Sectors

The Concertación's approach to the popular sectors and popular organizations exhibits a remarkable degree of continuity with the views held by political parties and party elites in 1986, as discussed in Chapter 6. Three principals guide its policies in this area. First, increased state resources are to be devoted to helping those most in need—the "victims" of the military regime's socioeconomic transformations. Second, demands for greater so-

18. It should be pointed out that this could be said of most other social movements in Chile at the time. For example, see ECO, various issues.
19. Some of the implications of this will be discussed in Chapter 9.

cial equity are to be subordinated to the government's need to reach an accommodation with the Right on institutional reform and the maintenance of macroeconomic equilibrium. Finally, the *Concertación* is committed to supporting the development of autonomous popular-sector organizational activity.

Despite sustained economic growth since 1984 leading to a substantial reduction in unemployment, 44.4 percent of all Chileans lived in poverty at the end of 1990.[20] Given the magnitude of the problem, the Aylwin government has acted on a variety of fronts in order to begin to pay back this "social debt" inherited from the military regime. The minimum wage was increased by 44.4 percent in June, although its real purchasing power, deflated by a consumer price index weighted for the consumption patterns of the poor (see Chapter 2), was still only 53.8 percent of what it had been in September 1981 (*Análisis Económico*, January–March 1991, 5).

To channel resources to those most in need, the Ministry for Planning and Cooperation was created in July 1990. Social expenditures were projected to reach their highest level in Chile's history. $2.142 billion would be spent in 1990, $336 million more than in the last year of the military regime, and expenditures planned for the period 1991–94 were more than double those of the military government from 1986 through 1989 (*La Epoca* 20 and 24 July 1990).

Repaying Chile's accumulated social debt, however, was just one of the many challenges the Aylwin government faced when it assumed office. Although Aylwin and the parties of the Concertación had won a decisive victory in the December 1989 elections, the new government would have to overcome numerous obstacles in its path toward a fully democratic regime free of the "authoritarian enclaves" inherited as part of the military regime's legacy (Garretón 1989a). Pinochet would remain as commander-in-chief of the Army essentially until *he* decided to step down. Laws were passed in the last months of the military regime to restrict the freedom of action of the incoming administration severely: for example, guaranteeing security of tenure for the vast majority of public-sector posts, speeding up

20. Figures on economic growth and unemployment can be found in *Análisis económico*, no. 1 (January–March 1991). The estimate for the poverty level, which compares to a level of 20 percent in 1970, is from a study conducted by the UN's Comisión Económica para América Latina y el Caribe (CEPAL) and is quoted in *Análisis*, 13 (29 October–4 November 1990): 3. A study conducted by the Programa de Economía del Trabajo (1989, 2) estimated the level of poverty in the Santiago metropolitan region in 1989 at 41.2 percent. Chile's level of poverty was roughly comparable to the 44 percent–level estimated for all of Latin America in 1989 by CEPAL. See CEPAL 1990.

privatizations of state enterprises and services, restricting the activities of remaining state enterprises, offering Supreme Court justices lucrative payments for their retirement in order to allow for the appointment of equally conservative—but much younger—replacements, and even committing substantial portions of state funds before the new government could enact its own budget.[21] Changing these and other restrictive laws, especially if it required modifying the constitution, would require compromise and accommodation with the political Right.

Moreover, the Aylwin government could scarcely ignore the economic situation. Having committed itself to preserving the core elements of the military regime's neoliberal economic model (Concertación 1989), the government had to maintain investor confidence and preserve macroeconomic equilibriums.[22] More radical redistributive policies were simply not feasible, and the Aylwin government only had to look to the economic crises of its immediate neighbors, Argentina and Peru, to recognize the importance of macroeconomic balance.

Under these circumstances, the popular sectors would have to wait until the political and economic situation could accommodate their demands. As Sergio Molina, the new minister for planning and cooperation, explained when he assumed office and announced the record social expenditures: "The government does want the disadvantaged sectors, especially the homeless, the unemployed, those who scarcely have what they require to live, to know that the principal task is to improve the anguished situation in which they live. This is the commitment of the president and those that work with him. But we do not want to fool them. The solutions are not immediate, but they are possible and for this reason we are optimistic" (*La Epoca* 20 July 1990, 35). Interior Minister Enrique Kraus, in his address inaugurating a series of discussion groups on proposed changes to the legislation governing *juntas de vecinos* in the municipality of Conchali on 16 August 1990, echoed this reality: "We are not asking for patience, we are asking for comprehension. The problems inherited from 17 years of the military regime cannot be solved in just 145 days."

21. These laws are commonly referred to as the *leyes de amarre*, which literally means "the binding laws." See Angell and Pollack 1990. The financial constraints the government faced during its first year in office are also discussed in *Análisis* 13 (7–13 May 1990): 19–21.

22. Ironically, the Aylwin government was forced to adopt a series of economic austerity measures upon taking office in order to contain inflationary pressures generated in 1988 and 1989. The military government had overheated the economy in order to win electoral support, first for Pinochet in the plebiscite and then for the Right in the 1989 elections.

Popular organizations have an important role to play in making this strategy viable. As Ricardo Solari, subsecretary general of the presidency, explained, "the great value of nongovernmental [popular] organizations is that their collaboration [with the government] leads to less pressures" (personal interview, Santiago, 10 August 1990). The government has even established a special office, the División de Organizaciones Sociales (DOS), to serve as the interface between itself and community organizations.

The DOS is founded on the assumption that a democratic regime requires a maximum number of autonomous organizations within society and that the government has an important role to play in facilitating their emergence:

> In order to carry through an increase in participation, it is essential that people organize themselves. In order to satisfy any type of aspiration, the population must provide itself with organic forms which can serve as interlocutors with the Government or other authorities. . . . The state function is to strengthen and promote the diverse forms of organization that the society creates, ensuring that they fall within the constitution and the law, but respecting their autonomy without restriction. (División de Organizaciones Sociales 1990, 2)

At the same time, the DOS must also "help ensure that the expectations created by the democratic process are realistic and not the precursors for new frustrations" (División de Organizaciones Sociales 1990, 2–3).

The DOS seeks to moderate popular expectations by reinforcing popular organizations as an alternative to state action for resolving problems faced by the popular sectors. In this way, the DOS hopes to build on the positive experiences of such organizational activity under the military regime: "There exists a tendency to look for the solution to all problems in government action. The experience of recent years in this area shows us that the energy and capacity of organized people is not substitutable in the process of democratization. The government can support, foment and accompany the protagonism of the citizenry, but it can never be a substitute for it" (División de Organizaciones Sociales 1990, 3).[23]

There is a great deal of agreement between the principals guiding the

23. One way in which the Aylwin government hopes to support such organizational activity is through leadership training programs. DOS plans for 1990 envisioned training 15,000 people. Personal interview, E. Pistacchio, director, DOS, Santiago, August 1990.

DOS's activities and many of the core values expressed in *lo popular*. The DOS's commitment to respecting the autonomy of popular organizations and the government's vision of popular organizations as spaces for effective democratic participation have already been mentioned. Similarly, the DOS in principal rejects the paternalism and manipulation characteristic of past governmental efforts to organize the popular sectors:

> The ideal of participation between 1964 and 1973 is very well preserved [in our policies]. But we have learned from the experience of the dictatorship that we cannot preserve ourselves as a paternalistic state. There is no policy of "popular promotion" like Frei and Allende [which was paternalistic]. Our policy is one of respect for the autonomy of the organizations. The state needs its intermediate organizations in order to strengthen itself, but respecting their autonomy. They are not organizations of the state, of a party. . . . They represent the interests of their members and not a government. (personal interview, E. Pistacchio, director, DOS, Santiago, August 1990)

Pistacchio added elsewhere:

> The autonomy of [social] organizations is not an ideological postulate, but the recognition of a cultural reality, a process that has been experienced since 1982, as well as earlier, that is the "positive" [legacy] . . . that the dictator has left us." (*La Epoca* 12 August 1990, 20)

The Concertación's policies regarding social organizations represent an important (and intentional) break with pre-1973 practices. They reflect important changes in the Chilean political system during the military regime—changes that may also augur well for their likely success.

Political Parties and the New Style of Politics

The commitment to greater pragmatism and coalition government expressed by political parties and party elites in 1986 appeared to become reality in 1990. It was evident in the success of the Concertación, but also in the central role played by party elites responsible for reaching a consensus

on virtually all major political decisions—Chile's "democracy by agreements." This is reminiscent of the elite accommodation that had characterized Chilean democracy well into the 1960s, but the way it has been
achieved has fundamentally changed the style in which Chilean politics is
conducted and the nature of Chilean political parties.

   In effect, political parties, together and individually, are trying to transcend Chile's infamous "three thirds" in which the electorate is sharply
divided into three competing camps—the Right, Center, and Left—on the
basis of uncompromising ideological positions (Garretón 1989a). Voting
patterns still roughly correspond to the same three-way split.[24] However,
the old Socialist Party–Communist Party axis on the Left appears to be
irrevocably broken by fundamentally divergent visions of Chile's future,
and by the close association of the Socialist Party (PS) with the Christian
Democratic Party (DC) and the Party for Democracy (PPD) in the Concertación. With several notable exceptions, absolute ideological positions have
been rejected by Chile's principal political parties in favor of a more
pragmatic approach to concrete problems based on consensus rather than
confrontation. There is a deliberate effort to avoid appeals to single
classes or groups in society, and instead emphasize national unity and
reconciliation after seventeen years of military rule.[25]

   24. In the 1992 municipal elections, the Center parties within the Concertación received
35.5 percent of the vote, with the largest share (28.97 percent) going to the Christian
Democrats. The moderate Left (the Socialist Party, the Party for Democracy, and independents,
all part of the Concertación) received 17.64 percent of the vote and the far Left (which was
not part of the Concertación) received 6.6 percent, for a combined total of 24.24 percent of
votes. The Right (the National Renovation Party, Independent Democratic Union, and smaller
groups, including the populist Union Center) received 37.77 percent. See La Epoca 30 June
1992, 9. This result compares with the 1973 congressional elections in which Center parties
received 32.8 percent of the vote, with 34.9 percent voting for parties of the Left and 21.3
percent voting for the Right. See Scully 1992.
   25. These changes reflect the evolution of most major Chilean political parties toward what
Robert Dix has described as the "catch-all" parties that are typical of most of Latin America:
"A catch-all party is one that eschews dogmatic ideology in the interests of pragmatism and
rhetorical appeals to the 'people,' 'the nation,' 'progress,' 'development,' or the like, that
electorally seeks (and receives) the support of a broad spectrum of voters that extends the
party's reach well beyond that of one social class or religious denomination, and that develops
ties to a variety of interest groups instead of exclusively relying on the organizational and
mobilizational assets of one (such as labor unions)" (Dix 1989, 26–27). It should be noted
that Dix seems to place the DC erroneously in this category before the military coup. As
shown in both Chapters 2 and 6, most analysts and Chilean politicians themselves appear to
agree that the DC's own dogmatic pursuit of a Christian Democratic ideology and its
unwillingness to seek pragmatic compromises with other political actors was one of the causes
of the breakdown of Chilean democracy. In fact, the DC's own self-criticism in this regard

A number of important changes have taken place within the political-party system since the beginning of 1987. The Renovated Left has been consolidated by the emergence of the PPD and the unification of the PS in late 1989. While sectors associated with the Traditional Left remain in the PS, the predominant tendency at the level of the national leadership is clearly associated with the process of socialist renovation (discussed in Chapter 6). This process of renovation has been further reinforced by the PS's participation in the Aylwin government and the continued close cooperation between the PS and the PPD.[26] The IC, however, has largely ceased to be a major political force after many of its most prominent leaders defected to either the PPD or the PS.

The strength of the Renovated Left in Chilean politics offers new possibilities for the emergence of a popular social movement. The tendency's apparent commitment to more fluid relations with social movements and more participatory notions of political democracy (as discussed in Chapter 6) are one reason. Another reason is the lack of organic ties between both the PS and PPD and the organized segments of the *poblaciones*. As shown in Chapter 6, only the IC had been able to insert itself effectively into this realm, and those ties have either been fragmented or lost with the demise of that party. This implies, regardless of what each party's actual intentions may be, less capacity to influence the emergence of a new social movement in the *poblaciones*, should one again begin to emerge.

The changes in the Traditional Left have been far more dramatic. In the aftermath of its equivocal policy concerning the plebiscite and its failure to win any seats in the newly elected Congress, the PC entered into what its own leadership publicly referred to as a crisis. The fact that the PC would even admit to the existence of such a crisis itself is a reflection of how deep the divisions within the party actually ran. The PC had long prided itself on having avoided significant internal divisions—in stark contrast to the

---

was one of the factors that led to the creation of the Concertación and the commitment to "democracy by agreements." Similarly, these and other changes that will be discussed shortly reflect the modernization of Chilean political parties. See Linz 1992.

26. The relationship between the PPD and the PS is not free of tensions. PS leaders played an important role in the PPD's formation as a way to circumvent the military regime's proscription of leftist parties, creating special problems when the PS itself was legalized because prominent figures often held leadership positions in both parties. Moreover, the two parties compete for many of the same voters and each has had fears of being "swallowed" by the other. But their close cooperation seems unavoidable given the undisputed leadership of Ricardo Lagos in the Renovated Left and the results of the 1992 municipal elections, in which both parties demonstrated a rough electoral parity.

266 Organizing Civil Society

PS—and its own survival during the military regime required that the party assume a unified public stance. With the military regime gone and its past policies in support of armed insurrection now in doubt, the party had to deal with the desertion of large numbers of militants at both the grassroots and elite levels.

In the *poblaciones*, many of these defections were by younger militants who had been attracted by the party's role in the protests. While a significant number of them joined either the PS or PPD due to substantive disagreements over PC policies, perhaps even more simply distanced themselves from party politics altogether. Many of these militants had little formal political training, in contrast to militants who had joined the party in earlier periods, suggesting that the ranks of the party were artificially swollen in the mid-1980s.[27]

A number of issues divided the PC leadership, but the most fundamental related to basic disagreements over democratization of internal party structures and the type of political alternative that the Left should represent given the collapse of Soviet-style communism.[28] The crisis was surpassed by mid-1991, when the PC emerged as a much smaller party. The Concertación has rebuffed all overtures of cooperation by the PC, and the PC can be expected to continue its attempt to cement the support of specific groups on the basis of appeals to particular interests that are perceived to have been dealt with inadequately by the government. These include the lack of affordable housing for the homeless, and wage demands in different sectors of the economy such as health care, education, mining, and so forth.[29]

27. Ironically, this also helps explain the slowness with which the PC has been able to adapt to the rapid pace of political change in the last few years. The substantial mass of new militants that entered the party under a specific set of political circumstances has acted as a constraint on political innovation or even a return to the party's traditional pragmatism prior to 1973.

28. The appropriateness of resorting to armed struggle and political violence, thereby abandoning any adhesion to political democracy, was not a significant cleavage in the PC or the Traditional Left. The FPMR had split several years earlier on this issue, with the larger segment maintaining its ties to the PC and supporting the party's more moderate line. The latter faction recently renounced any pretense to maintaining a paramilitary potential, proclaiming its intention to transform itself into a movement that would represent elements of the popular sectors that lack other channels for expressing their interests. See *Análisis* 14 (20–26 May 1991): 12–14. The MIR has also divided on this issue, with the MIR(Político) similarly pledging to integrate itself fully into Chile's democratic political process.

29. The PC formed the Movement of the Allendista Democratic Left (MIDA) in late 1991 in order to profile itself as a leftist opposition. See *Análisis* 15 (23 December 1991–5 January 1992): 10–12. The MIDA did surprisingly well in the 1992 municipal elections, surpassing even its own expectations by receiving 6.6 percent of the national vote.

While the PC may be tempted to assert control over popular organizations in order to further the party's electoral prospects, its own weakness and efforts to win renewed political legitimacy will make this more difficult, if not unlikely.[30]

In the Center, the DC has been confirmed as the dominant party in Chile. As such, its policies (as discussed in Chapter 6) regarding the popular sectors have formed the core of the Aylwin government's program in this area. The DC's continued desire to contain any potential radicalization of popular-sector demands could imply intensified efforts to control popular-sector organizational activities. But the DC is also conscious of the need not to appear to be seeking a hegemonic position within the political system. Ironically, its own political preponderance and commitment to maintaining the *Concertación* as a governing coalition may force it to accept more pluralism and autonomy within popular-sector organizations than might otherwise be the case.

Finally, the Right is still dominated by essentially the same two parties as in 1986: the UDI and the National Renovation Party (RN),[31] of which the RN is clearly the most important.[32] While the RN is much less concerned with establishing any organic ties with the popular sectors, the UDI has continued the efforts it began under the military regime to penetrate the *poblaciones*. This involves a new right-wing populism that is reminiscent of

30. Paradoxically, the numerous ex-PC militants could help spur a resurgence in popular-sector organizational activity in much the same way that former PC labor leaders did during the military regime. Many of these people have important organizational experience and a primary issue that drove a large number of them from the party was the party's excessive centralism and control of grassroots organizations. Whether these people joined other parties or simply retired from political party activity, many remain committed to working with social organizations. An illustrative example is that of a man in his mid-thirties who had been a member of the PC since the mid-70s and had risen to the party's central committee. From a modest background, he had worked organizing *pobladores* almost all of his adult life, even working for a church-sponsored organization for a number of years. He relinquished all leadership positions in the PC in late 1990 (although he had not formally resigned from the party) due to disagreements over the lack of internal democracy within the party and the party's efforts to manipulate popular organizations. While he had effectively retired from political organizing, he continued to work with popular-sector organizations and was even recently given a job within the DOS.

31. The RN was formerly known as the National Union Movement (MUN). It changed its name when it became legalized.

32. The RN has been the government's primary opposition partner in the political agreements that have characterized Chile's "democracy by agreements," even before Aylwin took office in 1990. With thirty-four deputies and thirteen senators, the RN is the second-largest party in Chile. See *Análisis* 14 (23–30 June 1991): 5.

the strategies employed by various political parties of the Center and Traditional Left prior to the 1973 coup.

A case in point is a series of three illegal land seizures organized by the UDI in August 1990. Approximately 800 families participated after having been assured by UDI militants that sympathetic local authorities would take advantage of the situation to find a solution to their housing situation. Most of the participants did not belong to any political party and few had ties to popular organizations (although community leaders and local party militants later became involved in order to help mediate the conflict). The UDI knew that the government would not tolerate such activity and hoped to embarrass it by highlighting its inability to solve the desperate housing situation. The UDI further hoped to undermine the government's human rights position by forcing a violent confrontation with the police. It sent what the police and government condemned as outside "provocateurs" to one of the land seizures when the participants refused to peacefully vacate the land and were dislodged by the police.[33]

At a more general level, the experiences of the past eighteen years have contributed to a new "style" of party politics. The PPD and the RN are the most obvious examples of this new style, but it is permeating all major political parties. Political parties are increasingly centering their activities around national electoral campaigns. This new electoralism emphasizes periodic mobilizations to get out the vote. In between elections, politics focuses on elite decision-making and agreements, opening up potential political space for the resurgence of local issues and concerns.

One factor influencing these trends is public perceptions of the problems with Chile's old style of democratic politics. As discussed in Chapters 5 and 6, both the popular sectors and political elites recognized a need to limit the role of political parties to a more narrowly circumscribed political realm that allowed for more autonomous activities by nonparty actors. Similar sentiments are also expressed by the general population at large (Garretón 1989b). This helps explain why part of the PPD's popularity clearly rests on its very novelty. As one of the few major new political

---

33. The above is based on several personal interviews with individuals at the time in Santiago, as well as reports in *La Epoca*. See in particular the editions of *La Epoca* for 6, 7, and 8 August 1990. In two of the land seizures, the participants voluntarily abandoned the seized land after authorities agreed to explore the possibility that they would be eligible to participate in lotteries for distributing the seized land that was not being used productively. Interestingly, PC militants appear to have played an important role in resolving the conflict after the UDI initially mobilized the land seizures.

parties to emerge under the military regime (the other two being the RN and the UDI), it has deliberately sought to appeal to voters who traditionally considered themselves to be "independents," and it explicitly eschews a style of party politics that subordinates all political activity to narrow partisan interests.[34]

The military regime has also transformed the Chilean state in ways that accentuate these trends. The tremendous reduction in the state's size, with the reduction and/or dismantling of government ministries and the privatization of large portions of the economy, has concomitantly limited the capacity of political parties to construct a massive apparatus through their access to state resources.[35] As Sergio Bitar, then secretary general of the PPD, noted, "a small state means that parties cannot grow through the state, but must be based in civil society" (speech before a local PPD meeting, Valparaiso, 14 August 1991).

This new relationship with civil society is not based on recruiting large numbers of party militants and erecting rigidly controlled party organizations in different spheres of society, as had been the practice in the past. Instead, people are encouraged to participate according to the particular issues and/or candidacies that appeal to them. A woman who worked for a church-sponsored institution that supported popular organizations and was a member of the PC explains: "if the people do not want to approach the parties [on the parties' terms], the parties will approach the people on the people's terms—it is happening. All parties are undergoing structural changes, changes in leadership, etc." (personal interview, Santiago, August 1990).

While the state was decreasing its role in Chilean society, it was also being decentralized. This further reinforces a new style of politics. Municipal governments now administer a number of governmental services that were

34. Garretón (1989b) and Scully (1992) argue there are no new major political parties because most of their leaders were active in politics prior to the coup. One should not overemphasize this historical continuity with traditional parties, given that they have explicitly tried to break with past organizational styles and structures. Moreover, many of their most prominent leaders, including Ricardo Lagos (the PPD's founding president), Sergio Bitar (the PPD's current president) and the RN's president Andrés Allamond, among others, were never active in electoral politics before 1973.

35. Central government expenditures as a percentage of GNP declined from 43.2 percent in 1972 to 32.8 percent in 1990. See World Bank 1992, 239. In terms of public-sector employment, approximately 95,000 jobs were lost between 1973 and 1979 alone. If the number of jobs that would have been created had public-sector employment expanded at its historical rate (an average of 3.84 percent per year 1940–70) are included, the total rises to almost 183,000. See Martínez and Tironi 1985, 69–70.

formerly the responsibility of central authorities. Primary and secondary education, basic health care services, low-income housing programs and programs designed to help those living in extreme poverty are now controlled by local governments. As a result, total local expenditures increased 2,500 percent between 1973 and 1987.[36] A high-level PPD official noted that "decentralized institutions mean that parties also have to decentralize. Local leaders worry about local problems, specific problems" (personal interview, Santiago, August 1990). Just as the centralized state apparatus no longer has the capacity to direct many aspects of everyday life, political parties must allow for greater initiative and independence at the grassroots levels. Similarly, party interests at the national level cannot determine all aspects of party activity. This was clearly borne out in the 28 June 1992 municipal elections, in which local leaders and issues predominated.

A good example of this is Jorge Arrate's bid to be mayor of Santiago. Arrate had just completed a term as president of the PS, yet he only managed a third-place showing (enough to guarantee him a seat on the city council). It is difficult to imagine that such a prominent national figure would have entered such a race before 1973 unless a victory could be assured—or that he could survive politically if he lost—yet Arrate knew that it would be extremely difficult for him to win and his political career hardly seems to have suffered as a result of this electoral setback.

Perhaps the best evidence of this new style of politics, however, is the widespread perception of declining citizen participation that corresponds to a distancing of the Concertación from its social bases. In the absence of elections, political parties feel less compelled to renew their ties with society. Moreover, the political dynamic created by efforts to reach elite accommodations on important policy decisions reinforces (if not necessitates) a noticeable deemphasis of mass participation and nonelectoral forms of participation.[37] A female *poblador* who has worked to organize the homeless and democratize *juntas de vecinos* best captured the increasingly common sentiments both within and outside of the *poblaciones*: "The role of politicians is different than it was before 1973. Then, they made the demands of the people their own. Now, they are very technical, very far from the demands of the people. They are trying not to undermine the economic model, but this has nothing to do with popular demands. They

---

36. G. Martelli Nobba (1989, 7).

37. Not surprisingly, the important exceptions to this have been those very parties that have had the least input into elite decision-making processes—the UDI and PC.

are worried about agreements among themselves. This is important for the country, but it does not say much for the problems of the people."

The problem of growing apathy and a lack of participation on the part of the citizenry became apparent in October 1990. The government organized its first mass rally since assuming power in order to welcome President Aylwin back to Chile after a successful trip abroad. It hoped to demonstrate that it, too, could successfully mobilize people after a series of events organized by the Right in September. Expectations were great: the DOS and the Concertación organized the event, Aylwin's popularity in public opinion polls was very high, even the rate of inflation (which was announced the day before the rally was scheduled) was low. But instead of the expected 50,000 people, only 10,000 showed up to hear the president's address (*Análisis* 13 [8–14 October 1990], 6–8).

There is little evidence to suggest that this apathy and lack of participation has changed since then. As Interior Minister Enrique Kraus lamented: "We have lost the capacity to mobilize [people]. The parties had deactivated themselves, the parliamentarians have had to learn the work of congressmen and the government has been preoccupied with its tasks in its offices, and we have distanced ourselves from the social base" (*Análisis* 14 [10–16 December 1990]: 21). More recently, after a Chilean soccer team won the America's Freedom Cup in June 1991, hundreds of thousands of Chileans took to the streets to celebrate in a manner reminiscent of the national protests against the military regime.[38] One commentator noted: "If political lessons can be obtained from a soccer episode, the evidence indicates that our people were capable of again vibrating with the struggle and confrontation. That the passion of the multitudes awakens with vigor when they visualize clear goals and when the people appreciate, as in this championship, that their participation can be decisive in achieving an objective, however limited [that objective] may be" (*Análisis* 14 [10–16 June 1991]: 3).

The significance of these changes in the Chilean political process for the possible emergence of new social movements or actors thus remains ambiguous. The potential space for such movements is clearly there, although no social group appears to be filling it. Moreover, the parties themselves continue to resist fundamental elements of change. This was

38. There were even reports of barricades being built in *poblaciones* and the number of people killed, injured, and arrested was comparable to a typical national protest in the mid-1980s.

apparent in the protracted negotiations over the democratization of municipal governments. The various political parties involved sought to maximize their own electoral prospects when deciding which form these governments would take and the timing of local elections. As a result, something that virtually all parties agreed was both necessary for the continued viability of Chilean democracy and inevitable was postponed in order to pursue purely partisan interests.

Paradoxically, the emergent style of electoral politics simultaneously generates a need for innovative forms of participation in order to close the gap between elected elites and their social bases, yet discourages their emergence by focusing political activity into periodic elections and engendering apathy. For the popular sectors, the issue is even more important given the continued existence of widespread poverty and the constraints on the Aylwin government in attempting to alleviate it.

Popular Organizations and the Return to Democratic Rule

Popular organizations, with the important exception of political organizations dedicated to coordinating party strategies during the national protests, have continued to show sustained growth in recent years. This is despite impressive economic growth and a significant decline in the level of unemployment. Subsistence organizations, for example, have continued to double in number every two years, with 2,237 subsistence organizations functioning in the Santiago metropolitan area in 1989, representing an active membership of just under 80,000 and helping to support over 206,000 people, well over ten percent of all *pobladores* (Razeto et al. 1990, 202).[39] The number of coordinating bodies in the Santiago metropolitan

39. It should be recalled, from Chapter 3, that subsistence organizations accounted for approximately half of all popular organizations in 1986 and are frequently referred to as "popular economic organizations." That percentage has risen with the dissolution of many explicitly political organizations. Razeto et al. (1990, 217–21) estimate that there were 529 other organizations in 1989, including senior citizens', women's, and human rights groups, which had approximately 10,700 members. The percentage of the total Santiago population who are the direct recipients of material support from subsistence organizations has also increased significantly, from 2.3 percent in 1986 to more than 3.5 percent in 1989 (Razeto et al. 1990, 224). The same study, using less conservative figures, estimates that the percentage of the total population receiving direct benefits from subsistence organizations may be as high as 4.15 percent (Razeto et al. 1990, 202). This compares to the approximately 12.5 percent of all workers who belonged to unions at the end of 1990, according to Ministry of Labor statistics. See *Análisis* 14 (15–21 April 1991): 25.

area also has grown significantly. In 1989, there were 102 such organizations, up from only 56 in 1986, although these largely assumed administrative and technical roles in the distribution of available resources (Razeto et
al. 1990, 223). Moreover, many subsistence organizations have adopted
new or redefined activities and goals in accordance with their members'
changing needs (Razeto et al. 1990), an important indicator of the level of
institutionalization that popular organizations have achieved.[40] Similarly,
many appear to be adapting well to substantially decreased support from
the Catholic Church.[41]

While organizational activity at the grassroots level remains relatively
strong, the public presence of popular-sector organizational activity is
extremely low. The popular sectors have lost even the pretense of being a
social actor with the eclipsing of the national protest movement. After the
dissolution of the CUP in 1988, there have been no systematic efforts from
within the popular sectors themselves to create any kind of popular social
movement, or even influence governmental policies. The popular sectors
appear to be demobilized from a political point of view.

A number of factors account for this. One factor, as discussed above, is
the general lack of citizen participation among all segments of Chilean
society that has characterized Chile's "democracy by agreements." In
addition, an important segment of the leadership that had emerged within
popular organizations has, at least for the present, tended to commit itself
to working within political parties instead of strengthening autonomous
popular organizations. These people are dependent upon political parties
for resources, and the central role parties play in Chilean politics makes

40. It should be recalled, from Chapter 1, that adaptability is an important indicator of
institutionalization. In addition to changing goals and activities, the mere fact that many
popular organizations continue to function after the transition suggests a considerable level of
institutionalization. A further indication of their level of institutionalization is the finding that
more than 84 percent of the subsistence organizations included in the Razeto study were either
stable or growing (Razeto et al. 1990, 210).

41. With the return to democracy, the church has taken the position that the responsibility
for resolving the social problems associated with poverty rests with the civilian government
and is instead concentrating its resources on more explicitly religious activities. The church
has been gradually distancing itself from popular-sector organizational activities; in 1991 it
began to cut virtually all ties with many of these organizations. For example, a handicraft
workshop that had been created in 1975 suddenly lost all of its support from the church in
early 1991, including help in marketing the tapestries ("arpillera") it produced and access to
parish buildings for conducting its activities. By August, the workshop had its own center for
carrying out its activities and was operating at least as successfully as it had while receiving
aid from the church.

leadership positions in them very attractive in comparison to the relative political isolation of popular organizations. Moreover, at least some are trying to represent the popular sectors within their respective parties in an effort to make traditional party structures more responsive to popular-sector interests and supportive of a future popular social movement.

Other members of popular organizations exhibit a certain distrust of any legal structures after so many years of operating outside of the law (ECO, June 1989). This distrust is only exacerbated by the very nature of the transition and the failure of the protest movement to force the military into making substantial concessions on constitutional reform. Similarly, legal recognition by even the democratic regime is sometimes seen as a restriction on the organization's ability to act autonomously, reflecting possible anarchistic elements in the collective identity *lo popular*. As one youth leader who ran for an elected seat on his *junta de vecinos* and lost explained:

> There is fear of legalizing *población* organizations through [existing] institutions. Their objectives will be determined by the political conjuncture rather than long-term objectives. For example, [our] youth group's goal is the construction of socialism. We cannot plan this now if we are legalized. . . . The only way to get resources is through legalization. All organizations, including cultural ones, become promoters of grand events [*espectáculos*] instead of developing [our own culture] because that requires a lot of resources (equipment, people to teach, etc.) [which the government will not provide]. (personal interview, Santiago, August 1990)[42]

For many who did not participate in popular organizations before the return of democracy, this fear of participation did not necessarily disappear with the change of regime. According to the woman quoted above who has been active in trying to democratize *juntas de vecinos*, "the average citizen does not participate yet. She is afraid. Thus, there is no neighborhood organization. The only people who participate are groups of party militants or people with more social consciousness who participated before" (personal interview, Santiago, August 1990).[43]

42. This general attitude toward legalization of popular organizations also undoubtedly reflects the lack of any democratic reform of municipal governments, a point that will be discussed below.

43. The same woman went on to point out how this fear was reinforced by the periodic discovery of mass graves of people who had "disappeared" during the military regime: "We are living in between two worlds. [Now] it is more relaxed, there is less fear, but finding bodies, etc., is reminding people of the fear."

Frustration and not knowing how to deal with it explain why the popular sectors appear so acquiescent. Many feel that the transition and Aylwin's victory would have been impossible without the active participation of the popular sectors, through voting and the role they played in the protest movement. While many party elites came to the conclusion that the protests were a failure (if not actually counterproductive), many leaders of popular organizations feel that the protests forced the military to respect constitutional provisions for the transition process.

These same people frequently express disillusionment with what they feel has been the exclusion of the popular sectors from the transition process and the political process in general (ECO, various issues). For them, the true winner has been the political class who took control over government decision-making (ECO, December 1989, 20–24). Many have even begun to question the motives of political parties that had worked with popular organizations during the military regime. A youth leader who had belonged to the Almeyda faction of the PS explained: "There is less [political] activity . . . in part because of deception by political parties. People have realized that they were used by parties of the Left. For example, the PC and illegal land seizures: it gave false expectations for solutions, utilizing [people's] problems" (personal interview, Santiago, August 1990). A former leader of the CUP expressed a common conclusion: "In sum, *pobladores* lost: Their structures, their organization, the capacity to have an effect on society. Their leadership has been disarticulated and discredited. It has been replaced by political representation" (personal interview, Santiago, August 1990).

The slow pace of change has also been a source of frustration. Despite the Aylwin government's pledge to address the social debt, there have been few changes in the day-to-day lives of many people (who perhaps had unrealistic expectations about what a return to democracy would mean). As one middle-aged woman active in organizing soup kitchens noted:

> People thought that with the new government there would be no more *ollas*, that there would be jobs for everyone. They thought the *ollas* would become microenterprises—productive workshops, "popular restaurants"—but this did not happen. Unemployment continues. The circumstances are not right. Moreover, the people lack the capacity [to create microenterprises]. (personal interview, Santiago, August 1990)[44]

44. To a certain extent, this suggests that people's expectations concerning a return to

Similarly, the pace of democratic reform has been slow in key areas. For example, Pinochet remains a vivid reminder of the power that the military and the Right still exercise. As the PS(A) youth leader quoted above noted, democratization "is still an incomplete task because Pinochet has not left."

This problem of limited democratization is particularly apparent at the local level, where popular organizations might most effectively influence government decision-making (see Chapters 1 and 5). Of the 335 mayors in Chile, all but fifteen were appointed by the military regime before the Aylwin government took office.[45] They could be replaced only after elections were held in June 1992—more than two years after Aylwin assumed office. In the meantime, there was little or no change in the officials with whom the *pobladores* had interacted at the local level.

The lack of democratically elected municipal governments also directly affects another principal institution through which the popular sectors can interact with the state: *juntas de vecinos*. In one of the last pieces of legislation enacted by the military government, a new law governing neighborhood organizations was promulgated in December 1989. Among other changes to the existing legislation, the new law allows for the creation of multiple *juntas de vecinos* in each recognized territorial division as a way to fragment a potential popular social movement. It also undermined efforts to democratize existing *juntas de vecinos* by allowing mayors to recognize alternative—but less representative—*juntas de vecinos* that were more sympathetic toward the Right. All municipal resources would then be channeled through these organizations, while the municipal government would turn a deaf ear to more democratically constituted *juntas de vecinos*. An official of a democratically elected *junta de vecinos* described a common problem in many *poblaciones*:

> The mayor does not want to recognize us. The mayor is from the UDI. . . . There is a parallel *junta de vecinos* that is recognized by

---

democracy were somewhat higher that they had been in 1986. This rise in expectations undoubtedly reflects the impact of the electoral process itself. It should be noted, however, that the popular sectors have continued to demonstrate a considerable degree of moderation in their political behavior since the return to democracy. This moderation is consistent with earlier findings.

45. President Aylwin was legally entitled to appoint fifteen mayors in strategic municipalities. The rest were selected by a Consejo de Desarrollo Comunal (CODECO) in each locality and these are structured to overrepresent the Right by, for example, ensuring that local businessmen account for half of the membership of each CODECO and excluding representatives of local labor unions. For more on the antidemocratic structure of local-level government

the mayor because he created it. He gave a lot of resources to it. There are 30 people in it [compared to approximately 150 who attend our assemblies]. The mayor is practically buying the people, dividing the *población*. . . . taking advantage of their poverty, buying their dignity. (personal interview, Santiago, August 1990)[46]

While people are frequently frustrated by the pace of change and the lack of popular participation, they are unsure of how to express such frustration. Whatever their specific disappointments may be, most members of popular organizations are happy that there has been a return to civilian rule and appear to be worried about the possibility of destabilizing the situation by applying excessive pressure on the government. They also have considerable respect for Aylwin and recognize that the 1980 constitution and the strength of the Right in the legislature limit his freedom to act. Many people are also simply waiting to see how the process of democratic reform unfolds.

Translating the experiences accumulated during the period of military rule into political practices that are appropriate for a democratic regime has proven difficult. Time and time again, leaders of different popular organizations referred to the difficulties they face in trying to adapt to the new possibilities opened up by the transition to democracy. A woman active in organizing *pobladores* in the northern sector of Santiago explained: "It has been difficult for the people to go beyond the past stage. It is like starting all over again. They say sixteen years was a long time and the people have almost lost the capacity to think. They still think [their organizations] are clandestine. They cannot believe that there is democracy, that they can organize" (personal interview, Santiago, August 1990).

When Aylwin assumed the office of president, the popular sectors lost an unambiguous enemy against whom they could organize. Mobilization, at least until 1987, emphasized confrontation and called upon the state to respond to specific demands for change. Now, with the transition to democracy over, the popular sectors have a more difficult task of developing

---

and the challenges this poses for the popular sectors, see Solervicens 1990 and Martelli Nobba 1989.

46. The Constitutional Tribunal declared unconstitutional governmental legislation that would have prohibited multiple *juntas de vecinos* in a given territorial district. See *Análisis* 14 (20–26 May 1991): 8. The effect of this finding, however, will be less detrimental once municipal governments are democratized since it will be more difficult for elected officials to ignore representative neighborhood bodies that are democratically constituted.

their own concrete proposals in order to influence politics. As a young man who worked with human rights groups for the Chilean Human Rights Commission during the 1980s explained:

> It was easier to organize activities against the dictatorship—to denounce it—than organize activities for generating proposals. A different kind of participation, of expression, is needed. For example, cultural events. There are still activities denouncing human rights violations, etc. These are good, but we need more and new activities. Proposals looking to the future must be made. Instead of a discourse about the past, we must work so that there will never again be torture, disappearances, etc. (personal interview, Santiago, August 1990)

A young female social worker, also active in human rights work, added: "We have to challenge ourselves to create. Before, everything was a demand against Pinochet. Now we must create what we want" (personal interview, Santiago, July 1990).

The lack of concrete proposals is perhaps the greatest shortcoming of popular organizations to date. At the grassroots level, popular organizations often exhibit a remarkable capacity for self-help and (so far at least) have refrained from placing excessive demands on the state. Yet their capacity to formulate policies and suggest alternatives is quite limited. One reason is that little technical assistance is available to help a popular social movement emerge with this kind of capacity. In contrast, the labor movement has historically enjoyed a high level of technical support and resources (ECO, November 1989).[47]

Another reason may be related to the kinds of popular organizations that emerged under the military regime. At the grassroots level, these organizations can be important sources of social change, serving as foci for democratic participation and collective self-help. Their very foundations within specific territorial communities, however, can limit their national

---

47. This imbalance is also a reflection of the Aylwin government's emphasis on trilateral negotiations among labor, business leaders, and the state. The reasoning behind these kinds of negotiations and their intrinsic limitations are discussed in Chapter 6. Negotiations between labor and business leaders, along with representatives of the state, have already resulted in significant changes in labor legislation and are generally considered a success by the government, regardless of the limited impact they have had on large segments of the popular sectors. See the interview with Labor Minister Rene Cortázar in *Análisis* 14 (6–12 May 1991): 4–6. Also see Epstein 1992 and Ruiz-Tagle 1992.

projection. One must begin to question the appropriateness of this organizational type for generating a new popular social movement under a democratic regime. The role for a popular social movement has changed with the return to civilian rule. Similarly, the demands which that new role places on popular organizations are, in a critical sense, much more difficult to respond to.

Perhaps a more appropriate organizational form to serve as the basis for a new popular social movement is the *junta de vecinos*, First established in the 1960s, *juntas de vecinos* enjoy institutionalized access to the state through now powerful local governments. Already, there is evidence that organizational experiences under the military regime are beginning to transform these traditional organizations in ways that resemble the popular organizations that emerged after the 1973 coup. As the human rights organizer quoted above explained:

> Popular organizations are in a process of rethinking [what it is to be] social actors in the new democracy. Old organizations are again being erected—*juntas de vecinos*. They are integrating themselves with another experience. . . . *Juntas de vecinos* can have offices for human rights, committees for the homeless, cultural committees, etc. All the organizations in each neighborhood [can be in the *junta de vecino*]. . . . This process of integration is taking place. *Juntas de vecinos* are looking for solutions for the problems of their neighborhoods. This institution could achieve an improved standard of living for its neighborhood when it is organized.

Similarly, the woman quoted above who was active in helping to democratize *juntas de vecinos* observed:

> *Juntas de vecinos* now include a much larger gamut of organizations—women's groups, *ollas*, etc. Young people—they have new modern motivations (communications, ecology), therefore *juntas de vecinos* must be modernized. . . . *Juntas de vecinos* have a different vision compared to the past. They are ultrademocratic—a lot of participation, decisions are made by consensus. . . . Traditionally, *juntas* were concerned with urban problems. They must look at new problems, those of popular organizations (homelessness, children, etc.). The old popular organizations will continue, with their own

autonomy. But if unified action is needed, they will turn to the *juntas de vecinos*.

Until now, the emphasis has been on the lack of mobilization by the popular sectors and their generally low levels of political participation; that is, the limited nature of popular-sector collective action. It should be recalled from Chapter 1 that collective action is just one dimension of the contribution that popular-sector organizational activity can make toward the democratization of civil society. The other dimension, which is important in and of itself, is the presence of a popular collective identity, independent of any collective action it might generate.

Despite the limitations imposed on *juntas de vecinos* by the lack of democratically elected local governments, their roles and activities appear to be expanding to reflect the ideals and organizational style that were associated with the emergent popular-sector collective identity, *lo popular*. In this way, *lo popular* continues to exert an influence in the *poblaciones* as the traditional institution of *juntas de vecinos* is restructured by *pobladores* to reflect changes in Chilean society and the challenges Chile faces after eighteen years of military rule. These efforts suggest that *juntas de vecinos* are becoming an important arena for integrating past experiences into the changed reality of democratic politics. This is consistent with the beliefs expressed by leaders of popular organizations in 1986.

Moreover, the popular organizations themselves continue to exhibit many of the same qualities that tended to generate and reproduce *lo popular* under the military regime (Razeto et al. 1990). At the grassroots level, values of community, participation, pluralism, and autonomy are still important to many members of popular organizations—despite the frustrations, uncertainty, and confusion associated with a transition to democracy. Satisfaction of consumption needs and an effective integration into society continue to guide participation in popular organizations. For example, as the man quoted above who worked with popular organizations in the northern sector of Santiago for a church-sponsored institution and who belonged to the PC explained: "I do not believe in paternalistic assistance for the people. It serves no purpose. People must demand the right to participate in society, through jobs, education, and health care." Another young man who has been actively involved with different cultural organizations during most of the 1980s described this more positive legacy left by the military regime:

Thanks to the dictator, we realized that there are more than just political and economic demands. There is also the right to be a person. . . . We continue working on conscientization, constructing a social movement, emphasizing territorial space—the *población*. To achieve a popular communication that expresses the demands of those who live in the *poblaciones*. . . . [Our cultural group] is more than the community. It is recovering the historical memory of the last sixteen years—the values that were created under the dictatorship, solidarity. They must be developed, taking advantage of the public space. (personal interview, Santiago, August 1990)

CONCLUSION

Civil society in Chile has been transformed by the experiences of the past eighteen years. It is certainly stronger and more developed than it was prior to 1973. A variety of self-constituted organizations have emerged within civil society, enjoying an unprecedented degree of autonomy from political parties. As such, they continue to challenge the traditionally dominant role played by political parties in the constitution of social actors. Popular organizations are also important strengthening Chilean civil society. Thousands of organizations have been formed since the imposition of military rule and continue to function despite the recent transition to a democratic regime. These organizations represent a new capacity to organize within civil society at the margin of partisan political activities. By their very existence, these organizations form a rich social fabric whose ultimate potential remains unrealized.

The limited role that the popular sectors as a collective actor played in the transition and their subsequent political demobilization reveal important insights into the nature of popular organizations. As the preceding chapters made clear, popular organizations under the military regime were conditioned in fundamental ways by the authoritarian experience itself. The absence of alternative channels for participation, particularly the weakening of political parties, created an essential space for the emergence of an alternative form of participation in the *poblaciones* of Santiago. The popular organizations that emerged were based on shared interests and a new collective identity, *lo popular*. Their development culminated in (largely unsuccessful) efforts by leaders of popular organizations to create a new popular social movement between 1986 and 1988. This failure, and the fact that these efforts emerged in two very different political contexts, highlights important limitations to the kind of popular-sector organizational activity that developed under the authoritarian regime.

First, as stressed throughout this study, the relationship between political parties and popular organizations remains problematic, at best. As direct responses to the changes induced in Chilean society by the period of military rule, popular organizations represent a potentially "new" actor and identity that frequently clashes with political parties as "old" actors attempting to adapt to those same changes. Their experience and far greater resources (now including direct access to the state) suggest that, for better or worse, political parties will ultimately be the decisive influence on the potential for a popular social movement to emerge, in any form. This trend is reinforced by the nature of Chilean politics, which focuses political activity into political-party channels dominated by a small political elite.

As suggested in the model of political-party base-level organization relations developed in Chapter 1, the relationship between popular organizations and political parties is a function of the scope and nature of the former's demands. As the level of popular-sector collective action approached forming a new popular social movement, the scope and nature of popular-sector demands peaked, bringing the incipient movement directly into competition with political parties.

A change had taken place, however, in the dynamic of this competitive relationship between 1986 and 1988. Whereas narrow-partisan interests led political parties to try to capture the incipient movement in 1986, as the possibility of an actual transition to democracy became increasingly imminent in 1987 and 1988, political parties joined together to dismantle the movement as part of their collective efforts to secure the transition. Generally abandoning self-interest and focusing on a goal clearly seen to be in the public interest, political parties were much more successful in preventing the emergence of a popular social movement in 1988 than in 1986. The result (which also reflects other factors pertaining to the transition and the nature of the popular sectors as a social category) has been the effective political demobilization of the popular sectors as a political actor in the new democratic regime.

This demobilization brings into relief the tension between forms of political participation that were most appropriate in an authoritarian context and those that are more efficacious in a democratic setting. The popular organizations that first emerged during the military regime may never be able to forge a new popular social movement. Their tendency toward fragmentation and limited ability to generate a political project that could transform them into a protagonist in Chilean politics may make that goal impossible. The demands of democratic politics and the ways in which the authoritarian experience conditioned the nature of popular organizations raise serious questions about the ability of these kinds of organizations to effectively represent popular-sector interests in the democratic political process.

It must also be stressed, however, that political parties and the Chilean state have also been changed as a result of the authoritarian experience, potentially creating opportunities at the local level for greater popular-sector input. Moreover, we may be already witnessing a gradual transformation of popular organizations as they, and the central elements of *lo popular*, are absorbed into *juntas de vecinos*. This transformation might prove to be a more effective way to ensure their integration into local levels of government, and into Chilean politics more generally.

The democratic qualities of popular organizations (and the experience that hundreds of thousands of *pobladores* have had in them) also offers an important force for civil society's democratization. The significance of these democratizing influences is ambiguous, given that the democratization of civil society is difficult to measure or even observe. Moreover, the local governments that interact with these tendencies at the base level remained undemocratic until well into 1992. Once again, the effects that these democratizing influences have had within civil society can already be seen in the way they are transforming the traditional institution of *juntas de vecinos*.

As Chilean democracy enters into its consolidation phase, this new strength in civil society and the democratizing influences of popular-sector organizational activity should contribute to making that task easier and more rapid. Changes in the Chilean state and party system can reinforce and further stimulate these positive processes by providing the necessary political space for more autonomous social movements. Whatever collective role that popular organizations and the popular sectors eventually come to play in a consolidated democratic regime, their contributions at the level of civil society will remain a lasting legacy of popular-sector organizational activity under the military regime.

9

POPULAR ORGANIZATIONS, THE DEMOCRATIZATION OF CIVIL SOCIETY, AND POLITICAL DEMOCRACY

Literally hundreds of popular organizations, involving hundreds of thousands of people, emerged in the *poblaciones* of Santiago after the 1973 military coup in response to the new needs and issues created by the authoritarian regime. They were clearly part of a process of the resurrection of civil society that had begun prior to and independently of a democratic transition. These organizations demonstrated an unprecedented level of autonomy from political parties, engaging in a variety of activities in the pursuit of a number of different objectives. They also were characterized by their participatory and democratic qualities. But to what extent have popular organizations contributed to the democratization of Chilean civil society? Perhaps even more important, what lessons does this experience offer for the reconstruction and consolidation of the new democratic regime in Chile?

POPULAR ORGANIZATIONS AND THE DEMOCRATIZATION OF CIVIL SOCIETY

The preceding chapters have shown that popular-sector organizational activity under the authoritarian regime was quite distinct from the type of organizational activity that predominated during the democratic period. The distinctive qualities of popular-sector organizations as they developed during the period of military rule are summarized in Table 29.

Fundamentally, a new type of popular organization had evolved under the authoritarian regime that exhibited greater autonomy vis-à-vis both the state and political parties. It was relatively complex and expressed a new popular collective identity, *lo popular*. This new organizational type did not emerge immediately or spontaneously after the military coup, but was the result of an evolutionary process strongly influenced by the changing political and economic context, support institutions such as the Catholic Church, and the organizational experiences accumulated by the popular sectors under the previous democratic regime.

The process through which popular organizations evolved also suggests their increasing institutionalization. This conclusion is supported by the continued existence and evolution of popular organizations after the transition to democracy. As noted in Chapter 1, the institutionalization of popular organizations is a prerequisite if they are to continue contributing to the democratization of Chilean civil society in the future. As the military regime attempted to ensure its own institutionalization by imposing a neoconservative project on Chilean society, popular organizations demonstrated an impressive level of adaptability in confronting the changing political, social, and economic situation in which the popular sectors found themselves. They have similarly continued to adapt to the changing context ushered in by the return to democratic rule. Moreover, popular organizations have displayed increasing levels of complexity, autonomy, and coherence—all important measures of institutionalization (Huntington 1968).

Today, popular-sector organizational activity is characterized by an interesting mix of continuity and change with respect to the previous two periods, as shown in Table 29. Most obviously, the state no longer represents the threat to popular organizations that it did during the military regime. But unlike the previous democratic period, the state is not the sole referent for the realization of popular-sector demands. Instead, it is one of many alternatives available to the popular sectors, and the state itself has adopted a policy of encouraging greater self-reliance on the part of popular organizations. While the church has distanced itself from popular-sector organizational activities, popular organizations are also seeking assistance from other nongovernmental organizations.

The return to political democracy has led to a shift in the locus of political activity back to traditional political channels. Political parties, in particular, are again the dominant actors in Chilean politics. This has

Table 29. Modalities of organizational activity in the *poblaciones*

	Under the Previous Democratic Regime	Under the Authoritarian Regime	Under the Current Democratic Regime
Relationship to external actors	State is the sole referent for seeking responses to demands.	Antagonistic relationship with state. Exclusion of popular sectors from political participation and access to the state. Popular organizations must resist regime's efforts to disarticulate all forms of popular-sector organization.	State is one referent for seeking responses to demands. State seeks to strengthen community organizations as an alternative to state action for resolving the problems of the popular sectors.
	Dependence on political parties for access to state. Limited autonomy.	Tension between political parties and popular organizations. Popular organizations are generally pluralist. High level of autonomy from political parties.	Tension between political parties and popular organizations at grassroots level less pronounced. Popular organizations continue to be pluralist. High level of autonomy from political parties.
	Limited relations with other external actors.	Importance of "support institutions," especially the Catholic Church, in stimulating popular-sector organizational activity. Excessive dependence on support institutions into late 1970s. Increasing importance of popular sector's own organizational initiative and organizational autonomy since then.	Limited church support for popular organizations compensated for by increasing importance of popular sectors' own organizational initiative, state programs and various nongovernmental organizations. Autonomy of organizations still stressed.

Table 29. *Continued*

	Under the Previous Democratic Regime	Under the Authoritarian Regime	Under the Current Democratic Regime
Organizational dynamic	Interparty competition for electoral support.	Alternative locus for political activity with the cessation of traditional political-party activity.	Return of traditional party activity has limited their political activity, which is now largely confined to working through *juntas de vecinos*.
	Absence of self-help	Self-help initiatives predominate.	Self-help initiatives still predominate.
Nature of demands	Particularistic. Little or no interest in systemic change and alternative forms of social organization.	Collective. High interest in systemic change and alternative forms of social organization.	Transition to democracy has muted demands for systemic change. Demands continue to be collective and popular organizations still represent alternative forms of social organization.
	Lack of sense of collective identity.	Strong sense of collective identity, *lo popular*. Limited efforts to create a popular social movement based on *lo popular*.	Continued strong sense of *lo popular*. No efforts to create a popular social movement.

coincided with a marked decrease in the political activities associated with popular organizations. Instead, there is a new tendency to channel such activity through *juntas de vecinos* and there are no efforts to create a popular social movement. But these traditional institutions for local-level participation appear to be undergoing an important evolution that reflects their absorption of many of the ideals associated with *lo popular* and the political activities of popular organizations during the period of military rule. Moreover, autonomy from political parties remains an important issue for popular-sector organizations, and political-party challenges to that autonomy—at least so far—are less severe than during the mid-1980s and the preceding democratic regime.

The institutionalization process experienced by popular organizations represents one of the most interesting paradoxes of Chile's authoritarian experience. As explained in Chapter 2, a primary characteristic of the Chilean political system under the democratic regime was the dominance of the political-party system over society, which impeded the development of the autonomous and self-constituted units characteristic of "civil" societies (see Glossary). The cessation of traditional political-party activity, combined with the new needs and interests of the popular sectors created by the imposition of authoritarian rule, provided the necessary political space for this institutionalization process to occur.

This institutionalization process was closely intertwined with the emergence of a new collective identity, *lo popular*, based on the shared dispositions of members of popular organizations and increasing levels of collective action organized around that identity. Both were reactions on the part of the popular sectors to changes in Chile's economic structure and the organization of Chilean society induced by the authoritarian regime. And regardless of the impact of the transition to democracy on the political mobilization of the popular sectors, the evolution of popular-sector organizational activity since then suggests that many of the ideals associated with *lo popular* have not disappeared. These ideals continue to influence not only the organization and functioning of the popular organizations that emerged under the military regime; they are conditioning the revitalization of *juntas de vecinos* in many *poblaciones* as well.

The discussion of *lo popular* in Chapter 4 highlighted the democratizing potential of popular organizations within society as a whole. But, as pointed out in Chapter 1, in order to maximize this potential, popular organizations must somehow coalesce and form a new popular social movement that seeks to transform civil society. In other words, the popular sectors must engage in new forms of collective action that transcend individual communities and reflect the ideals and interests embodied in *lo popular*.

The emergence of a popular collective identity and its capacity to generate new forms of popular collective action are two independent (but obviously related) empirical questions that will vary from case to case. Nor is there any necessary sequence in the emergence of a collective identity and its translation into collective action. Both can emerge more or less simultaneously, as ad hoc collective solutions to new social and economic needs are institutionalized on the basis of a collective identity that itself is born out of the deteriorating socioeconomic situation confronted by the urban poor.

In such a case, both the emergent collective identity and the organizations that embody it will tend to be more vulnerable to external factors—particularly a democratic transition that quickly thrusts political parties to the forefront of a rapidly changing political process. The degree of such vulnerability will, to a large extent, depend on the level of institutionalization that popular organizations are able to achieve during the authoritarian regime.

One cannot assume that the presence of a collective identity, no matter how firmly held, will automatically be translated into effective collective action. A variety of variables affect the process by which shared dispositions are transformed into collective action. In the case of popular-sector organizations, three such variables have already been discussed in Chapter 1: the ability of popular organizations to institutionalize themselves under the authoritarian regime; the nature of the transition from authoritarian rule; and the political-party system. Moreover, it is a *process*. While the ideal-typical culmination of this process would be the emergence of a popular social movement, such a movement did not emerge in Chile under the military regime and one may never emerge. Short of that, however, the popular sectors might achieve varying degrees and types of collective action.

Finally, one cannot assume that the significance of a popular collective identity is limited to its capacity for generating collective action. For example, it can help transform traditional democratic institutions such as *juntas de vecinos*. Similarly, the presence of a popular collective identity can influence party strategies in a variety of ways as parties seek popular-sector support. The efforts by political parties to appeal to popular sectors on the basis of a popular collective identity might actually undermine the potential for a popular social movement to emerge, to the extent that popular sectors perceive their interests and values as being faithfully represented in political parties without the need for an autonomous interlocutor in the form of a popular social movement.

Throughout this study, much emphasis has been placed on the importance of the *type* of relationship established between popular organizations and political parties for determining the prospects for popular-sector organizational activity. The typology of relations between social actors and political parties developed in Chapter 1 suggested that this relationship would vary between the two extremes: patron-client penetration of popular organizations by political parties and competition between popular organizations and political parties. The typology was based on a central hypothesis: Different types of actors (territorial or functional) have a proclivity for a given type of relation with political parties, depending on the scope and nature of their demands.

The findings presented here largely confirm the hypothesis. Tensions between popular organizations and political parties peaked as the scope and nature of interests expressed by popular organizations reached their maximum breadth in efforts to create a new popular social movement. During the military regime, most major political parties sought to penetrate popular organizations at the grassroots level. The Center and segments of the Renovated Left tried to do so by deliberately narrowing the scope of popular-sector demands in order to ensure more favorable political outcomes. The Traditional Left attempted to achieve the same end by very different means, appealing to more radical elements within the popular sectors in an effort to subordinate autonomous popular-sector organizational activity to the requirements of the Traditional Left's more radical (and orthodox) project for social change.

The potential for competition between political parties and a popular social movement persists into the current period, but its dynamic underwent significant change starting in 1987. Rather than seeking patron-client penetration of popular organizations, most major political parties began to focus on building massive electoral bases in preparation for periodic electoral contests—the first of which was the 1988 plebiscite. Changes in the state and the political-party system (not to mention civil society) have affected how political parties relate to civil society and seek to represent different segments within it. As suggested in Chapter 8, the ultimate implications of these changes for popular-sector organizational activity remain ambiguous. On the one hand, new opportunities have opened up for popular-sector participation in the political process. On the other, the dominant role of political parties has tended to generate apathy and low levels of citizen participation, punctuated by brief periods of mobilization during elections.

A useful way of illustrating these various possibilities is presented in Figure 6. Popular-sector political activity is characterized in terms of the two dimensions discussed at length throughout this study: collective identity and collective action. For example, when the popular sectors are characterized by both a weak sense of collective identity and low levels of collective action, popular organizations will tend to be atomized and short-lived. Their principal objective will be to satisfy the immediate material needs of their members. People will move in and out of organizations according to changes in their material situation and the availability of

Figure 6. Popular sector political activity

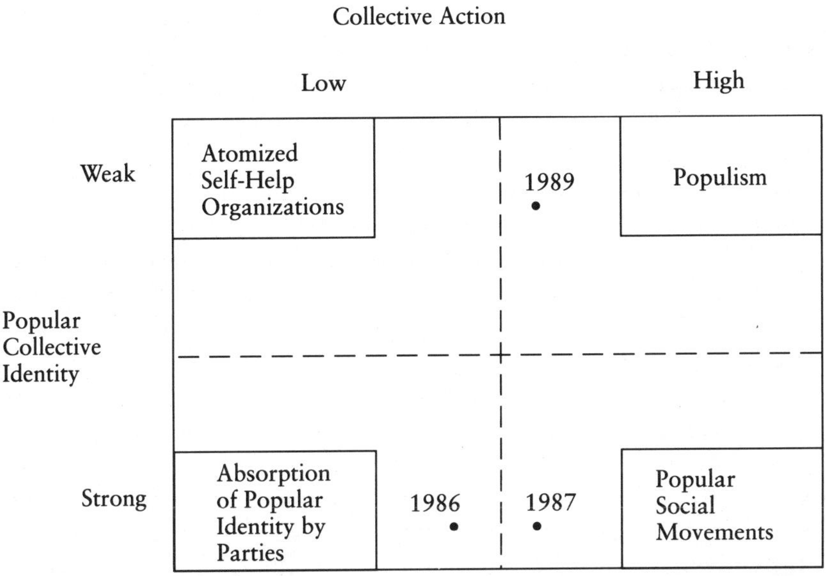

Collective Action

Low   High

Popular
Collective
Identity

	Low			High
Weak	Atomized Self-Help Organizations		1989 •	Populism
Strong	Absorption of Popular Identity by Parties	1986 •	1987 •	Popular Social Movements

alternative solutions. These organizations may seek patron-client relations with political parties and/or the state. Little or no effort will be made to coordinate activities with other popular-sector organizations, as they are viewed as potential competitors for limited resources.

If the popular sectors' collective identity is weak, but there is a relatively high level of popular-sector mobilization, the tendency is toward populism. Such mobilization tends to be spontaneous but "sponsored," and is a function of changing political circumstances (i.e., *la coyuntura*). The initiative for such mobilization comes from political parties, although in different circumstances the labor movement and the church may play an important mobilizational role. A principal defining characteristic of this scenario is that there is no popular-sector actor capable of mobilizing large numbers of the urban poor on the basis of distinct popular-sector interests and values. Participants in such mobilizations do so for a variety of reasons, and appeals for mobilization are based either on general calls for "elections," "democracy," and so forth, or on the interests of specific groups within the popular sectors as a whole, such as the proletariat and members of Christian base communities.

The presence of a strong sense of collective identity generates tendencies either toward the absorption of that collective identity by political parties or the emergence of an autonomous popular social movement capable of serving as interlocutor for the popular sectors with other political actors. In the former case, collective action on the part of the popular sectors qua autonomous social actor is nonexistent. Popular organizations tend to be multipurpose, and nonmaterial benefits from participation are important, often even the primary motivation for participation. A high level of institutionalization is achieved by popular-sector organizations at the base level.

In this scenario, there are various sporadic attempts by popular organizations to coordinate their activities at different levels, including the metropolitan, regional, and national levels. But these efforts are unable to progress very far. The issue of autonomy for an incipient popular social movement is critical, as political-party infighting and attempts to capture such a movement create divisions within the popular sectors that cannot be overcome. Efforts at popular-sector collective action may be further undermined by the parties' deliberate efforts to adapt their projects and party structures to accommodate popular-sector interests and norms, thereby diminishing the perceived need for a popular social movement.

The outcomes associated with this tendency will vary widely according to the degree and way in which popular-sector interests are reflected in party projects and structures. At one extreme, popular organizations are fragmented along party lines. There is an uneasy tension between political parties vying for popular-sector support and the intermittent efforts of popular-sector organizations to create autonomous structures capable of coordinating popular-sector organizational activities. At the other extreme, a political party (or a coalition of political parties) effectively absorbs the popular collective identity. In this case, political parties to varying degrees incorporate the popular sectors' concern with urban services, health care, the creation of employment opportunities, access to education, etc. into their party platforms. Parties also tend to become more democratic in their internal structures, creating a variety of channels for a more or less continual two-way interchange of ideas and opinions between the parties' elite and base levels.

On the opposite end of the horizontal axis in Figure 6, the popular collective identity serves as the basis for collective action. This occurs through the emergence of popular social movements that can claim to represent popular-sector interests as determined by that identity. It is characterized by the existence of a number of coordinating bodies that retain their autonomy independently of any political party. These organizations operate at a variety of levels. They coordinate popular-sector organizational activity within individual communities, as well as among various communities located close to one another. At an intermediate level, such coordinating bodies cover particular zones within major metropolitan areas and, ultimately, entire metropolitan regions or the nation as a whole.

Prior to the final demise of the CUP in 1988, the development of popular-sector organizational activity in Chile was clearly on a trajectory pointing toward the formation of a popular social movement. Popular organizations at the base level had achieved an important degree of institutionalization. In terms of a strong popular collective identity, by the mid-1980s the very survival of popular organizations was often dependent upon their capacity to produce and reproduce such a collective identity, *lo popular*, among their members. *Lo popular*, in turn, served as the basis for new forms of popular-sector collective action at levels that reached beyond the specific communities where each popular organization was located. It helped define popular-sector interests and demands in their interactions with other political actors and was ultimately to be represented through the CUP. This combination of a strong collective identity with growing levels of collective action would suggest that popular-sector organizational activity in Chile during the 1986–87 period was progressing toward the creation of a new popular social movement, and fell somewhere in the lower half of Figure 6. In 1986, the political parties undermined this process as they competed for control over the incipient movement. The failure of the first effort to create a popular movement gave way to the CUP's resurgence in 1987, as its leaders placed popular-sector interests ahead of partisan ones for the first time. This change in priorities was facilitated by the political parties' search for a new strategy to replace the now failed strategy of popular mobilization.

As a new opposition consensus regarding the transition process emerged, the importance of this collective identity in popular-sector collective action declined. Beginning with the demise of the CUP in 1988, collective action by the popular sectors beyond the community level was increasingly dominated by political parties, suggesting that it fell somewhere in the upper right-hand quadrant of Figure 6. *Pobladores* participated in massive numbers by registering to vote and voting, but no popular-sector actor was capable of mobilizing the urban poor on the basis of distinct popular-sector interests and values. Instead, the initiative for popular-sector mobilization came almost exclusively from political parties on the basis of general appeals for a return to democracy. This is true despite the continued influence of *lo popular* at the grassroots level within individual popular organizations.

This shift in the location of popular-sector political activity during and after the transition to democracy in Figure 6 highlights what may be the inherent tension (or contradiction) between a democratic civil society and political democracy (see Chapter 1). The scale of politics within modern nation-states and the centrality of political parties for organizing participation may constrain the maximization of citizen participation in ways inimical to the ideals that a popular social movement embodies. Similarly, to the extent that the urgency associated with political demands under a military regime and the lack of alternative channels for participation are critical for the emergence of popular organizations and the identity they embody, political democracy is likely to undermine the democratizing processes popular organizations represent. A major challenge facing not only the popular sectors, but also the architects of Chile's new democratic politics, is to find mechanisms that effectively deal with the problems (and possibilities) this poses.

POPULAR ORGANIZATIONS AND POLITICAL DEMOCRACY

To suggest that the popular sectors as a collective actor were progressively marginalized from Chile's transition process is not meant to imply that popular-sector interests were ignored by Chile's political elite. As noted in Chapter 8, the Concertación committed itself during the 1989 campaign to repaying the immense "social debt" accumulated during the years of military rule. Moreover, the Aylwin government recognized the role that popular organizations might play in Chile's new democratic regime.

Still, the lack of autonomous organizations capable of representing popular-sector interests historically has contributed to their subordination to the interests of other groups or actors in Latin America, particularly during periods of economic downturn when the popular sectors are most vulnerable (Hamilton 1985; Eckstein 1988; Alves 1989; Hagopian 1990; Waisman 1987; Stepan 1978). Nor, with the notable exception of Mexico, has this subordination contributed to political stability. Instead, it has

always come at the expense of such basic democratic principles as accountability and participation. As the historical record clearly shows, these
traditional patterns of popular-sector incorporation have not been favorable for sustaining stable democracies in Latin America, and at best
are compatible only with conservative and more exclusionary types of
democratic regimes (Karl 1990 and 1986).

Already, some of the more potentially destabilizing consequences of
populism are apparent in Chile. The PC-dominated Movement of the
Allendista Democratic Left (MIDA) did surprisingly well in the 1992
municipal elections, surpassing even its own expectations by receiving 6.7
percent of the national vote. MIDA declared itself formally in opposition
to the Aylwin government and campaigned largely on the need for a much
greater emphasis on social policies to help different disadvantaged groups.
A new right-wing populism has also emerged. Efforts by the UDI to
penetrate the *poblaciones* have already been discussed in Chapter 8, while
the wealthy businessman Javier Francisco Errázuriz managed to win over
15 percent of the presidential vote in 1989 on the basis of vague populist
appeals to the popular sectors and middle class. His "Center–Center
Union" party also performed remarkably well for a new party in the 1992
municipal elections, winning just over 8 percent of the national vote.
What conclusions can be derived from the experiences of popular-sector
organizational activity under the military regime for attempting to avert
potential problems associated with these populist tendencies?

The first conclusion is that the organized labor movement is not sufficient
to use as a representative of the popular sectors or as a mechanism for their
integration. Structural changes in the Chilean economy and the emergence
of new forms of popular organization imply that even with recent changes
in labor legislation and tripartite negotiations, the labor movement will not
be able to reassume its formerly central role, even though it will remain
very important.

There is a need to search for alternative bases of organization and
collective action if the popular sectors are to define their own interests
and defend them within society. The alternative embodied in popular
organizations as they emerged during the military regime may not be the
only (or even most appropriate) alternative, but it is an option that cannot
be ignored. As one woman who was a leader of a soup kitchen and a
coordinating body of soup kitchens in one of the municipal divisions within
Santiago explained, "The *poblaciones* are key. Workers must recognize that

their demands are in the *poblaciones*—work, health care, education, there are no limits to the *población* in the sense that everyone—students, workers, women—live in *poblaciones*."

The emergence of a popular collective identity under the authoritarian regime, and sporadic (albeit largely unsuccessful) efforts to create a popular social movement need to be taken into account by both academics and policymakers concerned with the integration of the popular sectors into the Chilean political system and society as a whole. One way to do so would be to encourage the positive tendencies already noted in the evolution of *juntas de vecinos* and the democratization of local governments. Political parties, by democratizing their own internal structures and absorbing elements of *lo popular* into their platforms, can ensure the effective integration of the popular sectors into the political system. At the same time, they can help mitigate the contradiction between democratizing civil society and political democracy in a positive way by obviating the perceived need to create a popular social movement. In this case, popular-sector political activity would again shift away from the populist pole towards the lower left-hand pole of Figure 6.

A second general conclusion concerns a critical issue facing all of Latin America today: Can these countries democratize, given the dramatic economic situations which they all face? The arguments presented here suggest that the popular collective identity is more concerned with *procedural rather than substantive demands*. It is possible for the urban poor to appreciate the immensity of the economic crisis confronting all of Latin America and focus their demands on the kinds of guarantees that only political democracy can provide. This should contribute to the consolidation of democratic regimes and add new importance to the procedural aspects of political democracy.

In looking toward the future, I want to emphasize that populism is not the only alternative awaiting the popular sectors. The organizational experiences that emerged during the long period of military rule can, with appropriate encouragement and support, provide the basis for new forms of incorporation. The democratic and participatory characteristics of that experience, moreover, suggest that such forms of incorporation will not only better serve the long-term interests of the popular sectors; they can also serve as important new pillars for the consolidation of Chilean political democracy to the benefit of all Chileans.

Whether it be through the incorporation of various aspects of *lo popular* into party platforms, the continued decentralization and democratization of political power, or even the emergence of a new popular social movement, the frequently perceived "threat" that society's disadvantaged masses pose to political stability can be mitigated in ways compatible with both political democracy and greater social justice. To make this possibility a viable alternative, political parties must demonstrate the necessary maturity to sacrifice possible short-term partisan interests and allow, even encourage, popular organizations to continue to develop under a democratic regime. They must, in effect, carry out their promises to decentralize the state, democratize their internal structures, and respect the autonomy of social organizations.

The political and social integration of the popular sectors has always been incomplete and subordinate to the interests of other social groups in Chile. Structural changes associated with the adoption of an import-substituting industrialization model in the late 1930s, Frei's "Revolution in Liberty" in the 1960s, and Allende's "Chilean Road to Socialism" in the early 1970s all implied increasing levels of democratization. They also improved the life chances and consumption possibilities of the urban poor. Yet none of these initiatives eliminated the gross social inequities associated with Chile's dependent economic development or prevented the ultimate breakdown of Chilean democracy with its dramatic consequences. New approaches to integrating the popular sectors into the political and socio-economic systems are required. These must incorporate both past failures and recent changes in Chilean society that are the result of prolonged military rule. The popular organizations that developed after 1973 may not provide the ultimate solution, but at least they suggest a promising direction for exploration in the search for solutions. After all, it is popular organizations that represent the most important response by the popular sectors to the consequences of past failures.

GLOSSARY

POPULAR SECTORS

A study of this nature must address the ambiguity and lack of clarity surrounding the concept of *popular sectors*, in both the social sciences literature and the current Latin American political discourse. At the root of this problem is the lack of a precisely defined sociological category capable of encompassing otherwise quite diverse categories of social actors. While it should be obvious that this category would not be exhausted by the concept of the "proletariat," the "working class" or even the "workers,"[1] it is not so apparent which groups and persons are encompassed within the so-called popular sectors and why.

Fundamentally, the notion of "popular sectors" in Latin America refers to the "disadvantaged" groups in highly segmented, unequal societies. While this distinction at first glance seems somewhat arbitrary and imprecise, it is less theoretically confused than a reference to the "lower classes," given the limitations of classical Marxist analysis for understanding heterogeneous social agglomerations. Instead, it directs attention toward a key defining characteristic of this sociological category: the popular sectors' limited life chances and consumption possibilities. Even in the context of the advanced, industrialized societies of Western Europe, the parties of the Left whose core constituency is organized labor must confront the constant

---

1. The obviousness of this conclusion becomes apparent by noting the diversity of groups included in more comprehensive analyses of the popular sectors, even when a precise definition of them is not provided. For example, see Ballón 1986; CLACSO-ILET 1985; and Garretón 1989a.

problem of balancing appeals to the class interests of labor and the necessity of seeking a wider "popular" base of support that is often crucial to their electoral success (Przeworski 1985). Such is the case despite the fact that, compared to the situation found in Latin America, the nature of people's relationship to the productive system in general is relatively unambiguous and state social welfare policies are more comprehensive in their scope and reach a much higher percentage of those in need.

In the societal contexts found in Latin America, the nature of the "popular sectors" is much more complex and heterogeneous. In addition to an organized working class (which is relatively weak in comparison to its European counterparts), the popular sectors in these societies include those workers with more or less regular employment in the formal economy but who lack any functional or class organization, the unemployed who are seeking employment, the increasingly large numbers of people associated with the informal or underground economy, as well as the *lumpenproletariat* who are largely outside of both the formal and informal economies.[2] Overlapping all of these, two groups in particular are frequently singled out for special consideration because of their important influence in any characterization of the popular sectors: the youth and women who live in the shantytowns.[3]

2. The heterogeneity of Latin American class structures is underscored by the typology of social classes developed by Portes (1985). Defining class on the basis of the position of individuals in the process of production, their control over the labor power of others, and their mode of renumeration, Portes concludes that Latin American societies are characterized by the presence of five distinct social classes: the dominant class, the bureaucratic-technical class, the formal proletariat, the informal petty bourgeoisie, and the informal proletariat. It is the formal and informal proletariat, along with a large proportion of the informal petty bourgeoisie, that generally would constitute the popular sectors as defined here. Although Portes does not directly address the issue of the class composition of the popular sectors, he would seem to agree with the general conclusions drawn here on the basis of his brief discussion of the multiclass nature of urban political movements.

The peasantry might also be considered as forming part of the "popular sectors," and many studies that discuss popular sectors include the peasantry. See CLACSO-ILET 1985; Cardoso and Faletto 1979. The reasons for such an inclusion are the subordinate position of the peasantry in Latin American societies and the large number of rural migrants who live in the communities where the popular sectors are concentrated. The peasantry has been excluded from the definition of popular sectors developed here because of the explicitly urban focus of the present study. The inclusion of the peasantry, however, would not significantly alter the basic conclusions drawn concerning the nature of the popular sectors in general.

3. The high proportion of young people in most developing countries, the dim prospects for their future and their tendency to seek more violent and radical solutions are among the reasons why this group is so important in understanding the nature of the popular sectors. See Valenzuela 1984; and Agurto, Canales, and de la Maza 1985. In recent years, women have

All of these sectors are disadvantaged in comparison to a minority composed of the middle and upper classes. The notion "popular" thus becomes associated with democracy in the sense that popular interests represent those of the vast majority in developing societies. The sense of being disadvantaged, or that other groups in society are in some way "privileged," forms a basis for distinctive popular cultures and common experiences. In a similar fashion, "popular" becomes associated with all that is indigenous to a society: traditional culture, values, art forms and beliefs, and so forth. While not rejecting all that is "foreign," influences from the developed industrialized nations tend to be associated with the "privileged" sectors and the popular sectors often see themselves as reservoirs of national identity.

The state, and the perceptions of the upper classes in general, also help define what is frequently identified with the concept of "popular." This may be especially true in countries such as Argentina, Brazil, Chile, and Uruguay, where recent authoritarian regimes took on a markedly "antipopular" aspect as a reaction to increasing populist tendencies under the democratic regimes that preceded them (Garretón 1989a; Portes and Kincaid 1985). Whereas popular sectors would tend to see themselves as society's disadvantaged sectors, they are the sectors with little or no stake in the political, social, and economic system from the perspective of the state and the upper classes. They pose the greatest potential threat, imagined or real, to the established order to the extent that they can be organized into a collective actor, and an element of at least latent fear thus sets popular sectors apart from the rest of society.[4] State educational, employment, health care, and welfare policies often benefit the upper and middle classes disproportionately, while popular sectors enjoy far fewer safeguards against the arbitrary use of the state's repressive apparatus.

In this interplay of influences, housing becomes a central issue for the popular sectors. Social pressure from the middle and upper classes, as well as economic realities, combine to concentrate popular sectors in specific communities, contributing to a common "popular life-style" associated

---

become key actors in popular-sector organizations in Latin America as the combination of economic hardship and political repression have thrust them into new roles. See Álvarez 1990; Jelin 1990; Jacquette 1989; Valenzuela 1987; Kirkwood 1986; Barrig 1986; and Stokes 1988. Both of these groups give a particular dynamic to popular-sector organizations.

4. The preoccupation with the potential danger to a society posed by the organization of its disadvantaged "masses" is not unique to either Latin America or this century. A particularly interesting example of this is Marx's analysis of the role of the *lumpenproletariat* in the French Revolution of 1848–51 (Marx 1963).

with overcrowding, substandard dwellings, and inadequate urban services, especially sewerage, drinking water, health care, and public education. At times a highly visible physical segregation of a society's poor from its well-off is maintained. The life chances of those who belong to the popular sectors are directly affected because of the educational and economic disadvantages that shantytown dwellers must overcome in order to achieve any level of social mobility.

Despite this, however, the heterogeneity of popular-sector interests must also be emphasized. They do not represent a single homogeneous class; in fact, the interests that correspond to each individual popular sector are often contradictory. Policies that favor one sector may find indifference in others and, given the competition for scarce resources, even active opposition. Though there may be a strong proclivity for popular sectors to drift toward the Left in terms of their political allegiances (to the extent that they have such allegiances), the different interests of particular sectors make it very difficult for any one political party to claim an exclusive hold on the popular sectors. Numerous parties, from the far Right to the far Left, compete for their support.

POPULAR AND BASE-LEVEL ORGANIZATIONS

Popular-sector organizations, or *popular organizations* for short, can be based on functional or territorial identities as lines of differentiation. The best example of a functional type of popular organization would be the labor movement. Perhaps the most common type of territorial popular organization would be the neighborhood councils in many Latin American cities. The key distinction is the primary basis for organization, whether it be a plant, an industry, or all the workers in a branch of the economy in the case of functional organizations, or all the neighbors on a specific block, a single shantytown, or all the shantytowns in a particular city in the case of territorial organizations. Territorial organizations can also be quite specific in their purpose, such as in the case of neighborhood health groups or local handicraft cooperatives. In such cases, membership is restricted to the residents of a clearly defined territory and the primary source of identification is that of "neighbor" (*vecino*)[5] (Tovar 1986b).

5. As this study makes clear, the concept of "neighbor" or *vecino* as used here implies more than residence in a particular geographic unit. It also implies membership in a community and presupposes a certain bond between the inhabitants of that community.

Base-level organizations are those formal groupings in which participation is most direct and generally face to face. It is here that the general population at large gains access to popular organizations. These organizations consist of the most basic units of popular organization and may form the foundations for higher-order structures of wider-ranging scope at the city, regional, and national levels. Individual organizations tend to be relatively small, with frequently ten to twenty-five members, thereby facilitating member communication and participation.

A distinction needs to be drawn between base-level actors and elite-level actors. Base-level actors are those who participate at the lowest organizational level in which the surrounding community or the immediate work environment are the principal foci. Beyond this level, mass participation is quickly attenuated and becomes a function of some form of representation by different levels of elites who in some manner aggregate the interests and concerns of their bases. Such a scheme is perhaps most developed in the labor movements of various countries, whose structure resembles a pyramid that links a large number of base-level organizations in different factories or worksites to a higher-order or peak organization composed of organizational elites.

The heterogeneity of popular sectors has significant implications for their effective organization. Whereas functional organizations are usually predominant in developed countries given the strength of contemporary labor movements, in developing countries such functional organizations tend to accentuate the differences associated with the popular sectors' heterogeneity. Viewed in terms of their relationship to the means of production, unionized workers, unorganized workers in the formal sector, workers in the informal sector, the unemployed seeking work, and the *lumpenproletariat* often have different objective interests. Obviously there is potential for conflicting interests between those enjoying stable employment in the formal sector (who tend to be most concerned with maintaining their job security) and the unemployed (who are often in a desperate search for work).[6]

Moreover, there often is no basis for effective organization along functional lines for significant popular sectors, such as the sector composed by

6. As Portes (1985) concludes, most current research on class structures in Latin America is still only tentative in nature. Actual patterns of interaction and conflict between different social classes is not sufficiently understood and future research should therefore seek to provide a more detailed description of such patterns. An objective of the current study is to develop an alternative perspective for understanding such patterns of class relations by focusing on territorially based organizations in the *poblaciones* of Santiago.

those in the informal economy and, very generally, women and youths. For members of the more traditional working class with ties to the formal economy, the position of individual workers and unions in general is frequently so precarious as to make effective organization very difficult. The nature of organizing around the workplace makes labor leaders relatively vulnerable to repression, while the labor movements in most Latin American countries have been weakened by the effect of new labor laws imposed by authoritarian regimes (Foxley 1983) or by democratic governments as a response to the economic crisis, as well as by the economic crisis itself, which has increased unemployment. Finally, the lack of employment security, which is a generalized condition in popular sectors in much of Latin America today, suggests that many will find that their functionally defined interests are subject to periodic and contradictory changes as people move between periods of unemployment and employment in either the formal or informal economies, unionized and nonunionized jobs, and so forth.

Territorial organizations, on the other hand, emphasize the shared interests of the popular sectors. The different popular sectors tend to live in the same shantytowns and urban slums. Important concerns such as basic urban services (sewerage, clean water, electricity, paved roads), children's education, health care, hunger, crime and delinquency, are shared by all of the inhabitants to one extent or another, and the "differences" that functional organizations emphasize lose at least some of their importance.

The definition of specific territories or, in this case, the establishment of shantytown and slum boundaries creates common interests that did not exist before. As argued above, these are often central to the concept of "popular" itself. They are also inherently political in nature, given that the establishment of such boundaries depends upon decisions by the state and that the resolution of the conflicting priorities that these interests give rise to (the provision of services, for example) requires state action at the local and/or national levels. This political nature is particularly true in reference to the areas inhabited by the poorer sectors in any society, which require some form of redirection of resources by the state, either directly by its own agencies or indirectly through appropriate incentives to attract private resources.

Moreover, since the organization of most popular sectors may not be feasible along functional lines, given the now classic problems associated with organizing collective action, especially those of the "free rider" and the lack of perceptible material benefits received by individuals as a result of their participation in the organization (Olson 1965), the territorial basis of popular organizations rests on the individual's "natural" identification with the concept of "neighbor" (Tovar 1986b), as a member of the community in which he or she lives. The idea of "neighbor" captures the common interests and demands that are associated with living in popular-sector communities; important shared interests related to life chances and consumption opportunities are intrinsic to the definition of the popular community or neighborhood itself and all neighbors share them more or less equally. As a member of a community, a common bond of solidarity emerges among the community's members. Problems of collective action that can seriously hinder the development of functional organizations lacking any similar overriding shared sense of identity are therefore much more easily resolved in popular organizations (cf. Wilson 1973). The same kind of daily contact that workers experience, which is so important for organizing them into labor movements, occurs frequently within the popular neighborhood or community, encompassing all of the different popular sectors residing there (Perlman 1976). For some groups, such as women and people employed in the informal sector, the community may be their only source of identity beyond their families.

MARGINALITY

In focusing on territorially based popular organizations, the concept of *marginality* becomes important. I mean here marginality in a concrete sense: state services in popular communities tend to be minimal to nonexistent, the basic rights of their inhabitants receive little or no protection under the law, and there is a dearth of opportunity for socioeconomic and cultural advancement. In this sense, marginality does not refer to the isolation of popular communities from the society at large or the contrast between the "traditional" and the "modern." The inhabitants of popular-sector communities often live in squalor and poverty; their interactions with the productive system, either through the formal or informal economy, do not provide them with economic security and often leave them without sufficient resources to properly feed, clothe, and care for themselves and their families. Their "marginality" is thus defined in terms of access to the basic necessities of life, as well as to the amenities of modern society, such as health care, education, and adequate housing, and the precariousness of their position when they do manage to secure a more acceptable situation for themselves.

POLITICAL ACTIVITY

First, while the focus in this study will be on the political activities of organizations, it must be remembered that much political activity may be produced independently of any organization, for example, in spontaneous protests. A distinction must also be drawn between direct political activity, which consists of conscious attempts to influence policy, and indirect political activity, which is more diffuse and takes place in a variety of arenas, often revolving around economic activities.

More generally, however, the scope of "politics," the proper boundary between the "public" and "private" spheres, is something that cannot be defined independently of a given social context. Indeed, competing concepts of politics and political activity provide one of the principal foci of this investigation. Struggles over the definition of what is "political" are a vital and unresolved part of political life, especially in polities undergoing or about to undergo some form of regime change.

But these competing conceptions can be considered a threshold: the point at which activities are considered to be political in nature by the principal actor or actors. A high threshold implies that only activities directly aimed at influencing policy, generally through political parties, are considered to be "political." A low threshold recognizes as "political" a variety of activities unconnected to political parties. Such activities may be intended, for example, to denounce existing policies only symbolically, that is, without any realistic hope of changing them. They also might represent an alternative model for the alleviation of societal problems that is contrary to the one being imposed by those in control of the state, such as through collective group solutions to problems of hunger or unemployment rather than relying on individualistic, market-oriented approaches.

State policies, especially under authoritarian regimes, are important in establishing the threshold for what is considered to be "political" by altering the benefits and, in particular, the costs of certain kinds of activities. Repression may have the effect of lowering the threshold of political activity by imposing heavy penalties on those activities that are labeled "subversive," thereby diverting collective action into informal, indirect channels. Moreover, there can be a shift over time, with activities becoming more self-consciously political. Such is the case with many base-level self-help organizations as their members gradually become more vocal and explicit in their demands for basic political change, recognizing that any real solutions for their socioeconomic problems will have to be political in nature as they overcome the fear of violent repression.

POPULAR SECTORS AND THE CONCEPT OF CLASS

Until now, the analysis has stressed the *heterogeneity* of the popular sectors when examined in terms of each sector's relationship to the productive structure. This very heterogeneity of the popular sectors has important, perhaps even paradoxical, implications for understanding the possibilities of class-based collective action in Latin America, as well as the nature of class conflict itself in dependent capitalist economies. Most obviously, the proletariat as a class is not likely to be either the primary agent for social change in Latin America or an adequate representative of the collective interests of the popular sectors as a whole. The potential for collective action on the part of popular sectors is best understood by focusing on territorially based popular organizations that address issues relating to the collective consumption opportunities and life chances of the popular sectors.

I do not imply, however, that Marxist class analysis, and particularly the notion of class conflict, is of little relevance to the study of the collective behavior of popular sectors. On the contrary, useful comparisons can be drawn between popular-sector organizational activity in Latin America and processes of working-class formation. This requires a multilayered conceptualization of class that distinguishes abstract notions of class from the concrete experiences of class relations in a given societal context. Borrowing from the seminal work of Ira Katznelson (1986, 1981), social classes can exist at four distinct levels: *structure* (level 1), *ways of life* (level 2), *dispositions* (level 3) and *collective action* (level 4).

Level 1 refers to the common elements shared by all capitalist economies (privately owned autonomous firms seeking to make profit-maximizing decisions, the commodification of labor, etc.) that shape capitalist development within specific nations and have no phenomenological referents. It is at this level that a heuristic distinction between collective capital and collective labor can be usefully made.

While the structural level clearly influences the social relations among classes in specific circumstances, a variety of other factors such as demography, cultural traditions, state organizations and policies, and geopolitics, are equally important. Level 2, ways of life, refers "to the social organization of society lived in by actual people in real situations" (Katznelson 1986, 16). Class relations at this level, Katznelson emphasizes, are not limited to the workplace. The development of industrial capitalist societies has been closely associated with the separation of the workplace from the place of residence. Moreover, residential communities themselves segregate according to the class position of their residents. "With these separations between work and home and between social classes in space," Katznelson concludes, "class relations are lived and experienced not only at work but also off work in residence communities" (1986, 16).

At both levels 1 and 2, social formations correspond closely to the structure of capitalist economies and classes are defined in terms of the position of their members in the productive system. Yet, as Katznelson points out, neither level can offer insights into how different classes think or act in any set of experienced circumstances. Such insights, in turn, can be found only by analyzing class at levels 3 and 4.

At level 3, classes are formed by groups with shared dispositions and it is at this level that one can attempt to understand how classes actually "think." Shared dispositions are formed through the interaction of people with one another and constitute cultural configurations within which people act. Referring specifically to the formation of working classes, Katznelson concludes: "The third level, that of dispositions, is not coextensive with class structures and class-based ways or life; nor, however, do dispositions simply mirror reality. Rather, they are plausible and meaningful responses to the circumstances workers find themselves in" (1986, 19).

Yet shared dispositions do not necessarily result in collective action. Level 4 therefore refers to "classes that are organized and that act through movements and organizations to affect society and the position of the class within it. This kind of behaviour is self-conscious and refers to activity that is more than just the common but unself-conscious shared behaviour of members of a class" (Katznelson 1986, 20).

Katznelson developed this multilayered conceptualization of class in order to understand, from a comparative perspective, processes of working-class formation in industrialized capitalist societies. If this same general approach to analyzing class in capitalist societies is applied to popular-sector organizational activity in Latin America today, it becomes readily apparent that such organizational activity may in fact be part of a process that resembles an actual or incipient process of class formation. Class formation, according to Katznelson, can be thought of as

> the conditional (but not random) process of connections between the four levels of class. . . . The content of each of the four levels of necessity will vary from society to society; no level need be under-stood or analyzed exclusively in class terms; and the connections between the levels are problematical and conditional. Questions about the content of each level and about the connections between levels of class constitute the very heart of the analysis of class formation. (1986, 21–22)

The evolution of cities is intimately tied to capitalist economic development[7] and a major aspect of that evolution is reflected in the emergence of shantytowns in most major Latin American cities since the end of the Second World War.[8] This study, moreover, is concerned specifically with the kinds of shantytown organizations that began to emerge in the late 1970s; I argue that their emergence and particular organizational form have been influenced by important recent changes in Latin American economies. Such changes have been the result of the economic crisis confronting the region as a result of the external debt problem and the world recession of the early 1980s. Particularly in the countries of the Southern Cone, they also represent the efforts of authoritarian regimes to

7. It is important to emphasize that the type of popular-sector activity being studied here is an essentially urban phenomenon. For a comprehensive review of the relationship between capitalist economic development and the evolution of urban social structures, see Katznelson 1981. Castells (1983) similarly stresses the influence of the international capitalist system on the emergence of urban grassroots social movements in capitalist societies. It should be noted, however, that Castells tends to emphasize a "world systems" approach to understanding capitalist development that obscures important national differences related to, for example, each country's unique experience with democratic and authoritarian rule, domestic social structures that reflect each country's particular insertion in the international system, and the types of class and/or elite compromises that have been struck. For a broad historical account of the development of cities that demonstrates the importance of economic trends in shaping that development, see Mumford 1961.

8. For a description of the growth of shantytowns in Latin American cities in the postwar period, see Stokes (1988).

impose new, neoconservative, capitalist economic-development models in their respective countries. The class structures of Latin American countries have been altered (Portes, 1985; Martínez and Tironi, 1985) and new economic needs have been generated. I argue that a variety of popular organizations have since emerged as part of an attempt by the urban poor to meet those new needs.

At levels 1 and 2 of class, the shantytown organizations that have become prevalent throughout much of Latin America represent changes in the ways that the specific classes included in the popular sectors—workers in the formal economy, workers in the informal economy, the unemployed seeking work and the *lumpenproletariat*—actually experience class relations given the changes in the development of the capitalist economy in their respective countries. Two of the principal questions addressed by the current study relate specifically to the other dimensions of class formation. First, to what extent do these organizations represent a new "popular" identity— something akin to "the shared dispositions" of level 3 of class? Second, if such a collective identity is present in these organizations, to what extent is it serving as the basis for new forms of collective action on the part of shantytown dwellers (level 4 of class)? In other words, are workers and members of the popular sectors joining these shantytown organizations because they are perceived (to paraphrase Katznelson) as "plausible and meaningful responses to the circumstances" in which the urban poor throughout Latin America are finding themselves? Can it be shown that shantytown dwellers are consciously joining these "organizations to affect society and the position of [a] class within it?" More generally, under what conditions would popular sectors be likely to (1) recognize their common interests and (2) organize around those interests in an effort to transform society?

This distinction between "shared dispositions" and "collective action" is particularly important in the current study. The conditions presented by an authoritarian regime may be particularly auspicious for the emergence of a popular identity in terms of shared dispositions, yet the very nature of the authoritarian regime and a later transition process may be inimical to the emergence of a new collective actor—an apparent paradox discussed at length in this study. The inability to transcend the level of shared dispositions and engage in new forms of collective action, however, should not be allowed to obscure the fact that new shared dispositions among members of the popular sectors may have emerged.

The appropriateness of using an analytic scheme associated with the formation of classes also seems apparent with reference to the initial argument that, fundamentally, the popular sectors represent the disadvantaged segments of highly segmented, unequal societies. While the precise makeup of the lower end of the social structure may be somewhat ambiguous when looked at in terms of the system of production, there is a close correspondence between the "advantaged" segments of society and the middle and upper classes. Their juxtaposition with the popular sectors in a given national context implicitly, if not explicitly, assumes conflicting class interests; for this very reason the popular sectors are often viewed as the greatest potential threat to the established order. It would be an error to assume that the heterogeneity of the popular sectors alone in any way denies the importance of Marxist analyses which stress the inherently conflictual nature of relations between those social classes or sectors of society that benefit from capitalist development and those that do not.

CIVIL SOCIETY

A principal focus of this study is on the processes through which a "civil society" is both constituted and democratized. Yet the concept of a "civil society" is extremely ambiguous.[9] This ambiguity largely reflects the existence of two competing models of civil society: the Continental, or corporate model and the market-oriented liberal model.

9. Perhaps the most relevant example of this ambiguity is the work of Antonio Gramsci (1971). In his conceptualization of civil society as the realm of hegemony and counterhegemony, Gramsci's work offers insights into the processes of domination. Gramsci's analysis of counterhegemony, particularly its origins in the actual "deviant" behavior of workers, also suggests a potential dimension for assessing the significance of popular-sector organizational activity. Moreover, Gramsci's principal distinction between domination as manifested through resort to the state's coercive apparatus and hegemony, also offers insight into how the resurgence of the coercive dimension of domination under authoritarian regimes may contribute to the emergence of counterhegemony by undermining the dominant social group's ability to exercise "intellectual and moral" leadership in civil society; cf. Femia 1975. Also cf. O'Donnell (1979), who argues that the undisguised resort to repression by bureaucratic authoritarian regimes in order to maintain themselves in power will ultimately contribute to the downfall of these regimes by mitigating against any possibility for legitimizing their rule over the longer term. Yet, Gramsci's work makes little reference to how society is actually organized, apart from the role that hegemony plays within it. As a result, it provides little or no basis for the comparative study of civil societies across capitalist countries or the evolution of civil society within a given country. These issues are very important, as will be demonstrated in the following.

In what can be described as the *corporate model of civil society*, society is composed of a series of self-constituted units and subunits. It is a "collectivist" vision of society, whose historical and ideational roots can be traced back to the struggles of twelfth-century European guilds and the formation of the first European towns in the thirteenth century.

Medieval craft-guilds set the pattern for the development of civil society based on their struggles with the aristocracy for corporate status. This same pattern of struggle for corporate status was soon replicated in the early formation of European towns. These towns, in turn, frequently reinforced the importance of collective identities by granting rights and obligations to guilds, often incorporating them directly into city government. The result of this historical process was the notion that rights and obligations should be granted to groups whose members would enjoy equal status within the group. Even the concept of freedom becomes associated with group autonomy and independence from external influences. There is a sense of "community," or belonging to a collective body. A person's social and economic standing, as well as his or her political rights and obligations—not to mention identity—become dependent on membership in a particular group.

Under such circumstances, membership can no longer be meaningfully considered as strictly "voluntary." Membership in a group becomes a prerequisite for identifying oneself and enjoying important rights, privileges, and opportunities. One is more or less at the mercy of the factors that determine the "community" to which one belongs—place of birth, a parent's profession, class, and so forth.[10]

With the emergence of the modern nation-state, the struggle for the establishment of collective rights against the resistance of feudal lords was replaced by a struggle against the centralizing tendencies of the state in the hands of a monarchic dynasty. Eventually, a new dynamic for the further development of civil society was created through the universalization of citizenship rights (Bendix 1964). The subunits of national society served as a counterweight to the development of the modern state. The equality of status within the various self-constituted units was augmented—and

10. A detailed discussion of the evolution of civil societies in terms of collective identities based on the patterns established by early European guilds can be found in Black 1984. It should be noted that Black's interpretation of "guild theory" corresponds to what is characterized here as the corporate model of civil society, while Black reserves the title "civil society" for the body of ideas that are associated here with the liberal model of civil society. In the following discussion, both models will be referred to in ideal terms. This explains the apparent disagreement between the views expressed here and those in Black, who argues that the two models have in fact both contributed to the development of modern society.

threatened—by the (fitful, uneven) extension of equal status to all members of the national society. The critical political problem facing Western European nation-states in the nineteenth century was whether, and to what extent, the extension of citizenship to the lower classes would be able to accommodate social protest. Both the socialist and nationalist movements of the nineteenth century should be seen as political, reflecting the political alienation of the working class seeking integration into the civic community: "Rather than engage in a millenarian quest for a new social order, the recently politicized masses protest against their second-class citizenship, demanding the right of participation on terms of equality in the political community of the nation-state" (Bendix 1964, 73).[11]

Civil society develops over a period of centuries in the context of struggles between self-constituted units competing over jurisdiction and in the pursuit of collective interests. This corporate model of civil society reflects a historical process shaped first by the struggle for the recognition of collective or corporate rights by early guilds and towns, and then by the dynamic created by expansion and struggle for the universalization of citizenship rights once modern nation-states replace medieval institutions. Through this process, civil society comes to consist of a rich social fabric formed by a multiplicity of territorially and functionally based units. There is an equality of status within these units, and these units in turn have a public or civic character that allows them to justify and act on behalf of their interests openly, in competition with one another, and to resist subordination to the rising power of the central (and, eventually, national) state. Such a development process may generate a "strong" or "resilient" civil society characterized by "institutionalized social pluralism": independent territorial communities; distinctive functional identities of social classes, economic sectors, and professions; ethnic and linguistic groups,

11. It is also interesting to point out a possible parallel between base-level organizational activity and mobilization, during and prior to the initiation of a democratic transition, and Bendix's characterization of nineteenth-century socialist and nationalist movements in that both may revolve around the political nature of the problem of integrating the lower classes into the national political community. Whereas this seems to be less so in Peru, where immediate economic concerns were apparently more central to early popular-sector mobilization (Tovar 1986a and 1986b; Stephens 1983), such a parallel seems to be consistent with some recent findings concerning base-level organizational activities and political views in Chile (Oxhorn 1988 and 1986; Huneeus 1987; Rodríguez and Tironi 1986; FLACSO 1986; Brunner 1986; Baño 1986). If such activity does reflect a purely political demand, it bodes more favorably for the successful consolidation of democracy than if the object of such activity was a more fundamental and immediate socioeconomic reform of society, or even the satisfaction of immediate economic needs, given the current economic crisis which Latin America confronts.

religions and sects; voluntary associations; gender and generational group-ings; and so forth, that acquire a recognized right to exist and openly defend their justifiable interests (Schmitter 1986).

To the extent that civil society reflects the corporate model of develop-ment, it affects the viability of a democratic regime. Schmitter has suggested that contemporary prospects for the successful consolidation of democratic political regimes after the demise of authoritarian regimes in Southern Europe are more favorable than in Latin America because the former (with the partial exceptions of Turkey and Greece) have more "resilient and viable" civil societies than their Latin American counterparts. The "root hypothesis" for such a conclusion, he argues, is

> that for an effective and enduring challenge to authoritarian rule to be mounted, and for political democracy to become and remain an alternative mode of political domination, a country must possess a civil society in which certain types of self-constituted units are capable of acting autonomously in defense of their own interests and ideals. Moreover, these identities must not only be dispersed throughout the country, they must also be capable of being concen-trated when the occasion demands, that is, they must be organized for coherent collective action. (1986, 6)

The public status, or "civicness," of these groups allows them to escape subordination to state authority and governmental manipulation, thereby contributing to eventual democratization. Moreover, the complex patterns of cleavage and identity that these groups reinforce help insulate the new democratic regime from a potential threat from the extreme Right and the far Left. By providing the moderate "democratic" Right and Left with greater opportunities for electoral successes, both are given a concomitant stake in the new democratic system. Similarly, as a result of their variegated civil societies, shifting coalitions of more moderate elements from the ranks of the previous authoritarian regime's supporters and opponents have been more likely to emerge and provide for democratic stability in these countries than in Latin American countries.

Several factors can help explain why civil society has not developed in the same way, or to the same extent, in Latin America as in Western Europe. In most of Latin America, the colonial heritage has had a lasting impact on the evolution of national civil societies (cf. Stein and Stein 1970). The patterns of colonial trade and administration were highly centralizing influences, concentrating economic, political, and social resources in a few major cities and ports throughout the region.[12]

After independence, these same cities quickly came to dominate the national political, economic, and social scenes in many countries, such as Argentina, Chile, and Peru. Unlike in Western Europe, competing power centers did not emerge in Latin America to contribute to the institutionalization of social pluralism. The cities that had acted as the centralizing link between the colonial power and the territory retained their grip on national politics after independence. These cities became national capitals, and colonial administrators generally were the first rulers of the new countries.

As the main link to the international economy, these principal cities served as the conduit for the export of primary products and the importation of manufactured goods and capital. Once the process of urbanization set in, the concentration of economic resources and power acted as a magnet for attracting new rural migrants. It is in these cities that national industries (and therefore jobs) tended to concentrate. Throughout Latin America, as the rural population began to fall, at least in relative terms, these same cities became population centers as well.

In Latin America, the rural elite (or oligarchy) often lives in the capital and is closely linked to the urban elite. Whereas in Western Europe the cities sought autonomy from the aristocracy in the countryside, trying to overcome the last vestiges of feudalism, in Latin America this source of societal cleavage was often secondary to the shared interests of those connected to the export economy. The weakness of this cleavage contributed to a further concentration of resources and power, as well as the blurring of identities that were important in forming variegated civil societies in Western Europe.

As Cardoso and Faletto (1979) demonstrate, the highly centralized polities characteristic of much of Latin America are to a large extent the result of each country's particular insertion into the international capitalist system. Civil societies in Latin America could not develop in the same way as they did in Western Europe because of the subordinate position of Latin American countries in the international economic system dominated by

12. A similar phenomenon also took place in Europe, as the discovery of the New World and the opening up of trade routes to the Far East had the effect of shifting the locus of economic activity away from the Mediterranean to the Atlantic. Unlike in Latin America, however, where the principal modern cities were first established according to the needs of colonial trade and empire, the cities of Europe already had existed for some time and, in any case, were far more numerous. See Black 1984.

the developed countries of Western Europe and, later, the United States. Differences in each country's natural resources, the timing of its incorporation into the international system, and different national patterns of class alliance and conflict all contribute to unique national histories marked by the structural constraints of dependent development.

In situations of dependency, from an economic point of view, "the accumulation and expansion of capital cannot find its essential dynamic component inside the [national economic] system" (Cardoso and Faletto 1979, xx). "External" interests and values from the dominant core countries of Western Europe and the United States are "internalized" by dominant local social classes who adopt them as their own and the nature of internal domination becomes closely intertwined with the dependent countries' subordinate position in the international capitalist system.

The constraints and opportunities created by a country's particular insertion into the international system allowed traditional locally dominant classes, especially the landed oligarchy, to retain political and economic power well into the twentieth century. New groups—such as a national bourgeoisie and middle classes, which emerge as a result of the state's expanding role in the economy—are gradually included in the distribution of wealth and political power on the basis of their shared interests resulting from common ties to the international system.

Industrialization, when it begins, exacerbates income concentration because it tends to mimic production patterns found in industrialized countries as a function of the needs of international capital rather than national development. It only provides for the partial inclusion of those workers associated with the modern, technologically advanced, sectors of the economy. The rest of society—the majority that constitutes the popular sectors—bear much of the burden for such "progress" as they are excluded from political and economic power. Cardoso and Faletto thus insist that because of its fundamentally dependent character in Latin America, "we do not mean by the notion 'development' the achievement of a more egalitarian or more just society" (1979, xxiii).

Whereas societal pluralism characterizes civil society in Western Europe, in Latin America the pattern seems to be more one of the concentration and centralization of economic and political resources and power. There is a blurring of potential sources of societal cleavage and a concomitant accentuation of others as a result of the extreme inequality between the major sectors and classes in society. Rather than being variegated, Latin American societies are characterized by a rigid and self-reinforcing social stratification that in turn, helps to explain the importance of the stark dichotomy between the haves and the have-nots. This stratification is reflected during the contemporary period in the broad meaning assigned to the idea of "popular" in Latin American social science and political discourse.

According to this corporate model, many potentially self-defined units are thus incapable of acting autonomously in the definition and defense of their interests and ideals. The notion of the *autonomy* of different societal units is crucial, because it explains why the mere appearance of numerous societal units in Latin America—such as an organized labor movement, numerous locally elected municipal governments, and the existence of a variety of voluntary organizations (women's and youth groups, federations of university students, various types of community councils, and so forth)—belies the existence of a resilient civil society. The virtual monopoly of national governments in many Latin American countries over the collection and distribution of resources and the setting of national priorities creates a centralizing tendency that has repercussions that seriously impair the emergence of the types of autonomous organizations central to the corporate model of civil society.

In terms of their autonomy, Latin American cities are generally at a disadvantage in comparison to European cities—at least those that were well established prior to the emergence of modern states with their centralizing tendencies. The concentration of the principal institutions that constitute the state (especially those with the broadest decision-making authority) in the capital, combined with the capital's general social, economic, and political dominance, severely impedes the autonomy of Latin American cities, as well as other societal units. This convergence of power and resources in the capital helps explain why the various elite groups competing for control over the state can monopolize the definition of societal interests and the struggles for the defense of these interests.

Somewhat paradoxically, this problem of autonomy may actually be worsened by the consolidation of strong political-party systems under democratic regimes. As a "political class" is created within the political parties, partisan interests begin to penetrate all spheres of society. Political parties competing for control of the state may gradually come to define the interests that social organizations express and defend.

The concentration of political, economic, and social resources and power, both geographically in the capital and in the state, requires a parallel concentration of authority and discretion at the elite levels of power in order to effectively compete for control over the state. Similarly, the administration of the state encourages a parallel centralization of party apparatus. Rather than act as a damper or brake in moderating polarizing tendencies at the national party level, social organizations controlled by these parties may magnify them throughout society. Political crises at the national party level easily become societal crises and the resultant polarization, which in effect represents the stratified nature of these societies, can threaten regime stability. Unlike the situation in Western Europe, where the close association between societal organizations and political parties is not viewed as a problem (and is often an important resource for Social Democratic and Labor parties in particular), in the "underdeveloped" civil societies of many Latin American countries this association can dangerously magnify contradictions and threaten the stability of democratic regimes.[13]

It should be acknowledged that there is a competing model of what a civil society is or should be, and this model is particularly relevant in those Latin American countries that have experienced the type of authoritarian rule being discussed here. This *liberal* model, first developed by the eighteenth-century political economist Adam Ferguson (1966) portrays the development of modern civil society as closely paralleling the spread of the market economy. Society is characterized as being composed of rational individuals who decide to live together in order to further their private, individual, interests. The ideas of community, collective fraternity in identity, and formal equality that characterize the corporate model of civil society decrease in importance as the market economy expands. Commerce, "the mighty engine which we suppose to have formed society, only tends to set its members at variance, or to continue their intercourse after the bands of affection have broken" (Ferguson 1966, 19). Personal gain becomes the principal motivation for individual behavior rather than the public good, as in the "illustrious states" of ancient Greece and Rome: "To the ancient Greek, or the Roman, the individual was nothing, and the public everything. To the modern, in too many nations of Europe, the individual is everything, and the public nothing" (Ferguson 1966, 56).

13. Given its long period of democratic government and history of a competitive party system, Chile best exemplifies the problems addressed here, and the issue of "autonomy" will be a central concern throughout this study. However, as discussed in Chapter 1, the issue of the autonomy of popular organizations from political parties has been important in many other contexts and countries, suggesting that Chile represents, albeit in a more extreme form, a generalized problem, or at least potential problem, for the emergence of civil societies along the lines of this European pattern.

This process by which civil society develops suggests as its ideal form a highly atomized society composed of individuals in the rational pursuit of their self-interest, in much the same way as the market and voting are characterized in classical economics. The individual becomes the focus for granting rights and reciprocal obligations. The rational maximization of individual interests, reconciled through the mechanism of the market when they conflict, becomes the driving force behind progress. Groups and group identities lose any sense of intrinsic value, and membership becomes solely a function of convenience and interest maximization (Black 1984). Individual freedom is valued above all, and requires for itself the rule of law and respect for private property. Voluntarism and the absence of coercion, in turn, justify the restriction of citizenship rights for those who are defined as incompetent or dependent, such as youths, illiterates, the poor, and the working class.

The ideal of "civil society" contained in the liberal model is very relevant to recent experiences in Latin America where authoritarian regimes have attempted to impose neoconservative "projects" for transforming society (Foxley 1983; Garretón, 1989a). The free rein these regimes have attempted to give to market forces in all spheres of society suggests that governments can have the creation of a certain type of civil society as an explicit or implicit goal. In restructuring economic and political institutions, as well as the nature of the system of incentives and disincentives they create (including the threat of violent repression of different types of activities and organizations in society), these authoritarian regimes may have important consequences for the directions in which civil society may or may not develop.

APPENDIX 1
Organizational Structure and Activities

Organization Type	Structure[a]	Activities
1. Human Rights Group	Treasurer, secretary; one delegate to coordinating body of *población*, parish pastoral council; two people for mobilization and propaganda; three for popular education	Discuss political situation; support for protests; support for people arrested; education for members (first aid, human rights); painted mural for *población*; planning education program on human rights for *población*
2. Self-Defense Group	None—3 or 4 leaders	Social/affective relations; efforts to provide youths with alternatives to drugs; political education; preparation for and participation in protests; plans: popular library in *población*
3. Women's Group	President, secretary, treasurer; two people in charge of health matters; two for legal matters; one delegate for the Legion of Mary (religious order); special commissions (e.g., work to support recent land-seizure near *población*)	Educational programs (health/hygiene, political, literacy, women's problems); fund raising (bake and sell bread, "*onces vendibles*,"[b] collect and sell used clothes); solidarity (various activities in support of land-seizure; collection of resources); provides first aid during protests; responsibility for consumers' co-op warehouse; social gatherings; sponsors short religious ceremonies.
4. *Junta de Vecinos*	President, secretary, treasurer; three directors; three people to review the group's accounts[c]	Programmed for weeklong celebration of *población*'s anniversary. Plans: improve *población* (e.g., install sewers); build a meeting place

		for cultural activities; programs for youth (problems of drugs and unemployment); form committee for the unemployed and those who need housing.
5. Women's Group	President, secretary, treasurer, two directors; one person in charge of knitting workshop; one person in charge of solidarity activities among members	End-of-year celebration for members and their children (food, presents); fund raising (*onces vendibles*, sell hot dogs, sell bread; hold raffles); knitting workshop; solidarity with members' problems.
6. Women's Group	President, treasurer, secretary, two directors.	End-of-year celebration for members and their children (food, presents); fund raising (*onces vendibles*, sell hot dogs, sell bread; hold raffles); solidarity with members' problems; fund for funeral expenses.
7. Women's Group	Delegate to a women's organization working in various *poblaciones*; One permanent delegate and one rotating delegate to coordinating body of *población*.	Education (parent-child and premarital relations, sexuality, women's rights, the political situation, the regime's policies); support soup kitchens; handicraft workshops; fund raising (sell french fries, *sopaipillas*,[d] used clothes); cultural events (*peñas*);[e] street activities/ mural painting with other groups (International Women's Day, May 1); protests (soup kitchen for participants).
8. Women's Group	Rotate positions on commissions for consumers' co-op, used-clothes sales, small-scale bread bakery, and four delegates to zonal coordinating body; commissions for special activities.	Fund raising (sell bread, *sopaipillas*, used clothes); consumers' co-op; co-organized independence day celebration for *población*; retreat for evaluating group's activities over the year; short-term loans between paychecks; solidarity with members who are ill; handicraft workshops; participate in *población*'s coordinating body.

9. Workers' Coop	President, secretary, treasurer; commissions: sports, finance, culture, discipline, welfare; delegates: two to federation of construction workers, two to coordinating body of *población*, one to organization of the relatives of the imprisoned and disappeared.	Formed legal union of construction workers; two retreats per year for evaluation of group's activities; participation in public acts and protests; Christmas gifts and celebration for members' children; co-organized independence day celebration for *población*; solidarity with members who are ill; support training for members; discuss political situation; worked with psychiatrist for a period; participate in *población*'s coordinating body.
10. Soup Kitchen	President, secretary, treasurer, person in charge of storehouse; committee for special activities : campaigns to raise money for school expenses, winter needs, Christmas, recreation.	Yearly campaigns to raise money for school supplies for children, winter needs (mattresses, blankets, clothes), Christmas (celebration and gifts for all children in *población*), recreation (trip to beach); celebration of soup kitchen's anniversary; literacy workshop; solidarity (support people involved in land-seizures, victims of March 1985 earthquake, hunger strikes in solidarity with other groups); feed participants in protests; *porotados*[f] to denounce hunger; *peñas*; cosponsor of a *colonia urbana*;[g] fund raising for supplies for the soup kitchen; participate in regional coordinating body for soup kitchens.
11. Cultural Group[h]	Treasurer.	*Peñas*, workshops: gardening, plans for guitar/music, art, popular education; work with young children; provide alternatives for young people.
12. Health Group	Treasurer.	Runs a small clinic with Chilean and foreign doctors; courses in health, first aid,

		hygiene and health rights; monitors nutrition in soup kitchen; gathers health statistics and deals with the health needs of children participating in *colonia urbana*; provides first aid during protests.
13. Union of Workers in the Informal Sector	Twelve-member executive committee: treasurer, secretary and individuals responsible for specific areas: youth, children, women, health, the soup kitchen, political matters, self-defense of the *población*, territorial coordination, preuniversity education, and person responsible for relations with various outside organizations.	Formed a legal union; workshops for young adults, children, politics, women, handicrafts; soup kitchen; health group; folk music group; sports club; various activities relating to protests.
14. Soup Kitchen—see No. 10.		
15. Soup Kitchen—see No. 10.		
16. Committee of People Seeking Housing	President, secretary, treasurer, one delegate per block (approx. sixty).	Welfare committee (solidarity with members' problems); youth organization; work on health problems (classes for health monitors); documentation of housing situation and collection of data on residents' economic situations; distribution of milk to children ages 1–6; lectures (housing alternatives, health); support activities of other organizations in *población* (cultural acts, protests, anniversary, Christmas celebration, etc.); organized soup kitchen and committee for unemployed people; organized land-seizure (1981); various petitions to municipal government.

17. Consumers' Co-op	Two couples run the co-op, work with one delegate from each of the sixty groups into which co-op is divided.	Buy merchandise in large volumes and sell at cost; formed theater group; organizing weeklong trip to the beach; fund raising for beach trip (raffles); celebration of co-op's anniversary; political education (videos, talk on nonviolent protest); seminars for married couples (sexual relations, parent-child relations).
18. Human Rights Group	President, vice president, secretary, treasurer.	Lectures and videos on human rights and the political situation; distribute pamphlets; statistics on repression; denounce repression (press releases); help for victims of human rights abuses; one 1-day retreat per year for evaluation of group's activities; exposition of cartridges, bullets, etc. used by security forces.
19. Handicraft Workshop	President, secretary, treasurer; two delegates to *población*'s coordinating body.	Handicraft workshop (knitting, painting, leather work, etc.); political education (discussions, lectures, videos for entire *población*); newsletter once per month (editorials, news analysis, recipes, etc.); lectures (health care, child care, public health service laws); participation in *población*'s coordinating body.
20. Youth Group	Individuals in coordinating body selected to be in charge of specific tasks as they arise (fund raising, publicity, etc.).	Political education, discussion of current political situation; lectures and movies for the *población*, emphasis on culture and recreation; support activities in *población*.
21. Human Rights Group	President, representative to the *población*'s coordinating body, secretary; various	Coordinate activities with the Vicaría de la Solidaridad (the Catholic Church) and the

	commissions (housing, education, health).	Chilean Human Rights Commission; lectures (justice in Chile, people arrested and "disappeared," the political situation); videos; *peñas* (theme of human rights, also for children and Christmas); training in human rights for members; collection of information on repression during protests and help for victims of repression; participation in *población*'s coordinating body.
22. Christian Base Community	n.a.	Health group; consumers' co-op; educational workshop; sponsor recreational activities for children, social gatherings for adults; home where group meets is used for church services; participation in the parish council and the *población*'s coordinating body.
23. Cultural Group	Six-person executive committee, monitors for workshops.	Organizes a cultural act for *población* once per month (folk music, discussion of various themes); informational newsletter once per month; women's group; various workshops for children (art, folk music); personal development workshop; three-day retreat to evaluate organization's activities and future plans.
24. *Colonia Urbana*	Four-member coordinating committee, committees for communication, finance, and recreation.	Summer camp in the *población* for children; organize protests; acts to denounce hunger, misery and repression; acts of solidarity with other groups; organizes recreational activities for children; organized sports competition in *población*; works with state-sponsored sports clubs; act to celebrate *colonia*'s anniversary; personal development

		workshop; campaign to collect food; *peñas*; fund raising (selling *sopaipillas*, used clothes).
25. Cultural Group—see No. 23.		
26. Women's Group	Two directors.	Handicraft workshop; discuss women's problems, the political situation; training in handicrafts; social activities (barbecue for members).
Cultural Group—see No. 23.		
Consumers' Co-op	President, secretary, treasurer; divided into five groups with president, secretary, treasurer; periodic commissions for cultural events (May 1 activity) and social commission (members' economic and health problems).	Buying and selling merchandise; solidarity with members' problems; cultural activities (*peñas*); family recreation days; Christmas celebration.
27. Discussion Group	Two different people direct each meeting; health committee.	Discuss and analyze the political situation; group interaction exercises; health committee; sports events; year-end event for children; celebration of anniversary of the arrival of a group of nuns.
28. Soup Kitchen	President, secretary, treasurer; women's workshop; men's workshop.	Fund raising (*peñas*, bake and sell bread); participates in *población*'s coordinating body.
Women's Workshop/ Group	President, secretary, treasurer.	Handicrafts (knitting, sewing); group interaction exercises and personal development sessions; retreat at beach.
29. Soup Kitchen—see No. 28.		
Women's Workshop/ group—see No. 28.		

30. Human Rights Group	President, vice president, secretary, treasurer.	Health-related activities (contacts with private medical clinic, first aid station during protests); political education (lectures and forums on political situation, each party's perspective on human rights, videos on repression); press releases/ conferences; solidarity activities with other groups; participation in protests (marches, barricades, hand out pamphlets, etc.): *peñas*; sports events.
31. People Affected By 1985 Earthquake	Sector has coordinating body with six members and is divided into six subcommittees.	Education (leadership formation, political situation, forums and lectures on the labor and *poblador* movements, courses in first aid, videos); petitions to municipal government and state agencies; organizes events for children (sports, poetry, etc.); sports activities; fund raising (sell used clothes, prepared food); organize and participate in protests.
Human Rights Group—see No. 30.		
32. Housing Co-op	Treasurer.	Fund raising to buy materials to build homes (sell used clothes, prepared food, sponsored a dance, show films, raffles, ask for donations, make and sell school clothes, collect newspapers and bottles).
Co-op for Buying Housing Plots[i]	None—UDI party sympathizers direct meetings.	People attend meetings to see if any land had been obtained or if food, clothes, etc. are available to help the neediest; discuss negative aspects of the protests.
33. None[j]		
34. Handicraft Workshop	President, secretary, treasurer, two or three directors;	Education (handicraft skills, leadership courses); activities

subcommittee for specific jobs; monitors who specialize in certain things and teach others.

to promote personal development and improve group-interaction; help *población* (provides first aid, help in organizing, help with family vegetable gardens); fund raising (*onces vendibles*, raffles, sell used clothes); anniversary celebration.

35. Handicraft Workshop

President, secretary, treasurer, person in charge of quality control; two delegates to the Vicaría de la Solidaridad and one to the *Movimiento Poblacional Solidaridad*; divided into knitting and macramé groups, each with one person in charge; social committee.

Expositions to sell handicrafts; fund from sales to buy food and distribute to members at end of year; weekly raffle of food (each member contributes one item and everyone wins once); social activities (teas once per month for members, anniversary celebration, barbecue on independence day); solidarity with members' problems; fund raising (films, sell used clothes); projects for family vegetable gardens, workshops for making ponchos and rugs, and a consumers' co-op.

36. Sports Club

President, secretary, vice president, treasurer, directorate; commissions for special activities.

Sports events; movies; yearly homage to member killed in a fight; anniversary celebration; independence day celebration for *población*; collection for members hurt in playing field and with other problems; planted trees around playing field.

37. Neighborhood Council[k]

President, secretary; person in charge of health, coordination and eradications;[l] one delegate per sector (twenty-four sectors).

Primary task is finding plots of land for moving people out of shantytown; work on problems of inhabitants (lack of bathrooms, potable water, and trash disposal; epidemics); operate small clinic; give Christmas toys to children.

38. Soup Kitchen

President, vice president, secretary, treasurer, person in charge of storehouse, person in charge of shifts in soup

Commissions ask bakery for bread, local merchants for food daily; solidarity with other organizations and kitchen; commissions to seek donations daily.

activities in *población*; provides food for people invited to *población*; participation in protests (food for people participating); sends petitions to municipality and local meat-packing company asking for assistance; discuss political situation; collections when member dies; fund raising (sells french fries; snacks); handicraft workshop to raise money for school books for members' children; participates in *población*'s coordinating body.

39. Home-building Co-op	Executive Committee; five groups, each with a coordinator and treasurer.	Executive committee coordinates work of *pobladores* who build homes for each other, a certain number of homes are built in each phase of the project; fund raising (sell *sopaipillas*, meat pies); social activities (barbecues, etc.); solidarity for ill people.
40. Handicraft Workshop	President, secretary, treasurer, delegate to *población*'s coordinating body; committee for the defense of women's rights, for the *colonia urbana*; literacy workshop; women's collective for women who never participated in a workshop.	Sell handicrafts through Vicaría de la Solidaridad and expositions; discuss political situation; solidarity with other groups and members (support hunger strikes, visit political prisoners, collections when a member is ill); course on how to cope with fear; literacy workshop; social activities; work with church (Christian base community, participate in various activities); participate in *población*'s coordinating body.

41. Neighborhood Council—see No. 37.

42. Handicraft Workshop—see No. 35.

43. Cultural Group	President, secretary, treasurer.	Cultural activities (theater, videos, paint street murals, daylong retreat in a park); solidarity campaigns (for *población* after an *allanamiento*,[m] participated in Campaign for Life with other groups, for young person with cancer, for victims of repression); political education (general and about the political situation); organize and participate in protests; group interaction exercises and personal development activities; fund raising (sell *sopaipillas*, raffles, *peñas*, street festival).
44. Soup Kitchen	President, treasurer, person in charge of supplies and the kitchen, secretary; special commissions (Christmas celebration).	Christmas celebration, toys for children; organized trip for members; fund raising (raffles, film-showings).
45. Family Vegetable Gardens	President, secretary, two directors	Members learn how to grow vegetables.
46. Soup Kitchen—see no. 38.		

a. Vital to the structure of all popular organizations is the assembly; that is, the meetings of the organization's entire membership and it is here that important decisions are discussed and made.

b. The organization prepares and sells a light meal in the early evening.

c. The *pobladores* were able to elect their own *junta de vecinos* because the previous members of the junta stole the group's municipal funds. Three people are in charge of reviewing the previous junta's accounts.

d. These are small fried breads made with squash.

e. These are cultural acts centering on folk music and sometimes include skits and original short plays.

f. A large pot of beans is cooked in a street and shared by *pobladores* as a symbolic form of protest.

g. Summer day-camp for *pobladores* in the *población*.

h. This group is recently reforming after a party militant nearly destroyed the organization by diverting its funds from an outside grant to activities intended to support his party.

i. The group was formed to help members gain access to plots of land on which they could eventually build houses. The group is sponsored by the pro-government UDI party and there are no collective activities for raising funds to buy the land. Few members had apparently received any land through the group.

j. This person was interviewed because he was a member of the youth branch of the Christian Democratic Party. He was not a member of a popular organization, but was planning to form a discussion group.

k. This neighborhood council was in the campamento Silva Henríquez. After the declaration of a state of siege in November 1984, the previous council was intervened and many of its members were sent into internal exile.

l. This is the government program under which the residents of the shantytown are relocated in *poblaciones* in other parts of Santiago.

m. These are combined military-police operations in which a *población* is sealed off, all adult males are detained and their documents checked, and houses are searched.

APPENDIX 2
Interview Methodology

Between June 1986 and January 1987, I conducted a total of forty-six interviews of leaders of popular organizations. The interview sample was designed to represent a general cross-section of organizational activity in the popular sectors. For the most part, only leaders of popular organizations were interviewed. Given the limited number of interviews that could be conducted, leaders were considered to be most likely to provide useful information because they tended to be more accustomed to dealing with outsiders and often had thought more about the kinds of issues being studied in the survey. These also were the people who were most actively involved in trying to forge a new popular collective identity.

Four variables were taken into account in selecting the people to be interviewed. First, an effort was made to distribute the sample among a variety of *poblaciones* in Santiago. Santiago is divided into five zones. The Northern Zone historically is characterized by the lowest level of popular-sector organizational activity and the Southern Zone is characterized by the highest. Since 1973, the Central Zone of Santiago has been characterized by extremely low levels of organizational activity. The principal government offices are located here and political-party activity previously had been quite high, leading to particularly intense repression after the coup. The Central Zone was also predominantly middle class until relatively recently, when, as a result of structural changes in the economy, many formerly middle-class people found themselves in situations of poverty. Big houses and whole buildings often were abandoned only to be occupied by a large number of people working in the informal economy for very low wages. The Western and Eastern Zones of Santiago have historically been characterized by intermediate levels of organizational activity.

Within each zone, particular *poblaciones* also have distinctive identities and historical tendencies. This often reflects how the *población* was created and when. If the *población* was created through a land-seizure or through a governmental program, the political party (or parties) that organized the land-seizure or were responsible for implementing the government programs tended to be the dominant party (or parties) in the *población*, even after the coup. Older *poblaciones*, which had sprung up as a result of urban migration prior to the first land-seizures in the late 1950s and early 1960s, or which were the result of the declining socioeconomic status of the area's residents, often lacked the predominant political influence of any single political party.

By focusing on the location of the *poblaciones* where interviews would be sought, an effort was made to control for the level of organization within the *población* (both historically and since the late 1970s) and the relative influence of the principal political tendencies within the popular sectors. A total of thirteen *poblaciones* were used in constructing the sample. One *población* (La Victoria) was characterized by a very high level of organization. In La Victoria, which was founded as a result of a land-seizure in the late 1950s, the Communist Party was by far the dominant political party. Seven people were interviewed from this *población*. Two other *poblaciones* were chosen because of the high level of organizational activity that characterized them prior to the coup and their differing experiences since then. Both also were characterized by a relatively high presence of members of the Revolutionary Left Movement (MIR). In one, Nueva Amanecer (formerly Nueva Habana),[1] the organizational activity was only recently beginning to reemerge and still remained relatively low within the *población* as a whole. In the other, Villa Francia, organizational activity remained at a moderately high level and the MIR maintained a relatively strong presence, in large part due to the presence of a particular priest and less post-coup repression. Three people were interviewed from Nueva Amanecer, and seven were interviewed from Villa Francia. Six people were also interviewed from Lo Hermida, a *población* with a moderately high level of organizational activity in Santiago's Eastern Zone.

Four different *poblaciones* were selected from the Northern Zone: Los Chorrillos, La Pencoya,[2] Remodalación (formerly "Angela Davis") and

1. Many *poblaciones* were officially renamed by the military regime because of the political significance of their original names.
2. La Pencoya is a large, relatively recent settlement on the northern edge of Santiago. It was formed by many contiguous *poblaciones* and is treated as one *población* for the purposes

Salto. This number in part was due to the lack of organizational activity in this zone, which necessitated going to several *poblaciones* in order to include an adequate number of people with a variety of experiences. The combined total of interviews from these *poblaciones* was thirteen.

Two *poblaciones* were selected because they were in areas where the Christian Democratic Party had historically been active. They were also characterized by relatively low levels of organizational activity. These were Villa O'Higgins and Villa La Reina. Three people were interviewed from each.

Finally, interviews were conducted in the Central Zone of Santiago, as well as one of the two large shantytowns (Silva Henríquez) created by successful land-seizures in 1983. Silva Henríquez was largely controlled by the pro-Pinochet Independent Democratic Union (UDI) and provided an interesting counterbalance to the other interviews. Of the two people interviewed from this shantytown, one was a UDI militant and the other had close ties to the UDI. Two people were also interviewed from the Central Zone.[3]

Once the *poblaciones* were identified, individual interviewees were selected according to three criteria: age, gender, and party affiliation. Age was considered an important variable because many of the participants in popular organizations were too young to have had meaningful memories or organizational experiences prior to the 1973 coup. Gender was considered in selecting interviewees in order to reflect the fact that, unlike many other kinds of organizations in Chile, women played a significant, and often dominant role in popular organizations. The breakdown of the interviewees according to age and gender is given in Table A-1.

Party affiliation was looked at to ensure that the majority of interviewees had no party affiliation or close party attachment and that the principal political parties would be represented among the party activists actually interviewed. In the end, nineteen of the forty-six people interviewed were either members of parties or "sympathizers." Someone who called herself a "sympathizer" generally had close ties to the party and often was close to

---

of this study. All of the *poblaciones* within La Pencoya generally exhibited very low levels of organization and they were formed under similar circumstances. Most important, the organizations that did exist usually had members living in different *poblaciones*. Of the thirteen interviews from the Northern Zone, five came from La Pencoya in recognition of its size.

3. Because of the Central Zone's unique history, it was difficult to distinguish meaningfully between *poblaciones*.

Table A-1. Interview sample by age and gender

	Male	Female	Total
Under 30	12	10	22
30 and Over	9	15	24
Total	21	25	

formally joining it. Table A-2 lists the various party affiliations of interviewees. Additional information regarding the individuals interviewed and the organization they belonged to is provided in Table A-3.

Interviews were usually conducted in the home of the interviewee. Sometimes they were conducted in the home of another *poblador*, in the interviewee's place of work or in the organization's meeting place. Three interviews were conducted in my home. The majority of the interviews were completed in one session, although a number of longer interviews required multiple meetings. Throughout this entire process of selecting interviewees, I was involved in a wide variety of participant-observer experiences throughout Chile with a number of different kinds of popular organizations, enabling me to identify particular *poblaciones* and organizations from which to draw interviewees. In many cases, I personally identified people to interview. In others, contacts were asked if they could suggest someone who fit certain characteristics, such as, for example, a middle-aged woman who was not a member of a political party and was active in the *población*'s soup kitchen.

Having spent a good deal of time in the *poblaciones* included in the

Table A-2. Party affiliations of interviewees

	Party							
	DC	IC	PC	PS[a]	MIR	Other	UDI	Total
Sympathizer		1			2		1	4
Militant	4	1	5	1 (N) 1 (SA)	1	MOC[b]	1	15

[a]Two factions of the Socialist Party were represented in the sample: The Nuñez faction and the Salvador Allende faction.

[b]*MAPU Obrero-Campesino,* a splinter group of the MAPU Party that had broken away from the Christian Democratic Party in the 1960s. It is a small Left party.

interview sample, it was not difficult to identify the most important or interesting organizations within each *población*. Some effort was made to include members of as wide a variety of organizations as possible. Most interviewees were active in more than one organization. Only seventeen belonged to a single organization. In all, the interviewees belonged to twenty-two different kinds of popular organizations. The following table lists the organizations to which interviewees belonged and summarizes some of the basic information concerning those organizations.

The interview consisted of 135 open-ended questions. Questions covered a variety of topics: how and why their organizations came into existence, the activities that they engaged in, the problems that the organization had confronted and how they were dealt with, relations between political parties and popular organizations, and the interviewees' opinions concerning political parties in general, the military regime and the coup, "democracy," political violence, and the protest movement.

The questionnaire was designed to see if a new popular collective identity was emerging from within the popular sectors themselves. As such, it was intended to probe the similarities in experiences, perceptions, and opinions among members of a wide variety of popular-sector organizations. Moreover, the issues to be addressed had to reflect the issues that the members of popular organizations themselves considered important. And this had to be done in a way that they could readily comprehend. The choice and wording of the questions reflected the author's own participant-observer experiences and was prepared in consultation with a number of researchers in Chile.

The questions were left open-ended for several reasons. First, I made a deliberate effort to minimize the influence of my own prejudices and experiences on the answers given by interviewees. This influence was an especially important concern, given the dearth of materials on the subject of a popular collective identity in Chile (or even on the opinions and experiences of the urban poor after the coup) that could have been used as a guide in formulating alternative responses from which interviewees could be asked to choose. Second, many of the interviewees were unaccustomed to being questioned on such a wide variety of issues, especially ones that were politically sensitive. By allowing interviewees to express themselves freely, they became more comfortable with the process and more involved in it.

In the various tables, it is apparent that not everyone answered every question. This does not reflect any lack of cooperation. Only rarely did an

Table A-3. Organizations to which interviewees belonged

Organization	Approx. Age of Org. at Time of Interview	No. of Members	External Actor Involved in Founding	Meeting Place
1. Human rights group	9 mos.	9	None	Church
2. Self-defense group	9 mos.	6	None	Homes
3. Women's group	5 yrs.	14	Priest, nun	Church
Consumer's co-op	2 yrs.	200 families	Priest	Church
4. Junta de Vecinos	3 mos.	9	None	Homes
5. Women's group	less than 1 year	12	Nun, missio[a]	Homes
6. Women's group	4 yrs.	22	Missio	Church
7. Women's group	1 yr.	12	None	Church
8. Women's group	n.a.	16	None	Church
9. Workers' co-op	10 yrs.	22	Priest	Church
10. Soup kitchen	3 yrs.	200–300	None	Org.'s own place
11. Cultural group	1 yr.	15	Missio	Church
12. Health group	3 yrs.	12	None	Org.'s own place
13. Union of workers in the informal sector	4 yrs.	43	None	Homes
14. Soup kitchen	3 yrs.	200	None	Org.'s own place
15. Soup kitchen	3 yrs.	200	None	Org.'s own place
16. Committee of people seeking housing	4 yrs.	60[b]	Metro	Church
17. Consumers' co-op	4 yrs.	600 families	Priest	Church
Workers' co-op	3 mos.	3	Priest	Church
18. Human rights	3 yrs.	10	Political party	Church
19. Women's group	3 yrs.	11	None	Homes

	Duration	Members	Sponsor	Meeting place
20. Youth group	4 yrs.	9	None	Church[c]
Group for children	6 yrs.	18	Church org.[d]	Church[c]
21. Human rights group	1 yr.	5	Chilean Human	Church
22. Christian-base community	2 yrs.	12 families	None	Member's home
23. Cultural group	8 yrs.	12	None	Org.'s own place
24. Colonia Urbana[e]	3 yrs.	15	None	Church
25. Cultural group	8 yrs.	12	None	Org.'s own place
26. Women's group	1 yr.	8	None	Org.'s own place
Cultural group	8 yrs.	12	None	Org.'s own place
Consumers' co-op	3 yrs.	250 families	Church	Church
27. Discussion group	2 yrs.	16	Nun	Church
28. Soup kitchen	2 yrs.	76	None	Member's home
29. Soup kitchen	2 yrs.	76	None	Member's home
Handicraft workshop	less than 1 yr.	15	None	Member's home
30. Human rights group	2 yrs.	15	None	Church
31. People affected by 1985 earthquake	1 yr.	120	METRO, church	Church
Human rights group	2 yrs.	15	None	Church
32. Housing co-op	less than 1 yr.	18	Missio	Church
Co-op for buying housing plots	less than 1 yr.	40	Political party	Member's home
33. None[f]	—	—	—	—
34. Handicraft workshop	2 yrs.	22	Solidaridad[g]	Church
35. Handicraft workshop	1 yr.	48	Solidaridad[g]	Church
36. Sports club	—	130	State	Org.'s own place
37. Neighborhood council[i]	2 yrs.	24	Party/state	Org.'s own place
38. Soup kitchen	5 yrs.	600	Group of exiles	Home of nonmembers
39. Home-building co-op	1 yr.	600	None	Org.'s own place
40. Handicraft workshop	12 yrs.	16	Nun	Church

Table A-3. *Continued*

Organization	Approx. Age of Org. at Time of Interview	No. of Members	External Actor Involved in Founding	Meeting Place
41. Neighborhood council[g]	2 yrs.	24	Party/state	Org.'s own place
42. Handicraft workshop	1 yr.	48	Solidaridad[g]	Church
43. Cultural group	less than 1 yr.	20	None	Church
44. Soup kitchen	4 yrs.	16 families	Nuns	Church
Mothers' center[i]	—[h]	27	State	Org.'s own place
45. Family vegetable gardening	less than 1 yr.	25	Solidaridad[g]	Member's home
46. Soup kitchen	5 yrs.	600	Group of exiles	Person's home

[a]This is an institution that works with popular organizations under the auspices of the Catholic Church.

[b]The committee is composed of one delegate for each block in the *población*, and there are sixty blocks in this *población*.

[c]This includes church parishes and buildings owned directly by the church or institutions under the church's direct auspices.

[d]This organization is affiliated with a Protestant church.

[e]This group organizes a summer camp in the *población* for young children.

[f]This person was interviewed because he was a member of the youth branch of the Christian Democratic Party. He was not a member of a popular organization, but was planning to form a discussion group in the near future.

[g]*Movimiento Poblacional Solidaridad*. This organization was created by the Christian Democratic Party to represent the party in the *poblaciones*. See Chapter 7.

[h]This is one of the organizations established by the state during the presidency of Eduardo Frei in the 1960s.

[i]This neighborhood council was in the campamento Silva Henríquez. After the declaration of a state of siege in November 1984, the previous council was intervened and many of its members were sent into internal exile.

[j]This person was required to join the organization, which is sponsored by the state, because her child attended public school.

interviewee refuse to answer a question (and their option to do so was always made very clear from the beginning), and in those few cases the interviewee would later answer the same question after he or she had become more relaxed and confident. Only once, in the first interview, did the interviewee refuse to answer a question.[4] When no response was given to a question, it was because the question had not been asked. With long interviews, averaging three hours, a large number of questions, and the tendency of interviewees to answer questions long before they came up on the questionnaire, questions were sometimes accidentally omitted.

The nature of the interview process has important limitations. It is not intended to be a "scientific" or random sample. Instead, the results represent a first effort to search for the existence of something new in the popular sectors. Having used an open-ended, semi-structured interview technique, answers were not readily codable and did not necessarily fit into neat categories. This shortcoming, however, makes the patterns that emerged all the more interesting because they were less influenced by the possible biases and prejudices of a more structured format. These observed patterns, in turn, can serve as the basis for future, more structured investigations.

Finally, the author also conducted fourteen interviews with national political-party elites. These elites represented the major political parties, from both the Right and the Left. They included the Independent Democratic Union, the National Union Movement, the Christian Democratic Party, the Christian Left, the more moderate Nuñez and more radical Almeyda factions of the Socialist Party, and the Communist Party. The interviews were substantially shorter than those with *pobladores*; generally seeking to probe each party's relations with the popular sectors and identify areas of potential agreement and disagreement between the parties and popular organizations over issues relating to popular-sector demands, the nature of democracy, the appropriateness of different opposition strategies and the role of the popular sectors in a future democracy.

4. When asked if she was a member of a political party, she said she was planning to join one that she could not name. However, she realized that from her answers—and given where she lived—it was clear that the party was an extreme left-wing one. She simply did not want to be on record as stating her intent to join.

APPENDIX 3
A Day in the Life of a Protest

The protest in the *poblaciones*[1] begins early. Before dawn, the "youth brigades" are awake, preparing to perform their assigned tasks. The used tires, wood, and gasoline that had been carefully hidden in the *población* over the preceding few weeks now had to be brought out in order to build the barricades that would prevent that day's first shift of workers from going to their jobs by stopping public transportation. Trenches had to be dug in dirt roads to make it more difficult for police and military vehicles to enter the *población*. The *miguelitos*[2] had to be distributed and scattered over the major access roads to the *población* and any major highways nearby.

At about the same time as the brigades are beginning their day's activities, the security forces begin to arrive. The cat-and-mouse game that serves as dynamic to the protests begins. As the barricades are dismantled, the streets swept clean of *miguelitos* and "suspicious"-looking *pobladores*—generally all males under the age of 25—are chased, tear-gassed, clubbed, and maybe arrested or shot at, the young *pobladores* retreat deep into the *población* and reemerge somewhere else to start the process all over again.

This very serious game continues for several hours, until around nine or

---

1. The following account is based on experiences in two separate *poblaciones* during different national protests. These experiences have been combined here in order to provide a general idea of what happens in the *poblaciones* on days of protest. They are typical of the experiences of most well-organized *poblaciones* in Santiago.

2. These are small, sharpened metal objects that vary in design and sophistication from *población* to *población*. They are used to puncture the tires of police and military vehicles, as well as any taxi or bus unlucky enough to pass over them. *Miguelitos* are usually designed so that one only has to throw them into the street. In *poblaciones* with a lot of unpaved roads, they may be partially buried in the ground the night before a protest.

ten, when those trying to go to work either had succeeded or given up. Throughout the *población*, people then begin to assess the day's activities so far. Which brigades had performed their assigned tasks? Which had not and why? Sometimes people oversleep or worried parents forbid their children to leave the house. Sometimes people are unlucky and walk into a military or police patrol.

People exchange information about who was hurt or arrested. Human rights groups attempt to keep records of the victims of repression. It is important to know who is arrested in order to make sure that the person is released quickly—and unharmed. As it turns out, on this day a young man—whom we shall call "Juan"—was assaulted by the police and taken to the stationhouse. No one is sure which police station he was taken to or what condition he was in when the police took him. But nothing could be done until people knew where Juan actually was. It was hoped that Juan was in a regular police station and not in the hands of the secret police. His mother, surrounded by Juan's younger brothers and sisters, is very worried. *If*, as people think, Juan was just walking through the *poblaciones* with other teenagers, he should be released in the early afternoon. But was that all he was doing?

Every hour, on the hour, the *población* comes alive with the sounds of Radio Cooperativa.[3] People eagerly listen to hear how the protest is progressing in other parts of Santiago. How many people did not show up to work? How many downtown shops were closed? How many bus and taxi drivers kept their vehicles in their garages? How severe is the repression? On this particular day, a very bizarre and tragic story was beginning to unfold as the first fragmented accounts of two young people who had been severely burned earlier that morning began to filter into Radio Cooperativa. The *población* became alive with the rumors—no one knew who was burned or why, or even how severely. Yet everyone sensed something horrible had happened.

It is mid-morning and things begin to slow down. Buses are fewer and farther in between. The military and the police begin to roam around more at random, looking for anything suspicious, but rarely entering too far into the *poblacion* where the tight confines of a shantytown made the results of any incursion unpredictable. To keep the spirit of the protest alive, an occasional barricade is erected, only to be quickly dismantled by the police and/or military armed with tear gas, shotguns, and machine guns.

3. Radio Cooperativa is owned and operated by the Catholic Church. It was the only reliable source of news in the *poblaciones* on days of protest.

Suddenly, there is some sort of commotion at the head of the principal street leading into the *población*. A fully loaded garbage truck had dumped tons of garbage at the intersection of that street and a major highway leading into Santiago—the ultimate barricade. The *pobladores* are ecstatic at their own ingenuity.

The morning progresses slowly. The silence is shattered by the taunts of young *pobladores* trying to provoke the young draftees into doing something foolish. From out of nowhere, the baritone voice of a young *poblador* shouts out obscenities and insults to eighteen-year-old draftees on a corner on the *población's* perimeter. The soldiers immediately draw their assault weapons, not knowing what to expect. Shots are fired, yet the voice continues. The soldiers, probably *pobladores* themselves, cautiously attempt to enter the *población*. The crowds that always gather on the major streets, assured that they are safely removed from the barricades and confrontations, watch with awe. People try to guess who the brave *poblador* might be. Slowly, protecting each other's flanks, the patrol of four or five soldiers advances down the alleys of the *población* toward the mysterious voice that continues to egg them on. Then, finally, the voice stops. The crowd's attention had been temporarily won and the soldiers had been very annoyed. This game was over and, fortunately, no one was hurt.

News continues to seep into the *población* in fragments. Juan was only walking through the *población* with friends and was only kicked around slightly. His "mistake" was to be a young man walking through the *población* on a day of protest without any identification. Members of the human rights group were also pretty sure where he had been taken, or at least they knew where most of those arrested in their sector of Santiago were being taken that day. But a new preoccupation began to grow. Did Juan remember to throw away the piece of paper he had had the previous night that noted the address of a house in the *población* where he was to retrieve materials for today's protest? Only time would tell.

More information was also becoming available about the report that two young people were burned alive that morning. Yes, two people had been found burned—and very severely. But who was responsible? Why were they found, apparently left for dead, miles away from any areas where the protest had been active?

In the meantime, a group of middle-aged women became enraged. A military patrol had broken into the house of an old woman, allegedly looking for someone, and she had been struck. Out of rage and frustration, but aware of the symbolism that their courage would represent for the rest of the *población*, they literally surrounded a police jeep. They screamed at the young police lieutenant to do something, to defend the honor of the *población* (which the police were supposed to protect) and the honor of the police force itself in the face of the military's apparent impunity. They appealed to the tradition of the *Carabineros*,[4] which the military regime had corrupted by turning them against their own people. But the women also appealed to the growing tension between the military and the *Carabineros*, who felt that the military government was using them as the scapegoat in its repressive activities.

Although nothing came of the incident—the *Carabineros'* hands were effectively tied when it came to the activities of the military—the women had made a point. They had made their point with the *Carabineros*, who themselves were made to feel helpless and impotent in the face of the military's privileged position. But these woman had also made another point, and this one was intended for the *pobladores*. They showed through their own actions that it was possible for *pobladores* to stand up to the police and at least attempt to defend what they felt was right.

By now, close to noon, the military had decided it was time to remove the tons of garbage blocking the road. Armed with shotguns, soldiers guarded over workers employed in the state's minimal employment program as they shoveled the mess into a truck. The *pobladores* were not going to stand idly by. Dozens of young men, hiding behind corners on side streets, approached the workers and began throwing rocks at the soldiers. Those too young to throw rocks relayed buckets full of rocks from throughout the *población* to those who could. Women, many of whom were mothers and some even grandmothers, chanted from behind, out of range from the soldiers' birdshot. For close to half an hour, the confrontation continued—rocks and words from the *pobladores* that were met by birdshot from the military. Again, through good fortune, no one had been hurt seriously. The military had refrained from using anything more lethal than tear gas and shotguns loaded with birdshot.[5]

But the *pobladores'* luck was to change. A crowd began to gather around one twenty-two-year-old man who was obviously in a lot of pain. He had lost an eye to birdshot and his friends were taking him to the chapel, where

---

4. The national police force.
5. The military frequently uses assault rifles against unarmed *pobladores* on days of protest and this accounts for most of the deaths registered on these days in the *poblaciones*. A number of deaths are also attributed to civilians who drive around *poblaciones* in unmarked cars, apparently shooting people at random.

an "emergency room" had been set up for the inevitable injuries that resulted on days of protests.[6]

The head priest in the *población*'s parish decided it was now time to halt the insanity. A huge crowd of people swarmed behind him as he approached the lieutenant in command of the cleanup crew at the head of the street. They argued, but the lieutenant backed down, not wishing a confrontation with the priest. The *pobladores* took courage in this and again began to chant and taunt the young soldiers, feeling shielded by the priest's presence. Finally, the priest had to silence his people and things were once again able to return to "normal."

At the opposite end of the same street where the priest was confronting the lieutenant, no more than ten blocks away, another crowd quickly formed. There was a different kind of excitement here. The people were cheering and giving a hero's greeting to four masked *pobladores* armed with machine guns—the *población*'s contingent of the Manuel Rodríguez Patriotic Front (FPMR). As the crowd at the other end of the street behind the priest began to disperse, the *población*'s own "guerrillas" left by a side street to go off to confront the military as the *pobladores* cheered them on. The FPMR had already completed its real job—the four "guerrillas" had given the *pobladores* something to be proud of.[7]

The protest came to an effective halt at mid-day. People ate lunch and rested. A soup kitchen offered to feed all of those who had participated in the day's activities. The streets are quiet; even the military and police relaxed their guard. News continued to come in small, inclusive pieces. Juan had definitely been located. He should be released within a few hours and appeared to be in good spirits. It looked as if he did not have the incriminating piece of paper on him when he was arrested, but no one could be sure until he was actually back in the *población*. It also was now clear that two teenagers—a young man who had recently returned to Chile from the United States where his mother, also a victim of the military's repression, was living in exile, and a young Chilean woman who had befriended him—had been severely burned and might die. Why they were burned was still unclear and rumors had begun to spread that the military

6. Although many *poblaciones* have their own state-sponsored medical clinics, these were closed by the government on days of protests.

7. The four members of the FPMR may or may not have engaged in an armed confrontation with the military. Such confrontations did take place occasionally and *pobladores* allegedly have been killed in such confrontations.

was responsible. Shivers of horror could be seen among those who listened as the news came in over the radio.

Late afternoon came and the young *pobladores* grew restless. More barricades were erected and dismantled by the security forces. Large crowds formed as whole families, many with children in strollers, came out to see what was going on. Whiffs of tear gas floated in the air and the occasional but familiar sound of automatic weapons being fired could be heard throughout the *población*. Buses are very rare now, but the unfortunate bus that chose to pass was immediately bombarded by a shower of rocks, with boys as young as seven or eight taking aim. The police, dressed in riot gear, responded with volleys of tear gas. The young protestors dispersed, often running into a nearby *población* where there were no barricades or *miguelitos* and where they might be able to hide. Busloads of riot police fanned out in the less active *población*, where they too felt more secure. The cat-and-mouse game continued, on again, off again, throughout the day. Tear-gas canisters landed randomly throughout both *poblaciones*. Mothers, supposedly safe within the confines of their homes, watching over children who are too little to have any idea of what is going on outside, were occasionally shocked as a tear-gas canister "accidentally"—no one knows for sure—crashed through a window. A mother had to move quickly—the gas can suffocate a small child when confined to the small, frequently poorly ventilated space that many call "home" in the *poblaciones*.

Juan finally came home. He was safe, and had remembered to destroy the incriminating note. Everyone was relieved. But there was also growing concern. The details of what had happened to the two young people found burned alive were now becoming much clearer. The young man had been taking pictures of the protest for an opposition magazine. When a small group of protestors was surprised by an early-morning military patrol, everyone had run. But the two teenagers could not escape. As eyewitness reports began to emerge, it became increasingly apparent that the military had poured gasoline over the two, lit them, and then dumped the bodies miles away. No one would dare touch the bodies for a number of hours, fearing military reprisals. Once the two were finally taken to a hospital, effective treatment was hampered by the military government's intransigence—it insisted that the two were the victims of their own Molotov cocktails and therefore terrorists—and shortages of even the most basic medical supplies in the public hospital to which the two were brought.[8]

8. The young man soon died of his injuries. The woman eventually went to Canada for

As night approached, the protest was winding down. People needed to rest and regroup for the next day's activities. But more than that, as darkness came, it was safer to be inside. The military was still present and the unmarked cars carrying armed civilians would soon start to circulate throughout Santiago. Shots could be heard throughout the night. The military usually would turn off either all of the electricity in the *poblaciones* or at least the streetlights—making it easier for them to hide and more dangerous for anyone to leave their home. And so ended a typical day of protest in the *poblaciones*.

---

treatment of her burns at the invitation of the Canadian government. Many of her family members also had to leave the country due to harassment by the military government's security apparatus.

REFERENCES

Acuerdo nacional para la transición a la plena democracia. 1985. Pamphlet. Santiago.

Agurto, I., M. Canales, and G. de la Maza. 1985. *Juventud chilena: Razones y subversiones.* Santiago: ECO-FOLICO.

Alvarado, L., R. Cheetham, A. Garat, and G. Rojas. 1973. "Movilización social en torno al problema de la vivienda," *Revista Latinoamericana de Estudios Urbanos Regionales (EURE)* 3 (April): 37–70.

Álvarez, S. E. 1990. *Engendering Democracy in Brazil: Women's Movements in Transition Politics.* Princeton: Princeton University Press.

Alves, M. 1989. "Interclass Alliances in the Opposition to the Military in Brazil: Consequences for the Transition Period." In S. Eckstein, ed., *Power and Popular Protest: Latin American Social Movements,* 278–98. Berkeley and Los Angeles: University of California Press.

Alwin, P. 1984. *La Alternativa democrática.* Santiago: Editorial Andante.

Análisis. Various issues.

Análisis Económico. (January–March 1991). No. 1.

Angell, A. 1972. *Politics and the Labour Movement in Chile.* London: Oxford University Press.

———. 1989. Trade Unions in Chile in the 1980s. Paper presented at the conference "Transformation and Transition in Chile, 1982–1989." University of California at San Diego, 13–14 March, Mimeographed.

Angell, A., and B. Pollack. 1990. "The Chilean Elections of 1989 and the Politics of the Transition to Democracy." *Bulletin of Latin American Research* 9 (1): 1–23.

Arellano, J. 1985. *Políticas sociales y desarrollo: Chile, 1924–1984.* Santiago: CIEPLAN.

Arrate, J. 1985. *La Fuerza democrática de la idea socialista.* Santiago: Ediciones del Ornitorrinco.

Arrate, J., et al. 1986. *Siete ensayos sobre democracia y socialismo en Chile.* Santiago: VECTOR, Centro de Estudios Económicos y Sociales.

Arriagada, G. 1985a. *Chile: El Sistema político futuro.* Santiago: Editorial Aconcagua.

———. 1985b. "Comentarios." In Centro de Estudios del Desarrollo, *El futuro democrático de Chile,* 198–204.

———. 1986a. *La Democracia cristiana: Un análisis de su estrategia y de las tareas políticas del periodo 1987–1990.* Paper presented before the Junta Provincial del Partido de Valparaíso, 6 June 1986. Mimeographed.

———. 1986b. "La Democracia cristiana y el Partido Comunista." In E. Frei et al., *Democracia Cristiana y Partido Comunista,* 9–86. Santiago: Editorial Aconcagua.

Asamblea Nacional de la Civilidad. *Demanda de Chile.* 1986. Pamphlet. Santiago.

Bachrach, P. 1967. *The Theory of Democratic Elitism: A Critique.* Boston: Little, Brown.

Ballon, E., ed. 1986. *Movimientos sociales y democracia: La Fundación de un nuevo orden.* Lima: DESCO.

Baño, R. *Lo social y lo político.* Santiago: FLACSO.

———. 1986. *Los Sectores populares frente a la política (algunos resultados de una encuesta).* Santiago: FLACSO, Documento de trabajo, no. 315.

Baraona, J. 1974. "La Evolución del movimiento laboral." In Dagmar Raczynski et al., *Los actores de la realidad chilena,* 101–71. Santiago: Editorial del Pacífico S.A.

Barber, B. 1974. *The Death of Communal Liberty: A History of Freedom in a Swiss Mountain Canton.* Princeton: Princeton University Press.

———. 1984. *Strong Democracy: Participatory Politics for a New Age.* Berkeley and Los Angeles: University of California Press.

Barrera, M. 1988. *Consideraciones acerca de la relación entre política y movimiento sindical: El Caso de Chile.* Santiago: Centro de Estudios Sociales, Materiales de Discusión, no. 6.

Barrera, M., and J. Valenzuela. 1986. "The Development of Labor Movement Opposition to the Military Regime." In J. Valenzuela and A. Valenzuela, eds., *Military Rule in Chile: Dictatorship and Opposition,* 230–69. Baltimore: Johns Hopkins University Press.

Barrig, M. 1986. "Democracia emergente y movimiento de mujeres." In Eduardo Ballon, ed., *Movimientos sociales y democracia: La Fundación de un nuevo orden,* 143–83. Lima: DESCO.

Barros, R. 1986. "The Left and Democracy: Recent Debates in Latin America." *Telos,* no. 68 (Summer): 49–70.

Bases de sustentación del régimen democrático. Profundización del Acuerdo Nacional Para la Transición a la Plena Democracia. 1986. Pamphlet.

Benavente, A. 1985. "Panorama de la izquierda chilena, 1973–1984." *Estudios Públicos,* no. 18 (Fall): 155–99.

Bendix, R. 1964. *Nation-Building and Citizenship: Studies of Our Changing Social Order.* New York: John Wiley and Sons.

Berquist, C. 1986. *Labor in Latin America.* Stanford: Stanford University Press.

Bitar, S. 1986a. *Chile: Experiment in Democracy.* Philadelphia: Institute for the Study of Human Issues.

———. 1986b. "La Urgencia de darle al país un camino," *Liberación* (March–April): 19–22.

Black, A. 1984. *Guilds and Civil Society in European Political Thought From the Twelfth Century to the Present.* London: Methuen.

Boeninger, E. 1984a. *La Concertación política y social: Problema y exigencia de la consolidación democrática.* Santiago: Centro de Estudios del Desarrollo, Documento de Trabajo, no. 9.

———. 1984b. *Participación: Oportunidades, dimensiones y requisitos para su desarrollo*. Santiago: Centro de Estudios del Desarrollo, Documento de Trabajo, no. 16.

———. 1985. *La Democracia: Unico proyecto posible para Chile*. Santiago: Centro de Estudios del Desarrollo, Documento de Trabajo, no. 21.

———. 1986. "The Chilean Road to Democracy." *Foreign Affairs* 64 (Spring): 812–32.

Boschi, R. 1984. *On Social Movements and Democratization: Theoretical Issues*. Stanford: Stanford–Berkeley Joint Center for Latin American Studies, Occasional Paper no. 9.

Brunner, J. 1986. *Notas sobre la situación política chilena a la luz de los resultados preliminarios de una encuesta!* Santiago: FLACSO, Material de discusión, no. 80.

Burdick, J. 1992. "Rethinking the Study of Social Movements: The Case of Urban Christian Base Communities in Urban Brazil." In A. Escobar and S. Alvarez, eds., *The Making of Social Movements in Latin America: Identity, Strategy and Democracy*, 171–84. Boulder: Westview.

Cademartori, J. 1988. Chile: Economic Aspects of Democratization. Paper presented at the Fourteenth International Congress of the Latin American Studies Association, New Orleans, 17–20 March.

Calderón, F., ed. 1986. *Los Movimientos sociales ante la crisis*. Buenos Aires: Universidad de las Naciones Unidas.

Calhoun, C. 1991. "The Problem of Identity in Collective Action." In J. Huber, ed., *Macro-Micro Linkages in Sociology*, 51–75. Newbury Park: Sage Publications.

Campero, G. 1986. "Luchas y movilizaciones sociales en la crisis: ¿Se constituyen movimientos sociales en Chile?: Una introducción al debate." In CLACSO-ILET, *Los movimientos sociales y la lucha democrática en Chile*, 9–19. Santiago: CLACSO-ILET.

———. 1987. *Entre la sobrevivencia y la acción política: Las Organizaciones de pobladores en Santiago*. Santiago: Estudios ILET.

Campero, G., and R. Cortázar. 1985. "Lógicas de acción sindical en Chile." In Comisión de Movimientos Laborales, CLACSO, *El sindicalismo Latinoamericano en los ochenta*, 133–58. Santiago: Comisión de Movimientos Laborales, CLACSO.

Campero, G., and J. A. Valenzuela. 1984. *El Movimiento sindical en el régimen militar chileno, 1973–1981*. Santiago: ILET.

Cardoso, R. 1983. "Movimentos sociais no Brasil Pós-64: Balanco crítico." In B. Sorj and M. H. Tavares de Almeida, eds., *Sociedade e Política no Brasil Pós-64*, 215–39. São Paulo: Brasiliense.

Cardoso, F., and E. Falleto. 1979. *Dependency and Development in Latin America*. Berkeley and Los Angeles: University of California Press.

Carta abierta al pueblo de Chile. October 1986. Pamphlet.

Castells, M. 1973. "Movimientos de pobladores y lucha de clases." *Revista Latinoamericana de Estudios Urbanos Regionales (EURE)* 3 (April): 9–35.

———. 1983. *The City and the Grassroots: A Cross-Cultural Theory of Urban Social Movements*. Berkeley and Los Angeles: University of California Press.

Central Committee, Partido Comunista de Chile. 1985. *Informe al Pleno del C.C. del Partido Comunista*.

Centro de Estudios del Desarrollo. 1985. *El Futuro democrático de Chile: 4 visiones políticas*. Santiago: Centro de Estudios del Desarrollo.

CEPAL. 1990. *Magnitud de la pobreza en América Latina en los años ochenta.* Santiago: Comisión Económica para América Latina y el Caribe and Programa de las Naciones Unidas Para el Desarrollo.

Chalmers, D. 1977. "The Politicized State in Latin America." In James M. Malloy, ed., *Authoritarianism and Corporatism in Latin America*, 23–45. Pittsburgh: University of Pittsburgh Press.

Cincuenta preguntas al Partido Comunista de Chile. 1984. Clandestine Press Conference, Communist Party of Chile, 23 January. Mimeographed.

CLACSO-ILET. 1986. *Los Movimientos sociales y la lucha democrática en Chile.* Santiago: CLACSO-ILET.

Collier, D. 1976. *Squatters and Oligarchs: Authoritarian Rule and Policy Change in Peru.* Baltimore: Johns Hopkins University Press.

Comisión Nacional de Verdad y Reconciliación. 1991. *Informe de la Comisión Nacional de Verdad y Reconciliación.* Santiago: La Nación.

Concertación de Partidos por la Democracia. 1989. *Programa de gobierno.* Santiago: Concertación de Partidos por la Democracia.

Consejo Nacional, Movimiento Democrático Popular. N.d. *El MDP y la Asamblea de la Civilidad: En el camino de la concertación social para terminar con la dictadura.* Pamphlet. Santiago.

Constitución Política de la República de Chile, 1980.

Cornelius, W. 1975. *Politics and the Migrant Poor in Mexico City.* Stanford: Stanford University Press.

Correa, P. 1985. "Comentarios." In Centro de Estudios del Desarrollo, *El futuro democrático de Chile*, 155–59.

Correa, E., and J. Viera-Gallo. 1986. *Iglesia y dictadura.* Santiago: CESOC.

Cortázar, R. 1987. "La No-transición a la democracia en Chile y el plebiscito de 1988." *Colección Estudios CIEPLAN* 22 (December): 111–28.

Corvalán, L. 1983. Discurso de Luis Corvalán, Secretario General del Partido Comunista de Chile pronunciado a traves de Radio Moscú (November). Mimeographed.

Cumplido, F. 1984. "El Concepto de constitución y de democracia del Grupo de los 24." *Opciones*, special edition (August): 191–97.

de la Maza, G., and M. Garces. 1985. *La Explosión de las mayorías: Protesta nacional, 1983–1984.* Santiago: ECO.

Departamento Nacional de Pobladores, Partido Socialista de Chile (Nuñez). N.d. *Documento de Trabajo.* Santiago. Pamphlet.

División de Organizaciones Sociales, Ministerio Secretaría General de Gobierno. 1990. *Estrategía de Participación para la Transición a la Democracia.* Santiago: División de Organizaciones Sociales, May.

Dix, R. 1989. "Cleavage Structures and Party Systems in Latin America." *Comparative Politics* 22 (October): 23–38.

Drago, R. 1986. *Una Propuesta de desarrollo local basada en la participación.* Santiago: VECTOR, Centro de Estudios Económicos y Sociales.

Duncan, G., and S. Lukes. 1963. "The New Democracy." *Political Studies* 11:156–77.

Duque, J., and E. Pastrana. 1971. Elementos teóricos para la interpretación de los procesos organizativo-políticos poblacionales. Santiago: Escuela Latinoamericana de Sociología. Mimeographed.

Eckstein, S. 1988. *The Poverty of Revolution: The State and the Urban Poor in Mexico.* Princeton: Princeton University Press.

————, ed. 1989. *Power and Popular Protest: Latin American Social Movements.* Berkeley and Los Angeles: University of California Press.

ECO, *Taller de Análisis Movimientos Sociales y Coyuntura.* January 1988–August 1990. Nos. 1–6.

La Epoca. Santiago. Various issues.

Epstein, E. 1992. Labor and Political Stability in the New Chilean Democracy: Three Illusions. Paper presented at the Seventeenth International Congress of the Latin American Studies Association, Los Angeles, 24–27 September.

Equipo de Estudios Poblacionales de CIDU. 1972. "Reivindicación urbana y lucha política: Los Campamentos de pobladores en Santiago de Chile." *Revista Latinoamericana de Estudios Urbanos Regionales (EURE)* 2 (November): 55–81.

Es tiempo de unir y de luchar. 1984. Clandestine Press Conference, 4–5 September, Communist Party of Chile. Mimeographed.

Escobar, A., and S. Alvarez, eds., 1992. *The Making of Social Movements in Latin America: Identity, Strategy and Democracy.* Boulder: Westview.

Escobar, J. 1986. *Persecución a la iglesia en Chile (Martirologio, 1973–1986).* Santiago: Terranova Editores, S.A.

Espinoza, V. 1983. *Tipos de acción poblacional y movimiento popular urbano en Chile.* Santiago: SUR, Working Paper, no. 18.

————. 1985. *Los Pobladores en la política.* Santiago: SUR, Working Paper, no. 27.

————. 1986. "Los Pobladores en la política." In CLASCO-ILET 1986, 31–52.

————. 1988. *Para una historia de los pobres de la ciudad.* Santiago: Ediciones SUR, Colección Estudios Historicos.

Evers, T. 1985. "Identity: The Hidden Side of New Social Movements in Latin America." In D. Slater, ed., *New Social Movements and the State in Latin America,* 43–71. Amsterdam: CEDLA.

Faletto, E., and E. Ruiz. 1970. "Conflicto político y estructura social." In Aníbal Pinto et al., *Chile, hoy,* 213–54. Mexico: Siglo Veintiuno Editores S.A.

Femia, J. 1975. "Hegemony and Consciousness in the Thought of Antonio Gramsci." *Political Studies* 23 (1):29–48.

Ferguson, A. 1966. *An Essay on the History of Civil Society.* Edinburgh: Edinburgh University Press.

Ffrench-Davis, R., and D. Razcynski. 1988. *The Impact of Global Recession and National Policies on Living Standards: Chile, 1973–87.* 2d ed. Santiago.

FLACSO. 1986. *Encuesta sobre la realidad socio-política chilena: Resultados preliminarios.* Santiago: FLACSO, Material de discusión, no. 81.

Fleet, M. 1985. *The Rise and Fall of Chilean Christian Democracy.* Princeton: Princeton University Press.

Flisfisch, A. 1987. *Incentivos y obstáculos a la cooperación política en el Chile autoritario.* Santiago: CED, Materiales Para Discusión, no. 187, August.

Foxley, A. 1983. *Latin American Experiments in Neoconservative Economics.* Berkeley and Los Angeles: University of California Press.

————. 1984. "Formas de la política despues del autoritarismo." *Colección Estudios CIEPLAN,* no. 15 (December): 203–10.

————. 1986. "The Neoconservative Economic Experiment in Chile." In J. Valenzuela and A. Valenzuela, eds., *Military Rule in Chile: Dictatorship and Opposition,* 13–50. Baltimore: Johns Hopkins University Press.

————. 1987. *Chile y su futuro: Un País posible.* Santiago: CIEPLAN.

Frente Patriótico Manuel Rodríguez, n.d. *Chile.* Pamphlet.

Frühling, H. 1984. "Repressive Policies and Legal Dissent in Authoritarian Regimes: Chile 1973–1981." *International Journal of Sociology of Law* 12:351–74.

———. 1985. *Reproducción y socialización de núcleos de resistencia: La experiencia de la Vicaría de la Solidaridad en Chile.* Santiago: Academia de Humanismo Cristiano, Programa de Derechos Humanos, Cuaderno de Trabajo, no. 2.

Furci, C. 1984. *The Chilean Communist Party and the Road to Socialism.* London: Zed Books.

Gallardo, B. 1985. *Las Ollas comunes de La Florida como experiencia de desarrollo de la organización popular.* Santiago: FLACSO, Documento de Trabajo, no. 248.

———. 1987. "El redescubrimiento del caracter social del hambre: Las Ollas comunes." In J. Chateau et al., *Espacio y poder. Los pobladores,* 171–201. Santiago: FLACSO.

Garretón, M. 1986. "The Political Evolution of the Chilean Military Regime and Problems in the Transition to Democracy." In G. O'Donnell, P. Schmitter, and L. Whitehead, eds., *Transitions from Authoritarian Rule: Southern Europe,* 95–122. Baltimore: Johns Hopkins University Press.

———. 1987a. "¿En que consistio la renovación socialista? Síntesis y evaluación de sus contendidos." In *La Renovación socialista,* 11–43.

———. 1987b. *1986–1987: Entre la frustración y la esperanza: Balance y perspectivas de la transición a la democracia en Chile.* Santiago: FLACSO.

———. 1987c. *Reconstruir la política: Transición y consolidación democrática en Chile.* Santiago: Editorial Andante.

———. 1989a. *The Chilean Political Process.* Boston: Allen and Unwin.

———. 1989b. "La Oposición política partidaria en el régimen militar chileno. Un proceso de aprendizaje para la transición." In M. A. Garretón and M. Cavarozzi, eds., *Muerte y Resurrección: Los partidos políticos en el autoritarismo y las transiciones del cono sur,* 395–465. Santiago: FLACSO.

———. 1989c. "Popular Mobilization and the Military Regime in Chile: The Complexities of the Invisible Transition." In S. Eckstein, ed., *Power and Popular Protest: Latin American Social Movements,* 259–77. Berkeley and Los Angeles: University of California Press.

———. 1990. *Partidos, transición y democracia en Chile.* Santiago: FLACSO, Documento de trabajo, no. 443, April.

Garretón, M., and T. Moulian. 1983. *La Unidad Popular y el conflicto político en Chile.* Santiago: Ediciones Minga.

Gazmuri, J. 1987. "Una nueva síntesis del socialismo chileno: Dispersión y vitalidad del socialismo. " In *La Renovación socialista,* 249–83.

Gil, F. 1966. *The Political System of Chile.* Boston: Houghton Mifflin.

Gil, F., R. Lagos, and H. Landsberger, eds. 1979. *Chile at the Turning Point: Lessons from the Socialist Years, 1970–1973.* Philidelphia: Institute for the Study of Human Issues.

Gómez, M. 1986. *El Discurso de los partidos comunistas de América Latina y el Caribe en las publicaciones del Movimiento Comunista Internacional.* Santiago: FLACSO, Documento de Trabajo, no. 295.

Gonzales, R. 1986. "1986: Nadie lo Hará Por Nosotros." *Liberación* (March–April): 4–7.

Gramsci, A. 1971. *Selections from the Prison Notebooks.* Edited by Q. Hoare and G. N. Smith. New York: International Publishers.

Gumucio, R. 1986. "La A.D. no tiene inconvenientes para conversar con la Derecha, pero sí con la Izquierda." *Liberación* (March–April): insert.

Gwynne, R. N. 1986. "The Deindustrialization of Chile, 1974–1984." *Bulletin of Latin American Research* 5:1–23.

Hagopian, F. 1990. "Democracy by Undemocratic Means: Elites, Political Pacts, and Regime Transition in Brazil." *Comparative Political Studies* 23 (July): 147–70.

Hamilton, N. 1985. *The Limits of State Autonomy: Post Revolutionary Mexico.* Princeton: Princeton University Press.

Hardy, C. 1985. *Estrategias organizadas de subsistencia: Los Sectores populares frente a sus necesidades en Chile.* Santiago: Programa de Economía del Trabajo, Academia de Humanismo Cristiano, Documento de Trabajo, no. 41.

———. 1986. *Hambre + Dignidad = Ollas Comunes.* Santiago: Programa de Economía del Trabajo, Academia de Humanismo Cristiano.

Hardy, C., and L. Razeto. 1984. *Nuevos actores y prácticas populares: Desafíos a la concertación.* Santiago: Centro de Estudios del Desarrollo, Documento de Trabajo, no. 47.

Hechos Urbanos. July 1986. No. 55.

Hechos Urbanos. October 1985. "Pobladores: Crisis de la acción reivindicativa y renacimiento comunitario." Special edition.

Hechos Urbanos. May 1983–November 1984. Nos. 21–37.

Held, D. 1987. *Models of Democracy.* Stanford: Stanford University Press.

Hersh, S. 1983. *The Price of Power: Kissinger in the Nixon White House.* New York: Summit Books.

Huneeus, C. 1987. *Los Chilenos y la política: Cambio y continuidad en el autoritarismo.* Santiago: CERC and ICHEH.

———. 1988. "El Sistema de partidos políticos en Chile: Cambio y continuidad." *Opciones,* no. 13:163–97.

Huntington, S. 1968. *Political Order in Changing Societies.* New Haven: Yale University Press.

International Commission of the Latin American Studies Association to Observe the Chilean Plebiscite. 1989. "The Chilean Plebiscite: A First Step Toward Redemocratization." *LASA Forum* 19 (Winter): 18–36.

La Izquierda chilena al país: Nuestra propuesta de concertación de la oposición para la lucha democrática. December 1986. Declaración del Conclave de la Izquierda.

Izquierda Cristiana. 1986. Nuestra concepción de partido: Principios de organización. Estatutos. Acuerdos del Ultimo Central (1986). Santiago: Izquierda Cristiana. Mimeographed.

Jacquette, J., ed. 1989. *The Women's Movement in Latin America: Feminism and the Transition to Democracy.* Boston: Unwin Hyman.

Jelin, E., ed. 1990. *Women and Social Change in Latin America.* London: Zed Books.

Karl, T. 1986. "Petroleum and Political Pacts: The Transition to Democracy in Venezuela." In G. O'Donnell, P. Schmitter, and L. Whitehead, eds., *Transitions from Authoritarian Rule: Southern Europe,* 192–219. Baltimore: Johns Hopkins University Press.

———. 1990. "Dilemmas of Democratization in Latin America." *Comparative Politics* 23 (October): 1–21.

Katznelson, I. 1981. *City Trenches: Urban Politics and the Patterning of Class in the United States.* New York: Pantheon Books.

———. 1986. "Working-Class Formation: Constructing Cases and Comparisons." In I. Katznelson and A. Zolberg, eds., *Working-Class Formation: Nineteenth-Century Patterns in Western Europe and the United States.* Princeton: Princeton University Press.

Kirkwood, J. 1986. *Ser política en Chile: Las Feministas y los partidos.* Santiago: FLACSO.

Lagos, R. 1985a. *Democracia para Chile. Proposiciones de un socialista.* Santiago: Pehuen Editores.

———. 1985b. "Las grandes tareas de la Reconstrucción." In Centro de Estudios del Desarrollo, *El futuro democrático de Chile,* 167–75.

Lechner, N. J. Brunner, and A. Flisfisch, eds. 1985. *Partidos y Democracia.* Santiago: FLACSO.

Levine, D., ed. 1986. *Religion and Political Conflict in Latin America.* Chapel Hill: University of North Carolina Press.

Levine, D., and S. Mainwaring. 1989. "Religion and Popular Protest in Latin America: Contrasting Experiences." In S. Eckstein, ed., *Power and Popular Protest: Latin American Social Movements,* 203–40. Berkeley and Los Angeles: University of California Press.

Liberación, March–April 1986, November 1986.

Linz, J. 1992. "Change and Continuity in the Nature of Contemporary Democracies." In G. Marks and L. Diamond, eds., *Reexamining Democracy: Essays in Honor of Seymour Martin Lipset,* 182–207. Newbury Park: Sage Publications.

Loveman, B. 1979. *Chile.* New York: Oxford University Press.

Macpherson, C. B. 1977. *The Life and Times of Liberal Democracy.* Oxford: Oxford University Press.

Mainwaring, S. 1986. *The Catholic Church and Politics in Brazil, 1916–1985.* Stanford: Stanford University Press.

———. 1987. "Urban Popular Movements, Identity, and Democratization in Brazil." *Comparative Political Studies* 20 (July): 131–59.

———. 1989. "Grass Roots Popular Movements and the Struggle for Democracy: Nova Iguaçu." In A. Stepan, ed., *Democratizing Brazil,* 168–204. Princeton: Princeton University Press.

Maira, L. 1986a. "Editorial." *Liberación* (January), 3.

———. 1986b. "Editorial." *Liberación* (March–April), 1.

———. 1986c. "El proceso de democratización y las opciones de recambio en Chile." *Liberación,* special edition (November), 1–13.

Mansbridge, J. 1980. *Beyond Adversary Democracy.* New York: Basic Books.

Martelli Nobba, G. 1989. "Juntas de vecinos, movimientos de pobladores y reforma municipal." In ECO, *Taller de Análisis Movimientos Sociales y Coyuntura,* no. 4 (July): 3–12.

Martínez, G. 1985. "Las Definiciones políticas e institucionales." In Centro de Estudios del Desarrollo, *El futuro democrático de Chile,* 57–75.

Martínez, J., and E. Tironi. 1985. *Las Clases sociales en Chile: Cambio y estratificación, 1970–1980.* Santiago: Ediciones SUR, Colección Estudios Sociales.

Marx, K. 1963. *The Eighteenth Brumaire of Luis Bonaparte.* New York: International Publishers.

McClintock, C. 1981. *Peasant Cooperatives and Political Change in Peru.* Princeton: Princeton University Press.

El Mercurio. 20 August 1991.

Mill, J. S. 1972. *Utilitarianism, Liberty, Representative Government: Selections from Auguste Comte and Positivism*. Edited by H. B. Acton. London: Dent.

Morales, E. 1987. "Políticas públicas y ámbito local: La Experiencia chilena." In Jordi Borja et al., *Descentralización del estado: Movimiento social y gestión local*. Santiago: FLACSO, 349–401.

Morales, E., H. Pozo, and S. Rojas. 1988. *Municipio, desarrollo local y sectores populares*. Santiago: FLACSO, Materiales de Difusión.

Morales, E., and S. Rojas. 1986. *Relocalización socio-espacial de la pobreza: Política estatal y presión popular, 1979–1985*. Santiago: FLACSO, Documento de Trabajo, no. 280.

Moran, T. 1974. *Multinational Corporations and the Politics of Dependence: Copper in Chile*. Princeton: Princeton University Press.

Movimiento Democrático Popular. 1985. *Saludo del Movimiento Democrático Popular a la concentración opositora "Chile Exige Democracia."* Pamphlet.

Mumford, L. 1961. *The City in History: Its Origins, Its Transformations, and Its Prospects*. San Diego: Harcourt Brace Jovanovich.

Nef, J. 1983. "The Revolution that Never Was: Perspectives on Democracy, Socialism, and Reaction in Chile." *Latin American Research Review* 17 (1):228–45.

Nuñez, R. 1985. "Comentarios." In Centro de Estudios del Desarrollo, *El futuro democrático de Chile*, 107–13.

———. 1986a. *Municipalización autoritaria y régimen democrático*. Santiago: VECTOR, Centro de Estudios Económicos y Sociales.

———. 1986b. Posición socialista frente a la empresa y la propriedad. Speech given before the Union Social de Empresarios y Ejecutivos Cristianos, Galerias Hotel, 17 July. Mimeographed.

———. 1987. "Las Tensiones principales en el proceso de renovación del pensamiento socialista chileno." In *La Renovación socialista*, 77–86.

O'Donnell, G. 1979. "Tensions in the Bureaucratic Authoritarian State and the Question of Democracy." In D. Collier, ed., *The New Authoritarianism in Latin America*, 285–318. Princeton: Princeton University Press.

O'Donnell, G., and P. Schmitter. 1986. *Transitions from Authoritarian Rule: Tentative Conclusions about Uncertain Democracies*. Baltimore: Johns Hopkins University Press.

O'Donnell, G., P. Schmitter, and L. Whitehead, eds. 1986. *Transitions from Authoritarian Rule*. Baltimore: Johns Hopkins University Press.

Olsen, J. 1983. *Organized Democracy: Political Institutions in a Welfare State—The Case of Norway*. Begen: Universitetsforlaget.

Olson, M. 1965. *The Logic of Collective Action: Public Goods and the Theory of Groups*. Cambridge: Harvard University Press.

Oppenheim, L. 1989. "The Chilean Road to Socialism Revisited." *Latin American Research Review* 24 (1):155–83.

Ortega, E. 1985. "Crisis, transición y estabilidad política." In Centro de Estudios del Desarrollo, *El futuro democrático de Chile*, 76–98.

Ortíz, E. 1985. "Socialismo, democracia y participación." In Centro de Estudios del Desarrollo, *El futuro democrático de Chile*, 176–89.

Ottone, E. 1986. "Democratización y nueva hegemonia en Chile." In J. Arrate et al., *Siete ensayos sobre democracia y socialismo en Chile*, 137–64.

Oxhorn, P. 1986. *Democracia y participación popular: Organizaciones poblacio-*

nales en la futura democracia chilena. Santiago: FLACSO, Contribución, no. 44.

———. 1988. "Organizaciones poblacionales, la reconstitución de la sociedad civil y la interacción elite-base." *Revista Mexicana de Sociologia* 50 (April–June): 221–37.

———. 1991. "The Popular Sector Response to an Authoritarian Regime: Chilean Shantytown Organizations Since the Military Coup." *Latin American Perspectives* 18 (Winter):66–91.

———. 1995. "From Controlled Inclusion to Coerced Marginalization: The Struggle for Civil Society in Latin America." In J. Hall, ed., *Civil Society: Theory, History and Comparison,* 250–77. Cambridge: Polity Press.

Paginas Sindicales. May 1983–November 1984. Nos. 55–65.

Pateman, C. 1970. *Participation and Democratic Theory.* Princeton: Princeton University Press.

Paulsen, F. 1988. "El Polémico congreso del PC." *Análisis* (12–18 December): 4–6.

Perlman, J. 1976. *The Myth of Marginality: Urban Poverty and Politics in Rio de Janeiro.* Berkeley and Los Angeles: University of California Press.

Pinto, A. 1970. "Desarrollo económico y relaciones sociales." In Aníbal Pinto et al., *Chile, hoy,* 5–52. Mexico: Siglo Veintiuno Editores S.A.

Portes, A. 1985. "Latin American Class Structures: Their Composition and Change during the Last Decades." *Latin American Research Review* 20 (3):7–39.

———. 1989. "Latin American Urbanization in the Years of the Crisis." *Latin American Research Review* 24 (3):7–44.

Portes, A., and M. Johns. 1986. Class Structure and Spatial Polarization: An Assessment of Recent Urban Trends in Latin America. Revised version of a paper written originally for the Symposium on Spatial Mobility and Urban Change, University of Utrecht, August.

Portes, A., and A. Kincaid. 1985. "The Crisis of Authoritarianism: State and Civil Society in Argentina, Chile and Uruguay." *Research in Political Sociology* 1:49–77.

Poulantzas, N. 1980. *State, Power, Socialism.* London: Verso and NLB.

Pozo, H. 1986. *Partidos políticos y organizaciones poblacionales I: Una reflexión problemática.* Santiago: FLACSO, Documento de Trabajo, no. 309.

Principios. September 1983, January–March 1984.

Programa de Economía del Trabajo. November 1989. Las organizaciones económicas populares: Situación y perspectivas en la transición. Santiago. Mimeographed.

Proyecto Alternativo: Seminario de profesionales técnicos humanistas cristianos. 1984. Vols. 1–3. Santiago: Editorial Aconcagua.

Przeworski, A. 1985. *Capitalism and social democracy.* Cambridge: Cambridge University Press.

Raczynski, D. 1974. "La Estratificación ocupacional en Chile." In Dagmar Raczynski et al., *Los actores de la realidad chilena,* 33–100. Santiago: Editorial del Pacífico S.A.

Razeto, L., A. Klenner, A. Ramirez, and R. Urmenteta, 1986. *Las organizaciones económicas populares.* 2d ed. Santiago: PET.

———. 1990. *Las Organizaciones económicas populares, 1973–1990.* 3d ed. Santiago: PET.

La Renovación socialista: Balance y perspectivas de un proceso vigente. 1987. Santiago: Ediciones Valentin Letelier.

Revista de CIEPLAN. July 1987. No. 9.

Riesco, G. 1985. "La Democracia y el rol de la Derecha Política." In Centro de Estudios del Desarrollo, *El futuro democrático de Chile*, 21–30.

Rodríguez, A. 1984. *Por una ciudad democrática*. Santiago: Ediciones SUR, Colección Estudios Sociales.

Rodríguez, A., and E. Tironi. 1986. Encuesta a pobladores de Santiago: Principales resultados. Preliminary version. Santiago: SUR. Mimeographed.

Rodríguez, J. 1985. *La distribución del ingreso y el gasto social en Chile—1983*. Santiago: ILADES.

Roxborough, I., P. O'Brien, and J. Roddick. 1977. *Chile: The State and Revolution*. New York: Holmes and Meier.

Ruiz Tagle, J. 1985. *El Sindicalismo chileno despues del Plan Laboral*. Santiago: Programa de Economía del Trabajo.

———. 1992. Desafíos del sindicalismo chileno frente a la flexibilización del mercado del trabajo. Paper presented at the Seventeenth International Congress of the Latin American Studies Association, Los Angeles, 24–27 September.

Salles, A. 1983. "Movimentos populares urbanos e suas formas de Organização Ligadas a Igreja." *Ciencias Sociais Hoje* 2 (Brasilia): 63–95.

Sanborn, C. 1988. ¿El futuro diferente? The Legacy of the 1970s for Peruvian Populism in the 1980s. Paper presented at the Fourteenth International Congress of the Latin American Studies Association, New Orleans, 17–19 March.

Sánchez, D. 1987. "Instituciones y acción poblacional: Seguimiento de su acción en el periodo 1973–1981." In J. Chateau et al., *Espacio y poder: Los pobladores*, 123–70. Santiago: FLACSO.

Schmitter, P. 1981. "Interest Intermediation and Regime Governability in Contemporary Western Europe and North America." In S. Berger, ed., *Organizing Interests in Western Europe*, 285–327. New York: Cambridge University Press.

———. 1983. "Democratic Theory and Neocorporatist Practice." *Social Research* 50 (Winter): 885–928.

———. 1986. "An Introduction to Southern European Transitions from Authoritarian Rule." In G. O'Donnell, P. Schmitter, and L. Whitehead, eds., *Transitions from Authoritarian Rule: Southern Europe*, 3–10.

Schneider, C. 1991. "Mobilization at the Grassroots: Shantytowns and Resistance in Authoritarian Chile." *Latin American Perspectives* 18 (Winter): 92–112.

Scully, T. 1992. *Rethinking the Center: Party Politics in Nineteenth- and Twentieth-Century Chile*. Stanford: Stanford University Press.

Secretaría Técnica, Comisión de Municipalización. 1984. *Municipalización y desarrollo de la comunidad. Bases de discusión*. Santiago: Instituto Chileno de Estudios Humanísticas, Proyecto Alternativa, preliminary document, no. 10.

Senate Intelligence Committee. 1975. *Covert Action in Chile, 1963–73*. Washington, D.C.: GPO.

Serrano, B. 1986. *Los Relegados de Lo Hermida*. Santiago: Ediciones Warriafilla.

El Siglo. June 1983, November 1983, February 1984, November 1986.

Sigmond, P. 1977. *The Overthrow of Allende and the Politics of Chile, 1964–1976*. Pittsburgh: University of Pittsburgh Press.

Singer, P. 1981. "Movimientos de bairro." In P. Singer and V. Caldeira Brant, eds., *São Paulo: O Povo em Movimento*, 83–108. Petropolis: Vozes/CEBRAP.

Smith, B. 1982. *The Church and Politics in Chile: Challenges to Modern Catholicism*. Princeton: Princeton University Press.

Solervicens, M. 1990. *Puente Alto: Desafíos de la transición en la comuna*. Santiago: Ediciones Las Alamedas.

Stallings, B. 1978. *Class Conflict and Economic Development in Chile, 1958–1973*. Stanford: Stanford University Press.

Stein, S., and B. Stein. 1970. *The Colonial Heritage of Latin America: Essays on Economic Dependence in Perspective*. New York: Oxford University Press.

Stepan, A. 1978. *The State and Society: Peru in Comparative Perspective*. Princeton: Princeton University Press.

Stephens, E. 1983. "The Peruvian Military Government, Labor Mobilization, and the Political Strength of the Left." *Latin American Research Review* 18 (2):57–93.

Stokes, S. 1988. Confrontation and Accommodation: Political Consciousness and Behavior in Urban Lower Class Peru. Ph.D. diss., Stanford University.

Taylor, M. 1982. *Community, Anarchy and Liberty*. Cambridge: Cambridge University Press.

Tironi, E. 1987. "Protesta, pobladores y democracia." *Revista de CIEPLAN*, no. 9 (July): 29–32.

Tocqueville, A. de. 1969. *Democracy in America*. Edited by J. P. Mayer. Garden City, N.Y.: Anchor Books.

Tovar, T. 1985. *Velasquismo y movimiento popular. Otra historia prohibida*. Lima: DESCO.

———. 1986a. "Barrios, Ciudad, Democracia y Política." In E. Ballon, ed., *Movimientos sociales y democracia: La Fundación de un nuevo orden*, 67–142. Lima: DESCO.

———. 1986b. "Vecinos y pobladores en la crisis." In E. Ballón, ed., *Movimientos sociales y crisis: El caso Peruano*, 113–64. Lima: DESCO.

Union Democrática Independiente. 1983. *Unión Democrática Independiente*. Santiago: Union Democrática Independiente.

———. 1986. *Chile Ahora*. Santiago: Union Democrática Independiente.

Valdés, G. 1986. "Carta de Gabriel Valdes presidente del Partido Democrata Cristiano a Germán Correa y Directiva del M.D.P." In E. Frei et al., *Democracia Cristiana y Partido Comunista*, 215–20. Santiago: Editorial Aconcagua.

Valdés, T. 1987. "El Movimiento de pobladores, 1973–1985: La Recomposición de las solidaridades sociales." In J. Borja et al., *Descentralización del estado: Movimiento social y gestión local*, 263–319. Santiago: FLACSO.

Valenzuela, A. 1977. *Political Brokers in Chile: Local Government in a Centralized Polity*. Durham: Duke University Press.

———. 1978. *The Breakdown of Democratic Regimes: Chile*. Baltimore: Johns Hopkins University Press.

———. 1989. "Chile: Origins, Consolidation and Breakdown of a Democratic Regime." In L. Diamond, J. Linz, and S. Lipset, eds., *Democracy in Developing Countries: Latin America*. 4:159–206. Denver: Lynne Rienner.

Valenzuela, A., and P. Constable. 1988. "Plebiscite in Chile: End of the Pinochet Era?" *Current History* (January): 29–33ff.

Valenzuela, J., and A. Valenzuela. 1986a. "Party Oppositions under the Chilean Authoritarian Regime." In J. Valenzuela and A. Valenzuela, eds., *Military Rule in Chile: Dictatorship and Opposition*, 184–229.

Valenzuela, J., and A. Valenzuela, eds. 1986b. *Military Rule in Chile: Dictatorship and Opposition*. Baltimore: Johns Hopkins University Press.

Valenzuela, E. 1984. *La Rebelión de los jóvenes*. Santiago: SUR.

Valenzuela, M. E. 1987. *La Mujer en el Chile militar: Todas íbamos a ser reinas.* Santiago: Ediciones Chile y America–CESOC ACHIP.

Vallier, I. 1970. *Catholicism, Social Control, and Modernization in Latin America.* Englewood Cliffs, N.J.: Prentice-Hall.

Varas, A. 1987. *De la violencia aguda al registro electoral: Estrategia y política de Alianzas del PC, 1980–1987*. Santiago: FLACSO, Documento de Trabajo, no. 362.

Venceremos. August 1986.

Vergara, P. 1984. *Auge y caída del neoliberalismo en Chile: Un Estudio sobre la evolución ideológica del régimen militar*. Santiago: FLACSO, Documento de Trabajo, no. 216.

———. 1986. "Changes in the Economic Functions of the Chilean State under the Military Regime." In J. Valenzuela and A. Valenzuela, eds., *Military Rule in Chile: Dictatorship and Opposition*, 85–116.

Vodanovic, H. 1988. *Una socialismo renovado para Chile*. Santiago: Editorial Andante.

Waisman, C. 1987. *Reversal of Development in Argentina*. Princeton: Princeton University Press.

Walker, I. 1990. *Socialismo y democracia: Chile y Europa en perspectiva comparada*. Santiago: CIEPLAN-Hachette.

Wilson, J. 1973. *Political Organizations*. New York: Basic Books.

World Bank. 1992. *World Development Report*. New York: Oxford University Press.

Yrarrázabal, J. 1985. "Una Perspectiva de Unidad Nacional Democrática." In Centro de Estudios del Desarrollo, *El futuro democrático de Chile*, 31–40.

Zaldivar, A. 1986. "Busguemos una solución para Chile por la razon y no por la fuerza." *Hoy* (July 28–August 3): supplement.

INDEX